Public Speaking

for College & Career

12e

Hamilton Gregory

Asheville-Buncombe Technical Community College

Mc
Graw
Hill

PUBLIC SPEAKING FOR COLLEGE & CAREER, TWELFTH EDITION

Published by McGraw Hill, a business unit of The McGraw Hill Companies, Inc., 1221 Avenue of the Americas, New York, NY 10020. Copyright © 2022 by Hamilton Gregory. All rights reserved. Printed in the United States of America. Previous editions © 2018, 2013, 2010, and 2008. No part of this publication may be reproduced or distributed in any form or by any means, or stored in a database or retrieval system, without the prior written consent of The McGraw Hill Companies, Inc., including, but not limited to, in any network or other electronic storage or transmission, or broadcast for distance learning.

Some ancillaries, including electronic and print components, may not be available to customers outside the United States.

This book is printed on acid-free paper.

1 2 3 4 5 6 7 8 9 LWI/LWI 26 25 24 23 22 21

ISBN 978-1-260-00710-7 (bound edition)
MHID 1-260-00710-3 (bound edition)
ISBN 978-1-260-86217-1 (loose-leaf edition)
MHID 1-260-86217-8 (loose-leaf edition)

Executive Portfolio Manager: *Sarah Remington*
Product Development Manager: *Dawn Groundwater*
Content Project Managers: *Rick Hecker; George Theofanopoulos*
Buyer: *Sandy Ludovissy*
Designer: *Beth Blech*
Content Licensing Specialist: *Sarah Flynn*

Cover Image: (clockwise): © *michaeljung/Shutterstock; fizkes/Shutterstock; Dave and Les Jacobs/Blend Images LLC; Hill Street Studios/Tobin Rogers/ Blend Images LLC; Jamie Farrant/Getty Images; Last Resort/Getty Images*
Compositor: *MPS Limited*

All credits appearing on page or at the end of the book are considered to be an extension of the copyright page.

Library of Congress Cataloging-in-Publication Data

Names: Gregory, Hamilton, author.
Title: Public speaking for college & career / Hamilton Gregory, Asheville-Buncombe Community College.
Other titles: Public speaking for college and career
Description: 12th edition. | New York : McGraw Hill LLC, 2022. | Includes bibliographical references and index.
Identifiers: LCCN 2020032762 | ISBN 9781260007107 (hardcover) | ISBN 9781260862171 (spiral bound)
Subjects: LCSH: Public speaking.
Classification: LCC PN4121 .G716 2022 | DDC 808.5/1—dc23
LC record available at https://lccn.loc.gov/2020032762

The Internet addresses listed in the text were accurate at the time of publication. The inclusion of a website does not indicate an endorsement by the authors or McGraw Hill Education, and McGraw Hill Education does not guarantee the accuracy of the information presented at these sites.

mheducation.com/highered

Dedicated to the memory of Merrell,
my beloved wife and best friend

Brief Contents

Contents

Part 3
Preparing Content

Part 4
Organizing the Speech

Preface

Public Speaking for College & Career supports the skills students need to succeed in the course and in their future careers, across the growing range of public speaking contexts. Informed by the latest research, the twelfth edition provides students with practical guidance and fresh examples that are anchored in students' real-world experiences. These features are supported by a suite of personalized study tools, customizable assessments, and interactive learning resources in McGraw Hill Connect.

McGraw Hill Connect: An Overview

McGraw Hill Connect offers full-semester access to comprehensive, reliable content and Learning Resources for the Public Speaking course. Connect's integration with most learning management systems (LMSs), including Blackboard and Desire2Learn (D2L), offers single sign-on and deep gradebook synchronization. Data from Assignment Results reports synchronize directly with many LMSs, allowing scores to flow automatically from Connect into school-specific gradebooks, if required.

Instructor's Guide to Connect for *Public Speaking for College & Career*

When you assign Connect you can be confident—and have data to demonstrate—that the learners in your course, however diverse, are acquiring the skills, principles, and critical processes that constitute effective public speaking. This leaves you to focus on your highest course expectations.

Tailored To You. Connect offers on-demand, single sign-on access to learners—wherever they are and whenever they have time. With a single, one-time registration, learners receive access to McGraw Hill's trusted content. Learners also have a courtesy trial period during registration.

Easy To Use. Connect seamlessly supports all major learning management systems with content, assignments, performance data, and SmartBook 2.0, the leading adaptive learning system. With these tools you can quickly make assignments, produce reports, focus discussions, intervene on problem topics, and help at-risk learners—as you need to and when you need to.

Public Speaking for College & Career SmartBook 2.0

A Personalized and Adaptive Learning Experience with Smartbook 2.0. Boost learner success with McGraw Hill's adaptive reading and study experience. The *Public Speaking for College & Career* SmartBook 2.0 highlights the most impactful public speaking concepts the student needs to learn at that moment in time. The learning path continuously adapts and, based on what the individual learner knows and does not know, provides focused help through targeted question probes and Learning Resources.

Enhanced for the New Edition! With a suite of new Learning Resources and question probes, as well as highlights of key chapter concepts, SmartBook 2.0's intuitive technology optimizes learner study time by creating a personalized learning path for improved course performance and overall learner success.

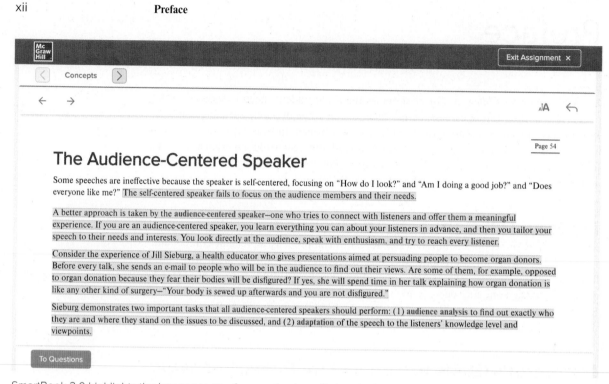

SmartBook 2.0 highlights the key concepts of every chapter, offering the learner a high-impact learning experience.

Hundreds of Interactive Learning Resources. Presented in a range of interactive styles, *Public Speaking for College & Career* Learning Resources support learners who may be struggling to master, or simply wish to review, the most important public speaking concepts. Designed to reinforce the most important chapter concepts—from topic selection and research skills to the outlining and delivery of presentations—every Learning Resource is presented at the precise moment of need. Whether video, audio clip, or interactive mini-lesson, each of the 200-plus Learning Resources was created for the new edition and was designed to give learners a lifelong foundation in strong public speaking skills.

Note Taking Strategies: Use a Note Taking Method

When taking notes, you should use a note taking method. This may be one you have developed yourself or one of the following options:

1. Create three columns and label them "Main Ideas," "Supports," and "Follow-Up." Place the speaker's key points and supporting details in the first two columns. The third column can be used as needed to record questions you might want to ask during a question and answer period or points of interest you would like to follow up on later.

2. Write one note per line. Later, use a highlighter to call out key points and a pen to circle anything you would like to follow up on. This method is useful if the speaker is talking quickly or does not clearly differentiate between main points and support.

More Than 1,000 Targeted Assessments. Class-tested at colleges and universities nation-wide, a treasury of engaging question probes—new and revised, more than 1,000 in all—gives learners the information on public speaking they need to know, at every stage of the learning process, in order to thrive in the course. Designed to gauge learners' comprehension of the most important *Public Speaking for College & Career* chapter concepts, and presented in a variety of interactive styles to facilitate student engage-ment, targeted question probes give learners immediate feedback on their understanding of the material. Each question probe identifies a learner's familiarity with the instruc-tion and points to areas where additional remediation is needed.

A Suite of Application-Based Activities. At the higher level of Bloom's, McGraw Hill's Application-Based Activities are highly interactive, automatically graded, online learn-by-doing exercises that provide students a safe space to apply their knowledge and problem-solving skills to real-world scenarios. Each scenario addresses key concepts that students must use to work through to solve communication problems, resulting in improved critical thinking and development of relevant skills.

Informed by the Latest Research. The best insights from today's leading public speaking scholars infuse every lesson and are integrated throughout *Public Speaking for College & Career*.

Fresh Examples Anchored in the Real World. Every chapter of *Public Speaking for College & Career* opens with a vignette exploring both public speaking challenges and successes. Dozens of additional examples appear throughout the new edition, each demonstrat-ing an essential element of the public speaking process. Whether learners are reading a chapter, working through a SmartBook 2.0 assignment, or reviewing key concepts in a Learning Resource, their every instructional moment is rooted in the real world. McGraw Hill research shows that high-quality examples reinforce academic theory throughout the course. Relevant examples and practical scenarios—reflecting interac-tions in school, the workplace, and beyond—demonstrate how effective public speaking informs and enhances students' lives and careers.

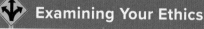

Examining Your Ethics

Suppose you are speaking in support of a good cause, but the statistics you want to use in your speech are complicated and hard to explain. You could convince your audience more easily if you made up some simplified statistics. Is it okay to fabricate a small amount of data so that they are easier for your audience to understand?

A. Yes, it's okay if the data are close to being accurate.
B. No, it is not okay.
C. Sometimes yes, sometimes no—it depends on the context.

For the answer, see the last page of this chapter.

Features. Critical-thinking skills are vital in the classroom, on the job, and in the community. Students who build these skills will be better speakers, listeners, and citizens as they strive to understand and evaluate what they see, hear, and read. The new edition of *Public Speaking for College & Career* includes a variety of boxed and end-of-chapter features to support student learning and enhance critical-thinking skills.

- **"Examining Your Ethics"** exercises provide real-world scenarios that pose ethical dilemmas and ask students to make a choice. Students can check their answers at the end of the chapter.

Tips for Your Career

TIP 4

Express Appreciation to a Speaker

Whenever you find a speech enjoyable or profitable, let the speaker know. No matter how busy or important he or she is, genuine feedback will be greatly appreciated.

After giving a speech, some speakers are physically and emotionally exhausted, and they sit down with a nagging doubt: Did it go okay? A word of thanks or a compliment from a listener is refreshing and gratifying. (If you can't express your appreciation in person right after the speech, write the speaker a brief note or send an e-mail or text message.)

Be sure to say something positive and specific about the content of the speech. A corporation president told of a commencement address he had delivered to a college several years before. "I sweated blood for a whole month putting that speech together and then rehearsing it

dozens of times—it was my first commencement speech," he said. "When I delivered the speech, I tried to speak straight from my heart. I thought I did a good job, and I thought my speech had some real nuggets of wisdom. But afterwards, only two people came by to thank me. And you know what? They both paid me the same compliment: they said they were grateful that I had kept the speech short! They said not one word about the ideas in my speech. Not one word about whether they enjoyed the speech itself. It's depressing to think that the only thing noteworthy about my speech was its brevity."

Sad to say, there were probably dozens of people in the audience whose hearts and minds were touched by the eloquent wisdom of the speaker—but they never told him.

- **"Tips for Your Career"** boxes in every chapter give students insight about the types of things they will need to think about as presenters in their professional lives.

- **"Building Critical-Thinking Skills"** features at the end of each chapter give students practice in this valuable skill.

Building Critical-Thinking Skills

1. When a person is truly and deeply listening to you, what behaviors do you detect in his or her tone of voice, facial expression, eyes, and overall body language?

2. Science writer Judith Stone wrote, "There are two ways to approach a subject that frightens you and makes you

Video Capture Powered by GoReact

With just a smartphone, tablet, or webcam, students and instructors can capture video of presentations with ease. Video Capture Powered by GoReact, fully integrated in McGraw Hill's Connect platform, doesn't require any extra equipment or complicated training. Create your own custom Video Capture assignment, including in-class and online speeches and presentations, self-review, and peer review.

With our customizable rubrics, time-coded comments, and visual markers, students will see feedback at exactly the right moment, and in context, to help improve their speaking and presentation skills and confidence.

- The Video Capture tool allows instructors to easily and efficiently set up speech assignments for their course that can easily be shared and repurposed, as needed.

- Customizable rubrics and settings can be saved and shared, saving time and streamlining the speech assignment process.

- Allows both students and instructors to view videos during the assessment process. Feedback can be left within a customized rubric or as time-stamped comments within the video-playback itself.

Access to just-in-time grammar and writing remediation, and originality detector. McGraw Hill's new Writing Assignment Plus tool delivers a learning experience that improves students' written communication skills and conceptual understanding with every assignment. Instructors can assign, monitor, and provide feedback on writing more efficiently and grade assignments within McGraw Hill Connect.

Connect Reports

Instructor Reports allow instructors to quickly monitor learner activity, making it easy to identify which learners are struggling and to provide immediate help to ensure those learners stay enrolled in the course and improve their performance. The Instructor Reports also highlight the concepts and learning objectives that the class as a whole is having difficulty grasping. This essential information lets you know exactly which areas to target for review during your limited class time.

Some key reports include:

Progress Overview report—View learner progress for all modules, including how long learners have spent working in the module, which modules they have used outside any that were assigned, and individual learner progress.

Missed Questions report—Identify specific probes, organized by chapter, that are problematic for learners.

Most Challenging Learning Objectives report—Identify the specific topic areas that are challenging for your learners; these reports are organized by chapter and include specific page references. Use this information to tailor your lecture time and assignments to cover areas that require additional remediation and practice.

Metacognitive Skills report—View statistics showing how knowledgeable your learners are about their own comprehension and learning.

Classroom Preparation Tools

Whether before, during, or after class, there is a suite of Gregory products designed to help instructors plan their lessons and to keep learners building upon the foundations of the course.

Annotated Instructor's Edition. The Annotated Instructor's Edition provides a wealth of teaching aids for each chapter in *Public Speaking for College & Career*. It is also cross-referenced with SmartBook 2.0, Connect, and other supplements that accompany *Public Speaking for College & Career*.

PowerPoint Slides. The PowerPoint presentations for *Public Speaking for College & Career* provide chapter highlights that help instructors create focused, yet individualized lesson plans.

Test Bank and Test Builder. The Test Bank offers multiple choice questions, true/false questions, fill-in-the-blank questions, and essay questions for each chapter. New to this edition and available within Connect, Test Builder is a cloud-based tool that enables instructors to format tests that can be printed and administered within a Learning Management System. Test Builder offers a modern, streamlined interface for easy content configuration that matches course needs, without requiring a download. Test Builder enables instructors to:

- Access all test bank content from a particular title
- Easily pinpoint the most relevant content through robust filtering options
- Manipulate the order of questions or scramble questions and/or answers
- Pin questions to a specific location within a test
- Determine the preferred treatment of algorithmic questions
- Choose the layout and spacing
- Add instructions and configure default settings

Remote Proctoring. New remote proctoring and browser-locking capabilities are seamlessly integrated within Connect to offer more control over the integrity of online assessments. Instructors can enable security options that restrict browser activity, monitor student behavior, and verify the identity of each student. Instant and detailed reporting gives instructors an at-a-glance view of potential concerns, thereby avoiding personal bias and supporting evidence-based claims.

Support to Ensure Success

- **Support at Every Step**—McGraw Hill's Support at Every Step site offers a wealth of training and course creation guidance for instructors and learners alike. Instructor support is presented in easy-to-navigate, easy-to-complete sections. It includes the popular Connect how-to videos, step-by-step guides, and other materials that explain how to use both the Connect platform and its course-specific tools and features. https://www.mheducation.com/highered/support.html

- **Implementation Consultant**—These specialists are dedicated to working online with instructors—one-on-one—to demonstrate how the Connect platform works and to help incorporate Connect into a customer's specific course design and syllabus. Contact your local McGraw Hill representative to learn more.

- **Learning Technology Representatives**—Learning Technology Representatives are local resources who work closely with your McGraw Hill learning technology consultants. They can provide face-to-face faculty support and training. http://shop.mheducation.com/store/paris/user/findltr.html

- **Digital Faculty Consultants**—Digital Faculty Consultants are experienced instructors who use Connect in their classrooms. These instructors are available to offer suggestions, advice, and training about how best to use Connect in your class. To request a Digital Faculty Consultant to speak with, please e-mail your McGraw Hill learning technology consultant.

CONTACT OUR CUSTOMER SUPPORT TEAM
McGraw Hill is dedicated to supporting instructors and learners. To contact our customer support team, please call us at 800-331-5094 or visit us online at http://mpss.mhhe.com/contact.php

Chapter-by-Chapter Changes to the New Edition

New and updated material in this edition of *Public Speaking for College & Career* reflects the latest research in the field and the current available technology. Chapter 4 presents an updated and increased focus on audience diversity in public speaking scenarios, including coverage of online presentations addressing international audiences. Integrated throughout Chapters 6 through 9, guidance for locating, evaluating, and documenting sources electronically reflects current research practices and helps students develop information literacy skills for a digital age. Chapters 15 and 16 feature two new sample student speeches with full video recordings available online, in the Connect Media Library.

Chapter 1 Introduction to Public Speaking: More examples relevant to students' lives, including examples reflecting diversity in public speaking scenarios

Chapter 2 Managing Nervousness: Updated coverage of public figures who experience speech anxiety; new chapter opening vignette

Chapter 3 Listening: New examples demonstrating the problems associated with poor listening skills; updated discussion of giving speakers a fair chance and showing respect as a listener in a different culture

Chapter 4 Reaching the Audience: Updated coverage for reaching a greater diversity of audiences, including guidance on customizing for different segments of the same audience, understanding gender and gender-biased language, addressing listeners with disabilities, an expanded explanation of the diversity of religious beliefs, and addressing audiences via online presentations; discussion of listeners with disabilities is now inclusive of disabilities that can't be seen, such as mental illnesses and psychological disorders

Chapter 5 Selecting Topic, Purpose, and Central Idea: Updated lists of general purposes to inform and persuade include topics aligned with student interest and current events

Chapter 6 Locating Information: Guidance for searching electronically better reflects current research practices; revised descriptions of types of periodicals distinguishes between mainstream and scholarly journals, and between opinion content and news content; updated coverage of search engines as a means of conducting research now includes tips for conducting advanced searches, as well as for searching for different types of content; updated section on conducting informal surveys and interviews electronically; Figure 5 and Table 1 examples reflect MLA 8e and APA 7e documentation guidelines

Chapter 7 Evaluating Information: Expanded and updated coverage of finding trustworthy information, applying critical-thinking skills, and analyzing Internet sites

Chapter 8 Supporting Your Ideas and Avoiding Plagiarism: Now includes section on avoiding plagiarism, in keeping with the chapter's focus on supporting ideas; refreshed examples of the types of support materials, and updated guidance around use of public domain, fair use, and royalty-free materials

Chapter 9 Presentation Aids: New guidance on making visual appeals to pathos; refreshed examples of effective and ineffective graphs, tables, and presentation slides feature throughout; updated section on using media includes definitions of synchronous, real-time, web-based presentations

Chapter 10 The Body of the Speech: New examples throughout, including new sample of the body of a speech on the topic of raising the driving age

Chapter 11 Introductions and Conclusions: New sample introduction and conclusion outlines on the topic of raising the driving age; new discussion of ethical use of hypothetical illustrations

Chapter 12 Outlining the Speech: New Tips for Your Career feature on speaking briefly when no time limit is set

Chapter 13 Wording the Speech: Revised section on the power of words warns against using loaded, deceptive, and inflated language; updated discussion and table illustrate proper use of gender-neutral pronouns and avoidance of gender-biased language; new Tips for Your Career feature examines the use of preferred gender pronouns in the professional sphere; new examples illustrate understanding denotation, controlling connotations, and using correct grammar

Chapter 14 Delivering the Speech: Updated discussion of volume explains how to make the best use of microphones; new examples illustrating the pitch and intonation, pauses, and rate of speech, as well as important forms of nonverbal communication; entirely new section on dialect and delivery; updated discussion of speaking in front of a camera; new chapter opening vignette

Chapter 15 Speaking to Inform: New table comparing and contrasting the different types of informative speeches; new student sample speech uses comparison–contrast pattern to present information on different types of health care plans (a video of the speech is available in the online Connect Media Library)

Chapter 16 Speaking to Persuade: New coverage of tackling controversial topics, including guidance on finding common ground, being respectful of opposing viewpoints, and striking a civil tone; new problem–solution outline on the topic of reducing the use of plastic shopping bags; new student sample persuasive speech on anti-bullying programs in schools (a video of the speech is available in the online Connect Media Library); new conflict-resolution exercise in Resources for Review and Skill Building

Chapter 17 Persuasive Strategies: Revised discussion of credibility including a new section on the importance of being accurate; updated examples illustrating deductive arguments and the range of fallacies; new chapter opening vignette

Chapter 18 Speaking on Special Occasions: Two new sample speeches of introduction; new model speeches of presentation and tribute

Chapter 19 Speaking in Groups: Entirely new section on showing respect during meetings; new Tips for Your Career feature explaining how to develop an "elevator speech"; new chapter opening vignette

Speeches Online

To view 29 videos of full-length sample student speeches and dozens of video speech clips, visit the media bank in the Gregory Connect site. Included in the media bank are all the major speeches presented in this text, plus many more, including 13 videos that are brand new to this edition. See below for a list of many of the full-length speeches available in Connect:

- All Eyes on Saturn
- Animal Helpers (Needs Improvement Version)
- Animal Helpers (Improved Version)
- The Deadliest Natural Disaster
- Do You Need Detox? (Improved Version)
- Failed to Get the Job? (Needs Improvement)
- Failed to Get the Job? (Improved Version)
- Fair Trade
- The Four-Day Work Week—Pros and Cons
- Gold Fever
- Hold Me a Spot: Campus Parking App
- House Arrest
- How to Hide Valuables
- Humanoid Robots
- Not as Healthy as They Sound
- One Slip—and You're Dead
- PPO or HDHP? How to Choose a Health Plan
- Public Schools Should Mandate Anti-Bullying Education
- Say No to Pit Bull Ban (Needs Improvement Version)
- Scars and Bruises
- Share a Bike for a Better Ride (Needs Improvement Version)
- She Did It
- Sleep Deficiency
- Speech of Acceptance
- Speech of Introduction
- Speech of Tribute
- Toast (Needs Improvement Version)
- Wedding Crashers
- What Is Absentee Voting? (Needs Improvement Version)
- Would You Vote for Aardvark?
- Your Body Needs Detoxification (Needs Improvement)
- Zoo Elephants

Acknowledgments

Over 200 instructors have reviewed this book in its successive editions. We are grateful to the reviewers for their insights, encouragement, and willingness to help.

For this edition, reviewers include Adam Bulizak, Hondros College of Nursing; Jim Crotty, The Modern College of Design; Joe Dennis, Piedmont College; Jill Dietze, Northeast Texas Community College; Anna Geffrard, Florida Career College–Margate; Minette Gentry-Hudson, Williamsburg Technical College; Carol Hayes, Forsyth Technical Community College; Dena Horne, Sam Houston State University; Michel Lain, Northeast Texas Community College; Nilam Patel, San Jacinto College South; Andrea Patterson-Masuka, Winston-Salem State University; and Gordon Young, Kingsborough Community College.

From the earliest days of this book, Betty Dvorson, an inspiring and popular instructor at City College of San Francisco, has shared lots of valuable advice and enthusiastic support. For their creative ideas, special thanks to Barbara Guess, Forsyth

Technical Community College; Ruth Bennett, Betty Farmer, and Jim Manning, all of Western Carolina University; and Tom W. Gregory, Trinity College in Washington, D.C.

This edition profited from the contributions of subject-matter experts Adam Bulizak, Joe Dennis, and Carol Hayes, who drew on their own experience as instructors and professionals in the field of communication to adapt the book to the needs and interests of today's college students. This edition also benefited from the support and vision of Sarah Remington, Portfolio Manager; Dawn Groundwater, Product Development Manager; Meghan Campbell, Director of Product Development; and Elizabeth Murphy, Product Developer, as well as the wholehearted backing of McGraw Hill executives David Patterson, Managing Director, and Michael Ryan, President of Higher Education.

For guiding the book through the production stages, thanks to Rick Hecker, Content Project Manager; Beth Blech, Designer; and Sarah Flynn, Content Licensing Specialist.

Special thanks go out to the team behind the scenes who built and continue to maintain speech assignment functionality on Connect: Irina Blokh-Reznik, Vijay Kapu, Swathi Malathi, Rishi Mehta, Bob Myers, Bhumi Patel, Dan Roenstch, Ayeesha Shaik, Kapil Shrivastava, and Udaya Teegavarapu.

A section in Chapter 14, "Speaking in Front of a Camera," was derived from the ideas and insights of three communication instructors: Stephanie O'Brien, a member of the Director's Guild of America who worked in Los Angeles on award-winning television series and motion pictures for 17 years as an assistant director and currently teaches communication and media studies courses at Asheville-Buncombe Technical Community College; Jan Caldwell, a communication instructor at the same college; and Melody Hays, Continuing Education Planner at Mountain Area Health Education Center in Asheville, North Carolina.

Thank you also to following individuals for ideas, inspiration, and support: Kenet Adamson, Jennifer Browning, Jan Caldwell, Angela Calhoun, Jim Cavener, Patricia Cutspec, Rebecca Davis, Michael Flynn, Lynne Gabai, Deborah L. Harmon, Cris Harshman, Melody Hays, Peggy Higgins, Patrizia Hoffman, David Holcombe, Rusty Holmes, Lisa Johnson, Dennis King, Erika Lytle, Deb Maddox, Mary McClurkin, Celia Miles, Stephanie O'Brien, Jim Olsen, Rolfe Olsen, Susan Paterson, Ellen Perry, Heidi Smathers, Beth Stewart, Mary Sugeir, and Heather Vaughn.

And to the hundreds of public speaking students who have made teaching this course a pleasant and rewarding task. From them most of the examples of classroom speeches have been drawn.

Public Speaking
for College & Career

Introduction to Public Speaking

OUTLINE

Benefits of a Public Speaking Course

The Speech Communication Process

The Speaker's Responsibilities

Speech Introducing Yourself or a Classmate

Quick Guide to Public Speaking

OBJECTIVES

After studying this chapter, you should be able to

1. Explain five benefits of a public speaking course.
2. Identify and explain the seven elements of the speech communication process.
3. Describe the main responsibilities that speakers have toward their listeners.
4. Prepare a speech introducing yourself or a classmate.

UPSET WHEN THEY DISCOVERED that African-American students were being barred from joining sororities on their campus, two University of Alabama students—Khortlan Patterson of Houston, Texas, and Yardena Wolf of Corvallis, Oregon—felt compelled to speak out. They led a march of 400 students and professors to the steps of the administration building, where they both gave speeches calling for an end to the segregated system.

Their message was heard loud and clear. University president Judy Bonner quickly proclaimed that "the University of Alabama will not tolerate discrimination of any kind," and a few days later, she announced that traditionally white sororities had invited 11 African-American students to join.[1]

Both Patterson and Wolf had taken a public speaking course, so they knew how to plan a speech and manage their nerves. Patterson says she calmed herself by focusing on "the message [she] wanted to convey."[2] Wolf used positive thoughts: "I realized that it wasn't really about me, rather about the bigger picture, and that not speaking wasn't an option."[3]

Patterson and Wolf not only displayed courage by speaking out, but they also demonstrated that public speakers can touch lives and make contributions to society.

University of Alabama students Khortlan Patterson, left, and Yardena Wolf speak out against the university's segregated sorority system.

© Dave Martin/AP Images

Benefits of a Public Speaking Course

Many college graduates say that of all the courses they took, public speaking proved to be one of the most valuable.[4] Here are some of the reasons:

1. **You learn how to speak to an audience.** Being able to stand up and give a talk to a group of people is a rewarding skill you can use throughout your life. Imagine yourself in these public speaking scenarios:

   - In one of your college classes, you must give a presentation for a group project.
   - At a training event in the workplace, you inform colleagues of a new policy or procedure.
   - You connect with college students across the nation by participating in a podcast focusing on how to adjust to college life.

2. **You learn skills that apply to one-on-one communication.** Although the emphasis of this course is on speaking to groups, the principles that you learn also apply to communication with individuals.[5] Throughout your lifetime you will be obliged to talk in situations such as these:

   - It is very common to be asked in a job interview, "Tell me about yourself." You want to appear confident and charismatic as you share insight into who you are and highlight what sets you apart from others. In a public speaking course you will learn strategies to give an effective impromptu response presenting a well-organized and persuasive message.
   - You sit down with a bank executive to ask for a loan so that you can buy a new car. The skills of nonverbal communication (such as eye contact and facial expression) that you learn in a public speaking course should help you convey to the banker that you are a trustworthy and reliable person who will repay the loan.

   After taking a public speaking course, many students report that their new skills help them as much in talking to one person as in addressing a large audience.

3. **You develop the oral communication skills that are prized in the job market.** With the advancement of technology and the ever-changing needs of business, what skills are employers looking for? According to LinkedIn's 2019 survey, companies are looking for these five soft skills:

   1. Creativity
   2. Persuasion
   3. Collaboration
   4. Adaptability
   5. Time management

   Technical knowledge in your field is important, but can you effectively communicate your expertise and work well with others?

   - Paul Petrone of LinkedIn Learning tells us that "strengthening a soft skill is one of the best investments you can make in your career, as they never go out of style."[6]
   - Canadian business executive Dan Pontefract argues that we should not use the term *soft skills* to refer to professional leadership skills.[7]
   - Elena Douglas, CEO of Knowledge Society, advises: "In a world of uncertainty and constant change, there is no doubt that having a full range of social and emotional skills will help young people thrive as citizens and employees."[8]

4. **You learn in an ideal environment for gaining experience and building confidence.** The classroom is a safe place to practice and develop your skills. No one will deny you a job or a loan on the basis of your classroom speeches. Your audience is friendly and sympathetic—all your classmates are going through the same experience.

The critiques given by your instructor and by fellow students are valuable parts of the course. If, for example, you say "um" or "uh" so often that it distracts your listeners, you are probably unaware of this unconscious habit. Being told of the problem is the first step toward correcting it.

If you are like most students, your public speaking class will help you gain self-confidence. You will enjoy the pride that comes from meeting a challenge and handling it successfully.

5. **You can make a contribution to the lives of other people.** While attending a funeral service for a beloved aunt, former student Karen Walker heard the minister give a brief eulogy and then say, "Would anyone like to say a few words?"

A few people went to the microphone and shared some memories, but most audience members were silent. "I wanted to pay tribute to my aunt, but I was too scared," said Walker. "I felt really bad because there were a lot of important things about my aunt and her life that were never said." A few years later, Walker took a public speaking class, and a year or so afterward, she attended another funeral—for her grandfather. "This time I vowed that I would not pass up the opportunity to honor a wonderful person. I asked to be part of the service, and I spoke about my childhood memories of my grandfather."

Greta Thunberg, a 16-year-old environmental activist with Asperger's, demonstrates how one voice can spark a global discussion through her impassioned speech at the UN to raise awareness about climate change. This young Swedish girl's speech was shared around the world and her words ignited discussions on both sides of the issue.

Stephanie Keith/Stringer/Getty images

The eulogy, said Walker, was appreciated by her family members, who told her that she had expressed beautifully what they would have said if they had possessed the courage and the skills to stand up and speak. "It gave me a good feeling to know that I could represent the family in this way," she said.

Being able to speak in public—offering a toast, sharing information, providing encouragement, attempting persuasion—can bring pleasure and joy to yourself and to others. Walker said that her success was possible because of what she had learned in her public speaking class.

The Speech Communication Process

When a speaker gives a speech, does communication take place?

Sometimes yes, sometimes no—because *speaking and communicating are not the same thing.* You can speak to a listener, but if the listener does not understand your message in the way you meant it to be understood, you have failed to communicate it.

For example, at a business dinner at a restaurant in Atlantic City, New Jersey, Joe Lentini told the server that he knew little about wine and asked her to "recommend something decent." She suggested a bottle of cabernet sauvignon sold under the name Screaming Eagle, and she said the price was "thirty-seven fifty." Lentini thought she meant $37.50, and he approved. But when the bill arrived at the end of the meal, he was astonished and dazed to see that the cost was $3,750.[9]

This incident illustrates that speaking and communicating are not synonymous. As a slogan of the Hitachi Corporation puts it: "Communication is not simply sending a message. It is creating true understanding—swiftly, clearly, and precisely."

To help you send messages that truly communicate, it is helpful to understand the process of speech communication. As we discuss the process, use Figure 1 as a visual reference.

Elements of the Process

The speech communication process has seven distinct components.

Speaker

speaker
the originator of a message sent to a listener.

When you are a **speaker**, you are the source of a message that is transmitted to a listener. Whether you are speaking to a dozen people or 500, you bear a great responsibility for the success of the communication. The key question that you must constantly ask yourself is not "Am I giving out good information?" or "Am I performing well?" but, rather, "Am I getting through to my listeners?"

Listener

listener
the receiver of the speaker's message.

The **listener** is the recipient of the message sent by the speaker. The true test of communication is not whether a message is delivered by the speaker but whether it is accurately received by the listener. "A speech," says management consultant David W. Richardson of Westport, Connecticut, "takes place in the minds of the audience."[10]

If communication fails, who is to blame—the speaker or the listener? It could be either, or both. Although speakers share part of the responsibility for communication, listeners also must bear some of the burden. They must focus on the speaker, not daydream or text a friend. They must listen with open minds, avoiding the tendency to prejudge the speaker or discount a speaker's views without a fair hearing.

Figure 1
The Speech Communication Process
In this model of the speech communication process, a **speaker** creates a **message** and sends it via a **channel** to the **listener,** who interprets it and sends **feedback** via a channel to the speaker. **Interference** is whatever impedes accurate communication. The **situation** refers to the time and place in which communication occurs.

The speech communication process is often dynamic, with communicators sending and receiving messages in rapid sequence, sometimes even simultaneously. In this informal business presentation, the speaker sends messages while receiving feedback (both verbal and nonverbal) from listeners. At various times, a speaker and a listener may exchange roles.

Pressmaster/Shutterstock

Message

The **message** is whatever the speaker communicates to the listeners. The message is sent in the form of *symbols*—either *verbal* or *nonverbal.*

Verbal symbols are words. It's important for you to recognize that words are not things; they are *symbols* of things. If you give me an apple, you transfer a solid object from your hand to mine. But if you make a speech and you mention the word *apple,* you do not transfer a concrete thing. You transfer a verbal symbol.

message
whatever is communicated verbally and nonverbally to the listener.

Nonverbal symbols are what you convey with your tone of voice, eyes, facial expression, gestures, posture, and appearance.

So far, the process sounds simple, but now we enter a danger zone. As a speaker transmits verbal and nonverbal symbols, the listeners must receive and interpret them. Unfortunately, listeners may end up with a variety of interpretations, some of them quite different from what the speaker intended. Consider our simple word *apple*. One listener may think of a small green fruit, while another conjures an image of a big red fruit. One listener may think of crisp tartness, while another thinks of juicy sweetness.

If such a simple word can evoke a variety of mental pictures, imagine the confusion and misunderstanding that can arise when abstract words such as *imperialism, patriotism,* and *censorship* are used. The term *censorship* may mean "stamping out filth" to some listeners, but it may mean "total government control of the news media" to others.

As a speaker, use symbols that are clear and specific. Don't say, "Smoking may cause you a lot of trouble." The phrase "a lot of trouble" is vague and might be interpreted by some listeners to mean "coughing," by others to mean "stained teeth," or by still others to mean "cancer." Be specific: "Smoking is the leading cause of lung cancer."

Sometimes a speaker's verbal symbols contradict his or her nonverbal symbols. If you say to an audience at the end of a speech, "Now I would like to hear your views on this subject," but your expression is tense and your voice sounds irritated, the listeners are getting a mixed message. Which will they believe, your words or your nonverbal behavior? Listeners usually accept the nonverbal behavior as the true message. In this case, they will conclude that you do *not* welcome comments.

Make sure the nonverbal part of your message reinforces, rather than contradicts, the verbal part. In other words, smile and use a friendly tone of voice when you ask for audience participation.

Channel

channel
the pathway used to transmit a message.

The **channel** is the medium used to communicate the message. In everyday life, you receive messages via televisions, phones, the Internet, and direct voice communication. For public speaking, your main channels are auditory (your voice) and visual (gestures, facial expressions, visual aids). You can also use other channels—taste, smell, touch, and physical activity—which will be discussed in the chapter on presentation aids.

Feedback

feedback
verbal and nonverbal responses made by a listener to a speaker.

Feedback is the response that the listener gives the speaker. Sometimes it is *verbal,* as when a listener asks questions or makes comments. In most public speeches, and certainly in the ones you will give in the classroom, listeners wait to give verbal feedback until the question-and-answer period.

Listeners also give *nonverbal* feedback. If they are smiling and nodding their heads, they are obviously in agreement with your remarks. If they are frowning and sitting with their arms folded, they more than likely disagree with what you are saying. If they are yawning, they are probably bored or weary. "A yawn," wrote English author G. K. Chesterton, "is a silent shout."[11]

If you receive negative feedback, try to help your listeners. If, for example, you are explaining a concept but some of your listeners are shaking their heads and giving you looks that seem to say "I don't understand," try again, using different words to make your ideas clear.

Tips for Your Career

Seek Feedback

Some speakers develop unconscious habits when they speak, such as smoothing their hair or straightening their clothes. The best way to discover and discard these quirks is to get feedback from your listeners in the form of an evaluation. Although feedback is valuable for pinpointing delivery problems, it is even more important as a way to assess the *content* of your speech: are your remarks enlightening or confusing to the listeners?

You don't need an evaluation of every speech in your career, but you should seek feedback occasionally. Strive to get both positive input and constructive suggestions so that you can keep the good and eliminate the bad. Here are four good methods:

1. **Ask several friends or colleagues to critique your speech.** Don't make an imprecise request like "Tell me how I do on this" because your evaluators will probably say at the end of your speech, "You did fine— good speech," regardless of what they thought of it, to avoid hurting your feelings. Instead give them a specific assignment: "Please make a note of at least three things that you like about the speech and my delivery, and at least three things that you feel need

improvement." Now your listeners know exactly what you need. As a result, you are likely to get helpful feedback.

2. **Use an evaluation form.** Distribute sheets to all listeners, asking for responses to a series of questions about your delivery and the content of your speech. To protect anonymity, you can have someone collect the forms.

3. **Ask a small group of listeners to sit down with you after a meeting to share their reactions.** This is especially useful in finding out whether the listeners understood and accepted your message. Try to listen and learn without becoming argumentative or defensive.

4. **Record your presentation on video.** Invite colleagues to watch the video with you and help you evaluate it. Because many people are *never* pleased with either themselves or their speeches on video, colleagues often can provide objectivity. For example, an introduction that now seems dull to you might strike your colleagues as interesting and captivating.

Interference

Interference is anything that blocks or hinders the accurate communication of a message. There are three types:

- *External* interference comes from outside the listener: someone coughing, people talking on their smartphones, or broken air-conditioning that leaves the listeners hot and sticky.

- *Internal* interference comes from within the listener. Some listeners might be hungry or tired or sick, or they might be daydreaming or worrying about a personal problem. As a speaker, you can help such listeners by making your speech so engaging that audience members want to listen to you.

- *Speaker-generated* interference can occur if you distract your listeners with unfamiliar words, confusing concepts, or bizarre clothing.

interference
anything that obstructs accurate communication of a message.

Sometimes listeners will try to overcome interference—for example, straining to hear the speaker's words over the noise of other people talking. But too often, listeners will fail to make the extra effort.

When you are a speaker, stay alert for signs of interference and respond immediately. For example, if a plane roars overhead, you can either speak louder or pause while it passes.

Situation

The **situation** is the context—the time, place, and circumstances—in which communication occurs. Different situations call for different behaviors. In some settings, speakers can crack jokes and audiences can laugh, while in others, speakers must be serious and listeners should remain silent.

Time of day determines how receptive an audience is. Many listeners, for example, become sluggish and sleepy about an hour after a big meal. If you give a presentation during that period, you can enliven it by using colorful visual aids and hands-on activities.

When you prepare a speech, find out as much as possible about the situation: What is the nature of the occasion? How many people are likely to be present? Will the speech be given indoors or outdoors? Once you assess these variables, you can adapt your speech to make it effective for the situation.

The Process in Everyday Life

So far, our discussion might suggest that speech communication is a simple process: a speaker sends a message, a listener provides feedback—back and forth, like a tennis match. But in everyday life, the process is usually complex and dynamic. Instead of speaker and listener taking turns, communicators often send and receive messages at the same time.

For example, you go into your boss's office to ask for a raise. As you start your (verbal) message, she is giving you a friendly, accepting smile, a (nonverbal) message that seems to say that she is glad to see you. But as your message is spelled out, her smile fades and is replaced by a grim expression of regret—negative feedback. "I wish I could give you a big raise," she says, "but I can't even give you a little one." As she is saying these last words, she interprets your facial expression as displaying disbelief, so she hastily adds, "Our departmental budget just won't permit it. My hands are tied." And so on—a lively give-and-take of verbal and nonverbal communication.

The Speaker's Responsibilities

When you give a speech, you should accept certain responsibilities.

Maintain High Ethical Standards

The standards of conduct and moral judgment that are generally accepted in a society are called *ethics*. In public speaking, the focus on ethics is on how speakers handle their material and how they treat their listeners. Speakers should be honest and straightforward with listeners, avoiding all methods and goals that are deceitful, unscrupulous, or unfair. "Examining Your Ethics" boxes throughout the book will help you exercise your skills at points where ethical issues are discussed.

Let's examine three important ethical responsibilities of the speaker.

Never Distort Information

As an ethical speaker, you should always be honest about facts and figures. Distorting information is not only dishonest—it's foolish. Let's say that in your career, you persuade some colleagues to take a certain

 Examining Your Ethics

Suppose you are speaking in support of a good cause, but the statistics you want to use in your speech are complicated and hard to explain. You could convince your audience more easily if you made up some simplified statistics. Is it okay to fabricate a small amount of data so that they are easier for your audience to understand?

A. Yes, it's okay if the data are close to being accurate.
B. No, it is not okay.
C. Sometimes yes, sometimes no—it depends on the context.

For the answer, see the last page of this chapter.

course of action but it is later discovered that you got your way by distorting facts and statistics. In the future, your colleagues will distrust everything you propose—even if you have sound logic and impeccable evidence on your side. "A liar will not be believed," said the ancient Greek writer Aesop, "even when he [or she] speaks the truth."[12]

Respect Your Audience

Some speakers talk down to their listeners. Speaking in a scolding, condescending tone, one speaker told an audience of young job-seekers, "I know you people don't believe me, but you're wasting your time and money if you pay a consultant to critique your résumé." When speakers are condescending or disrespectful, they are likely to lose the respect and attention of the audience. Their credibility is damaged.

Humorist Will Rogers once said, "Everybody is ignorant, only on different subjects" and "There is nothing as stupid as an educated man if you get him off the thing he was educated in."[13] When you are the expert on a subject, remember that your "ignorant" listeners are experts on topics within their own realm of knowledge and experience.

Reject Stereotyping and Scapegoating

A **stereotype** is a simplistic or exaggerated image that humans carry in their minds about groups of people. If you were asked to give a speech to raise funds for a homeless shelter, you might have difficulty generating sympathy because many people have a negative stereotype of homeless people, referring to them as "bums" and assuming them to be addicted to alcohol or drugs.

stereotype
an oversimplified or exaggerated image of groups of people.

Like all stereotypes, this one is unfair, as illustrated by the story of Dave Talley, a homeless man in Tempe, Arizona, who found a backpack containing a laptop computer and $3,300 in cash. He turned in the backpack, which had been lost by Bryan Belanger, a student at Arizona State University. Belanger said he had withdrawn the money from his bank account to buy a new car after his old one had been wrecked. As for Dave Talley, he said he had no hesitation about turning in the lost items. "Not everybody on the streets is a criminal," he said. "Most of us have honor and integrity."[14]

You should reject stereotypes because they force all people in a group into the same simple pattern. They fail to account for individual differences and the wide range of characteristics among members of any group. For example, a popular stereotype depicts lawyers as dishonest. Some lawyers are dishonest, yes, but many are sincere advocates who make positive contributions to society.

While avoiding stereotyping, you also should reject its close cousin, scapegoating. A **scapegoat** is a person or a group unfairly blamed for some real or imagined wrong. In recent years, the alleged decline in the quality of education in the United States has been blamed on public school teachers, who have been vilified as incompetent and uncaring. While there may be some teachers who deserve such labels, most are dedicated professionals who care deeply about their students.

scapegoat
an individual or a group that innocently bears the blame of others.

Enrich Listeners' Lives

Before a speech, some speakers make remarks such as these to their friends:

- "I hope not many people show up."
- "When I ask for questions, I hope nobody has any."
- "I want to get this over with."

Often a speaker makes these comments out of nervousness. As you will see in the chapter on managing nervousness, speech anxiety is a normal occurrence that can be motivated by a variety of understandable reasons. However, such remarks show that the speaker is focused on his or her own emotions rather than on the audience.

Instead of viewing a speech as an ordeal, consider it an opportunity to enrich the lives of your listeners. One of my students, Mary Crosby, gave a classroom speech on poisonous spiders—what they look like, how to avoid them, and what to do if bitten. She had spent six hours researching the topic. If the 17 of us in the audience had duplicated her research, spending six hours apiece, we would have labored for 102 hours. Thus, Crosby saved us a great deal of time and effort and, more importantly, gave us useful information. Most of us probably never would have taken the time to do this research, so her speech was all the more valuable.

Take Every Speech Seriously

Consider two situations that some speakers erroneously assume are not worth taking seriously: classroom speeches and small audiences.

Classroom speeches.   Contrary to what some students think, your classroom speeches are as important as any speeches that you may give in your career or community, and they deserve to be taken seriously. They deal with real human issues and are presented by real human beings. Teachers look forward to classroom speeches because they learn a lot from them, such as how to save the life of a person choking on food, how to garden without using pesticides, how to set up a tax-free savings account for their children, and so much more.

Small audiences.   Some speakers mistakenly think that if an audience is small, they need not put forth their best effort. Wrong. You should try as hard to communicate with an audience of 5 as you would with an audience of 500. James "Doc" Blakely of Wharton, Texas, tells of a colleague who traveled to a small town in the Canadian province of Saskatchewan to give a speech and found that only one person had shown up to hear him. He gave the lone listener his best efforts, and later that listener started a national movement based on the speaker's ideas.[15]

Speech Introducing Yourself or a Classmate

A speech introducing yourself or a classmate to the audience is often assigned early in a public speaking class. The speech gives you an opportunity to use an easy topic to gain experience. It also gives you and other members of the class a chance to learn key information about one another so that future classroom speeches can be tailored to the needs and interests of the audience.

Strive to show your audience what makes you or your classmate interesting and unique. Unless your instructor advises otherwise, you may include the following items:

Background Information
- Name
- Hometown
- Family information
- Work experience
- Academic plans
- Postgraduation goals

Unique Features
- Special interests (hobbies, sports, clubs, etc.)
- One interesting or unusual thing about you or your classmate
- One interesting or unusual experience

The last three items are especially important because they give the audience a glimpse into the qualities, interests, and experiences that make you or your classmate unique.

Sample Self-Introduction Speech

Rachel Chavez introduces herself to a public speaking class.

The Sun Is Free

INTRODUCTION

My name is Rachel Chavez, and I am from San Diego, California. I am majoring in environmental science.

BODY

I am very interested in solar energy. I have a part-time job installing solar panels for a company that is owned by my two older brothers. It is hard work, climbing up on roofs and installing panels, but it is very rewarding.

At the end of a job, I ask customers to turn on their system and then look at the electric meter. Because of the extra solar energy flowing in, they can see that their meter has started running in the opposite direction. In other words, they are sending power back to the grid—they are now making money. In two or three years, they will have earned the equivalent of all the money they spent on buying and installing the solar system.

CONCLUSION

You can see why I love solar energy. I hope that in the years ahead, I can help move this country further and further down the road toward free energy from the sun for everybody.

Sample Speech Introducing a Classmate

In this speech, Chris Richards introduces classmate Utsav Misra.

A Grand Passion

INTRODUCTION

Utsav Misra, who is a sophomore, comes to us all the way from India, and he's the first person in his family to go to college. He is majoring in culinary arts.

BODY

At the moment, Utsav's grand passion in life is cricket, which is the most popular sport in India. He grew up playing cricket, and he's trying to organize a cricket club on our campus. Not only is he recruiting international students who know the sport well, but he's also trying to recruit students who have never played the sport. Cricket is becoming more and more popular in the United States. Today over 80 American colleges have cricket clubs.

For those of you who don't know what cricket is all about, it's similar to baseball. Pitchers are called bowlers, and they throw the ball toward an opposing batsman, who tries to prevent the ball from hitting the wicket behind him. A wicket is made up of three upright wooden poles that are hammered into the ground. Utsav tells me that cricket involves a lot more than what I've told you, and the rules can be a bit complicated for Americans. But it's like any sport. Once you learn the rules, it's fun to play and it's fun to watch.

CONCLUSION

For one of his speeches in this class, Utsav is planning to give you an introduction to cricket. He will show you a cricket ball and a bat, and he will use videos so that you can understand what's going on when you see a cricket match on TV. I, for one, am eager to learn about this intriguing sport.

If you are excited about vacationing in Hawaii—including jumping off Maui's famous Black Rock—you have a good speech topic.

© Shutterstock/Jeanne Provost

Quick Guide to Public Speaking

To help you with any major speeches that you must give before you have had time to study this entire book, we will take a look at the key principles of preparation and delivery.

The guide below assumes that you will use the most popular method of speaking—extemporaneous—which means that you carefully prepare your speech but you don't read or memorize a script. Instead you look directly at your listeners and talk in a natural, conversational way, occasionally glancing at notes to stay on track.

The extemporaneous style and three other methods of speaking—manuscript (reading a document), memorization (speaking from memory), and impromptu (speaking with little or no time to prepare)—will be fully discussed in the chapter on delivering the speech.

Preparation

Audience. The goal of public speaking is to gain a response from your listeners—to get them to think, feel, or act in a certain way. To reach the listeners, find out as much as you can about them. What are their ages, genders, racial and ethnic backgrounds, and educational levels? What are their attitudes toward you and the subject? How much do they already know about the subject? When you have completed a thorough analysis of your listeners, adapt your speech to meet their needs and interests.

Topic. Choose a topic that is interesting to you and about which you know a lot (either now or after doing research). Your topic also should be interesting to the listeners—one they will consider timely and worthwhile. Narrow the topic so that you can comfortably and adequately cover it within the time allotted.

Purposes and central idea. Select a general purpose (to inform, to persuade, etc.), a specific purpose (a statement of exactly what you want to achieve with your audience), and a central idea (the message of your speech boiled down to one sentence). For example, suppose you want to persuade your listeners to safeguard their dental health. You could create objectives such as these:

> *General Purpose:*   To persuade
>
> *Specific Purpose:*   To persuade my listeners to take good care of their teeth and gums

Next, ask yourself, "What is my essential message? What big idea do I want to leave in the minds of my listeners?" Your answer is your central idea. Here is one possibility:

> *Central Idea:*   Keeping your mouth healthy can contribute to your overall health.

This central idea is what you want your listeners to remember if they forget everything else.

Gathering of materials. Gather information by reading books and periodicals (such as magazines and journals), searching for information on the Internet, interviewing knowledgeable people, or drawing from your own personal experiences. Look for interesting items such as examples, statistics, stories, and quotations. Consider using visual aids to help the audience understand and remember key points.

Organization.   Organize the body of your speech by devising two or three main points that explain or prove the central idea. To continue the example from above, ask yourself this question: "How can I get my audience to understand and accept my central idea?" Here are two main points that could be made:

I. Medical researchers say that poor oral health can lead to diabetes, heart disease, pneumonia, and some types of cancer.
II. Know how to protect your teeth and gums.

The next step is to develop each main point with support material such as examples, statistics, and quotations from experts. Underneath the first main point, these two items could be used to illustrate the health risks of poor oral health:

- Researchers at Columbia University's School of Public Health tracked 9,296 men and women for 20 years and found that those participants who developed gum disease had a much greater risk of becoming diabetic than participants without gum disease.
- A recent study published in the *New England Journal of Medicine* established that having gum disease significantly increases the chances of developing heart disease.

Under the second main point, discuss the needs to brush and floss daily, to use antibacterial mouthwash, and to get a professional cleaning from a dental hygienist twice a year.

Transitions.   To carry your listeners smoothly from one part of the speech to another, use transitional words or phrases, such as "Let's begin by looking at the problem," "Now for my second reason," and "Let me summarize what we've covered."

Introduction.   In the first part of your introduction, grab the attention of the listeners and make them want to listen to the rest of the speech. Attention-getters include fascinating stories, intriguing questions, and interesting facts or statistics. Next, prepare listeners for the body of the speech by stating the central idea and/or by previewing the main points. Give any background information or definitions that the audience would need in order to understand the speech. Establish credibility by stating your own expertise or by citing reliable sources.

Conclusion.   Summarize your key points, and then close with a clincher (such as a quotation or a story) to drive home the central idea of the speech.

Outline.   Put together all parts of the speech (introduction, body, conclusion, and transitions) in an outline. Make sure that everything in the outline serves to explain, illustrate, or prove the central idea.

Speaking notes.   Prepare brief speaking notes based on your outline. These notes should be the only cues you take with you to the lectern.

Practice.   Rehearse your speech several times. Don't memorize the speech, but strive to rehearse ideas (as cued by your brief speaking notes). Trim the speech if you are in danger of exceeding the time limit.

Delivery

Self-confidence.   Develop a positive attitude about yourself, your speech, and your audience. Don't let fear cripple you: nervousness is normal for most speakers. Rather than trying to banish your jitters, use nervousness as a source of energy—it actually can help you come across as a vital, enthusiastic speaker.

Approach and beginning.   When you are called to speak, leave your seat without sighing or mumbling, walk confidently to the front of the room, spend a few moments standing in silence (this is a good time to arrange your notes and get your first sentences firmly in mind), and then look directly at the audience as you begin your speech.

Eye contact.   Look at all parts of the audience throughout the speech, glancing down at your notes only occasionally. Avoid staring at a wall or the floor; avoid looking out a window.

Speaking rate.   Speak at a rate that makes it easy for the audience to absorb your ideas—neither too slow nor too fast.

Expressiveness.   Your voice should sound as animated as it does when you carry on a conversation with a friend.

Gestures are an important part of delivery.   Musician Jake Shimabukuro, a ukulele virtuoso and composer from Honolulu, Hawaii, uses effective gestures during a presentation in Pasadena, California.

© Richard Shotwell/Invision/AP Images

Clarity and volume.   Pronounce your words distinctly and speak loud enough so that all listeners can clearly hear you. Avoid verbal fillers such as *uh, ah, um, er, okay, ya know*.

Gestures and movement.   If it is appropriate and feels natural, use gestures to accompany your words. They should add to, rather than distract from, your message. You may move about during your speech, as long as your movements are purposeful and confident—not random and nervous. Don't do anything that distracts the audience, such as jingling keys or riffling note cards.

Posture and poise.   Stand up straight. Try to be comfortable, yet poised and alert. Avoid leaning on the lectern or slouching on a desk.

Use of notes.   Glance at your notes occasionally to pick up the next point. Don't read them or absentmindedly stare at them.

Enthusiasm.   Don't simply go through the motions of "giving a speech." Your whole manner—eyes, facial expression, posture, voice—should show enthusiasm for your subject, and you should seem genuinely interested in communicating your ideas.

Ending and departure.   Say your conclusion, pause a few moments, and then ask—in a tone that shows that you sincerely mean it—"Are there any questions?" Don't give the appearance of being eager to get back to your seat, such as by pocketing your notes or by taking a step toward your seat.

Tips for Your Career

Avoid the Five Biggest Mistakes Made by Speakers

In a survey, 370 business and professional leaders were asked to name the most common mistakes made by public speakers in the United States today. Here are the most common ones:

1. **Failing to tailor one's speech to the needs and interests of the audience.** A *poor* speaker bores listeners with information that is stale or useless. A *good* speaker sizes up the listeners in advance and gives them material that is interesting and useful.

2. **Using PowerPoint ineffectively.** If used wisely, PowerPoint slides can be wonderful, but if used poorly, they can irritate an audience. The chapter on aids will give you tips on creating effective slides.

3. **Speaking too long.** If you want to avoid alienating an audience, stay within your time limit. Time yourself when you practice, and refrain from ad-libbing and going off on tangents when you give your speech.

4. **Being poorly prepared.** A good speech does not just happen. The speaker must spend hours researching the topic, organizing material, and rehearsing the speech before he or she rises to speak. As many speakers have discovered, slapping together a presentation a few hours beforehand is not sufficient. You need at least two weeks to prepare.

5. **Being dull.** A speech can be made boring by poor content or by poor delivery. To avoid being dull, you should (a) choose a subject about which you are enthusiastic, (b) prepare interesting material, (c) have a strong desire to communicate your message to the audience, and (d) let your enthusiasm shine during your delivery of the speech.

Source: Survey by the author of 370 business and professional leaders, February–March 2011.

Listeners get bored if a speech is uninteresting or too long.
© Tomas Rodriguez/Corbis

Resources for Review and Skill Building

Summary

A public speaking course helps you develop the key oral communication skills (speaking well and listening intelligently) that are highly prized in business, technical, and professional careers. You gain both confidence and experience as you practice those skills in an ideal environment—the classroom—where your audience is friendly and supportive.

The speech communication process consists of seven elements: speaker, listener, message, channel, feedback, interference, and situation. Communication does not necessarily take place just because a speaker transmits a message; the message must be accurately received by the listener. When the speaker sends a message, he or she must make sure that the two components of a message—verbal and nonverbal—don't contradict each other.

Communicators often send and receive messages at the same time, creating a lively give-and-take of verbal and nonverbal communication.

Speakers should maintain high ethical standards, never distorting information, even for a good cause. They should respect their audiences and avoid a condescending attitude. They should reject stereotyping and scapegoating.

Good communicators don't view a speech as an ordeal to be endured, but as an opportunity to enrich the lives of their listeners. For this reason, they take every speech seriously, even if the audience is small.

Key Terms

channel, *8*	listener, *6*	situation, *10*
feedback, *8*	message, *7*	speaker, *6*
interference, *9*	scapegoat, *11*	stereotype, *11*

Review Questions

1. Name five personal benefits of a public speaking course.

2. Why is speaking not necessarily the same thing as communicating?

3. What are the seven elements of the speech communication process?

4. If communication fails, who is to blame—the speaker or the listener?

5. If there is a contradiction between the verbal and nonverbal components of a speaker's message, which component is a listener likely to accept as the true message?

6. What two channels are most frequently used for classroom speeches?

7. Why are communication skills important to your career?

8. What are the three types of interference?

9. What are stereotypes? Give some examples.

10. According to a survey, what are the five biggest mistakes made by public speakers?

Building Critical-Thinking Skills

1. Describe an instance of miscommunication between you and another person (friend, relative, salesperson, etc.). Discuss what caused the problem and how the interchange could have been handled better.

2. Interference can block effective communication. Imagine you are a supervisor and you are giving important instructions at a staff meeting. You notice that a few employees are not receiving your message because they are carrying on a whispered conversation. What would you do? Justify your approach.

3. Who is the most engaging public communicator (politician, teacher, religious leader, etc.) you have ever encountered? What are the reasons for his or her success?

Building Teamwork Skills

1. Working in a group, analyze a particular room (your classroom or some other site that everyone is familiar with) as a setting for speeches (consider the size of the room, seating, equipment, and potential distractions). Prepare a list of tips that speakers can follow to minimize interference and maximize communication.

2. For each member of a group, take turns stating your chosen (or probable) career. Then, working together, imagine scenarios in that career in which oral communication skills would play an important part.

Examining Your Ethics

Answer: B. Making up data is never acceptable or ethical. It is okay to summarize complicated data for your audience, but be sure to tell them that you did so, and never alter data to suit your agenda.

End Notes

1. Kayla Webley, "Revolution on Sorority Row," *Marie Claire,* www.marieclaire.com (accessed September 19, 2015).

2. Khortlan Patterson, e-mail interview, June 25, 2014.

3. Yardena Wolf, e-mail interview, August 9, 2014.

4. Hamilton Gregory, e-mail survey of 742 business and professional speakers (91 percent of the 487 who said that they had taken either a college public speaking course or a communication course with a public speaking component rated the course as "highly valuable").

5. Gerhard Gschwandtner, *The Pocket Sales Mentor* (New York: McGraw-Hill, 2006), p. 199.

6. Paul Petrone, "The Skills Companies Need Most in 2019— And How to Learn Them," LinkedIn Learning, January 1, 2019, https://learning.linkedin.com/blog/top-skills /the-skills-companies-need-most-in-2019–and-how-to-learn -them (accessed October 10, 2019).

7. Dan Pontefract, "The Big Problem with LinkedIn's List of Top Skills," *Forbes*, January 22, 2019, www.forbes .com/sites/danpontefract/2019/01/21/the-big-problem -with-linkedins-list-of-top-skills/#b724dac143cf.

8. Elena Douglas, "The Softs Skills Gap," *The Australian*, August 17, 2018, p. 37.

9. "I Read It in the Tabloids," *The Week* magazine, November 21, 2014, p. 14.

10. David W. Richardson, management consultant, Westport, Connecticut, e-mail interview, May 9, 2000.

11. G. K. Chesterton, BrainyQuote, brainyquote.com (accessed September 23, 2015).

12. *Aesop's Fables,* Bartleby.com, www.bartleby.com (accessed September 20, 2015).

13. Will Rogers, "From Nuts to Soup" (syndicated column number 90), *The New York Times*, August 31, 1924.

14. Bradley Blackburn, "Person of the Week: Arizona Homeless Man Dave Tally Turns in Lost Backpack with $3,300," *ABC News*, https://abcnews.go.com /US/PersonOfWeek/arizona-homeless-man-turns-lost -backpack-3300/story?id=12191814 (accessed January 6, 2016).

15. James ("Doc") Blakely, professional speaker, Wharton, Texas, e-mail interview, November 13, 2007.

Managing Nervousness

OBJECTIVES

After studying this chapter, you should be able to

1. Identify and describe the five fears that can cause nervousness.

2. Explain why nervousness can actually help a public speaker.

3. Apply techniques that can be used before and during a speech to manage nervousness.

EMMA WATSON, an actor and activist best known for her role in the *Harry Potter* series of films, struggled with fear and anxiety before delivering a speech about feminism to the United Nations. Her nervousness is visible in her trembling hands and voice as she begins her speech. "I really didn't think I had it in me," she later said.

But as Watson continues her speech, she relaxes and trusts her abilities—and her extensive preparation. She displays confidence and passion, she delivers her message clearly and eloquently, and she keeps her audience engaged. After a dramatic call to action at the end of her speech, the audience members respond with applause and a standing ovation. Even though she had a shaky start, she overcame her nervousness and delivered a very successful speech. (You can watch her speech on YouTube by searching for "Emma Watson at the HeForShe Campaign 2014—Official UN Video.")

If you experience nervousness as a public speaker, you are not alone. Most people—even public figures like Emma Watson—suffer from stage fright when called upon to

speak in public.[1] In fact, when researchers ask Americans to name their greatest fears, the fear of speaking to a group of strangers is listed more often than fear of snakes, insects, lightning, deep water, heights, or flying in airplanes.[2]

Using the tips offered in this chapter, you can manage your nervousness and become a confident speaker.

Reasons for Nervousness

Is it ridiculous to be afraid to give a speech? The answer is, simply, no. It is not unusual for beginning speakers to feel nervous, even while chiding themselves that there's no good reason to be scared. But that is just plain wrong: there are many valid reasons to be scared about public speaking, including the five below.

1. **Fear of being stared at.** If you haven't had experience being the center of attention, it can be unnerving to have all eyes in a room focused on you.

2. **Fear of failure or rejection.** If you are like most people, you are afraid of looking stupid. You ask yourself, "What if I make a fool of myself?" or "What if I say something really dumb?"

3. **Fear of the unknown.** New events, such as your first job interview, can be scary because you cannot anticipate the outcome. Fortunately, this fear usually eases in public speaking as you gain experience. You develop enough confidence to know that nothing terrible will happen.

4. **A traumatic experience in the past.** You may have painful memories of a humiliating event in a classroom or a presentation that flopped.

5. **Social anxiety.** Because of your genetic makeup or temperament, you may be awkward, uneasy, or apprehensive in public. You may feel defensive around other people and fearful of being evaluated and judged.

All of these reasons are understandable, and you do not need to feel ashamed if any of them apply to you. Recognizing them is an important step in learning how to manage your nervousness.

The Value of Fear

In the first hour of a public speaking class, many students express the same goal: to eliminate all traces of nervousness. They are often surprised to learn that a certain amount of fear can actually help them give a good speech. In other words, *you should not try to banish all your fear and nervousness.*

You *need* fear? Yes. When accepted and managed, fear energizes you; it makes you think fast. It gives you vitality and enthusiasm. Here is why: When you stand up to give a speech and fear hits you, your body's biological survival mechanisms kick in. You experience the same feeling of high alert that saved our cave-dwelling ancestors when they faced hungry wolves and either had to fight or flee to survive. Though these mechanisms are not as crucial in our day-to-day lives as they were to our ancestors, this system is still nice to have for emergencies: if you were walking down a deserted street one night and someone threatened you, your body would release a burst of **adrenaline** into your bloodstream, causing freshly oxygenated blood to rush to your muscles so you could fight ferociously or retreat quickly. The benefit of adrenaline can be seen in competitive sports; athletes *must* get their adrenaline flowing before a game begins. The great home-run slugger Reggie Jackson said during his heyday, "I have butterflies in my stomach almost every time I step up to the plate. When I don't have them, I get worried because it means I won't hit the ball very well."[3]

Many musicians, actors, and public speakers have the same attitude. Singer Beyoncé says, "I think it's healthy for a person to be nervous. It means you care—that you work hard and want to give a great performance. You just have to channel that nervous energy into the show."[4] In public speaking, adrenaline infuses you with energy. It enables you to

adrenaline
a hormone, triggered by stress, that stimulates heart, lungs, and muscles and prepares the body for "fright, flight, or fight."

think with greater clarity and quickness. It makes you come across to your audience as someone who is alive and vibrant. Elayne Snyder, a speech teacher, uses the term **positive nervousness,** which she describes in this way: "It's a zesty, enthusiastic, lively feeling with a slight edge to it. Positive nervousness is the state you'll achieve by converting your anxiety into constructive energy. . . . It's still nervousness, but you're no longer victimized by it; instead you're vitalized by it."[5]

positive nervousness
useful energy.

If you want proof that nervousness is beneficial, observe speakers who have absolutely no butterflies. Because they are 100 percent relaxed, they usually give speeches that are dull and flat, with no energy or zest. There is an old saying: "Speakers who say they are as cool as a cucumber usually give speeches about as interesting as a cucumber." One speaker, the novelist I. A. R. Wylie, said, "I rarely rise to my feet without a throat constricted with terror and a furiously thumping heart. When, for some reason, I *am* cool and self-assured, the speech is always a failure. I need fear to spur me on."[6]

Another danger of being too relaxed is you might get hit with a sudden bolt of panic. A hospital official told me that she gave an orientation speech to new employees every week for several years. "It became so routine that I lost all of my stage fright," she said. Then one day, while in the middle of her talk, she was suddenly and inexplicably struck with paralyzing fear. "I got all choked up and had to take a break to pull myself together," she recalled.

Many other speakers have had a similar experience. It is easy to get too relaxed, and then get blindsided by sudden panic. For this reason, if you find yourself overly calm before a speech, tell yourself to be alert for danger. Try to encourage "positive nervousness"—this can help you avoid being caught off-guard.

Guidelines for Managing Nervousness

A complete lack of fear is undesirable, but what about the other extreme? Is *too much* nervousness bad for you? Of course it is, especially if you are so incapacitated that you forget what you were planning to say, or if your breathing is so labored that you cannot get your words out. Your goal is to keep your nervousness under control so that you have just the right amount—enough to energize you, but not enough to cripple you. You can achieve a good balance by following the tips below.

In the Planning Stage

By giving time and energy to planning your speech, you can bypass many anxieties.

Choose a Topic You Know Well

Nothing will unsettle you more than speaking on a subject that is unfamiliar to you. If you are asked to do so, consider declining the invitation (unless, of course, it is an assignment from an instructor or a boss who gives you no choice). Choose a topic you are interested in and know a lot about—or want to learn more about. This will give you enormous self-confidence; if something terrible happens, like losing your notes, you can improvise because you know your subject. Also, familiarity with the topic will allow you to handle yourself well in the question-and-answer period after the speech.

Prepare Yourself Thoroughly

Here is a piece of advice given by many experienced speakers: *the very best precaution against excessive stage fright is thorough, careful preparation.* You may have heard the expression "I came unglued." In public speaking, solid preparation is the "glue" that will hold you together.[7] Joel Weldon of Scottsdale, Arizona (who quips that he used

Examining Your Ethics

Mick was nervous and lacked confidence in his ability to choose a good topic, so he gave a speech about meteors that his friend Aditya had created. Aditya was quite knowledgeable about astronomy and had created a good speech, but Mick himself did not know much about meteors. Which of the following are valid arguments against Mick's behavior?

A. His delivery might be shaky because of unfamiliarity with the subject matter.

B. He is guilty of plagiarism, passing off someone else's work as his own.

C. Not knowing his topic very well, he risks embarrassment if he is unable to answer simple questions during the question-and-answer period.

For the answer, see the last page of this chapter.

to be so frightened of audiences that he was "unable to lead a church group in silent prayer"), gives his personal formula for managing fear: "I prepare and then prepare, and then when I think I'm ready, I prepare some more." Weldon recommends five to eight hours of preparation for each hour in front of an audience.[8]

Start your preparation far in advance of the speech date so that you have plenty of time to gather ideas, create an outline, and prepare speaking notes. Then practice, practice, practice. Don't just look over your notes—actually stand up and rehearse your talk in whatever way suits you: in front of a mirror, a video camera, or a live audience of family or friends. Don't rehearse just once—run through your entire speech at least four times. If you present your speech four times at home, you will find that your fifth delivery—before a live audience—will be smoother and more self-assured than if you had not practiced at all.

Never Memorize a Speech

Giving a speech from memory courts disaster. Winston Churchill, the British prime minister during World War II, is considered one of the greatest orators of the twentieth century, but even he had to learn this difficult lesson as a young man. In the beginning of his career, he would write out and memorize his speeches. One day, while giving a memorized talk to Parliament, he suddenly stopped. His mind went blank. He began his last sentence all over. Again his mind went blank. He sat down in embarrassment and shame. Never again did Churchill try to memorize a speech. This same thing has happened to many others who have tried to commit a speech to memory. Everything goes smoothly until they get derailed, and then they are hopelessly off the track.

Even if you avoid derailment, there is another reason for not memorizing: you will probably sound mechanical. Your audience will sense that you are speaking from your memory and not from your heart, and this will undermine your impact.

Visualize Yourself Giving an Effective Speech

Let yourself daydream a bit: picture yourself going up to the lectern, a bit nervous but in control of yourself, and then giving a forceful talk to an appreciative audience. This visualization technique may sound silly, but it has worked for many speakers and it may work for you. Notice that the daydream includes nervousness. You need to have a realistic image in your mind: nervous, but nevertheless in command of the situation and capable of delivering a strong, effective speech.

positive imagery
visualization of successful actions.

This technique, often called **positive imagery**, has been used by athletes for years. Have you ever watched professional golf on TV? Before each stroke, golfers carefully study the distance from the ball to the hole, the rise and fall of the terrain, and so on. Many of them report that just before swinging, they imagine themselves hitting the ball with the right amount of force and watching it go straight into the cup. Then they try to execute the play just as they imagined it. The imagery, many pros say, improves their game.

Positive imagery works best when you can couple it with *believing* that you will give a successful speech. Is it absurd to hold such a belief? If you fail to prepare, yes, it is absurd. But if you spend time in solid preparation and rehearsal, you are justified in believing you will be successful.

Whatever you do, don't let yourself imagine the opposite—a bad speech or poor delivery. Negative thinking will add unnecessary fear to your life in the days before your speech and rob you of creative energy—energy that you need for preparing and practicing.[9]

Know That Shyness Is No Barrier

Some shy people think that their temperament blocks them from becoming good speakers, but this is erroneous. Many shy introverts like Kristin Stewart, Johnny Depp, Selena Gomez, Vanessa Hudgens, Justin Timberlake, Lady Gaga, and Beyoncé have prospered in show business.[10] Many less-famous people also have succeeded. "I used to stammer," says Joe W. Boyd of Bellingham, Washington, "and I used to be petrified at the thought of speaking before a group of any size." Despite his shyness, Boyd joined a Toastmasters club to develop his speaking skills. Two years later, he won the Toastmasters International Public Speaking Contest by giving a superb speech to an audience of more than 2,000 listeners.[11]

Kristen Stewart is a shy introvert.

Kristy Sparow/Contributor/ Getty images

Shift Focus from Self to Audience

Before a speech, some speakers worry about whether listeners will like them. This is a big mistake, says Johnny Lee, a specialist in preventing workplace violence who manages his nervousness by focusing on his audience rather than on himself. To worry about yourself and your image, he says, "is a kind of vanity—you are putting yourself above your audience and your message."[12] To some experienced speakers, like Lee, focusing on yourself is an act of inexcusable selfishness. Instead of worrying about whether listeners like you, focus on the audience and try to fulfill their interests, needs, and desires.

One good way to shift the focus from self to audience is to change your "self-talk." Whenever you have a self-centered thought such as "I will make a total idiot out of myself," substitute an audience-centered thought such as "I will give my listeners information that will be useful in their lives." This approach eases your anxiety and also empowers you to connect with your audience.

Plan Visual Aids

In addition to adding spice and interest to a speech, visual aids reduce anxiety because you can shift the audience's stares from you to your illustrations. Also, moving about as you display your aids siphons off some of your excess nervous energy. Your aids don't have to be elaborate, and you don't need many—sometimes one or two will suffice.

Make Arrangements

At least several days before you give your speech, inspect the location and anticipate any problems: Is there an extension cord for the multimedia projector? Do the windows have curtains or blinds so that the room can be darkened? Is there a whiteboard and a marker? Some talks have been ruined and some speakers turned into nervous wrecks because, at the last moment, they discover that there isn't an extension cord in the entire building.

Devote Extra Practice to the Introduction

Because you will probably have the most anxiety at the beginning of your speech, you should spend a lot of time practicing your introduction.

Most speakers, actors, and musicians report that after the first minute or two, their nervousness eases and the rest of the event is relatively easy. German opera singer Ernestine Schumann-Heink said, "I grow so nervous before a performance, I become sick. I want to go home. But after I have been on the stage for a few minutes, I am so happy that nobody can drag me off."[13] Perhaps happiness is too strong a word for what you will feel, but if you are a typical speaker, the rest of your speech will be smooth sailing once you have weathered the turbulent waters of the first few minutes.

Immediately before the Speech

Here are a few tips for the hours preceding your speech.

Verify Equipment and Materials

On the day of your speech, arrive early and inspect every detail of the arrangements you have made. Is the equipment you need in place and in good working order? If there is a public-address system, test your voice on it before the audience arrives so that you can feel at ease with it. Learn how to adjust the microphone.

Get Acclimated to Audience and Setting

It can be frightening to arrive at the meeting place at the last moment and confront a sea of strange faces waiting to hear you talk. If you arrive at least one hour early, you can get acclimated to the setting and chat with people as they come into the room. In this way, you will see them not as a hostile pack of strangers but as ordinary people who wish you well.

If possible, during your talk, refer to some of the audience members with whom you have chatted: for example, "I was talking to Gabriela Ramirez before the meeting, and she told me about the problems you have been experiencing with getting customers to pay their bills on time." In this way, you make your listeners feel valued, and you make yourself seem connected to them.

Danielle Kennedy of Sun Valley, Idaho, says that when she began her speaking career, she was so nervous she would hide out in a bathroom until it was time for her to speak. Now, she says, she mingles with the listeners as they arrive and engages them in conversation. "This reminds me that they are just nice people who want to be informed. I also give myself pleasant thoughts. Things like: 'Can you imagine, these people drove 100 miles just to hear me. I am so lucky. These people are wonderful.' I get real warm thoughts going by the time I get up there."[14]

Use Physical Actions to Release Tension

Greet listeners as they arrive.

Shutterstock / violetblue

Adrenaline can be beneficial, providing athletes and public speakers with helpful energy, but it also has a downside. When your body goes on high alert, you get pumped up and ready for action, but you also get a racing heart, trembling hands, and jittery knees. If you are an athlete, this is no problem because you will soon be engaged in vigorous play that will drain off excess nervous energy. As a public speaker, you don't have that outlet. Nevertheless, there are several tension releasers you can use:

- Take three slow, deep breaths and hold them. To prevent hyperventilating, be sure to inhale slowly and exhale slowly.

- Do exercises that can be performed without calling attention to yourself. Here are some examples: (1) Tighten and then relax your leg muscles. (2) Push your arm or hand muscles against a hard object (such as a desktop or a chair) for a few moments, and then release the pressure. (3) Press the palms of your hands against each other in the same way: tension, release . . . tension, release . . .

During the Speech

Here are proven pointers to keep in mind as you deliver a speech.

Pause before You Start

All good speakers pause a few seconds before they begin their talk. This silence is effective because (1) it is dramatic, building up the audience's interest and curiosity; (2) it makes you look poised and in control; (3) it calms you; and (4) it gives you a chance to look at your notes and get your first two or three sentences firmly in mind.

Many tense, inexperienced speakers rush up to the lectern and begin their speech at once, thus getting off to a frenzied, flustered start. They think that silence is an undesirable void that must be filled up immediately. To the contrary, silence is a good breathing space between what went before and what comes next. It helps the audience focus.

Deal Rationally with Your Body's Turmoil

If you are a typical beginning speaker, you will suffer from some or all of the following symptoms as you begin your talk:

- Pounding heart
- Trembling hands
- Shaky knees
- Dry, constricted throat
- Difficulty breathing
- Quivering voice
- Flushed face

You are likely to suffer the most during the first few minutes of a speech, and then things get better. However, if your symptoms get worse as you proceed, it might be because your mind has taken a wrong path. Examine the two paths diagrammed in Figure 1. If you take Route A, you are trapped in a vicious circle. Your mind tells your body that disaster is upon you, and your body responds by feeling worse. This, in turn, increases your brain's perception of disaster.

You can avoid this rocky road by choosing Route B, in which your mind helps your body stay in control. The mental trick is to remind yourself that nervousness is an ally that can help energize you. Tell yourself that your symptoms, rather than being a prelude to disaster, are evidence that you are energized enough to give a good speech.

Think of Communication, Not Performance

Regard your challenge as *communication* rather than *performance*. Dr. Michael T. Motley of the University of California, Davis, says that speakers who suffer from excessive anxiety make the mistake of thinking of themselves as *performing* for listeners, whom they see as hostile evaluators. Such people say, "The audience will ridicule me if I make a mistake. I'll be embarrassed to death." But in fact, says Dr. Motley, audiences are more interested in hearing what you have to say "than in analyzing or criticizing how [you] say it." Audiences "usually ignore errors and awkwardness as long as they get something out of a speech."[15]

When you stop worrying about "How well am I performing?" and start thinking about "How can I share my ideas with my audience?" two things usually happen: (1) your anxiety comes down to a manageable level and (2) your delivery improves dramatically.

Figure 1
The Alternative Paths That a Speaker Feeling Stressed Might Take

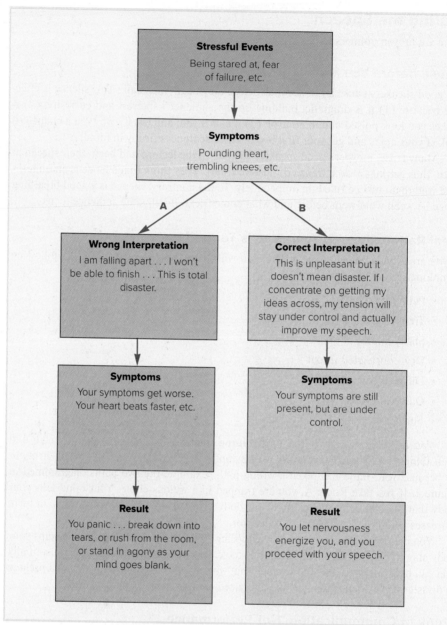

If you treat speechmaking as a dialogue with your listeners rather than as a performance, you will tend to talk *with* them instead of *to* them; you will tend to speak conversationally rather than in a stiff, unnatural way.

When one student, Maxine Jones, began her first classroom speech, her voice sounded artificial and cold; but after a few moments, she sounded animated and warm, as if she were carrying on a lively conversation. This caused her to become more interesting and easier to follow. Later she explained her transformation: "At first I was scared to death, but then I noticed that everyone in the room was looking at me with curiosity in their eyes, and I could tell that they really wanted to hear what I was saying. I told myself, 'They really *care* about this information—I can't let them down.'

So I settled down and talked to them as if they were my friends. I got so involved with explaining things to them that I didn't worry too much about being scared."

What Jones discovered is confirmed by athletes. Most tennis players, for example, are gripped by nervous tension before a match, but if they concentrate on hitting the ball, their tension recedes into the background. Likewise, public speakers may be filled with anxiety before a speech, but if they concentrate on communicating with the audience, their anxiety moves to a back burner, where it provides energy for the task.

Know That Most Symptoms Are Not Seen

Some speakers get rattled because they think the audience is keenly aware of their thumping heart and quaking hands. You, of course, are painfully aware of those symptoms, but—believe it or not—your audience is usually oblivious to your body's distress. Remember that people are sitting out there wanting to hear your ideas. They are not saying to themselves, "Let's see, what signs of nervousness is this person displaying?"

Some students, after a speech, report being embarrassed about their jittery performance, whereas the other listeners in the class saw no signs of nervousness. Everyone was listening to the ideas and failed to notice the speaker's discomfort. Various studies have found the same thing to be true: audiences are unaware of the symptoms that speakers think are embarrassingly obvious.[16] In other words, you are probably the only one who knows that your knees are shaking and your heart is pounding.

Olivia Mitchell, a presentation trainer and member of the Toastmasters club, notes, "You don't look as nervous as you feel." After a speech, Mitchell will often ask her students to rate their anxiety on a scale from 1 to 10, where 10 is the most nervous. She writes, "The presenter might say they were '8' on the scale. Then we ask the other participants what they thought [of the speaker's nervousness]. They'll say '3.'" Mitchell observes that the audience can't see your heart racing, they can't tell your mouth is dry, and they don't know that your shaky voice isn't how you normally sound. If you're a nervous presenter, it's likely your audience can't tell.[17]

Never Mention Nervousness or Apologize

Though most signs of nervousness are not visible, there may be times when an audience does notice your nervousness—when, for example, your breathing is audibly labored. In such a case, resist the temptation to comment or apologize. Everyone knows that most people get nervous when they talk in public, so why call attention to it or apologize for it?

Commenting about nervousness can create two big dangers. First of all, you might get yourself more rattled than you were to begin with. Take the case of a teacher who was giving a talk to a PTA meeting one night. In the middle of her remarks, she suddenly blurted out, "Oh my god, I knew I would fall apart." Up to that time, the audience had not been aware of any discomfort or nervousness. She tried to continue her talk, but she was too flustered. She gave up the effort and sat down with a red face. Whatever internal distress she was suffering, had she said nothing about her nervousness, she could have dragged herself through the speech. When she sat down, it was clear that several members of the audience felt irritated and disappointed because they had been keenly interested in her remarks. Perhaps they even thought her selfish for depriving them of the second half of her speech, simply because she was nervous. This may sound insensitive, but it underscores an important point: your listeners don't care about your emotional distress; they only want to hear your message.

The second risk of mentioning symptoms is that your audience might have been unaware of your nervousness before you brought it up, but now you have distracted

Tips for Your Career

Prepare for Memory Lapses

A psychologist tells of the time when he was speaking at a convention as the presiding officer. At one point, he wanted to praise an associate who was sitting next to him at the head table for her hard work in planning the convention. "As I began my words of tribute," he said, "my mind suddenly went blank, and I couldn't remember her name! It was awful. This was a woman I had worked with for years. She was like a sister."

Fortunately, he said, everyone was wearing name tags, so he leaned over, saw her name, and used it in his remarks—without the audience suspecting his memory lapse.

Such lapses are common, but don't be alarmed. There is a simple solution: prepare a card with all basic information—names, dates, websites—and keep the card with your other notes for easy access.

This "card trick" is used by many ministers, politicians, and other public speakers. "When I perform weddings, even if I'm an old friend of the couple," says one minister, "I have their names printed in big letters on a card that I keep in front of me."

Use a card for any familiar passages, such as the Lord's Prayer or the Pledge of Allegiance, that you are supposed to recite or to lead the audience in reciting. You may never need to read the card, but it's nice to have a backup in case of emergency.

Please don't misinterpret this tip to mean that you should write out an entire speech. Brief notes—a few words or phrases—are still recommended. Use the "card trick" only for names, numbers, and wordings that must be recalled with complete accuracy.

At public ceremonies, like this wedding, many ministers avoid embarrassment by having key information (such as the names of the bride and groom) on a card in front of them.

©Ned Frisk/Blend Images LLC

them from your speech and they are watching the very thing you don't want them to scrutinize: your body's behavior. If you say, "I'm sorry that my hands are shaking," what do you think the audience will pay close attention to, at least for the next few minutes? Your hands, of course, instead of your speech. Keep your audience's attention focused on your ideas, and they will pay little or no attention to your emotional and physical distress.

Don't Let Your Audience Upset You

If you are like some speakers, you get rattled when you look out at the audience and observe that most listeners are poker-faced and unsmiling. Does this mean they are displeased with your speech? No. Their solemn faces have nothing to do with you and your speech. This is just one of those peculiarities of human nature: in a conversation, people will smile and nod and encourage you, but when listening to a speech in an audience, most of them wear a blank mask. The way to deal with those stony faces is to remind yourself that your listeners want you to succeed; they hope that you will give them a worthwhile message. If you are lucky, you will notice two or three listeners who obviously appreciate your speech—they nod in agreement or give you looks of approval. Let your eyes go to them frequently. They will give you courage and confidence.

If you are an inexperienced public speaker, you may get upset if you see members of an audience whispering to one another. You may wonder, "Are these people making negative comments about me?" If the listeners are smiling, it can be even worse. You ask yourself, "Did I say something dumb? Is there something wrong with my clothes?" If this happens to you, keep in mind that your rude listeners are probably just sharing some personal gossip. If they *are* whispering about something you've said, it's not necessarily negative. They may be whispering that they agree with you 100 percent.

What if you see faces that look angry or displeased? Don't assume the worst. Some people get a troubled look on their face whenever they concentrate on a speaker's message. Michelle Roberts, a defense attorney in Washington, DC, studies the facial expressions of every juror when she addresses the jury during a trial, but she has learned that frowning faces do not necessarily signify disapproval. She says about jurors, "Sometimes they seem like they're scowling and actually they're with you."[18]

What if a listener stands up and walks out of the room? For some inexperienced public speakers, this feels like a stunning personal defeat. Before you jump to conclusions, bear in mind that the listener's behavior is probably not a response to your speech: he or she may have another meeting to attend, may need to use the rest room, or may need to take an emergency phone call. But what if the listener is indeed storming out of the room in a huff, obviously rejecting your speech? In such a case, advises veteran speaker Earl Nightingale, "don't worry about it. On controversial subjects, you're bound to have listeners who are not in agreement with you—unless you're giving them pure, unadulterated pap. Trying to win over every member of the audience is an impossible and thankless task. Remember, there were those who disagreed with wise, kind Socrates."[19]

Act Poised

To develop confidence when you face an audience, act as if you already are confident. Why? Because playing the role of the self-assured speaker can often transform you

Actress Moran Rosenblatt listens to a speaker at a film festival in Berlin. Is she displeased with the speaker's remarks? Is she bored? Don't jump to conclusions. Perhaps this is just her habitual expression when listening to an interesting topic.

©John MacDougall/AFP/Getty Images

into a speaker who is genuinely confident and poised. In various wars, soldiers have reported that they were terrified before going into combat, but nevertheless they acted brave in front of their buddies. During the battle, to their surprise, what started off as a pretense became a reality. Instead of pretending to be courageous, they actually became so. The same thing often happens to public speakers.

Look Directly at the Audience

If you are frightened of your audience, it is tempting to stare at your notes or the back wall or the window, but these evasions will only add to your nervousness, not reduce it.

Force yourself to establish eye contact, especially at the beginning of your speech. Good eye contact means more than just a quick, furtive glance at various faces in front of you; it means "locking" your eyes with a listener's for a couple of seconds. Locking eyes may sound frightening, but it actually helps calm you. In an article about a public speaking course that she took, writer Maggie Paley said, "When you make contact with one other set of eyes, it's a connection; you can relax and concentrate. The first time I did it, I calmed down 90 percent, and spoke . . . fluently."[20]

Don't Speak Too Fast

Because of nervous tension and a desire to "get it over with," many speakers race through their speeches. "Take it slow and easy," advises Dr. Michael T. Motley of the University of California, Davis. "People in an audience have a tremendous job of information-processing to do. They need your help. Slow down, pause, and guide the audience through your talk by delineating major and minor points carefully. Remember that your objective is to help the audience understand what you are saying, not to present your information in record time."[21]

To help yourself slow down, rehearse your speech in front of friends or relatives and ask them to raise their hands whenever you talk too rapidly. For the actual delivery of the speech, write reminders for yourself in large letters on your notes (such as "SLOW DOWN"). While you are speaking, look at your listeners and talk directly to them in the same calm, patient, deliberate manner you would use if you were explaining an idea to a friend.

Get Audience Action Early in the Speech

While it's a bit unnerving to see your listeners' expressionless faces, in some speeches, you can change those faces from blank to animated by asking a question. (Tips on how to ask questions will be discussed in the chapter on introductions and conclusions.) When the listeners respond with answers or a show of hands, they show themselves to be friendly and cooperative, which reduces your apprehension. When they loosen up, you loosen up.

Eliminate Excess Energy

For siphoning off excess energy during the speech, you can use visual aids (as mentioned earlier) and these two tension releasers:

- Let your hands make gestures. You will not have any trouble making gestures if you simply allow your hands to be free. Don't clutch note cards or thrust your hands into your pockets or grip the lectern. If you let your hands hang by your side or rest on the lectern, you will find that they will make gestures naturally. You will not have to think about it.

- Walk around. Though you obviously should not pace back and forth like a caged animal, you can walk a few steps at a time. For example, you can walk a few steps to the left of the lectern to make a point, move back to the lectern to look at your notes for your next point, and then walk to the right of the lectern as you speak.

In addition to reducing tension, gestures and movement make you a more exciting and interesting speaker than someone who stands frozen to one spot.

Accept Imperfection

If you think that you must give a perfect, polished speech, you put enormous—and unnecessary—pressure on yourself. Your listeners don't care whether your delivery is perfect; they simply hope that your words will enlighten or entertain them. Think of yourself as a package deliverer; the audience is more interested in the package than in how skillfully you hand it over.

Making a mistake is not the end of the world. Even experienced speakers commit a fair number of blunders and bloopers. If you completely flub a sentence or mangle an idea, you might say something like, "No, wait. That's not the way I wanted to explain this. Let me try again." If you momentarily forget what you were planning to say, don't despair. Pause a few moments to regain your composure and find your place in your notes. If you can't find your place, ask the audience for help: "I've lost my train of thought—where was I?" There is no need to apologize. In conversation, you pause and correct yourself all the time; to do so occasionally in a speech makes you sound spontaneous and natural.

If you make a mistake that causes your audience to snicker or laugh, try to join in. If you can laugh at yourself, your audience will love you—they will see that you are no "stuffed shirt." Some comedians deliberately plan "mistakes" as a technique for gaining rapport with their audiences.

Welcome Experience

If you are an inexperienced public speaker, please know that you will learn to manage your nervousness as you get more and more practice in public speaking, both in your speech class and in your career. You should welcome this experience as a way to further your personal and professional growth.

One student, at the beginning of the course, said that she just *knew* she would drop out of the class right before her first speech. She stayed, though, and developed into a fine speaker. She later got a promotion in her company partly because of her speaking ability. "I never thought I'd say this," she admitted, "but the experience of giving speeches—plus learning how to handle nervousness—helped me enormously. Before I took the course, I used to panic whenever I started off a talk. I had this enormous lump in my throat, and I thought I was doing terrible. I would hurry through my talk just to get it over with." But as a result of the course, she said, "I learned to control my nervousness and use it to my advantage. Now I'm as nervous as ever when I give a speech, but I make the nervousness work *for* me instead of *against* me."

In your career, rather than shying away from speaking opportunities, seek them out. An old saying is true: experience is the best teacher.

Like most public speakers, singer Shawn Mendes sometimes makes mistakes. Regarding a concert in Philadelphia, he says, "I fumbled my words on stage. I was between songs and meant to tell the fans to 'sing along if you know the words,' but it came out as an entirely jumbled sentence of gibberish."
©Brad Barket/iHeartMedia/Getty Images

Resources for Review and Skill Building

Summary

Nervousness is a normal, understandable emotion experienced by most public speakers. There are many reasons for jitters, but five of the most common are fear of being stared at, fear of failure or rejection, fear of the unknown, a traumatic experience in the past, and social anxiety. There is no reason to be ashamed if any of them apply to you.

Instead of trying to eliminate nervousness, welcome it as a source of energy. Properly channeled, "positive nervousness" can help you give a better speech than you would deliver if you were completely relaxed.

The best way to avoid excessive, crippling nervousness is to pour time and energy into preparing and practicing your speech. Then, when you stand up to speak, deal rationally with your nervous symptoms (such as trembling knees and dry throat). Remind yourself that the symptoms are not a prelude to disaster but instead are evidence that you are energized enough to give a good speech. Never call attention to your nervousness and never apologize for it; the listeners are more interested in your message than your emotional state. Focus on getting your ideas across to the audience. This will get your mind where it belongs (on your listeners, not yourself), and it will help you move your nervousness to a back burner, where it can still simmer and energize you without hindering your effectiveness.

Key Terms

adrenaline, *22*   positive imagery, *24*   positive nervousness, *23*

Review Questions

1. What are the five common reasons for speakers' nervousness?

2. Why are fear and nervousness beneficial to the public speaker?

3. Why is delivering a speech from memory a bad method?

4. Is shyness a liability for a speaker? Explain your answer.

5. How can a speaker reduce excessive tension before a speech?

6. Explain the idea "Think of communication, not performance."

7. Does an audience detect most of a speaker's nervous symptoms? Explain your answer.

8. Why should you never call attention to your nervousness?

9. Why should speakers not be upset when they see the unsmiling faces of their listeners?

10. Why should a speaker act as if he or she is confident?

Building Critical-Thinking Skills

1. In an experiment, psychologist Rowland Miller asked college students to do something embarrassing, such as singing "The Star-Spangled Banner," while classmates watched. Those students who reported a great degree of embarrassment thought that their classmates would consider them fools and like them less, but Miller found just the opposite: the classmates expressed greater regard for the easily embarrassed students after the performance than before. What lessons can a public speaker draw from this research?

2. Imagine that while you are speaking to an audience, you notice that (a) everyone is very quiet, (b) a man in the front is rubbing his neck, and (c) a woman is looking in her purse. Using two columns on a piece of paper, give a negative interpretation of these events in the left column, and then give a positive interpretation in the right column.

3. Many musicians make a distinction between "good nervousness" and "bad nervousness." What does this distinction mean? How does it apply to public speakers?

4. Is it a good idea for speakers to focus during their speech on whether their clothes, grooming, and overall image are pleasing to the audience? Defend your answer.

Building Teamwork Skills

1. In a group, make a list of the nervous symptoms that group members have experienced before and during oral communication in public. (This may include being asked for comments during a class discussion.) Then, discuss ways to control nervousness.

2. Worrying about future events, say mental-health therapists, can be helpful at certain times and harmful at other times. In a group, discuss the pros and cons of worrying using examples from everyday life. Then, decide which aspects of speech preparation and delivery deserve to be worried about and which do not.

Examining Your Ethics

Answer: A, B, and C. Not knowing much about the topic can worsen speech anxiety and can cause embarrassment in the question-and-answer period. Plagiarism is a form of theft and is always unethical.

End Notes

1. "Conquering Stage Fright," Anxiety and Depression Association of America, www.adaa.org/understanding-anxiety/social-anxiety-disorder/treatment/conquering-stage-fright (accessed January 7, 2016).

2. "Fear/Phobia Statistics," Statistic Brain Research Institute, www.statisticbrain.com (accessed September 24, 2015); Joan Acocella, "I Can't Go On! What's behind Stagefright?," *The New Yorker,* August 3, 2015, p. 69.

3. Reggie Jackson, interview during an ABC sports telecast, October 2, 1984.

4. Beyoncé, quoted by Caleb Hsu, http://blog.sonicbids.com/how-to-deal-with-performance-anxiety-on-and-off-the-stage (accessed January 11, 2020).

5. Elayne Snyder, Speechcoach, www.speechcoach.com (accessed May 16, 2015).

6. I. A. R. Wylie, quoted by Pushp Lata, *Communicate or Collapse: A Handbook of Effective Public Speaking* (New Delhi: Prentice-Hall of India, 2007), p. 22.

7. Adair Linn Nagata, "Cultivating Confidence in Public Communication," *Journal of Intercultural Communication,* no. 7 (2004), pp. 177–97.

8. Joel Weldon, professional speaker, Scottsdale, Arizona, e-mail interview, December 4, 2000.

9. Tammie Ronen, *The Positive Power of Imagery* (New York: Wiley, 2011), p. 46.

10. P. Close, "15 Celebrities You Didn't Know Were Shy," *PopCrush,* July 5, 2017, https://popcrush.com/shy-celebrity-loners-introverts-gallery/.

11. Joe W. Boyd, professional speaker, Bellingham, Washington, e-mail interview, December 4, 2000.

12. Johnny Lee, director of Peace at Work, Raleigh, North Carolina, e-mail interview, October 5, 2005.

13. Ernestine Schumann-Heink, quoted by Deborah Daiek and Nancy Anter, *Critical Reading for College and Beyond* (New York: McGraw-Hill, 2003), p. 341.

14. Danielle Kennedy, professional speaker, Sun Valley, Idaho, e-mail interview, June 8, 2000.

15. Michael T. Motley, "Taking the Terror out of Talk," *Psychology Today,* January 1988, p. 49.

16. Colette R. Hirsch et al., "Self-Images Play a Causal Role in Social Phobia," *Behaviour Research and Therapy,* August 2003, pp. 909–21.

17. Olivia Mitchell, "Anxiety and Public Speaking: What Everyone Ought to Know," https://speakingaboutpresenting.com/nervousness/anxiety-and-public-speaking/.

18. Michelle Roberts, quoted in David Segal, "Verdict: The Defense Can't Rest Too Often," *The Washington Post,* July 3, 1999, p. A14.

19. Earl Nightingale, *Communicate What You Think* (Chicago: Nightingale-Conant Corp., 2001), Audiocassette #11.

20. Maggie Paley, "Modern Image Signal: Voice," *Vogue,* August 1984, p. 412.

21. Michael T. Motley, "Taking the Terror out of Talk," *Psychology Today,* January 1988, p. 49.

Listening

OUTLINE

OBJECTIVES

After studying this chapter, you should be able to

1. Explain the difference between hearing and listening.
2. Describe eight key techniques to effective listening.
3. Define three major responsibilities that listeners have toward speakers.
4. Give and receive evaluations of speeches.

AIR FORCE TECHNICAL SERGEANT Marquis Mullins and his daughter Anya are giving their full attention to a speaker at an Independence Day celebration in Washington, DC. They are displaying the attributes of ideal listeners—eyes focused on the speaker, signaling their engagement with what the speaker is saying.

They also illustrate one of the key points of this chapter: when listeners are absorbed and attentive, they not only learn a lot—they also help energize and encourage the speaker.

When listeners are fully engaged, they help energize the speaker.

Kevin Dietsch-Pool/Getty Images

Figure 1
Samantha Rudolph tries to recruit college students to work for ESPN, but a listening error by some students blocks effective communication.

Introduction to Listening

Can you remember key ideas from a speaker's presentation 24 hours after you listen to it? Before you answer, consider this:

Samantha Rudolph gives presentations on college campuses throughout the United States to try to recruit students to work at ESPN, the popular sports network (Figure 1). During a presentation at one college, she spent most of her time talking about the many ESPN jobs that are available at headquarters in Connecticut, but at one point, she mentioned that there are also a number of positions available in other states.[1]

The next day, a professor who sent her Mass Communication class to listen to the presentation discussed ESPN job opportunities with her students. She was surprised to learn that at least half the class believed that Rudolph had given the following message: "If you can't live in Connecticut, you can forget about working for ESPN."

The students who failed to listen carefully were not stupid, and we should not feel superior to them. All of us face a challenge when we listen to a presentation. We don't have printed words to linger over and reread if necessary. All we have is oral communication, which is written on the wind—fast-moving and impermanent.

Although listening effectively is a challenging task, you can become a better listener by employing the techniques discussed in this chapter. These techniques should also help you become a better speaker. As you gain more awareness of the difficulties of the listening process, you will be able to plan your presentations to ensure that you give listeners messages that are clear and memorable.

The Problem of Poor Listening Skills

A parent says to a child, "Are you listening to me?"

The child replies, "I hear you. I hear you."

Although in conversation we sometimes use the words *hear* and *listen* interchangeably, we should not treat them as synonyms. **Hearing** occurs when your ears pick up

hearing
the process by which sound waves are received by the ear.

sound waves transmitted by a speaker. **Listening** involves making sense out of what is being transmitted. In the words of Keith Davis, a business professor at Arizona State University, "Hearing is with the ears, but listening is with the mind."[2]

listening
the act of interpreting and evaluating what is being said.

Listening is a major part of daily life. We spend an estimated 50 to 70 percent of our communication time listening, but research shows that most of us are not very effective as listeners. In a 1957 article in *Harvard Business Review*, researchers Ralph G. Nichols and Leonard A. Stevens describe their seminal study on listening at the University of Minnesota. They found that immediately following a short presentation, the average listener remembers only 50 percent of what he or she heard. After two months, the information retained drops to 25 percent.[3]

While failing to retain information can lead to negative outcomes, miscomprehending and distorting the information we hear can be disastrous. Consider the pilot who misinterprets instructions while taxiing at an airport, leading to a crash and multiple deaths and injuries. Or the health care worker who misunderstands patient care instructions, leading to a fall, an error in dosage calculation, or worse. Among 400 companies in the United States and the United Kingdom, misunderstandings lead to roughly $37 billion in costs each year due to confusion about employee policies, business processes, and job functions.[4]

How to Listen Effectively

Many businesses have discovered that they can boost productivity and sales by teaching their employees to listen more effectively. Here are some key techniques.

Prepare Yourself

Listening to difficult material is hard work, so prepare yourself as thoroughly as a runner prepares for a race.

Prepare yourself *physically*. Get enough sleep the night before. Consider exercising right before the speech or lecture. For example, if you suspect you will become drowsy in a warm classroom mid-afternoon, take a brisk walk beforehand to make yourself alert.

Prepare yourself *intellectually*. If the subject matter of the speech is new or complex, conduct research or do background reading beforehand. By previewing the information, you prime your brain to make connections between the content of the speech and what you already know. This helps you comprehend the speech and retain the information provided. As the American philosopher Henry David Thoreau once said, "We hear and apprehend only what we already half know."[5]

Be Willing to Expend Energy

When you watch a comedian on TV, do you have to work hard to pay attention? Of course not. You simply sit back and enjoy the humor. It is easy, effortless, and fun. If you are like many listeners, you assume that when you go to a presentation on a difficult subject, you should be able to sit back and absorb the content just as easily as you grasp a comedian's jokes. But this is a major misconception. Listening effectively to difficult material requires work. You must be alert and energetic, giving total concentration with your eyes, ears, and mind.

According to Dr. Ralph G. Nichols, who did pioneering work on listening skills at the University of Minnesota, listening "is characterized by faster heart action, quicker circulation of the blood, and a small rise in body temperature."[6]

If you tend to drift away mentally whenever a speaker begins to talk about unfamiliar or difficult material, try to break yourself of the habit. Vow to put as much energy as necessary into paying attention.

Listen Analytically

You should analyze a speech, not to nitpick or poke holes in it, but to help yourself understand and remember the speaker's message. Here are two elements to analyze:

Focus on main ideas.   After a speech, some listeners remember the interesting stories and fascinating visuals, but they can't tell you the points that the speaker was trying to make. Look for the key ideas of the speech.

Evaluate supports.   Effective speakers use stories, statistics, and quotations to explain, illustrate, or prove their main points. As a listener, you should evaluate those supports, asking yourself these questions:

- Do the supports seem to be accurate and up-to-date?
- Are they derived from reliable sources, or are they merely hearsay?
- Do they truly explain or prove a point?

Listening analytically helps you become a better listener. It also helps you improve the quality of your own speeches, because you can avoid the mistakes you see in the speeches of others. For an example of how to analyze, see Figure 2, which involves note taking, our next subject.

Take Notes

Note taking facilitates effective listening in two key ways:

1. *Note taking helps you remember.* Studies show that people who take notes in meetings and lectures retain far more information than people who don't take notes.[7]

2. *Note taking helps you stay focused on the speaker.* Because it prevents your mind from wandering, it is a good idea to take notes on *all* speeches, even if you eventually throw away the notes. One of my colleagues explains:

> I take notes at any talk I go to. I review the notes right after the meeting to solidify the key points in my mind. Afterwards, I may save the notes for my files or for some sort of follow-up, but I usually throw them away. This doesn't mean that I had wasted my time by taking notes. The act of writing them helped me to listen analytically. It also—I must confess—kept me from daydreaming.

Note taking is effective only if you take notes systematically. Follow these strategies:

Don't try to write down everything.   Jot down just the key information. If you try to record one sentence after another, you will wear out your hand, or worse, you might fall into the habit of transcribing without evaluating.

Take notes by hand.   People who type notes on a laptop during an oral presentation tend to copy down what they hear word for word. People who take notes by hand, however, have to interpret, process, and summarize the information, because they can't write as quickly as they can type. As a result, those who take notes by hand tend to remember the content of the speech better than those who use a computer.[8]

Summarize.   Put the speaker's ideas into your own words. This will help ensure that you understand the speaker's message. If you can't summarize a speaker's message to yourself or a friend, that is a good sign that you do not understand the material.

Speaker's Words

"Hackers are able to get into e-mail, Facebook, and bank accounts because most people use easy-to-guess passwords, according to the *New York Times*. Amichai Shulman is the chief technology officer at Imperva, a company that makes software to block hackers. He says that the most popular passwords are 123456, iloveyou, password, abc123, and america. The solution is to use a long password that mixes letters and numbers. But be careful. The password should be complex—for example, tp38jqx72wkw—instead of something simple, such as ilovemycat6789."

Figure 2
Option A and Option B show two methods of note taking.

Option A
The speaker's message is analyzed and sorted. (See text for details.)

Main ideas	Support	Follow-up
Hackers can access accounts	email, Facebook, bank	
Passwords too simple	123456, iloveyou, america	Are people just lazy?
Solution - long, with letters & numbers	tp38jqx72wkw	Too hard to memorize?

Option B
Because it is sometimes hard to distinguish between main ideas and subpoints while a speaker is talking, some listeners jot down one item per line.

Hackers can access accounts
email, Facebook, bank
Passwords too simple
123456, iloveyou, america - Are people just lazy?
Solution - long, with letters & numbers
tp38jqx72wkw - Too hard to memorize?

Later, the listener can analyze the notes, using a highlighter to focus on key ideas and a red pen for follow-up items.

Hackers can access accounts
email, Facebook, bank
Passwords too simple
123456, iloveyou, america - Are people just lazy?
Solution - long, with letters & numbers
tp38jqx72wkw - Too hard to memorize?

Tips for Your Career

Take Notes in Important Conversations and Small-Group Meetings

Whenever your supervisors and colleagues talk to you (either one-on-one or in a group meeting) about work-related matters, take notes. Not only does this give you a written record of important discussions, but it also is a compliment, a nonverbal way of saying "Your ideas are important to me— so important that I want to make sure I get them down correctly." Contrary to what some may think, taking notes does not signify to others that you have a poor memory.

One of the most common complaints of employees is that "the boss never listens to what we say." So, if you are ever in a supervisory position, take notes when an employee comes to you with a suggestion. Doing so demonstrates that you value the employee's comments and are prepared to take action if necessary. Even if you can't take action, you have shown that you truly listen and value input.

Use a note taking method.   If you have not already developed a method that works well for you, consider using one of the two methods in Figure 2. In Option A, the first column is labeled "Main ideas," and the second column is labeled "Support." Enter the speaker's key points in the first column and any supporting points in the second column. Use the third column, titled "Follow-up," to keep track of questions you want to ask during the question-and-answer period, or items that you want to conduct research on later (for example, you might remind yourself: "Get more info on this"). You should use the Follow-up column only as needed.

Option B is a good choice when a speaker talks fast or does not clearly distinguish between main points and supports. Write one note per line. Later, use a highlighter to mark the key ideas. In pen, circle any items that you need to follow up on.

Soon after a presentation, review your notes.   If necessary, clarify them while the speaker's words are still fresh in your mind. If any parts of your notes are vague or confusing, seek help from another listener or, if available, the speaker—he or she will be flattered.

Resist Distractions

Four common types of distractions make concentrating on a speech difficult:

- **Auditory**—people coughing or whispering, a cell phone ringing, loud noises in the hallway
- **Visual**—an interesting poster left over from a previous meeting, an intriguing listener seated nearby, people walking into or out of the room
- **Physical**—hunger, a headache or stuffy nose, an uncomfortable seat, a room that is too hot or too cold
- **Mental**—daydreams, worries, preoccupations

Mental distractions are often caused by the fact that your mind runs faster than a speaker can talk. As a listener, you can process speech at about 500 words per minute, while most speakers talk at 125 to 150 words a minute. This gap creates a lot of mental spare time, and we can easily start daydreaming or thinking of unrelated matters.

How can you resist distractions? By using rigorous self-discipline. Prepare yourself for active listening by arriving in the room a few minutes early and getting yourself situated. Find a seat that is free from distractions, such as blinding sunlight or friends who might want to whisper to you. Make yourself comfortable, lay out paper and a pen for

TIP 2

Tips for Your Career

Learn How Listeners Show Respect in Different Cultures

While Gail Opp-Kemp, an American artist, was giving a speech on the art of Japanese brush painting to an audience that included visitors from Japan, she was disconcerted to see that many of her Japanese listeners had their eyes closed. Were they turned off because an American had the audacity to instruct Japanese in their own art form? Were they deliberately trying to signal their rejection of her?

Opp-Kemp later found out that her listeners were not being disrespectful. Japanese listeners sometimes close their eyes to enhance concentration. Her listeners were paying tribute to her by meditating upon her words.

Someday you may be either a speaker or a listener in a situation involving people from other countries or backgrounds. Learning how different cultures signal respect can help you avoid misunderstandings. Here are some examples:

- In the deaf culture of North America, many listeners signify applause not by clapping their hands but by waving them in the air.

- In some cultures (both overseas and in some groups in North America), listeners are considered disrespectful if they look directly at the speaker. Respect is shown by looking in the general direction of the speaker but avoiding direct eye contact.

- In some countries, whistling by listeners is a sign of approval, while in other countries, it is a form of jeering.

You can find more information about different cultural practices around speaking and listening by typing a phrase like "India speaking customs" into Google or another search engine. Additionally, the library staff at your college or university can help you with cultural research.

Sources: Stella Ting-Toomey, *Communicating across Cultures* (New York: Guilford Press, 2012), pp. 114–29; Adam D'Arpino, "11 American Behaviors That Are Considered Rude around the World," Mental Floss, mentalfloss.com (accessed November 19, 2015).

Nick Dolding/Getty images

taking notes, and clear your mind of personal matters. When the speech begins, concentrate all your mental energies on the speaker's message.

Avoid Fake Listening

Many members of an audience look directly at a speaker and seem to be listening, but in reality they are just pretending. Their minds are far away.

If you engage in fake listening, you might miss a lot of important information, but even worse, you risk embarrassment and ridicule. Imagine that you are engaged in fake listening during a meeting and your boss suddenly asks you to comment on a statement that has just been made. You don't have a clue. You've been caught.

If you have the habit of tuning out speakers while pretending to listen, one of the best ways to force yourself to pay attention is to take notes, as discussed earlier.

Give Speakers a Fair Chance

Don't reject speakers because you dislike their looks, their clothes, or the organization they represent. Instead, focus on their message, which might be interesting and worthwhile.

The Chinese character for "the act of listening" includes (1) ear, (2) self, (3) eyes, (4) undivided attention, and (5) heart. Why do you think these components are included?

Shi Yali/Shutterstock

If speakers have ragged delivery, or they seem shaky and lacking in confidence, don't be too quick to discount the content of their speech.

Kimberley Mason, a community advocate and parent–teacher organization leader who ran for Columbus City Schools Board of Education, noted that many power brokers chose not to listen to her because she was an "outsider" to the political process.

> While running for office, I ran into titles, power, and position. Rather than listen to me and take me seriously, some individuals would try to intimidate or confuse me by pulling me out of my comfort zone, or pressuring me to speak on unfamiliar topics.
>
> What I have learned in life, and throughout my campaign, is that sticking to your truth allows you to stay in your comfort zone, and reduces disparities in titles, power, and position. This way, you can have open conversations with anyone in the room, no matter who they are.

In most cases, you should give speakers a fair chance. You may be pleasantly surprised by what you learn.

Control Emotions

During many question-and-answer periods, audience members verbally attack a speaker for putting forward a position that was not actually the speaker's stance. These audience members were not practicing careful listening.

Some listeners don't listen well because they have a powerful emotional reaction to a topic or to some comment the speaker makes. Their strong emotions cut off intelligent listening for the rest of the speech. Instead of paying attention to the speaker's words, they "argue" with the speaker inside their heads, or think of ways to retaliate in the question-and-answer period. They often jump to conclusions, convincing themselves that the speaker is saying something that he or she is not actually saying.

When you are listening to speakers who seem to be arguing against some of your ideas or beliefs, make sure you understand exactly what they are saying. Hear them out, and *then* prepare your counterarguments.

The Listener's Responsibilities

As discussed in the introduction to public speaking chapter, the speaker who is honest and fair has ethical and moral obligations to his or her listeners. The converse is also true: the honest and fair listener has ethical and moral obligations to the speaker. Let's examine three of the listener's primary responsibilities: to show courtesy and respect, to provide encouragement, and to find value in every speech.

Show Courtesy and Respect

Are you a polite listener? To make sure that you are not committing acts of rudeness, keep the following points in mind.

Follow the Golden Rule of Listening

If you were engaged in conversation with a friend, how would you feel if your friend yawned and fell asleep? Or started reading a book? Or talked on a cell phone? You would be upset by your friend's rudeness, wouldn't you?

Many people would never dream of being so rude to a friend in conversation, yet when they sit in an audience, they are terribly rude to the speaker. They fall asleep, study for a test, check their e-mail or text messages, or carry on a whispered conversation with their friends.

Fortunately, a public speaking class cures some people of their rudeness. One student realized his rudeness to speakers after being in their position:

> I had been sitting in classrooms for 12 years and until now, I never realized how much a speaker sees. I always thought a listener is hidden and anonymous out there in a sea of faces. Now that I've been a speaker, I realize that when you look out at an audience, you are well aware of the least little thing somebody does. I am ashamed now at how I used to carry on conversations in the back of class. I was very rude, and I didn't even know it.

Follow the golden rule of listening: "Listen unto others as you would have others listen unto you." When you are a speaker, you want an audience that listens attentively and courteously, so when you are a listener, you should provide the same response.

Is this woman justified in being upset because her date is talking to a friend during lunch?
Stockphoto4u/Getty Images

Reject Electronic Intrusion

During a meeting or presentation, if you read and send text messages, play games on your phone, or browse the Internet on your laptop, you are sending a strong, clear message to the speaker: "You are not important to me, and your comments don't merit my respect and my attention."

To be courteous, keep your eyes and attention on the speaker. Follow these rules:

- Before a meeting begins, turn off all electronics that might ring or make other noise, and put them away. Remove headphones or earbuds, even if they are not connected to devices.

- Never talk on a cell phone or headset. Even whispers are distracting.

- Don't send or read text messages. "People mistakenly think that tapping is not as distracting as talking," says Nancy Flynn, executive director of the ePolicy Institute. "In fact, it can be more distracting. And it's pretty insulting to the speaker."[9]

- Unless you have an emergency situation, turn your phone to silent mode. Even a vibrating phone can be noisy and distracting. Also, if you get up and leave the room to respond to a friend's casual call, you are creating an unnecessary disruption.

Sometimes the rules above can be broken, such as in cases like these:

- If it's appropriate and approved by the speaker, you may take notes on a tablet, laptop, or smartphone. Show the speaker that you are paying attention by looking at him or her frequently (rather than keeping your eyes focused nonstop on your computer). If you play games, text, or browse, the speaker will sense what you are doing and think that you are being disrespectful.

- In some classes or training sessions, you will be encouraged or even required to use an electronic device as part of the learning process. As suggested above, look at the speaker frequently to convey that you are connected to him or her.

- If you are on call (for example, if you are a firefighter or a paramedic), or if you are awaiting news related to an ongoing emergency, go to the speaker in advance and explain the situation. Set your phone to vibrate and sit near the door if you can. If you get a call, leave the room quietly and answer the phone well away from the door.

Beware the Pitfalls of Multitasking

We all multitask every day, combining such simple acts as driving a car and listening to music. When the tasks are easy and routine, this isn't a problem. However, multitasking is a bad strategy in two situations: (1) when the tasks are complex, and (2) when you

Tips for Your Career

Confront Electronic Rudeness

If you are like most speakers, you will be irritated or even unnerved if you see listeners who are immersed in their private world of electronic devices. It is hard to communicate effectively with people who are tuning you out.

What can you do to capture their full attention?

If possible, forbid the use of electronic devices. Many speakers—including corporate executives and military officers—ban the use of smartphones and tablets during meetings and presentations. Some companies require employees to put their electronic devices on a table as they enter a conference room.

What if you lack the power to order a ban? If possible, ask the person in charge of a group to request—before you rise to speak—that all equipment be turned off. But what if those strategies aren't possible and you see that some of your listeners are using electronic equipment? Try saying something like this: "I hate to inconvenience anyone, but I have a problem. I have trouble concentrating on what I want to say when I look out and see people working on their computers or talking on their cell phones. I would appreciate it if you would help me out and turn off your equipment while I'm speaking." By emphasizing *your* difficulties rather than attacking *their* rudeness, you enhance your chances of gaining compliance.

One final strategy that has been successful for some speakers is to use an attention-getter in the introduction of your speech that is so compelling that the audience becomes totally absorbed in listening to you. (Samples of attention-getters are presented in the chapter on introductions and conclusions.)

If you saw these rude listeners in your audience, how would you handle the situation?

Shutterstock/Sean De Burca

may insult or alienate other people. Here is some important information that you need to know.

Multitasking can mar your performance.   Although multitaskers think they are performing all activities effectively, studies show that their comprehension suffers. For example, researchers at Cornell University arranged for two groups of students to listen to the same lecture and then take a test immediately afterward. One group was allowed to use their laptops to browse the Internet during the lecture, while the other group was asked to keep their laptops closed. When tested, the students with open laptops remembered significantly less information from the lecture than did the students with closed laptops.[10]

Many other research studies show that in complex tasks, multitaskers of all ages are more likely to misunderstand information and make mistakes.[11] René Marois, a psychology researcher at Vanderbilt University, says, "Our research offers neurological evidence that the brain cannot effectively do two things at once."[12] Note the key word: *effectively*.

Multitasking can hurt you professionally.   Because they are considered discourteous or inattentive, multitaskers may be given extra work or unpleasant assignments, passed over for promotions, or even fired.[13] Here are some example incidents:

- An executive at a top hospital lost her job because she "disrespected" the board of directors by "working on her laptop during presentations, firing off e-mails, and focusing on her own projects instead of participating or listening to the chair and other speakers," according to *The Cost of Bad Behavior,* a book by professors Christine Pearson of the Thunderbird School of Global Management and Christine Porath of the University of Southern California.[14]

- A woman in British Columbia was fired for texting during a meeting. She was seen as not being a "team player." A tribunal eventually found that she was dismissed without fair cause under Canadian law, but only after a long and public legal battle that damaged the woman's reputation.[15]

- Danielle Gregory, a judge in Marion County (Indiana) Juvenile Court, lost her job because while she was "on the bench conducting court sessions," she sent "multiple text messages" to friends instead of giving her full attention to the discourse in the courtroom, reports *WTHR-TV Eyewitness News* in Indianapolis.[16]

What if nobody complains to you about texting? Is it okay? Hank London of Pacifica, California, who leads workshops on career development, says, "Just because coworkers, supervisors, or clients don't say anything about your [texting while in meetings], doesn't mean they haven't taken notice." Your rudeness, he warns, can come back to haunt you.[17] In some cases, people may develop a dislike for you without being aware of the subconscious reason for their antagonism.

Provide Encouragement

Encourage the speaker as much as possible by giving your full attention, taking notes, leaning slightly forward instead of slouching back in your seat, looking directly at the speaker instead of at the floor, and letting your face show interest and animation. If the speaker says something you particularly like, nod in agreement or smile approvingly.

The more encouragement a speaker receives, the better his or her delivery is likely to be. Most entertainers and professional speakers say that if an audience is lively and enthusiastic, they do a much better job than if the audience is sullen or apathetic. Even if just a few people are displaying lively interest, their nods, smiles, and eager eyes can inspire and energize the speaker. Many performers draw energy from their audience; for example, Alicia Keys once said, "When I'm on stage, my interaction with the audience is something that really makes me come alive. It's a feeling like no other. The energy of the crowd fuels something new inside."[18]

When we help a speaker give a good speech, we are doing more than an act of kindness. We are creating a payoff for ourselves because the better the speaker, the easier it is to listen. And the easier it is to listen, the better we will understand, remember, and gain knowledge.

Rude employees are sometimes given extra work.

Nomad Soul/Shutterstock

When listeners are fully engaged, they help encourage and energize the speaker.

wavebreakmedia/Shutterstock

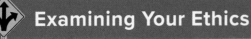

Examining Your Ethics

Consider this scenario: a group on your campus has decided to invite a controversial speaker with a known track record of hate speech and denouncing marginalized groups. As an ethical listener, what should your response be?

A. Attend the speech and listen attentively, giving the speaker your full respect.
B. Organize or attend a protest outside of the speech, providing an alternative to the speaker's message.
C. Avoid the speech entirely.

For the answer, see the last page of this chapter.

Find Value in Every Speech

Sometimes you will be obliged to hear a speech that you feel is boring and worthless. Instead of tuning out the speaker, try to exploit the speech for something worthwhile. Make a game of it: see how many diamonds you can pluck from the mud. Is there any new information that might be useful to you in the future? Is the speaker using techniques of delivery that are worth noting and emulating?

If a speech is so bad that you honestly cannot find anything worthwhile in it, use it as a how-not-to-do-it lesson. Ask yourself, "What can I learn from this speaker's mistakes?" Here is an example of how one business executive profited from a poor speech:

> At a convention recently I found myself in an extremely boring seminar (on listening, ironically enough). After spending the first half-hour wishing I had never signed up, I decided to take advantage of the situation. I turned my thought, "This guy isn't teaching me how to run a seminar on listening," into a question: "What is he teaching me about how *not* to run a seminar?" While providing a negative example was not the presenter's goal, I got a useful lesson.[19]

"When life hands you a lemon, make lemonade" some wise person once advised. If you look for value or a how-*not*-to-do-it lesson in every poor speech, you will find that the sourest oratorical lemon can be turned into lemonade. "Know how to listen," the Greek writer Plutarch said 20 centuries ago, "and you will profit even from those who talk badly."[20]

Speech Evaluations

Both evaluators and speakers profit from a speech evaluation. Evaluators gain insights into what works and what doesn't work in speechmaking, and speakers can use suggestions to improve their speaking skills.

When Evaluating

Evaluating speeches should not be limited to a public speaking class. You also can apply these techniques to speeches that you hear in your career.

Establish criteria.   Before you listen to a speech, decide upon the criteria for judging it. This will keep you from omitting important elements. For classroom speeches, your instructor may give you a checklist or tell you to analyze certain features of a speech. Otherwise, you can use the "Quick Guide to Public Speaking" found in the chapter on introduction to public speaking for your criteria.

Listen objectively.   Keep an open mind. Don't let yourself be swayed emotionally by the speaker's delivery or appearance. If, for example, a speaker sounds ill at ease and uncertain, this doesn't necessarily mean that her arguments are inferior. Don't let your own biases influence your criticism; for example, if you are strongly against gun control,

Tips for Your Career

Express Appreciation to a Speaker

Whenever you find a speech enjoyable or profitable, let the speaker know. No matter how busy or important he or she is, genuine feedback will be greatly appreciated.

After giving a speech, some speakers are physically and emotionally exhausted, and they sit down with a nagging doubt: Did it go okay? A word of thanks or a compliment from a listener is refreshing and gratifying. (If you can't express your appreciation in person right after the speech, write the speaker a brief note or send an e-mail or text message.)

Be sure to say something positive and specific about the *content* of the speech. A corporation president told of a commencement address he had delivered to a college several years before. "I sweated blood for a whole month putting that speech together and then rehearsing it dozens of times—it was my first commencement speech," he said. "When I delivered the speech, I tried to speak straight from my heart. I thought I did a good job, and I thought my speech had some real nuggets of wisdom. But afterwards, only two people came by to thank me. And you know what? They both paid me the same compliment: they said they were grateful that I had kept the speech short! They said not one word about the ideas in my speech. Not one word about whether they enjoyed the speech itself. It's depressing to think that the only thing noteworthy about my speech was its brevity."

Sad to say, there were probably dozens of people in the audience whose hearts and minds were touched by the eloquent wisdom of the speaker—but they never told him.

but the speaker argues in favor of it, be careful to criticize the speaker's ideas fairly and objectively.

Take notes.   Jot down your observations throughout the speech so that you capture key elements.

Look for both positive and negative aspects.   Emphasize the positive (so that the speaker will continue doing what works well) in addition to pointing out opportunities for improvement.

Give positive comments first.   When it comes to public speaking, most people have easily bruised egos. If you start out a critique with negative remarks, you can damage the speaker's confidence and self-esteem. Always begin by discussing his or her strengths. Point out positive attributes that might seem obvious to you but may not be obvious to the speaker. For example, you might say, "You looked poised and confident." Try ending with a positive comment, as well, so that your critical feedback is "sandwiched" between positive feedback.

Couple negative comments with positive alternatives.   When you point out a flaw, immediately give a constructive alternative. For example, you can inform a speaker that she seems to be reading long sentences from a script, and then you can suggest an alternative: "Use note cards with just a few words on each card so that you can look at the audience most of the time and sound conversational."

In most cases, ignore nervousness.   Because most people cannot help being jittery, don't criticize nervousness—unless you can give a useful tip. For example, it is unhelpful to say, "You looked tense and scared," but it is helpful to say, "Your hands trembled when you held your note cards, and this was distracting. Next time, put your notes on the lectern."

Be specific. Instead of saying, "You need to improve your eye contact," say, "You looked at the floor too much rather than at the audience." Instead of "You did great," say, "Your introduction captivated me, and your stories were extremely interesting."

When Receiving Evaluations

To get maximum benefit from evaluations, follow these guidelines:

Don't be defensive. Try to understand criticism and consider its merits. Don't argue or counterattack.

Seek clarification. If an evaluator makes a comment that you don't understand, ask for an explanation.

Strive for improvement. In your next speech, try to correct problem areas. But don't feel that you must eliminate all errors or bad habits at once.

Resources for Review and Skill Building

Summary

Listening effectively is often a difficult task, but it can be rewarding if you are willing to make the effort. Guidelines for effective listening include the following:

1. Prepare yourself intellectually and physically. Do background research to maximize your understanding of the new material in the speech. Get some exercise before the speech if necessary.
2. Listen analytically. Focus on main ideas and evaluate supports.
3. Take notes, not only to record key points but also to keep your mind from wandering.
4. Resist distractions, both external and internal. Use rigorous self-discipline to focus on the speaker's remarks.
5. Avoid fakery. Don't pretend to be listening when in fact your mind is wandering. This kind of behavior can settle into a hard-to-break habit.

6. Give every speaker a fair chance. Don't discount a speaker because of personal appearance or the organization he or she represents.
7. Control your emotions. Don't mentally argue with a speaker or else you might misunderstand what he or she is really saying.

As a listener you have three important obligations to a speaker: show courtesy and respect, provide encouragement, and find value in every speech. The more support you give a speaker, the better the speech will be, and the more you will profit from it.

Evaluating speeches can help you improve your own speechmaking skills. Look for both positive and negative aspects of a speech, and give specific, constructive suggestions. When you are on the receiving end of evaluations, don't be defensive. Try to understand the criticism and then make improvements.

Key Terms

hearing, *38*

listening, *39*

Review Questions

1. What is the difference between *hearing* and *listening*?

2. Name at least four problems caused by ineffective listening.

3. What is the difference between listening to easy material and listening to complex material?

4. List at least two ways in which you can prepare yourself physically and intellectually to listen to a speech.

5. What two speech elements should a listener examine analytically?

6. List two advantages of taking notes during a speech.

7. The text lists four types of distractions: auditory, visual, physical, and mental. Give two examples of each type.

8. How can texting during a meeting hurt you in your career?

9. When you are a listener, how can you encourage a speaker?

10. When you evaluate a speech, how should you handle both the positive and the negative aspects that you observe?

Building Critical-Thinking Skills

1. When a person is truly and deeply listening to you, what behaviors do you detect in his or her tone of voice, facial expression, eyes, and overall body language?

2. Science writer Judith Stone wrote, "There are two ways to approach a subject that frightens you and makes you feel stupid: you can embrace it with humility and an open mind, or you can ridicule it mercilessly." Translate this idea into advice for listeners of speeches.

Building Teamwork Skills

1. In a group, conduct this role play: One student gives an impromptu speech describing his or her classes this term, while all the other group members exhibit rude behaviors (such as texting, chatting, and browsing the Internet). Then the speaker discusses how he or she felt about the rudeness. If time permits, let other group members play the speaker's role.

2. Working in a group, compile a list of the attributes that would describe "the ideal listener" for a speech. Then do likewise for a conversation. In what ways are the lists similar and different?

Examining Your Ethics

Answer: B. These situations can be difficult to approach, but language that incites violence and hatred against marginalized people should not be respected or tolerated. While avoiding the speech entirely is not unethical, the most ethical response is to protest, distract from, or end the speech in question, if it cannot be stopped in advance.

End Notes

1. Samantha Rudolph, Associate Director of Stats and Information, ESPN network, e-mail interview, February 15, 2011.

2. Keith Davis, quoted in "How to Be a Better Listener," The Small Business Knowledge Base, www.bizmove .com (accessed June 5, 2015).

3. R. G. Nichols and L. A. Stevens, "Listening to People," *Harvard Business Review,* September 1957, https://hbr .org/1957/09/listening-to-people.

4. "The Costs of Poor Listening," Innolect, innolectinc .com/services-overview/the-cost-of-poor-listening (accessed January 7, 2016).

5. Henry David Thoreau, *I to Myself: An Annotated Selection from the Journal of Henry D. Thoreau,* ed. Jeffery S. Cramer (New Haven, CT: Yale University Press, 2012).

6. Dr. Ralph G. Nichols, quoted in William V. Beasley, "Effective Listening," *Truth Magazine* 20, no. 8 (February 19, 1976), pp. 7–9.

7. Cindi May, "A Learning Secret: Don't Take Notes with a Laptop," *Scientific American,* June 3, 2014, scientificamerican .com (accessed September 27, 2015); Andreas Kapardis, *Psychology and Law: A Critical Introduction,* 3rd ed. (Cambridge: Cambridge University Press, 2010), p. 189.

8. C. May, "A Learning Secret: Don't Take Notes with a Laptop," *Scientific American,* June 3, 2014, www .scientificamerican.com/article/a-learning-secret-don-t -take-notes-with-a-laptop/.

9. Alex Williams, "At Meetings, It's Mind Your Blackberry or Mind Your Manners," *The New York Times,* June 22, 2009, www.nytimes.com (accessed September 27, 2015).

10. Helene Hembrooke and Geri Gay, "The Laptop and the Lecture: The Effects of Multitasking in Learning Environments," *Journal of Computing in Higher Education,* www.ugr.es (accessed September 27, 2015).

11. David E. Mayer, director of the Brain, Cognition and Action Laboratory at the University of Michigan, and René Marois, director of the Human Information Processing Laboratory at Vanderbilt University, as quoted by Steve Lohr, "Slow Down, Multitasker, Especially If You're Reading This in Traffic," *The New York Times,* March 25, 2007, www.nytimes.com (accessed September 27, 2015).

12. René Marois, PhD, Department of Psychology, Vanderbilt University, quoted by Dave Crenshaw, *The Myth of Multi-tasking* (San Francisco: Jossey-Bass, 2008), p. 18.

13. Christine Pearson, "Sending a Message That You Don't Care," *The New York Times,* May 15, 2010, www.nytimes .com (accessed September 27, 2015); Blue Avocado (Food-for-Thought for Nonprofits), "Ground Rules for the New Generation," www.blueavocado.org (accessed September 27, 2015); Donald G. Zauderer, "Workplace Incivility and the Management of Human Capital," www.dzauderer.com (accessed September 27, 2015).

14. Christine Pearson and Christine Porath, *The Cost of Bad Behavior* (New York: Portfolio, 2009), p. 111.

15. M. Zeidler, "Texting at Work Wasn't Just Cause for Termination, B.C. Tribunal Rules," *CBC News,* July 18, 2019, www.cbc.ca/news/canada/british-columbia /texting-during-meeting-fired-1.5227941.

16. Sandra Chapman, "Judge Loses Job over Texting during Hearings," *WTHR-TV Eyewitness News* (Indianapolis, IN), www.wthr.com (accessed September 27, 2015).

17. Hank London, "To Tweet or Not to Tweet?," *Hank London's Blog,* http://hanklondon.com (accessed September 27, 2015).

18. M. Pleasant, "Alicia Keys Talks Inspiration, Family, and Prayer with ORIGIN Magazine," *HuffPost,* September 1, 2013, www.huffpost.com/entry/alicia-keys-interview -origin-magazine_n_3845400.

19. Anonymous speaker quoted by Ronald B. Adler and Jeanne Marquardt Elmhorst, *Communicating at Work,* 8th ed. (New York: McGraw-Hill, 2005), p. 125.

20. "Plutarch Quotes," Goodreads, goodreads.com (accessed November 19, 2015).

Reaching the Audience

OUTLINE

OBJECTIVES

After studying this chapter, you should be able to

1. Describe the difference between a speaker who is audience-centered and one who is not.

2. Define audience analysis and audience adaptation and state why they are important.

3. Use interviews and surveys to gain information about an audience in advance.

4. Define diversity and explain how speakers can be responsive to diverse audiences.

5. Describe how speakers can adapt to varying levels of audience knowledge, attitudes, and interest level.

6. Explain how speakers should adapt to the occasion (time limit, purpose, and size of audience).

7. Describe how a speaker can adapt to the audience during a speech.

WHAT IS THE MOST IMPORTANT RULE for public speaking? Many veteran speakers would say that it is to care deeply about your audience.

One speaker who has a reputation for caring deeply about her audiences is Kimberly Wright Cassidy, president of Bryn Mawr College in Pennsylvania. Cassidy gives talks to high schools, colleges, community groups, and professional associations. Before each presentation, she tries to find out as much as she can about the interests and needs of her future listeners. Then she tailors her remarks in an effort to give them a rich and satisfying experience.

Even before she became a college president, Cassidy had established herself as a caring person. At her inauguration, one of her former students, Aybala Warner Ozturk, said, "As an undergrad I enrolled in President Cassidy's Ed Psych course, a class that our president is still teaching today. For me, that class was transformative. First and foremost it forced me to wake up at 8am, something I swore to never do in college. More importantly, I was willing to see the early hours of the morning because of the passion and academic rigor President Cassidy encouraged in the classroom. She always made time for her students, serving as a true advocate for our education and showing interest and care in our lives while pushing us to higher academic achievements."[1]

To become a listener-oriented speaker like Cassidy, you should develop techniques for connecting with an audience. In this chapter we will look at these techniques and how you can use them in both college and career settings.

On the occasion of her inauguration as president of Bryn Mawr College, Kimberly Wright Cassidy agrees to a "selfie" with five of the students who listened to her inauguration speech.

Clem Murray/The Philadelphia Inquirer/AP Images

The Audience-Centered Speaker

Some speeches are ineffective because the speaker is self-centered, focusing on "How do I look?" and "Am I doing a good job?" and "Does everyone like me?" The self-centered speaker fails to focus on the audience members and their needs.

audience-centered speaker
one who tries to establish a meaningful connection with listeners.

A better approach is taken by the **audience-centered speaker**—one who tries to connect with listeners and offer them a meaningful experience. If you are an audience-centered speaker, you learn everything you can about your listeners in advance, and then you tailor your speech to their needs and interests. You look directly at the audience, speak with enthusiasm, and try to reach every listener.

Consider the experience of Jill Sieburg, a health educator who gives presentations aimed at persuading people to become organ donors. Before every talk, she sends an e-mail to people who will be in the audience to find out their views. Are some of them, for example, opposed to organ donation because they fear their bodies will be disfigured? If yes, she will spend time in her talk explaining how organ donation is like any other kind of surgery—"Your body is sewed up afterwards and you are not disfigured."

audience analysis
collecting information about audience characteristics.

Sieburg demonstrates two important tasks that all audience-centered speakers should perform: (1) **audience analysis** to find out exactly who they are and where they stand on the issues to be discussed, and (2) **adaptation** of the speech to the listeners' knowledge level and viewpoints.

adaptation
adjusting one's material and delivery to meet listeners' needs.

This process of analysis and adaptation is sometimes called **customizing**, a crucial strategy in the business world. If you are a web designer, you would find out what features each client needs and then build the website accordingly. For a blogger, you would need to create a comments section; for a band, you would need to include an audio player for music clips; and for a vacation destination, you would add links to local hotels, restaurants, and entertainments. Customizing in public speaking means tailoring a speech to fit a particular audience.

customize
to make or alter to a customer's specifications.

Here are some guidelines for customizing speeches.

Prepare a separate analysis of each audience.   Don't assume that if a speech works well with one group, it will surely succeed with another. Sometimes it will, but sometimes it won't.

Imagine an instructor giving a talk to a group of graduate students and her message is well-received with much laughter and applause. So sweet was her success that she delivered the same message to a group of incoming first-year students at orientation. Her speech was a dud. She failed to consider the new students had a different educational background and a different set of experiences. They needed a different speech.

Customize for different segments of the same audience.   Many audiences contain subgroups, with the people in each subgroup sharing the same needs and level of understanding. Try to reach all the subgroups. For example, in a speech on traveling abroad, one subgroup—young parents—may want information on activities for children, while

---

⬧ Examining Your Ethics

A registered nurse is scheduled to give a presentation to a group of first-year college students about maintaining healthy lifestyles while in school. She plans to inform them that tanning beds can cause premature skin aging as well as increase the risk of skin cancer. As she gathers information about her audience in advance, she discovers that several of her future listeners visit tanning salons regularly. What should she do?

A. Drop the information about tanning beds to avoid offending some listeners.
B. Mention the issue but downplay it and recommend that listeners do research and decide for themselves.
C. Keep the information and emphasize medical studies about the harm caused by tanning beds.

For the answer, see the last page of this chapter.

Tips for Your Career

Be Sensitive to Audience Discomfort

Some speakers like to keep a room's temperature on the chilly side so that their listeners stay alert. Alertness is a good goal, of course, but audiences can't be alert to a speaker's message if they are shivering and miserable.

Don't let audience discomfort undermine the effectiveness of your speech. Keep the room temperature from being too hot or too cold. Make sure the microphone amplification is neither too loud nor too soft (you can ask listeners for feedback). If a meeting lasts a long time, give periodic breaks. If your presentation is right before a scheduled meal, be sure to end on time (even if it means shortening your remarks)—hungry listeners quickly become irritated with a speaker who keeps them from a meal.

another subgroup—older travelers—may want information on discounts for seniors. A third subgroup—domestic partners with no children—may want information on night life.

Never sacrifice ethical principles. Customizing does not mean telling listeners whatever would make them happy—regardless of truth. An ethical speaker never lies or distorts information.

Getting Information about the Audience

A speaker's worst nightmare is being laughed at by listeners. This came true for Lawrence B. Gibbs. When he was Internal Revenue Commissioner, he spoke to an audience of 1,000 tax preparers at a convention in Las Vegas, and he tried to brag about how smoothly the latest tax preparation season had been. Some people, he said, had made "gloomy predictions that this tax-filing season would drive taxpayers crazy, confuse them unmercifully, or break them financially. [*Dramatic pause*] It just hasn't happened, folks!"[2]

The convention hall exploded with laughter. The tax preparers had just finished a tax season in which the scenario that Gibbs dismissed as nonexistent had (from their perspective) actually occurred. Regardless of whose viewpoint was accurate, Gibbs had revealed that he knew nothing about his listeners' feelings and experience. If he had spoken with just a few of the members of the audience beforehand, he could have escaped public ridicule.

You can avoid this kind of blunder by finding out as much as possible about your listeners—their backgrounds and what they know and don't know. Two good ways to collect information about them are interviews and surveys.

Interviews

Start by interviewing the person who invited you to speak. Find out all that you can about the listeners' knowledge level, attitudes, needs, interests, and backgrounds. Get details about the occasion, such as the purpose of the event, other speakers on the program, size of audience, and most importantly, your time limit. Next, ask for the names and contact information of a few prospective listeners and interview them to find out what they already know about your subject, what ideas and information they are hoping to receive from your speech, and whether any particular approach (such as visual aids) works well with this group. When you start your speech, you can thank the people you interviewed by name. Doing so will add to your credibility because it shows your desire to meet the needs and interests of your listeners.

Surveys

Another good way to get information about your audience is to conduct a survey in advance of your speech, using a questionnaire to poll listeners' knowledge, interests, and attitudes. For a classroom speech, work with your instructor to decide how and when to distribute the questionnaire. For a career or community speech, try to get permission to contact your future listeners through an electronic channel that is common among them, such as an e-mail distribution list, a Facebook page, or a LinkedIn group.

open-ended question
a question that permits a broad range of responses.

closed question
a question requiring only a short, specific response.

A questionnaire can have two kinds of questions: **open-ended questions**, which encourage respondents to elaborate on their views, and **closed questions**, which give respondents preselected options, such as yes/no, true/false, and multiple choice. In Figure 1, the first question is open-ended, while all the rest are closed.

Let's suppose you are planning a speech on why most people need to add more vegetables to their daily diet, and you want to find out what your listeners know about vegetables and what their attitudes are. The questionnaire in Figure 1 shows some sample questions.

The first question is open-ended so that you can get a picture of how your future listeners view vegetables. Do they dislike them? It is helpful to know the listeners' attitudes. The rest of the questions are designed to help you decide what to include in your speech. For example, the second question probes whether the listeners know that a multivitamin pill does not substitute for vegetables. If all respondents indicate that they already know this, you can omit it from your speech. The fourth question investigates whether your listeners understand what vegetables can and cannot do for the body.

Here are some guidelines for surveys:

- Keep it short. One page is ideal. Most people will not fill out a long document.
- Phrase questions in a way that doesn't suggest the answer you want or anticipate. Instead of "Do you resist eating vegetables because your parents tried to force them on you?" ask, "If you don't like to eat vegetables, can you explain why?"
- Test your questionnaire in advance with a few friends or colleagues who can point out any confusing questions.

Sometimes the results of a survey can be included in a speech as a point of interest. In your speech on vegetables, for example, you can say, "According to my survey, half of you think that fresh foods are always healthier than frozen foods. But nutrition researchers have found that frozen vegetables are often healthier than fresh produce sold in supermarkets. Why? Because vegetables chosen for freezing tend to be processed at their peak ripeness. That's the time when they are loaded with maximum nutrients."

Audience Diversity

In most presentations, you are likely to see a wide diversity of listeners, including gender, age, educational backgrounds, occupations, religions, economic and social statuses, nationalities, cultures, physical abilities, and sexual orientations. To be a successful communicator, you should welcome the opportunity to meet the needs of *all* listeners, not just those who are like you.

Figure 1

Types of Survey Questions

Open-ended	1.	What is your emotional reaction when you hear the word vegetables? (Jot down a few words or sentences.)
Simple options	2.	Do vitamin supplements provide all of the necessary nutrients that are contained in vegetables? Yes ☐ No ☐ Not sure ☐
Multiple choice	3.	Which one of the following statements is correct? ☐ Iceberg lettuce contains no nutrients. ☐ Fresh foods are always healthier than frozen foods. ☐ Cooked carrots are healthier than raw carrots. ☐ Colorless foods like white cabbage have low nutritional value.
Checklist	4.	What are the health benefits of a diet rich in vegetables? (Check all that are true.) ☐ Lower blood pressure ☐ Reduced risk of some cancers ☐ Improved vision ☐ Higher intelligence ☐ Improved digestion
Scale	5.	"The average person does not eat as many vegetables as he or she should." Strongly Agree Agree Not sure Disagree Strongly Disagree ○ ○ ○ ○ ○
Ranking	6.	Which of these vegetables do you eat most often? Rank them in order, from 1 (most often) to 5 (least often). _____ Corn _____ Carrots _____ Onions _____ Tomatoes _____ Potatoes

Gender

Gender can be defined as those traits that are considered masculine or feminine and are influenced by social norms. But be aware that not all of your audience members will conform to traditional views of gender and consider themselves to carry both masculine and feminine traits. Also, not all of your audience members may conform to the binary definition of gender and consider themselves more fluid. Rather than answer to traditional pronouns *he* or *she*, you may have an audience member who refers to the self as *they/them*. You want to use more inclusive language that recognizes the fluidity of gender.

Be more inclusive with your word choice and avoid making assumptions based on gender stereotypes. Men may become irritated by a speaker who assumes that only

gender-biased language
words based on gender stereotypes.

females are interested in issues concerning how to express your emotions to your partner. And women would be annoyed by a speaker who suggests that only men are interested in new gaming technology. Listeners can lose respect for a speaker who uses **gender-biased language**—that is, words that convey stereotypes about men or women. Instead of saying "an engineer should apply his math skills," say "engineers should apply their math skills." Instead of "the best man for the job," say "the best person for the job." (Gender-biased language is discussed in more detail in the chapter on wording the speech.)

Don't make assumptions about marriage and sexual orientation. For example, don't assume that everyone is married or is heterosexual. Instead of announcing to employees, "You and your husband or wife are invited to the party," say, "You and your partner are invited to the party."

Age

If you have a variety of ages represented in your audience, be sensitive to the interests, attitudes, and knowledge of all your listeners, giving explanations or background whenever necessary. If, for example, you talk about a new trend in music that is popular with young people, give a brief explanation for the benefit of older audience members.

Be careful about making generalizations concerning any age group. For an audience of older people, for example, you are wise to consider the fact that many people suffer hearing loss as they age, but you shouldn't jump to the conclusion that you must shout during your speech. Not all older people are hard of hearing, and those who are might be wearing hearing aids.

Educational Background

Find out the educational level of your listeners. Avoid talking over their heads, using concepts that they may not understand. Also avoid the other extreme: talking down to your listeners and treating them as if they are ignorant.

Define terms whenever necessary. Fred Ebel, past president of a Toastmasters club in Orlando, Florida, talks about his experience with one audience: "I told a joke which referred to an insect called a praying mantis. I thought everyone knew what a praying mantis was. But I was greeted by silence that would have made the dropping of a pin sound like a thunderclap. Several listeners came up to me and asked, 'What is a praying mantis?'"[3]

Occupation

Knowing your listeners' occupational background can help you shape your remarks. Let's say you give speeches on résumé padding. To a group of students, you might want to point out how one's career can be ruined if an employer finds out that an employee lied on a résumé. To a group of human resource managers, you can give tips on how to detect false information. To a group of lawyers, you can discuss legal action that can be taken against someone who has lied on a résumé.

Religious Affiliation

Knowing the religious affiliations of your audience will give you good clues about their beliefs and attitudes. Keep in mind that as our culture becomes more globally diverse, you may encounter audience members with different Christian faiths; Non-Christian faiths such as Judaism, Islam, Hindu, or Buddhism; or those who are unaffiliated with a religious faith and are atheist or agnostic. If you are giving an informative speech on current armed conflicts in other parts of the world, be considerate of your audiences' religious background and avoid language that may alienate some of your listeners.

Although religious background can give you clues about your audience, be cautious. You cannot assume that all members of a religious group subscribe to official doctrines and pronouncements. A denomination's hierarchy, for example, may call for a stop to the production of nuclear weapons, but the majority of the members of that denomination may not agree with their leaders' views.

Economic and Social Status

Be sensitive to the economic and social status of your listeners so that you can adapt your speech accordingly. Suppose you are going to speak in favor of an economic stimulus package intended to create new manufacturing jobs. If your listeners are blue-collar workers or unemployed, they will probably be favorably disposed to your ideas before you even begin. You therefore might want to aim your speech at encouraging them to support political candidates who endorse the stimulus program. However, if your listeners are wealthy members of the business community, many of them may be opposed to your ideas because they fear higher taxes, or they cannot easily relate to the people whom the stimulus would most benefit. Therefore, you could aim your speech at showing how new manufacturing jobs can contribute to the overall prosperity of the community, and you could spend time discussing the facts that concern the audience members most, such as taxes, labor union involvement, or political implications.

International Listeners

The world today is a "global village" with interlocking interests and economies, and you must know how to interact with customers and associates from many different countries. Whether you are speaking on campus, in the community, or in your career, any audience you face is likely to include people for whom English is a second language.

taboos
acts prohibited by social custom.

To reach international listeners, consider the following:

Respect taboos. Every culture has its own set of **taboos,** and violating them can undermine a speaker's credibility. Stacie Krajchir of Venice Beach, California, who works around the world as a television producer, says, "I have a habit of putting my hands on my hips when I talk." In Indonesia, she was told that "when you stand that way, it's seen as a sign of rudeness or defiance."[4]

You can avoid taboos by educating yourself about a culture—a task that will be discussed below.

Learn nonverbal signals. Body language cues such as eye contact vary from country to country. American business executives assume a person who won't look them in the eye is evasive and dishonest, but in many parts of Latin America, Asia, and Africa, keeping your eyes lowered is a sign of respect.[5] A few years ago, some Americans who were trying to negotiate a contract with Japanese executives were happy to see nods of assent throughout the meeting but were later stunned when the Japanese rejected their proposal. The Americans were unaware that in Japan a nod doesn't mean agreement; it signifies only that the listener understands what is being said.[6]

Although nonverbal cues vary from culture to culture, there are some cues that are recognizable everywhere. First and foremost is the smile, which Roger Axtell, an international behavior

In American culture, this posture is fine, but in some cultures, putting hands on hips signals disrespect.

iofoto/Shutterstock

Is a smile a universal cue?

Shutterstock/Charlotte Purdy

expert, calls the most understood and most useful form of communication in the world.[7] As a Mexican-American proverb puts it: *Todos en el mundo sonreímos en el mismo idioma*—"Everyone in the world smiles in the same language." (The smile discussed here is the natural involuntary expression that all people make when they are happy—not variations such as the embarrassed smile of someone caught in a shameful act.)

Conduct research.   If you are like most people, you don't have time to become well-versed in all the cultures in the world, but you can focus on cultures that are likely to be represented in an upcoming presentation. Here are a couple of ways to prepare:

1. Get insights by browsing websites specializing in international cultures. Books and articles also can be good sources, but make sure they are recent because cultural information can become outdated.

2. Contact knowledgeable people. You can use social media sites like Facebook to consult people who live in or visit the country you have questions about. Or, you can find an expert on your campus or in your community whom you can interview face-to-face.

Be careful with jargon and slang.   Avoid using idiomatic expressions, such as "cramming for an exam," "bite the bullet," and "the ball is in your court," as they are often not familiar to non-native English speakers. If you must use jargon, such as *interface* or *virtual reality,* explain or illustrate each term.

Maintain a serious, formal tone.   Americans are accustomed to speakers using a humorous and informal approach to public speaking, but American presenters who adopt this tone with international audiences are often viewed as frivolous and disrespectful. Telling jokes and coming across as "laid-back" can destroy the effectiveness of a presentation.

If possible, provide handouts covering some of your main points a day or two before a presentation.   Most non-native speakers of English have greater comprehension when reading than when listening. If they read the material beforehand, they can find out the meaning of any terms they don't understand, and when they come to the actual presentation, they will have a knowledge base that will maximize their understanding of your remarks. Be sure to avoid giving out lengthy material immediately before or during a meeting, for reasons discussed in the chapter on presentation aids.

Provide visual and tactile learning.   To make sure that your words are understood, can you use visual aids or demonstrations to illuminate your ideas? Can you provide any hands-on experiences?

Online presentations.   It is important to understand how technology offers a broad audience on an international level. You may post a speech on YouTube or share a speech on social media and cultural understanding is essential for success using these channels of communication.

Tips for Your Career

Work Closely with Interpreters

Use interpreters if there is a chance that some listeners will not hear or understand your message. For example, you might use a sign-language interpreter for deaf listeners and a language interpreter for non-English-speaking listeners. Here are some tips for using interpreters effectively:

• Because interpreters say that they stumble less and make fewer misinterpretations when they know the speaker's message in advance, provide a copy of your outline to the interpreter well before the event.

• If possible, ask him or her to rehearse with you several times and to alert you if any elements in your speech are likely to be misunderstood.

• In your opening remarks, introduce the interpreter to the audience and express your appreciation for his or her assistance.

• When using a language interpreter, you will probably employ the popular *consecutive interpretation* method, in which you and the interpreter take turns. Say only a few sentences at a time, so that neither language group gets weary of waiting its turn. A less-frequent method is *simultaneous interpretation,* in which the translation is rendered into a separate microphone a few seconds later for listeners wearing headphones. At large international meetings, a speech may be translated into many languages simultaneously.

• To demonstrate your desire to connect with all listeners, learn a few words and phrases from sign language and/or another language to sprinkle into your presentation. Practice with a fluent user to make sure you are giving an accurate rendition.

• Even if all listeners are using the services of a sign-language interpreter, you should still talk directly to the listeners, not to the interpreter.

Sean Berdy, who was born deaf, uses American Sign Language to translate the words of Constance Marie Lopez at a press conference in Pasadena, California. Both Berdy and Lopez are actors on the ABC TV series *Switched at Birth.*

Chris Pizzello/AP Images

America's Diverse Cultures

The same sensitivity you show toward international listeners should be extended to ethnic, racial, religious, and other groups in the United States. Below are some suggestions for showing respect to all cultures and groups.

Avoid ethnocentrism.   The belief that one's own cultural group is superior to other groups is known as **ethnocentrism**. People who are ethnocentric view the customs and standards of other groups as inferior or wrong.

    In most cases, different customs are not a matter of right and wrong but of choice and tradition. In some African-American churches, listeners shout affirmative responses during a sermon, while in some other churches, listeners remain silent. One custom is not superior to the other; they are simply different.

ethnocentrism
judging other cultures as inferior to one's own culture.

Learn the expectations and viewpoints of different cultures and groups.   Let's say you are a manager giving an informal training talk to a group of employees and you try to encourage them to ask questions as you go along. Some of the Asian-American

Many American audiences today have a diverse ethnic composition, in part because 700,000 immigrants become U.S. citizens each year. A native of Jamaica, Marine Corporal Everton Bryon, left, and a native of the Dominican Republic, Army Specialist Johanna Abreu, became U.S. citizens in a naturalization ceremony in Arlington, Virginia. Every year, 9,000 service members become American citizens.

Source: Courtesy of U.S. Defense Dept./Sergeant First Class Doug Sample

employees, however, never ask questions. Before you conclude that these employees are uninvolved and uninterested, keep in mind that for some Asian Americans, asking questions is considered a disrespectful challenge to the speaker's authority.

If you don't know much about the attitudes and viewpoints of an American ethnic group, interview a few representative audience members beforehand to learn about their backgrounds and needs. Also, ask for advice from associates who have had experience communicating with the kinds of listeners to whom you will be speaking.

Focus on individuality. Although becoming informed about group differences is important, treat your knowledge as possible clues, not as absolute certainties. In the example above, notice that we spoke of *some* Asian Americans—not all. Be sensitive to possible cultural differences; treat these listeners primarily as individuals who may have characteristics that do not coincide with those of other Asian Americans. In dealing with diverse groups, be sensitive to possible differences and special needs, but as much as possible, focus on the individuality of each listener.

Never ridicule any group.   Some people think that if no members of a particular group are present, it is okay to make insulting jokes. It is *never* okay. Such slurs are offensive and unfunny to many people who don't belong to the group being ridiculed, and they will automatically lose respect for a speaker who uses them.

Listeners with Disabilities

People with disabilities are active in the workplace and in their communities. How can speakers know what accommodations to make? Simply ask the most qualified sources of information—persons with disabilities themselves. Don't be afraid of making a social blunder. If some listeners have hearing impairments, for example, you can ask them where they would like you to stand during your presentation.[8]

Here are some general tips for being sensitive to listeners with disabilities:

- Before you ask your audience to gather around you for a demonstration, or involve them in an activity, be sure to determine if listeners with disabilities can participate. Encourage them to do so.

- Many people, without realizing it, treat adults with disabilities as if they were children. Don't use first names unless you are using first names with all others present. Don't speak in an exaggerated, condescending manner. Don't talk down to anyone.

- Don't equate physical limitations with mental limitations. The fact that a listener is in a wheelchair has nothing to do with that person's mental abilities.

- You can certainly offer help to a person with a disability if it seems needed, but don't insist on helping if your offer is declined.

- Never take the arm of a person with a mobility or visual impairment. Instead, offer your arm.

- Remember that not all disabilities are visible. According to the Higher Education Research Institute at UCLA, 11.9 percent of first-year population students have a mental illness, or "Hidden Disability," such as attention deficit/hyperactivity disorder and psychological disorders.[9]

Now let's look at tips for specific types of disabilities.

Listeners with Mobility Impairments

- Try to remove barriers that would limit wheelchair access. Whenever there is a choice, ask the listener where he or she would like to sit—don't assume that he or she would prefer to be in the back or the front of the room.
- Never patronize people in wheelchairs by patting them on the head or shoulder.
- Shake hands with people in wheelchairs like you would with anyone else.
- Don't lean against or hang on someone's wheelchair. It is part of that person's personal space.[10]

Listeners Who Are Deaf or Hearing Impaired

- If hearing-impaired listeners must see your mouth to understand your words, try to avoid turning away. At the same time, don't put them in a spotlight by standing directly in front of them and looking at only them.
- "It is not necessary to exaggerate your words," says Deborah L. Harmon, a college counselor for students with disabilities, "although it may be appropriate to slow your rate of speech slightly when talking with people who are hearing-impaired."
- Whenever possible, speakers should augment their remarks with visual aids, says Harmon. "Write technical terms on a board when first introduced" so that deaf audience members can see how the terms are spelled and thus can figure out their pronunciation.[11]
- Be aware that many people in the deaf community refer to deafness not as a disability, but as a culture in and of itself.[12]

Listeners Who Are Blind or Visually Impaired

- Talk in a normal voice. Just because a person has limited vision, don't assume that he or she has a hearing impairment, too.
- Don't touch or call a guide dog, says Harmon. Trying to play with it interferes with the performance of its duties. These animals are highly trained work dogs that will not disrupt a speech. They don't need to be soothed or distracted by you.[13]
- Don't assume that listeners who are blind or visually impaired will not want copies of your handouts. "Even if they can't read them at the meeting," says Sharon Lynn Campbell of St. Louis, Missouri, "they may want to have them read aloud later."[14]
- If you say to a listener who is blind, "Do you see what I mean?" or a similar phrase, there is no need to become flustered or apologetic. The listener realizes that you are using a common phrase out of habit and that you intend no insult.

For a speech on gambling, don't assume that all your listeners know what blackjack is. Find out in advance.

Ingram Publishing

Audience Knowledge

Thomas Leech, a business consultant in San Diego, California, tells of a manager at an electronics firm who was asked to explain a new electronics program to a group of visiting Explorer Scouts. "He pulled two dozen visuals used for working meetings, went into great detail about technical aspects, and spoke of FLMs and MOKFLTPAC," says Leech. "He was enthusiastic, knowledgeable, and totally ineffective, since his audience was lost for about 44 of his 45 minutes."[15]

This man made a common mistake: failing to speak at the knowledge level of his listeners. To avoid this mistake, find out what your listeners know and don't know about your subject, and then adapt your remarks to their level.

If your pre-speech analysis shows that your listeners know a lot about your topic, you can skip an explanation of basic concepts and go straight into advanced material. On the other hand, if your analysis shows that listeners know little or nothing about your topic, you will need to start at a basic level and add advanced material as you go along. Avoid overwhelming them with more information than they can comfortably absorb.

So far, so good, but now comes the tricky part. What should you do if some of your listeners know a lot about your subject and others know nothing? Whenever possible, the solution is to start off at a simple level and add complexity as you go along (and tell your audience that this is what you will do). For example, if you are speaking on identity theft to a mixed audience, you can hold the attention of everyone by saying something like this: "I realize that some of you know little about identity theft, while some of you have already been victims. So, to bring everyone up to speed, I want to begin by defining what identity theft is, and then I'll get into the nitty-gritty of how you can prevent the crime." Regardless of their level of knowledge, listeners usually appreciate this kind of sensitivity.

Audience Psychology

Your listeners do not see the world the same way you do because they have lived different lives with different experiences, different mistakes, and different successes. To further your understanding of your listeners, assess their level of interest and their attitudes.

Interest Level

Through interviews or surveys, ask your listeners whether they are interested in your topic. If they seem indifferent or bored, your challenge is to generate interest during the speech. Let's say you are planning to speak on the possibility of the Federal Reserve raising the federal funds rate. That sounds boring, so you would need to show listeners how raising the rate could impact their wallets. For example, you could quote NBC reporter Kristin Wong, who says, "Your credit card's interest rate is probably variable, meaning it can and will change along with the Fed's rate. If you carry credit card debt, this means you can expect to pay more in interest over time."[16]

To keep an audience interested throughout the entire speech, avoid getting bogged down in tedious, technical material. Use interesting examples, lively stories, and captivating visuals. All of these techniques will be discussed in more detail in later chapters.

attitude
a predisposition to respond favorably or unfavorably toward a person or an idea.

Attitudes

Attitudes are the emotional inclinations—the favorable or unfavorable predispositions—that listeners bring to a speech. Each listener's attitudes are derived from a complex inner web of values, beliefs, experiences, and biases.

Figure 2
When student speaker Najuana Dorsey invited her classmates at Georgia Southern University to try cricket cake, she managed to bring her listeners closer to her position.

Courtesy of Georgia Southern University

Before your speech, try to determine your listeners' attitudes—negative, neutral, or positive—toward your goal, you as a speaker, and the occasion.

Attitudes toward the Goal

Unfavorable.   If listeners are negative toward your goal or objective, you should design your speech either to win them over to your views or—if that is unrealistic—to move them closer to your position.

When Najuana Dorsey, a student at Georgia Southern University, planned a speech on the desirability of insects as a source of protein for low-income people in impoverished countries, she knew (from a questionnaire) that her classmates were repulsed by the idea of anyone eating insects. So she devised a plan to change their attitude. In the early part of her speech, she gave solid scientific data about the nutritional value of insects. Near the end, she pulled out a cricket cake and said, "The crickets are roasted, and they taste like pecans. Why don't you try just one bite?" Despite initial squeamishness, all but one of her classmates ended up eating an entire piece, finding the cake to be surprisingly delicious. On after-speech evaluation sheets, students indicated that they now agreed with Dorsey's contention that insects could help alleviate hunger in the world.[17] (See Figure 2.)

Neutral.   If your listeners are apathetic or neutral, try to involve them in the issue, and then win them over to your side. For example, if an audience seems unconcerned about the extinction of hundreds of species of plants every year, you can tell them of the many medicines that are derived from plants. Digitalis, which is derived from the leaves of the foxglove plant, is used to treat heart disease. "Who knows," you can say, "if one of the many plants that will disappear from Earth this year contains an ingredient that could have saved your life someday?" What you are trying to do, of course, is show that the issue is not a faraway abstraction but a real concern that could affect listeners' own lives.

Favorable.   If your audience is favorably disposed toward your ideas, your task is to reinforce their positive views and even motivate them to take action. For example, you might give a pep talk to members of a political party in your community, urging them to campaign on behalf of the party's candidate in an upcoming election.

Attitudes toward the Speaker

Listeners will have a negative attitude toward a speaker if they suspect that he or she is unqualified to speak on a particular subject. This skepticism can be overcome if the person introducing you states your credentials and expertise. Otherwise, you can establish your credibility yourself at the beginning of your speech. Angie Chen, a student speaker, gave a classroom speech on acupuncture. During her introduction, she revealed that she had grown up in China, had undergone acupuncture treatment herself, and had watched it be performed on friends and relatives. Though Chen did not claim to be a medical expert, her summary of her experiences showed that she knew a great deal about the subject.

You also can enhance your credibility by explaining how you got your information. Let's say you give a report on recovery programs for drug addicts in your community. In your introduction, it is appropriate to mention that you have read two books on the subject and interviewed a local expert on chemical dependency. This is not bragging; it is simply a way to let the audience know that your information is based on solid research.

Attitudes toward the Occasion

Sometimes listeners are irritated because they have been ordered to attend—they are a "captive audience"—and because they think the meeting is unnecessary. With such audiences, give a lively presentation geared to their precise needs. If possible, show an awareness of their situation and your desire to help.

One speaker had to address a group of disgruntled employees who were required to attend a 4 P.M. meeting to listen to her suggestions about filling out employee self-evaluations—a topic they felt was a waste of time. At the beginning she said, "I know you'd rather be somewhere else right now, and I know you think this meeting is pointless, but let's make the best use of our time that we can. I have talked to several of you about your concerns, and I'd like to zero in on them and see if we can improve the situation. And I promise to be finished by 5, so we can all go home." Her comments, she said, caused the listeners to lean forward and listen attentively to her presentation.

The Occasion

Find out as much as you can about the occasion and the setting of your speech, especially when you are giving a speech in your community or at a career-related meeting. Some issues to ask about include your time limit, your expectations, other events on the program, and the audience size; pay special attention to the issue of time limit.

Time Limit

Many public occasions are marred by long-winded speakers who drone on and on, oblivious to the lateness of the hour and the restlessness of the audience.

Picture a minister who spoke for over an hour giving a Mother's Day sermon at a Sunday morning service. At one point he says, "I know I'm going on too long, but . . ."

Tips for Your Career

Be Prepared to Trim Your Remarks

One of the most exasperating situations you can face is when, because of circumstances beyond your control, your speech comes at the end of a long, tedious meeting when listeners are weary and ready to leave. Often the best response is to trim your speech. As the following incident shows, the audience will be grateful:

An all-day professional conference was supposed to end at 3:30 P.M. so that participants would have plenty of daylight for driving back to their hometowns. Unfortunately, most of the speakers on the program exceeded their time limit, and the final speaker found himself starting at 3:18. Without commenting on the insensitivity of the other speakers, he started out by saying, "How many of you would like to leave at 3:30?" Every hand went up. "I will end at 3:30," he promised. Though it meant omitting most of his prepared remarks, the speaker kept his promise. One of the participants said later, "We appreciated his sensitivity to us and his awareness of the time. And he showed class in not lambasting the earlier speakers who stole most of his time. He showed no anger or resentment."

Here's a technique to consider: when invited to speak at meetings where there are several speakers, prepare two versions of your speech—a full-length one to use if the other speakers respect their time limits and a shorter version if events dictate that you trim your remarks.

Some members of the congregation may get upset because they had reservations at a restaurant (Mother's Day is the busiest day of the year for restaurants). Some people might have roasts in the oven, while others have elderly parents waiting to be picked up. The overlong sermon becomes a frustration and a source of resentment.

Always find out how much time has been allotted for your speech, and *never* exceed the limit. This rule applies when you are the sole speaker and especially when you are one of several speakers. If four speakers on a program are supposed to speak for only 10 minutes apiece, imagine what happens when each speaks for 30 minutes. The audience becomes fatigued and inattentive.

Some speakers have absolutely no concept of time. If you are giving a group presentation for class and each student in your group is allotted 5 minutes, what happens when two group members speak over 10 minutes? How will their going over on time affect the group grade? Sometimes speakers get too comfortable and get off point. Practicing your speech at home and timing yourself will help you keep within time limits. If you tend to be a talkative speaker, follow the wise formula of President Franklin D. Roosevelt to make a compelling speech and exit gracefully:[18]

- Be sincere.
- Be brief.
- Be seated.

Expectations

Actor Steve Martin upset a lot of listeners one evening when he appeared at the 92nd Street Y in New York City and talked about art history. The audience of 900, who had paid $50 each to hear him, had assumed he would talk about his film and television career as a comedian. Many of the listeners complained by phone and e-mail the next day, and the Y issued an apology and promised to send a $50 gift certificate to any unhappy listener.[19]

If listeners expect one thing, and you present another, they may be disappointed, even angry. Find out in advance the purpose of a meeting or presentation, and then make sure you give listeners the kind of material they are expecting.

Other Events on the Program

Find out all that you can about other events on a program. Are there other speakers on the agenda? If so, on what topic will they speak? It would be disconcerting to prepare a speech on how to protect yourself from identity theft online and then discover during the ceremony that the speaker ahead of you is talking on the same subject.

Even more alarming is to come to a meeting and find out that you are not just giving a speech but also debating someone on your topic. Obviously you need to know such information in advance so that you can anticipate the other speaker's argument and prepare your rebuttal.

Audience Size

It can be unsettling to walk into a room expecting an audience of 20 but instead finding 200. Knowing the size of your audience ahead of time will help you not only prepare yourself psychologically but also plan your presentation. Will you need extra-large visual aids? Will you need a microphone?

It's easier to connect with your listeners if they are close to you physically. If you have relatively few listeners, and they are scattered throughout a big room or are all clumped together in the back rows, ask them to move to the front and center. Because some listeners dislike having to move, you may have to appeal for their cooperation by saying something like, "I hate to bother you, but it will save my throat if I don't have to shout."

Adapting during the Speech

Adapting your speech to your audience, so important during the preparation stages, also must take place during the actual delivery of the speech. Be sensitive to your listeners' moods and reactions, and then make any appropriate adjustments that you can.

For example, one student, Lester Petchenik, used a portable chef's stove to demonstrate how to cook green beans amandine. At one point, he sprinkled a large amount of salt into his pan—an action that caused several members of the audience to exchange glances of surprise. Noticing this reaction, Petchenik ad-libbed, "I know it looks like I put too much salt in, but remember that I've got three pounds of green beans in this pan. In just a moment, when you taste this, you'll see that it's not too salty." (He was right.)

Try to overcome any barriers to communication.   Sometimes, for example, audiences are unable to focus on your remarks because of people walking in late. In this case, you can pause until the newcomers have settled in. John Naber of Pasadena, California, an Olympic gold medalist in swimming, says that he once gave a speech in a room with poor acoustics. Realizing the audience would have trouble understanding him if he stayed at the lectern, he said, "I moved into the middle of the group and walked among them as I spoke."[20]

Be sensitive to the mood of the audience.   You can tell if listeners are bored, drowsy, or restless by observing their body language. Are they yawning, letting their heads droop down, averting their eyes from the speaker, or fidgeting in their seats? Sometimes they are listless not because your speech is boring but because of circumstances beyond your control. It is eight o'clock in the morning, for example, and you have to explain a technical process to a group of conventioneers who have stayed up partying half the night.

Try to "wake up" a listless audience.   For droopy listeners, here are some techniques you can use: (1) Invite audience participation by asking for examples of what you are talking about or by asking for a show of hands of those who agree with you. (2) Rev up your delivery by moving about, by speaking slightly louder at certain points, or by speaking occasionally in a more dramatic tone.

Resources for Review and Skill Building

Summary

To be an effective speaker, concentrate your attention and energies on your audience, and have a strong desire to communicate your message to them. Analyze the listeners beforehand and adapt your materials and presentation to their needs and interests.

To get information about an audience, you can interview the program director, you can interview a few future listeners, or you can conduct a survey of your listeners.

A wide diversity of listeners—men and women of different ages, nationalities, ethnic groups, religions, economic levels, and physical abilities—are likely to be in your audiences.

When speaking to international audiences, learn as much as you can about the culture of the listeners. Learn nonverbal signals, be careful with jargon and slang, and maintain a serious, formal tone. If possible, provide handouts covering some of your main points a day or two before a presentation.

Extend the same sensitivity to America's diverse cultures. Avoid ethnocentrism, the belief that one's own cultural group is superior to other groups. Learn the expectations and viewpoints of different cultures, but treat your knowledge as possible clues, not absolute certainties. As much as possible, treat listeners primarily as individuals who may have characteristics that do not coincide with those of others in their cultural group.

Try to accommodate the needs of listeners with disabilities. If you are in doubt about what they need, simply ask them. Never treat adults with disabilities as if they were children, and don't equate physical limitations with mental limitations.

Analyze and adapt your presentations to such factors as age, gender, educational levels, occupations, religious affiliations, and economic and social status.

Consider your listeners' level of knowledge about your material, their level of interest in your subject matter, and their attitudes toward the goal, the speaker, and the occasion.

Analyze the occasion to gather details about the time limit, audience expectations, other events on the program, and the number of people who will attend.

Be prepared to adapt to the needs of the listeners during the speech itself. Be sensitive to the cues that indicate boredom, restlessness, or lack of understanding.

Key Terms

adaptation, *56*

attitude, *66*

audience analysis, *56*

audience-centered speaker, *56*

closed question, *58*

customize, *56*

ethnocentrism, *63*

gender-biased language, *60*

open-ended question, *58*

taboo, *61*

Review Questions

1. What is an *audience-centered* speaker?

2. What is meant by audience analysis and adaptation?

3. How can a speaker get advance information about an audience?

4. What are taboos, and why are they an important concern for a speaker?

5. Do international audiences usually prefer a presentation that is humorous and informal or one that is serious and formal? Explain your answer.

6. What is ethnocentrism?

7. Who is the best source of information about the needs of listeners with disabilities, and why?

8. What approach should you take if listeners have an unfavorable attitude toward your speech goal?

9. What guidelines should be followed for a speech to an audience that knows little or nothing about your topic?

10. What might happen if you give a speech that is different from the one the audience was expecting?

Building Critical-Thinking Skills

1. Several websites provide ready-made speeches that public speakers are welcome to use as their own. Aside from the dishonesty involved, why would using such speeches be a mistake?

2. At what time of day are you normally least alert? What conditions in a room (such as temperature and noise) cause you to be inattentive? Now imagine that you are a listener in these circumstances. What would a speaker need to do to keep you awake and engaged?

3. Why is it insulting to assume that all persons in a wheelchair want to sit in the back of a room?

4. While you are waiting to give a speech, you discover that the person speaking just before you is covering the same topic. When you stand up, what will you do and say?

Building Teamwork Skills

1. Work with a group to create a questionnaire aimed at finding out where an audience stands concerning one of these issues: (a) Should "vicious" breeds of dogs such as pit bulls be outlawed? (b) Should the legal drinking age be changed? (c) Should pain sufferers be given medical marijuana? Use all the types of questions shown in Figure 1.

2. In a group, create a list of 10 examples of American slang or jargon that might be misunderstood by visiting physicians from Hong Kong who speak British English.

Examining Your Ethics

Answer: C. The speaker should neither omit nor water down her information, especially since she believes it can prevent long-term harm.

End Notes

1. Aybala Warner Ozturk, remarks at the inauguration of Kimberly Wright Cassidy, Bryn Mawr College, inside. blogs.brynmawr.edu (accessed September 25, 2015).

2. Greg Anrig Jr., "Taxpayers' Revenge," in *How to Manage Your Taxes,* a booklet published by *Money* magazine, pp. 2–3.

3. Fred Ebel, "Know Your Audience," *Toastmaster,* June 1985, p. 20.

4. Perry Garfinkel, "On Keeping Your Foot Safely out of Your Mouth," *The New York Times,* www.nytimes.com (accessed September 28, 2015).

5. Joe Navarro, "The Body Language of the Eyes," *Psychology Today,* www.psychologytoday.com (accessed September 28, 2015).

6. Edward Daimler, travel agent, San Diego, California, telephone interview, September 12, 2005.

7. Axtell is quoted in Mary Ellen Guffey, *Business Communication,* 7th ed. (Mason, OH: Thomson South-Western, 2011), p. 92.

8. "Strategies for Working with People Who Have Disabilities," University of Washington, www.washington .edu (accessed November 21, 2015).

9. "College Students with 'Hidden' Disabilities: The Freshmen Survey Fall 2010," HERI Research Brief, Higher Education Research Institute at UCLA Home of the Cooperative Institutional Research Program, April 2011, www.heri.ucla.edu/PDFs/pubs/briefs/HERI _ResearchBrief_Disabilities_2011_April_25v2.pdf.

10. Deborah L. Harmon, *Serving Students with Disabilities* (Asheville, NC: Asheville-Buncombe Technical Community College, 1994), pp. 7–9.

11. Deborah L. Harmon, *Serving Students with Disabilities* (Asheville, NC: Asheville-Buncombe Technical Community College, 1994), p. 9.

12. Allegra Ringo, "Understanding Deafness," *The Atlantic,* www.theatlantic.com (accessed September 28, 2015).

13. Deborah L. Harmon, *Serving Students with Disabilities* (Asheville, NC: Asheville-Buncombe Technical Community College, 1994), p. 9.

14. Sharon Lynn Campbell, "Helping the Toastmaster of Disability," Toastmasters International, www.toastmasters .org (accessed September 29, 2015).

15. Thomas Leech, San Diego, California, consultant, "Tips and Articles," Winning Presentations, www .winningpresentations.com (accessed September 28, 2015).

16. Kristin R. Wong, "5 Ways a Fed Rate Hike Could Affect Your Pocketbook," *NBC News,* www.nbcnews.com (accessed January 8, 2015).

17. Najuana Dorsey, interview via the Georgia Southern University Marketing and Communications Department, May 1, 2001.

18. "Franklin D. Roosevelt Quotes," Goodreads, www .goodreads.com (accessed November 21, 2015).

19. Felicia R. Lee, "Comedian Conversation Falls Flat at 92nd Street Y," *The New York Times,* www.nytimes .com (accessed September 28, 2015).

20. John Naber, professional speaker, Pasadena, California, telephone interview, November 12, 2000.

Selecting Topic, Purpose, and Central Idea

OBJECTIVES

After studying this chapter, you should be able to

1. Select appropriate and interesting speech topics.
2. Specify the general purpose of a speech.
3. Develop a clear, concise specific purpose statement for every speech you prepare.
4. Develop a clear, coherent central idea for every speech you prepare.
5. Understand how the specific purpose and the central idea fit into the overall design of a speech.

WHEN HE WAS A HIGH SCHOOL STUDENT in a small city in India, Amol Bhave was bored with his classes. Then one day while surfing the Internet, he discovered a repository of online video courses from Massachusetts Institute of Technology (MIT).

Bhave immediately signed up. The courses were free, and he found them interesting and challenging. He performed so well that the prestigious school gave him a full scholarship. He excelled in engineering and computer science classes and became a teaching assistant.

Because of his academic success, Bhave is invited to give talks to students and television audiences, and he always chooses a topic about which he is passionate: why

During a television
program sponsored by
The New York Times
in New York City, MIT
student Amol Bhave
explains why he is
enthusiastic about
online courses.

Neilson Barnard/Getty Images

people should take advantage of online courses, which are often free, to
gain valuable information and learn new skills.[1]

For Bhave, choosing a topic for a speech is easy. But some speakers—on
campus and beyond—select topics they are not passionate about, and
they end up boring the audience. Other speakers are enthusiastic about
their topics, but they fail to have clear objectives. They meander and
roam, causing listeners to become irritated and confused.

To help you avoid these mistakes, the first half of this chapter shows how
to choose a good topic, and the second half explains how to develop
clear objectives using three valuable tools: general purpose, specific
purpose, and central idea.

Selecting a Topic

For some speeches that you will give as part of a job, your topic will be chosen by someone else. Your boss, for example, may instruct you to present a new policy to your fellow employees.

In most public speaking classes, students are permitted to choose their own topics—a freedom that causes some students a great deal of agony, as they moan to friends, "I have to give a speech next week and I can't think of a thing to talk about." Don't let yourself get stuck at this stage. Choose your topic far in advance, because you will need to spend your time and energy on researching, outlining, and practicing. If you are indecisive and delay, you may find yourself without enough time to prepare the speech adequately.

While you are taking this course, keep a notepad or smartphone handy and record ideas for topics as they come to you so that you will have a stockpile from which to draw. In the weeks ahead, you can add to your list as you come up with more ideas.

Here are some important points to bear in mind as you look for a topic.

Select a Topic You Care About

Has anything ever happened to you that was so exciting or interesting or infuriating you could hardly wait to tell your friends about it? That's the way you should feel about your speech topic. It should be something you care about, something you are eager to communicate to others. Are you exhilarated by the sport of kayaking? Speak on how to get started in kayaking. Are you angry over the rising number of car thefts in your community? Speak on how to foil car thieves.

Enthusiasm is contagious. If you are excited, your excitement will spread to your listeners. If you are not excited about your topic, you are likely to do a lackluster job of preparing the speech, and your delivery will probably come across as dull and unconvincing.

Select a Topic You Can Master

A nightmare scenario: You give a speech on a subject about which you know very little. In the question-and-answer period, some listeners (who know the subject well) point out your omissions and errors.

Imagine you are interested in mountain biking, but you know little about the subject and one of your audience members is an experienced mountain biker. Make things easy for yourself. Speak on a subject with which you are already thoroughly familiar—or about which you can learn through research.

Here are several ways to probe for topics about which you already know (or can learn) a lot.

Sharing Personal Experiences

If you are permitted to choose your own topic, start your search with the subject on which you are the world's foremost expert—your own life.

"But my life isn't very interesting or exciting," you might say. Not so. Maybe you are not an international celebrity, but there are dozens of aspects of your life that could make compelling speeches. Here are some examples, all involving students:

- After a friend was defrauded by a student-loan scam, Christina Morales researched the crime and told classmates how to find honest, reliable lenders for student loans.

- Michael Kaplan demonstrated how to make a crepe (a type of thin pancake) filled with spinach, cheese, and tomato.
- Yuna Paragas gave a classroom speech on how she responded to a malicious effort to embarrass her on a social media site.

These students were *ordinary* people who chose to speak on *ordinary* aspects of their lives, but their speeches turned out the way all good speeches should turn out—interesting. When you are searching for a topic, start by looking for intriguing experiences in your own life.

To help you assess your interests, you can create a personal inventory using the categories shown in Figure 1. After you have filled in the inventory, go back and analyze the list for possible speech topics. You may want to ask a friend or an instructor to help you.

Figure 1
A Personal Inventory, as Filled in by One Student

Name: ___Rachel Zamora___

Personal Inventory

Jot down as much information about yourself as you can in the categories below.

Work experience (past and present)
  Radiology intern, St. Francis Hospital
  Volunteer assistant, children's cancer ward
  Part-time server, Thai restaurant

Special skills or knowledge
  Managing money (I'm paying my way through college)
  Making hospital patients feel relaxed and comfortable

Pastimes (hobbies, sports, recreation)
  Swimming
  Chatting on Facebook
  Watching movies

Travel
  New York City
  Grand Canyon
  Yosemite
  Yellowstone

Unusual experiences
  Encountering a black bear in Yosemite
  Helping build a house for Habitat for Humanity

School interests (academic and extracurricular)
  Magnetic resonance imaging (MRI)
  Hanging out with International Club students

Concerns or beliefs (politics, society, family, etc.)
  Society must stop cutting funds for elementary schools
  We need to find a cure for multiple sclerosis
  More money should be spent on solar energy research

A college classroom speech on volcanoes changed the course of Jonathan Castro's life.

Ammit Jack/Shutterstock

All the items in this inventory are potentially good speech topics. The best one would be whichever the student is most eager to share with the audience.

Exploring Interests

Can you identify a topic that intrigues you—a topic that you have always wanted to know more about? If you choose such a topic, you will not only have fun researching, but you will also gain a stockpile of new and interesting information.

Your topic might even influence the direction of your life. In a first-year public speaking class at Humboldt State University in California, Jonathan Castro chose a topic that he had always wanted to investigate—volcanoes. Preparing and delivering the speech ignited a passionate interest that led Castro to choose volcanology as his life's work. After graduating from Humboldt, he earned a PhD in geology at the University of Oregon, and today he is a volcano specialist at Oberlin College.[2]

Even if it doesn't change the course of your life, an intriguing topic can yield benefits. One student had always wanted to know the safest options for investing in the stock market. She researched and gave a speech on the subject, and a year later, she used the information to make her own investments.

Brainstorming

brainstorming
generating many ideas quickly and uncritically.

If the methods already discussed don't yield a topic, try **brainstorming** (so called because it is supposed to create intellectual thunder and lightning). In brainstorming, you write down whatever pops into your mind. For example, if you start off with the word *helicopter,* the next word that floats into your mind might be *rescue* and then the next word might be *emergencies,* and so on. Don't censor any words. Don't apply any critical evaluation. Simply write whatever comes into your mind. Nothing is too silly or bizarre to put down.

Using a sheet of paper (with categories such as those in Figure 2), jot down words as they come to your mind. When you finish brainstorming, analyze your list for possible topics. Don't discard any possibility until you have chosen a topic.

One student's brainstorming notes are shown in Figure 2. Let's examine one category, Current Events, in which the student started with "depletion of fish in oceans," a serious global issue. This led him to jot down "mercury in tuna," perhaps due to various forms of pollution. This prompted him to think of "farm fish, "followed by "tilapia" and "salmon"—two common types of farm fish. This led him to think of the future of food and the fishing industry. Finally, his brainstorm produced the idea of "genetically modified food." Later, as he analyzed the list, he chose to speak on the use of genetically engineered salmon to combat environmental issues surrounding the fishing industry.

You may be wondering why you should put all this down on paper. Why not just let all your ideas float around in your mind? The advantage of writing down your thoughts is that you end up with a document that can be analyzed. Seeing words on a page helps you focus your thinking.

Exploring the Internet

An enjoyable way to find topics is to travel around the Internet. Here are some sample approaches:

- For current events, you can visit news media sites, such as those of *The New York Times, ABC News, MSNBC News,* Pew Research, and *BBC World News,* and then browse through various sections (Health, Technology, Business, etc.).

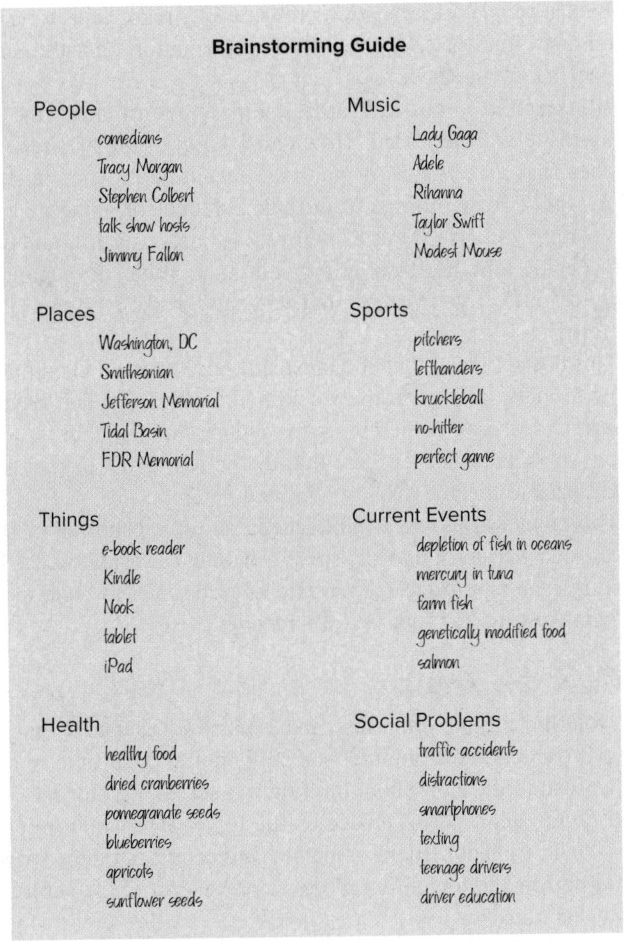

Brainstorming Guide

People
- comedians
- Tracy Morgan
- Stephen Colbert
- talk show hosts
- Jimmy Fallon

Music
- Lady Gaga
- Adele
- Rihanna
- Taylor Swift
- Modest Mouse

Places
- Washington, DC
- Smithsonian
- Jefferson Memorial
- Tidal Basin
- FDR Memorial

Sports
- pitchers
- lefthanders
- knuckleball
- no-hitter
- perfect game

Things
- e-book reader
- Kindle
- Nook
- tablet
- iPad

Current Events
- depletion of fish in oceans
- mercury in tuna
- farm fish
- genetically modified food
- salmon

Health
- healthy food
- dried cranberries
- pomegranate seeds
- blueberries
- apricots
- sunflower seeds

Social Problems
- traffic accidents
- distractions
- smartphones
- texting
- teenage drivers
- driver education

Figure 2
One Student's Entries on a Brainstorming Guide

- For general-interest articles, look through the websites of National Public Radio, *Psychology Today*, and *National Geographic*.
- Social media outlets and web databases can be helpful tools for finding inspiration. If you are stumped, try browsing Facebook, Twitter, YouTube, Wikipedia, or another informational hub that you are familiar with. Make notes about what catches your attention. Most of these sites are not adequate bibliographic sources on their own, but they can help you cycle through lots of ideas quickly and give you a jumpstart.

Select a Topic That Will Interest the Audience

To engage your audience, choose a topic that is timely, worthwhile, and interesting. A talk on why people decide to take vacations would be dull and obvious—everyone already

Examining Your Ethics

For her next speech in a public speaking class, Adrienne wants to recycle the key materials that she developed in a research paper in a psychology class last semester. Which course of action should she take?

A. Ask her speech instructor for permission to recycle the old materials in her upcoming speech.
B. Recycle the old materials in her speech without informing anyone of her decision.
C. Recycle the old materials in her speech but state clearly in the introduction that she did her research in another class.

For the answer, see the last page of this chapter.

Suppose you want to know if "extreme" roller coasters are safe, but you don't know if your classmates are interested in the topic. You may query six of them, and if they all express great interest, you know this is a good topic.

Shutterstock/Allen. G

knows that people take vacations to get away, relax, and experience something different and fun. Instead, give a lively presentation on sightseeing in Boston or backpacking in the Rockies.

"I'm excited about my topic," some students may say, "but I'm afraid the audience will be bored. How can I know?" Most listeners are bored by speeches that give them no personal enrichment. Their attitude is "What's in it for me?" To see things from their perspective, imagine a typical listener approaching you five minutes before your presentation and saying, "I'm trying to decide whether to stay for your talk. What do I stand to gain by listening to you?" If you realize that you can't make a compelling case, change your topic.

This doesn't mean that you must show listeners a dollar-and-cents gain, such as how to make money on the stock market. Perhaps their payoff is simply the pleasure of learning something new and fascinating. For example, you could explain why scientists anticipate that by the year 2100, extinct animals could be brought back to life and displayed in zoos.[3]

Two other ways to determine whether a topic is boring or interesting are to (1) ask your instructor and (2) survey classmates several weeks before your talk by asking them to rate several potential speech topics as "very interesting," "moderately interesting," or "not very interesting."

Narrow the Topic

Once you find a topic, you often need to narrow it. Suppose that you want to give a speech on weather; 5 minutes—or 20—is not enough time to adequately cover such a broad topic. How about limiting yourself to just storms? Again, 5 minutes would be too short to do justice to the topic. How about one type of storm—thunderstorms? This subject perhaps could be handled in a 5-minute speech, but it would be advisable to narrow the topic even more—to one aspect of the subject: "how to avoid being struck by lightning."

Narrowing a topic helps you control your material. It prevents you from wandering in a huge territory and allows you to focus on one small piece of ground. Instead of talking on the vast subject of elections, you might limit yourself to explaining how some states conduct voting online.

Ask yourself this question: "Is my topic one that can be adequately and comfortably discussed in the time limit I've been given?" If the honest answer is no, you can keep the topic, but you must narrow the focus.

Here are some examples of broad topics and how they can be narrowed:

Too Broad:	Native Americans
Narrowed:	Shapes, colors, and legends in Pueblo pottery
Too Broad:	Prisons
Narrowed:	Gangs in federal and state prisons
Too Broad:	Birds
Narrowed:	How migrating birds navigate

An important way to narrow your topic is to formulate a specific purpose, which will be discussed later in this chapter. First, let's take a look at your general purpose.

The General Purpose

Establishing a **general purpose** for your speech will help you bring your topic under control. Most speeches have one of the following purposes:

general purpose
the broad objective of a speech.

- To inform
- To persuade
- To entertain

Other purposes, such as to inspire, to pay tribute, and to introduce, will be discussed in the chapter on special occasion speeches.

To Inform

In an informative speech, your goal is to give new information to your listeners. You can define a concept (such as ransomware); explain a situation (why honeybees are essential for agriculture); demonstrate a process (how earthquakes occur); or describe a person, place, or event.

Your main concern in this kind of speech is to have your audience understand and remember new information. You are in effect a teacher—not a preacher, a salesperson, or a debater.

Here is a sampling of topics for informative speeches:

- The pros and cons of Internet dating sites
- Bullies in the workplace
- How your credit score is figured
- Bride kidnapping in Kyrgyzstan

To Persuade

Your aim in a persuasive speech is to win your listeners to your point of view. You may want them to change or discontinue a certain behavior (for example, convince them to stop buying ivory and other products from elephants) or prompt them to take action (for instance, persuade them to buy and drive an all-electric car).

In this kind of speech, you can try to persuade people to do the following:

- Bike, walk, or use public transportation.
- Adopt a plant-based diet.
- Donate money for autism research.

To Entertain

An entertaining speech is aimed at amusing or diverting your audience. It is light, fun, and relaxing.

Some students mistakenly think that an entertaining speech is a series of jokes. Although jokes are an obvious component of many entertaining speeches, you can amuse or divert your audience just as easily with other types of material: stories, anecdotes, quotations, examples, and descriptions. (For more details, see the chapter on special occasion speeches.)

Here are some examples of topics for entertaining speeches:

- My life with a parrot named Alex
- The five most outrageous excuses for absenteeism at work
- Being an "extra" in a Hollywood movie

Tips for Your Career

Examine Your Hidden Purposes

Professor Jane Tompkins confessed that earlier in her career, while teaching at Columbia University, she was more concerned about making a good impression than meeting students' needs. She was focused on "three things: (a) to show the students how smart I was, (b) to show them how knowledgeable I was, and (c) to show them how well-prepared I was for class. I had been putting on a performance whose true goal was not to help the students learn but to perform before them in such a way that they would have a good opinion of me."

If other speakers were as candid as Professor Tompkins, they would admit that they, too, often have hidden, unstated objectives that are far afield from listener-focused purposes such as "to inform" or "to persuade." If their purposes were written out, they might look like this:

- To dazzle my boss with my presentation skills
- To get listeners to like me and consider me smart and funny

Hidden objectives are not necessarily bad. We all have unstated goals such as looking our best and delivering a polished speech. But we should watch for ulterior purposes that make us self-centered and insensitive to our listeners' needs.

Source: Jane Tompkins, "Pedagogy of the Distressed," *College English* 52, no. 6 (October 1990).

The Specific Purpose

specific purpose
the precise goal that a speaker wants to achieve.

After you have chosen a topic and determined your general purpose, your next step is to formulate a **specific purpose**, stating exactly what you want to accomplish in your speech. Here is an example:

Topic:	Student loans
General Purpose:	To inform
Specific Purpose:	To tell my listeners how to find student loan services that are trustworthy and fair

The specific purpose is an important planning tool because it can help you bring your ideas into sharp focus so that you don't wander aimlessly in your speech and lose your audience.

Let's say you choose "protection of the environment" as a topic for a speech. It's a good topic, but much too broad—you might make the mistake of cramming too many different issues into the speech. How about "protecting national parks"? Now your topic is more manageable, especially if you devise a specific purpose that focuses on just one park:

Topic:	Preserving Yosemite National Park
General Purpose:	To persuade
Specific Purpose:	To persuade my audience to support steps to reverse overcrowding and neglect in Yosemite National Park

Now you have a sharp focus for your speech. You have limited yourself to a topic that can be covered adequately in a short speech.

Here are some guidelines for formulating a specific purpose statement.

Begin the Statement with an Infinitive

An **infinitive** is a verb preceded by *to*—for example, *to write, to read.* By beginning your purpose statement with an infinitive, you clearly state your intent.

infinitive
a verb form beginning with "to."

Poor: Solar energy

Better: To explain to my audience how to use solar energy to power all home appliances

For informative speeches, your purpose statement can start with such infinitives as "to explain," "to show," and "to demonstrate." For persuasive speeches, your purpose statement can start with infinitives such as "to convince," "to prove," and "to get the audience to believe."

Include a Reference to Your Audience

Your specific purpose statement should refer to your audience. For instance, "To convince my listeners that . . ." This may seem like a minor matter, but it serves to remind you that your goal is not just to stand up and talk but also to communicate your ideas to real flesh-and-blood human beings.

Poor: To explain how some employers are using psychological tests to determine whether prospective employees are honest

Better: To explain to my listeners how some employers are using psychological tests to determine whether prospective employees are honest

Limit the Statement to One Major Idea

Resist the temptation to cover several big ideas in a single speech. Limit your specific purpose statement to only one idea.

Poor: To persuade the audience to support efforts to halt the destruction of rain forests in Central and South America, and to demand higher standards of water purity in the United States

Better: To persuade the audience to support efforts to halt the destruction of rain forests in Central and South America

In the first example, the speaker tries to cover two major ideas in one speech. Although it is true that both themes pertain to the environment, they are not closely related and should be handled in separate speeches.

Make Your Statement as Precise as Possible

Strive to formulate a statement that is clear and precise.

Poor: To help my audience members brighten their relationships

Better: To explain to my listeners three techniques people can use to communicate more effectively with loved ones

The first statement is fuzzy and unfocused. What is meant by "to help"? What is meant by "brighten"? And what kind of relationships are to be discussed: marital, social, business? The second statement is one possible improvement.

Achieve Your Objective in the Time Allotted

Don't try to cover too much in one speech. It is better to choose a small area of knowledge that can be tightly focused than to select a huge area that can't be covered completely.

Poor: To tell my audience about endangered species

Better: To convince my audience that international action should be taken to prevent poachers from slaughtering elephants

The first statement is much too broad for a speech; you would need several hours to cover the subject. The second statement narrows the topic to one animal so that it can be covered easily in a short speech.

Don't Be Too Technical

You have probably sat through a speech or lecture that was too technical or complicated for you to understand. Don't repeat this mistake when you stand at the lectern.

Poor: To explain to my listeners the biological components of the *Salmonella enterica* bacterium, a common cause of food poisoning

Better: To explain to my audience the steps to take to avoid food poisoning

The first statement is too technical for the average audience. Many listeners would find the explanation tedious and over their heads. The second statement focuses on valuable information that people can use to safeguard their health.

The Central Idea

Picture a counselor from an alcohol rehabilitation center speaking to a college class on alcoholism and giving many statistics, anecdotes, and research findings. You did not hear the speech, but afterward, you overheard some of the listeners arguing about it. Several contended that the speaker's message was "Drink moderately—don't abuse alcohol," while others thought the speaker was saying, "Abstain from alcohol completely." Still others said they were confused—they didn't know what the speaker was driving at.

If you give a speech and people later wonder or debate exactly what point you were trying to make, you have failed to accomplish your most important task: to communicate your **central idea**.

central idea
the key concept of a speech.

The central idea is the core message of your speech expressed in one sentence. It is the same as the *thesis sentence, controlling statement,* or *core idea*—terms you may have encountered in English courses. If you were forced to boil down your entire speech to one sentence, what would you say? *That* is your central idea. If, one month after you have given your speech, the audience remembers only one thing, what should it be? *That* is your central idea.

As we will see in later chapters, the central idea is a vital ingredient in your outline for a speech. In fact, it *controls* your entire speech. Everything you say in your speech should develop, explain, illustrate, or prove the central idea. Everything? Yes, everything—all your facts, anecdotes, statistics, and quotations.

If you are unclear in your own mind about your central idea, you will be like the counselor who caused such confusion: listeners will leave your speech wondering, "What in the world was that speaker driving at?"

Devising the Central Idea

Let's imagine that you decide to give a speech on why governments should spend money to send powerful radio signals into outer space. The specific purpose statement of your speech might look like this:

Specific Purpose: To persuade my listeners to support government funding of radio transmissions into outer space

How are you going to persuade your audience? Can you simply say, "Folks, please support radio transmissions into outer space"? No, because merely stating your position won't sway your listeners. To convince them, you need to sell the audience on a central idea that, if believed, might cause them to support your position:

Central Idea: Most scientists agree that radio transmissions are the best means for making contact with extraterrestrial civilizations (if any exist).

If you can sell this idea, you will probably succeed in your specific purpose: to persuade the listeners to support public funding of radio transmissions. They will be persuaded because the central idea is so intriguing: Most people like the notion of communication with aliens from faraway planets, and if most scientists back the idea, it cannot be considered far-out and impractical. "Yes," the listeners will say, "let's spend some of our tax dollars to find other life."

After you decide on a central idea, your task in preparing the rest of the speech is to find materials—such as examples, statistics, and quotations—to explain and prove the central idea. In this case, you would need to explain the technology and cite the testimony of eminent scientists who support radio transmissions into space.

Some students have trouble distinguishing between the specific purpose and the central idea. Is there any significant difference? Yes. The specific purpose is written from your point of view—it is what *you* set out to accomplish. The central idea is written entirely from the listeners' point of view—it is the message *they* go away with.

To learn to distinguish between the specific purpose and the central idea, study the examples in Table 1.

Table 1 **How Topics Can Be Developed**

Topic	General Purpose	Specific Purpose	Central Idea
Space junk	To inform	To inform my audience about the dangers of "space junk" (dead satellites and bits of expended rocket stages) that orbits the Earth	More than 9,000 pieces of debris orbit the Earth, threatening commercial and scientific satellites.
Buying a car	To persuade	To persuade my audience to avoid high-pressure sales tactics when buying a car	By comparing prices and using reputable car guides, consumers can avoid being "taken for a ride" by car salespeople.
Driving tests	To entertain	To amuse my audience with the true story of my abysmal failure to pass my first driving test	Taking the test for a driver's license is a scary and sometimes disastrous event.

Central Idea for a persuasive speech: Sugar consumption by children should be limited because of the risk of weight gain and diabetes.

© McGraw-Hill Education

In planning your speech, write the specific purpose statement first—before you start gathering material. In many cases, you will be able to write the central idea immediately afterward. Sometimes, however, you may need to postpone the central idea until you have completed your research. For example, let's say you are planning a speech on the use of steroids by athletes and bodybuilders. Here is your goal:

Specific Purpose: To convince my audience not to use steroids for building muscle

You haven't done any research yet, so you can't really write a central idea. But after you spend a few days studying articles on steroids, you are able to create your central idea:

Central Idea: Individuals who chronically use steroids risk kidney and liver damage.

Guidelines for the Central Idea

1. **Include only one central idea in your speech.** Why not two? Or three? Because you will be doing well if you can fully illuminate just one big idea in a speech. If you try to handle more than one, you run the risk of overwhelming the listeners with more information than they can absorb.

2. **Put the central idea on paper.** Writing it down gives you a clear sense of the direction your speech will take.

3. **Limit the central idea to a single sentence.** Whenever theatrical producer David Belasco was approached by people with an idea for a play, he would hand them his business card and ask them to write their concept on the back. If they protested that they needed more space, that proved they didn't have a clear idea.

4. **Make an assertion rather than an announcement or a statement of fact.** A common mistake is to formulate the central idea as a mere announcement:

   Ineffective: I will discuss robots as surgeons. *(This is a good topic, but what idea does the speaker want to communicate?)*

   Another mistake is to put forth nothing more than a statement of fact:

   Ineffective: Several operations at Johns Hopkins Medical Center have been performed by surgeons using robots. *(This is interesting, but it is just a fact—a piece of information that can be included in the speech but does not stand alone as an overarching theme.)*

   Now let's turn to a better version—one that makes an assertion:

   Effective: Robots are valuable assistants in surgery because they can work with great precision and no fatigue. *(This is a good central idea because it asserts a worthwhile point that can be developed in a speech.)*

5. **Let the central idea determine the content of the entire speech.** As you prepare your outline, evaluate every potential item in light of the central idea. Does Fact A help explain the central idea? If yes, keep it. If no, throw it out. Does Statistic B help prove the central idea? If yes, keep it. If no, throw it out.

Overview of Speech Design

How do the items discussed in this chapter fit into the overall design of a speech? If you look at Figure 3, which is an overview of a typical plan for a speech, you will see this chapter's items—general purpose, specific purpose, and central idea—listed in the top oval, labeled "Objectives." These items are planning tools to help you create a coherent speech. They are *not* the opening words of your speech. The bottom oval, "Documentation," is also a planning tool and does not represent the final words of a speech. The actual speech that you deliver is shown in the rectangles: Introduction, Transition, Body, Transition, and Conclusion.

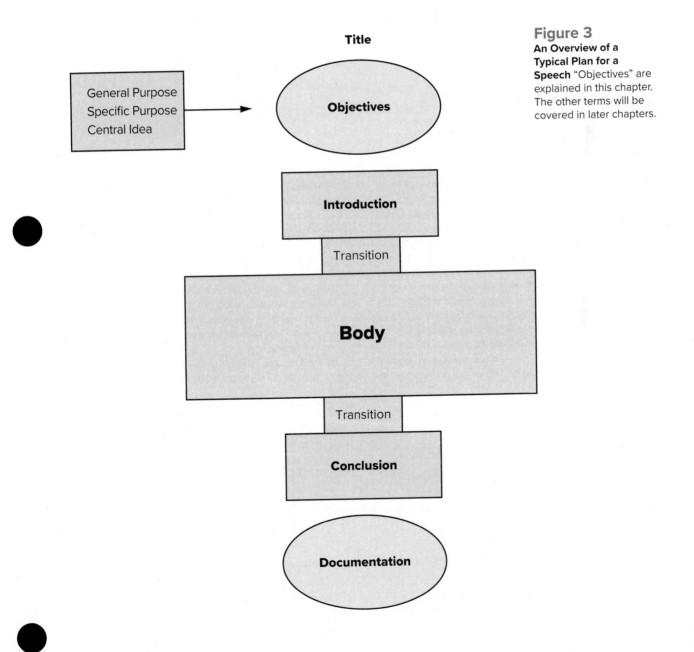

Figure 3
An Overview of a Typical Plan for a Speech "Objectives" are explained in this chapter. The other terms will be covered in later chapters.

Don't make the mistake of assuming that a speaker should create the rectangles from top to bottom, in the order in which they appear. For reasons that will be obvious later, it makes sense to work on the body first, and then tackle the introduction and the conclusion.

Let's pause a moment to consider where we are headed. The next seven chapters will show you how to build a strong speech. First, we will look at how to find good primary research materials and finesse them with raw materials. Next, we will examine how to develop the body of the speech, the introduction, and the conclusion. Finally, we will discuss how to arrange all the parts in your outline and your speaking notes.

All this work may seem wasteful of your time and energy, but in the long run, it pays rich dividends. It channels your thinking and prevents you from scattering your efforts across too wide a field. It helps you fashion an orderly, understandable speech, increasing the chances that you will enlighten, rather than confuse or bore, your listeners.

Resources for Review and Skill Building

Summary

In choosing a topic for your speech, think of subjects (1) about which you care a great deal, (2) about which you know a lot (either now or after you complete your research), and (3) that your audience will find interesting.

In looking for topics, start with yourself. What personal experiences might yield an interesting speech? If you want to go outside your own life, explore topics that intrigue you—subjects about which you have always wanted to know more.

Other methods for finding a topic include brainstorming (writing down ideas that come to your mind) and exploring websites that list subjects for college papers and speeches. Be sure to choose a topic narrow enough for the time allotted.

After you choose a topic, decide upon your general purpose in speaking (such as to inform, to persuade, or to entertain) and then formulate your specific purpose—exactly what you hope to accomplish in the speech. Follow these guidelines: (1) Begin the statement with an infinitive. (2) Include a reference to your audience. (3) Limit the statement to one major idea. (4) Make your statement as precise as possible. (5) Make sure you can achieve your objective in the time allotted. (6) Don't be too technical.

Next, write out your central idea: the one key idea that you want your audience members to remember even if they forget everything else in the speech. Make sure the central idea is phrased as an assertion rather than an announcement or a statement of fact.

In the long run, these preliminary steps will help you organize your ideas in a coherent, understandable form.

Key Terms

brainstorming, *78*

infinitive, *83*

central idea, *84*

specific purpose, *82*

general purpose, *81*

Review Questions

1. When a speaker is enthusiastic about his or her ideas, how do listeners usually react?

2. Name the three main strategies for selecting a good speech topic.

3. How does brainstorming work?

4. List three *general* purposes for speeches.

5. Are jokes required for an entertaining speech? Explain your answer.

6. What are hidden purposes, and how should you handle them?

7. List the six criteria discussed in this chapter for writing a specific purpose statement.

8. What is the central idea of a speech?

9. What is the difference between the specific purpose and the central idea?

10. For the central idea, is an assertion or an announcement better? Explain your answer.

Building Critical-Thinking Skills

1. If handled poorly, "painting a room" could be a boring topic. How would you make it interesting to an audience of college students?

2. "Telling about white collar crime." How could you improve this statement of specific purpose?

3. If the central idea of a speech is "The best computer passwords relate to obscure places and events known only to you," what do you think the specific purpose is?

4. Narrow the following broad subjects to specific, manageable topics:

   a. Outdoor recreation
   b. Musical groups
   c. Illegal drugs
   d. Saving money
   e. Climate change

5. All but one of the specific purpose statements below are either inappropriate for a brief classroom speech or incorrectly written. Identify the good one, and rewrite the bad ones so that they conform to the guidelines in this chapter:

   a. To inform my audience of the basics of quantum inelastic scattering and photodissociation code
   b. To inform my listeners about being creative on the job, getting raises, and being an effective manager
   c. To explain to my audience how to perform basic yoga exercises
   d. How persons with disabilities can fight back against job discrimination
   e. Immigration since 1800
   f. To persuade my audience to be careful

Building Teamwork Skills

1. Before you meet, each group member should list five potential speech topics. In your group, evaluate each topic: Is it interesting and appropriate for a classroom speech?

2. In a group, brainstorm topics that would be boring or inappropriate for speeches in your class. Choose one person to write down the topics. Remember that no one should criticize or analyze during the brainstorming session. Afterward, the group (or the class) can discuss each choice (Does everyone agree? Why is the topic inappropriate?).

3. Follow the instructions for item 2, except brainstorm topics that would be interesting and appropriate for speeches in your class.

Examining Your Ethics

Answer: A. You should know—and respect—your instructor's policy. Some instructors may give permission, while others may prefer that you conduct fresh research.

End Notes

1. Laura Pappano, "How Colleges Are Finding Tomorrow's Prodigies," *Christian Science Monitor*, www.csmonitor.com (accessed June 16, 2015); "Roll Over IIT, MIT Is Here," *The Telegraph* (Calcutta, India), www.telegraphindia.com (accessed June 16, 2015); Avijit Chatterjee, "Short Cut to MIT," *The Telegraph* (Calcutta, India), www.telegraphindia .com (accessed December 7, 2015).

2. Jonathan Castro, Oberlin College, e-mail interview, May 14, 2015.

3. Michio Kaku, *Physics of the Future* (New York: Doubleday, 2011), pp. 160–64; Marcus Hall, ed., *Restoration and History* (New York: Routledge, 2010), pp. 288–30.

Locating Information

OBJECTIVES

After studying this chapter, you should be able to

1. Understand why the Internet is sometimes a less-desirable source than traditional library materials.

2. Develop research strategies for finding materials quickly and efficiently.

3. Take advantage of the services and materials offered by librarians and libraries.

4. Locate useful materials on the Internet.

5. Recognize the value of deriving material from experiences, investigations, and surveys.

6. Conduct effective interviews with experts.

7. Take notes with precision, care, and thoroughness.

RADIO HOST AND COMEDIAN Pete Dominick is frequently asked to comment on a wide range of issues on cable news and political talk shows. Host of the *Stand Up!* podcast, Dominick regularly appears as a political pundit on MSNBC and has also been featured on SiriusXM, CNN, and HBO's *Real Time with Bill Maher.*

As a pundit, Dominick is often asked to give his opinion on breaking political news, so he always stays up-to-date on what is happening in the world. "I'll read *The New York Times* and *The Washington Post*, as well as some political blogs, to see what they're reporting," he says.

But his research doesn't end there. On big issues—especially ones that he knows he will discuss on air—Dominick will dig deeper. "I'll look up the experts who were

Pete Dominick is a political pundit, comedian, and host of the *Stand Up!* podcast.
Roy Rochlin/Getty Images

interviewed and examine them further to see what they've published and where their expertise lies," he explains, adding that he takes a lot of notes while researching to help formulate his talking points.

As a long-time political talk show host, Dominick is well-versed on many topics. Over the years, he has interviewed hundreds of experts on a wide range of issues, and that has helped him form his political opinions. Although he admits he certainly has his biases—every thinking human does—he dislikes the "black or white" approach that often clouds political debate.

"We're often put in a position to see a binary—two things cannot be true at once," he said. "But two things can be right at once." For example, a person may feel that abortion is wrong, but is not in favor of the government making a law outlawing abortion. Dominick goes on to add, "We don't need to be forced into political boxes."

Additionally, when it comes to commenting on issues, Dominick is always careful to keep his life experience in check. "My personal experience is limited," he said. "I always try to bring in other people to hear about their experience."

Dominick's approach is a good model for all public speakers. Research multiple sources and dig deeper to find out what the experts are saying. Additionally, talk to others who may have more relevant experience. And don't get caught in the binary trap.

91

Misconceptions about Research

A common misconception about research is that by conducting a simple Google search for information, one will find numerous reliable sources. Although it is true that an Internet search will yield *numerous* results, they will not necessarily be *reliable*. The reality is that many websites contain inaccurate or misleading information, especially concerning controversial or disputed issues.

The important thing is to not limit your research to traditional Internet searches. Most college libraries subscribe to online academic databases where students can access academic research and articles without stepping foot in the physical library. Additionally, there are many hard-copy resources at the library that can be beneficial in research. Students can also conduct their own field research, interviewing experts on their topic or conducting surveys.

Figure 1 gives an overview of the major research options and a sampling of the resources that you can use. All these resources will be discussed in this chapter. The next chapter will cover how to evaluate the information that you find.

Finding Materials Efficiently

To avoid research that is unproductive and irrelevant, use the following techniques.

Begin with a Purpose Statement

Decide the specific purpose of your speech before you start your research. It will focus your efforts.

Some students find it helpful to turn the purpose statement into a question. For example, "To inform my listeners how they can determine if their drinking water is free of dangerous contamination" could be asked as "How can we know if our water is safe to drink?"

Whichever form you use, write it out and keep it in front of you at each step of your research. It will guide your efforts and prevent wasted time.

Plan Your Time

To give yourself ample time before the speech date, start your research far in advance. Determine the materials and resources you will need, and then create a schedule. (See a sample schedule in Figure 2.)

Figure 1

Research Options

The resources shown here sometimes overlap. For example, many college libraries provide access to online academic journals that can be accessed online (usually with a college ID).

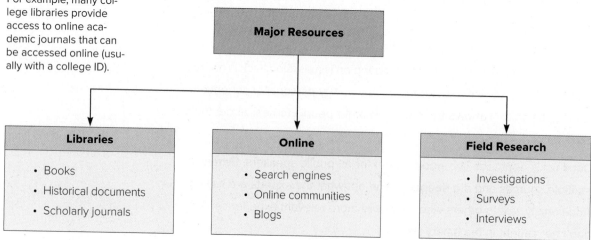

		My Research "To-Do" List
☐	Feb. 4	7 - 9 p.m.	Do Google search for topic. Study the top results
☐	Feb. 5	9 - 11 a.m.	Go to library and discuss topic with reference librarian. Examine hard copy materials
☐	Feb. 5	6 - 8 p.m.	Search academic databases recommended by librarian
☐	Feb. 6	9 a.m.	Schedule Interview with "expert" on topic
☐	Feb. 9	6 - 8 p.m.	Review research, prepare questions for Interview
☐	Feb. 10	1 - 2 p.m.	Conduct Interview with expert source
☐	Feb. 10	2 - 3 p.m.	Review Interview notes
☐	Feb. 11	1 - 5 p.m.	Compile research Into outline, breaking into 2-3 main points

Figure 2
Sample Schedule
Check off items as they are completed.

Be sure to call to arrange personal interviews early in the process so that the interviewees can fit you into their schedules.

Libraries

Libraries offer a treasury of resources for your speeches. Several valuable library resources can be used online without setting foot in the physical building. However, visiting a library—whether it be a campus library, public library, or specialized library—can still be invaluable for sound research. The greatest assets of libraries are those who work there, specifically reference librarians.

Getting Help from Librarians

Some people are reluctant to approach a librarian for help because they fear they will be bothersome. However, the main role of librarians is not to place books on shelves but to help patrons, so don't be shy about asking for help.

In most libraries, the person who is best able to help you with your research is called a **reference librarian**. This person is a specialist who has training and experience in tracking down information. Whether you're trying to locate a specific piece of information, or looking for help on where to start your research, visit the reference desk and ask a librarian for help.

"Don't spin your wheels and waste a lot of time if you get stuck or encounter something confusing," said Kathy Herrlich, a librarian at Northeastern University. "A reference librarian can save you time and help you find better information, more efficiently. For example, we can suggest a couple of the best databases for your topic." Also, she says, if a library fails to have what you are looking for, a librarian can provide referrals to other sources and collections outside your campus—at another library, for example, or a community agency.[1]

reference librarian
a specialist in information retrieval.

A reference librarian can be very helpful in finding information.
bikeriderlondon/Shutterstock

Books

Here are some tips on using books:

Use your library's catalog. The catalog, an online compilation of all books owned by the library, permits you to make a quick search in at least three categories: (1) author's name, (2) title, and (3) subject.

Pay attention to the date of publication because an old book may be useless for some research (such as current events). Another important item is the call number, which tells where a book is located in the library's stacks. If you have any problem finding a book, ask a librarian for help.

Some catalogs will indicate whether a book is already checked out and will permit you to place a "hold" on it. As soon as it is returned to the library, it will be reserved for you.

Consult reference materials.   Reference materials such as atlases, handbooks, and almanacs are carefully researched and double-checked for accuracy.

Find previews.   Sometimes, when an entire book is not readily available, you can still find key information by searching online for previews. Let's say you are researching the challenges that will face astronauts when they land on Mars someday, and you want to know how hot or cold it will be. Go to a site like Amazon, search for a book on travel to Mars, and enter the keyword "temperature." For example, if you find the book *How We'll Live on Mars* and search for "temperature," you will find preview pages that include this passage:

> Landing near the equator allows the astronauts to take advantage of milder temperatures that can reach 70 degrees Fahrenheit on a summer day. But at night, the temperature easily reaches minus 100 degrees.[2]

If this passage provides the key information you need, you have saved yourself the time and effort you would have spent tracking down the book itself.

Periodicals

scholarly journal
a publication that contains peer-reviewed research conducted by experts in the field.

Libraries provide access to articles in two types of periodicals: mainstream publications (such as *The Wall Street Journal* and *National Geographic*), and **scholarly journals** (such as *African Studies Quarterly* and *Harvard Health Journal*).

Most people are familiar with articles from mainstream publications, the kind of information found in popular newspapers, magazines, and news websites (like huffingtonpost.com). The information offered in mainstream publications is valuable; however, it is important to distinguish between opinion content and news content. For example, *The New York Times* is an excellent source for national and international news, but it also contains a very popular opinion section that is often liberal in its views. When using news outlets for research, make sure you are citing news content, not opinion content.

While mainstream publications provide insight on a broad range of topics, scholarly journals provide greater depth of information on specific topics. Scholarly journals are often peer reviewed, which means that other experts in the field examine the work of the author and approve the work before publication. Unlike news publications, which are written for the mainstream public, scholarly journals are highly specialized and written for fellow academics. This can make journals difficult to read. However, because the articles are vetted by experts in the field before publication, the information offered is invaluable. (See a table breaking down the advantages of mainstream publications and scholarly journals in Table 1.)

Whether researching mainstream publications or scholarly journals, articles are available in two formats:

1. *Print.* Libraries carry a wide variety of publications and keep past issues.

	Mainstream Publications	Scholarly Journals
Easy to read	Yes	No
Vetted by experts	No	Yes
Widely available	Yes	No
Accessible at library	Yes	Yes

Table 1
Referencing Periodicals

2. *Electronic.* Most libraries have searchable databases (such as ProQuest and EBSCO) that are available to you as a student or patron. Typically you will need a student ID or password to access this material. Ask the librarian if you need help accessing these online journals.

Electronic databases provide information in three forms:

1. *Citation.* A **citation** is a basic bibliographical reference that includes the title of the article, the name(s) of the author(s), the name of the magazine, the publication date, and page numbers.

citation
basic facts about a source.

2. *Abstract.* An **abstract**, or brief summary, of an article is designed to give you enough information to decide whether you want to see the complete text of that article. Sometimes the abstract itself gives you all the information you need.

abstract
summary of key information.

3. *Full text.* Some databases offer complete or **full-text** articles.

full text
every word of a document.

Interlibrary Loan

If your library does not have a book or an article that you want, librarians can seek help from other libraries, using **interlibrary loan**. A book can be borrowed, often at no cost to you, and an article can be photocopied (you pay only the copying fee).

Because a book or an article may take a few days or even weeks to arrive, make your request as far ahead of speech day as possible.

interlibrary loan
sharing of materials and services among libraries.

Online Research

A plethora of information is available online. It can be difficult to find what you need. Here are some effective tools for locating information.

Search Engines

A **search engine** finds documents on the Internet that match the keywords you have provided. Usually search engines will return results in order of relevance—the most relevant at the top, the least relevant at the bottom. However, companies can pay to have their websites posted at the top of the page for a specific keyword search, so it's important to look beyond the first few results when conducting research.

search engine
a service that lets you search for keywords on Web pages throughout the world.

You can save time by learning the advanced features that are available on your favorite search engine. For example, Google, the most popular search engine, allows you to limit a search to a certain domain or website. If you are investigating classroom cheating at colleges, you can put keywords like "classroom cheating site: .edu" in the search box, and all of the results will come from educational institutions. Likewise, the keywords "classroom cheating site: umich.edu" will yield results only from the University of Michigan website.

Another way to limit search results is to make use of "advanced search" options within Google and other search engines. Additionally, the following techniques can help narrow your search:

- **Put the search query in quotes** to ensure your results include all words in the query. For example, if you google *Portuguese water dog*, the search engine will be prompted to find results with any of those three words, netting more than 43 million results. On the other hand, googling "Portuguese water dog" prompts the search engine to find only results that match your search exactly as you typed it, netting under 3 million results.
- **Use the hyphen (-)** to prompt the search engine to filter out a specific word. Using the above example, you might decide to filter out results that include breeders. Google "Portuguese water dog" -breeders. This search yields just over 1.8 million results.
- **Use AND** to make your search more specific. AND (must be all caps) prompts the search engine to include only results with the initial phrase *and* the word/phrase you place after AND. For example, if you were interested in searching only for Portuguese water dogs and the claim that it is a hypoallergenic dog, search "Portuguese water dog" AND "hypoallergenic dogs" to get under 30,000 results.

A Google image search for "Portuguese water dog" can help you find several images that you can use to compliment your presentation.

Joe Dennis

Google also offers several options to help find different types of content. Under the search box, users can narrow their results to news, videos, images, maps, shopping, and more. This can be very helpful in speech research. Using the "Portuguese water dog" search example, you can easily find photos to compliment your speech slides by clicking on "images," videos of the furry pet in action under "videos," and news stories featuring Portuguese water dogs by clicking on "news."

Google also offers limited access to scholarly journals on its specialized search engine, Google Scholar (scholar.google.com), and access to the full text or excerpts of some books on Google Books (books.google.com).

Online Communities and Personal Blogs

In addition to consulting websites, you can tap the experiences and insights of people around the world who are eager and willing to share their knowledge and viewpoints. Here are three ways to find them.

Groups and Forums

Groups and forums are message centers where people who have similar interests can share ideas and observations. Sponsored by Facebook, Yahoo!, and other Internet companies, groups and forums cover just about any subject you can imagine. For example, if you are interested in watching and protecting whales, you will find dozens of groups or forums that provide commentary, as well as photos and videos, on whales.

For a researcher, the vital part of a group or forum is its archives. Messages are organized by "threads"—that is, all the messages that deal with an original query can be viewed, one after another. For example, one person asked for comments about a company that was offering her a college scholarship. In response, over a dozen people from different geographic regions posted messages warning that they had been defrauded by the company's scholarship scam. All those messages, organized by thread, can be viewed sequentially in the archives.

Blogs

A **blog** is a website that posts material that the blogger (the person or organization that owns the site) wants to share with the world.

blog
frequently updated online log.

For researchers, the most useful blogs are those that give the latest news in a particular field and provide links to other sources. For example, *The Health Care Blog* (thehealthcareblog.com) reports on current developments in the health care system, with links to related websites.

Many blogs permit readers to post responses or comments, thereby performing some of the same functions as groups and question-and-answer sites.

Blogs are included in the results of the search engines listed above. If you want to isolate them, add *blog* to your keyword.

Question-and-Answer Sites

Question-and-answer services sometimes provide information that you cannot get anywhere else on the Internet. But beware: the quality varies. Some sites have top people in a given field, but other sites have self-proclaimed experts whose expertise may be dubious, or even dangerous.

field research
firsthand gathering of information.

Some well-known sites are Ask.com and Quora.com. Additional sites can be found by typing "ask the experts" and "ask an expert" into Google.

Field Research

Field research means gathering information firsthand by observing, surveying, interviewing, or being part of some activity.

Experiences and Investigations

As you gather materials for a speech, don't overlook your own personal experiences, which can bolster your key points. For example, if you escaped serious injury in a car accident because you were wearing a seat belt, you can use the story to supplement national statistics on the value of seat belts.

You can also undertake investigations. David Marcovitz, a medical student at Vanderbilt University, investigated what food stamp recipients can afford to eat. For five straight days, he spent only one dollar for each of his three meals—the amount of money the average food stamp recipient could spend in Nashville, Tennessee, at the time of his experiment. For lunch one day, he had to limit himself to half an apple, a carrot, and a cold-cut sandwich made with day-old bread. His investigation left him hungry and helped him walk in the shoes of his future low-income patients and have empathy for them.[3]

Medical student David Marcovitz found out what it's like to be a food stamp recipient.

Larry McCormack/The Tennessean/AP Images

Informal Surveys

Nearly everyone has answered a survey at some point in their life, whether it's a company-sponsored survey about a shopping experience at a specific store or an online survey about politics. In most cases, these surveys are carefully developed by social scientists to be as statistically sound as possible.

While such surveys are time-consuming and require a certain level of expertise to develop, students should not be afraid to conduct informal surveys as part of their speech research. For example, if you are giving a speech on student loan debt, you might post a question on Facebook asking friends if they have student loan debt, how much debt they anticipate amassing before graduation, and how concerned they are about their debt. For those who do not want to post that information publicly, you can invite them to send you a direct message with the information.

The results you get could be impactful in your speech. For example, if you receive 20 responses and 17 friends indicated they have debt, you can open your speech by saying, "In an informal survey I conducted among my friends on Facebook, 85 percent of them said they have student loan debt." Then you can use the comments they provided over their level of concern about the debt to demonstrate why this topic is important.

In addition to using Facebook, you can conduct surveys via e-mail utilizing a survey-maker site like surveymonkey.com, or you can distribute paper questionnaires in person. For more information, see the discussion of surveys in the chapter on reaching your audience.

Interviews with Experts

Bestselling author Frederick Forsyth has written spy novels that have been acclaimed for their authenticity and accuracy. For his research, he says he avoids "all online fact searching because so much is either rubbish or inadequate." He elaborated, "I seek out the expert steeped in knowledge of his subject and ask for an hour of his time. I usually secure everything I need and probably several extraordinary anecdotes that would never be found on the Internet."[4]

Like Forsyth, many speakers and writers have discovered that interviews with experts—people who are highly knowledgeable about a topic—can yield valuable facts and insights. Often these experts can provide up-to-date information not yet available in magazines or books.

Let's look at two avenues for interviews: electronic and personal.

Electronic

Electronic communication via e-mail and social networks (such as Facebook) can be an excellent tool for interviewing experts. To find knowledgeable people on the Internet, visit websites or social media sites on your topic and click on links that take you to the authors' information. If you already know the name of an expert, you can use a search engine to try to find his or her e-mail address. Another option is to go to the website of the organization with which the expert is affiliated. If a scholar teaches at a certain university, you can visit the school's website, click on the directory of faculty members, and then locate the professor's e-mail address.

Personal

For face-to-face interviews, where can you find experts? For many college students, there are experts available on several topics right on their own college campus. Search your school's website for a faculty member's area of expertise. Or you can head to that department's building/office and ask if there is a professor available to talk about a specific topic. For example, if you are researching the impacts of violent programming in media, consider going to your school's mass communications department and psychology department to find an expert on the topic. Professors are usually delighted when students inquire about their area of expertise.

Once you've exhausted campus resources, look at the larger community beyond the campus. Are any businesses or agencies involved in your subject? If so, e-mail or call them to ask for the appropriate expert. If you are speaking on snakebites, for example, call the nearest zoo and ask to speak to the chief herpetologist.

If you are lucky, there can sometimes be a wonderful bonus from an interview: you might develop a rewarding professional contact or personal friendship. Don't let fear of rejection deter you. Some students have the idea that the knowledgeable people they want to interview are so important and so busy they will have no time for a "lowly" student. On the contrary, most people love to be interviewed about a topic for which they are passionate. If this surprises you, think about yourself for a moment: when a friend asks you for advice, don't you enjoy holding forth as an "expert"? The same is true of knowledgeable people in your community: they are flattered to be interviewed by a student.

Examining Your Ethics

Jennifer conducts research as part of her plan to convince her audience that frequent use of cell phones can cause brain cancer. She interviews three different cancer specialists, all of whom say that her theory is possible but highly unlikely. In her speech, which approach should she take?

A. Quote the specialists as saying the theory is possible, but omit the "highly unlikely" qualifier.
B. Avoid any mention of the interviews and find specialists whose findings support the speaker's argument.
C. Report that all three specialists found the theory to be possible but highly unlikely.

For the answer, see the last page of this chapter.

Preparing for an Interview

Before an interview, there are a few things you should do.

Make an appointment.   Never drop by and expect the person to agree to an interview on the spot. When you call or e-mail to line up the appointment, explain what you are trying to find out and how much time you are requesting.

Conduct research before the interview.   If you learn the basic facts about your subject beforehand, you can ask questions that will be right on target, yielding good information. Doing your homework can also help you avoid asking embarrassing questions. Suppose you are interviewing a neurologist about brain injuries suffered by Iraq War veterans and you ask, "Where is Iraq?" The expert may resent you wasting her time as she spoon-feeds you elementary material you should already know.

There are two other advantages of doing research before an interview: (1) If you are confused by something in your reading, the expert may be able to clarify. (2) If you are unable to find vital information in your research, the expert can often supply it or tell you where to find it.

Prepare questions.   Decide ahead of time exactly what questions you want to ask, and write them down. Be sure to put the most important ones first—in case you run out of time. If possible, e-mail the most important questions ahead of time to help the interviewee prepare for the interview.

Even though you have your questions prewritten, allow for flexibility during the interview. You may find out new information during the interview that will require you to change your questions. For example, in an interview about brain injuries suffered by Iraq War veterans, your neurologist source might mention a new treatment that is being developed for such cases. This would be good information for your speech—probe on this topic further even though it was not in your original line of questioning.

Decide how to record the interview.   Since human memory is highly fallible, you need a system for recording the interview. Most interviewers use either or both of the following methods:

1. *Writing down key ideas.* Jot down key ideas only. If you try to write down every word the person is saying, you will be completely absorbed in transcribing sentences instead of making sense out of what is being said.

2. *Using a recorder.* Smartphones with audio or video recording capabilities and video cameras are ideal when you want to get a word-for-word record of the interview.

If you want to use a recorder, seek permission from the interviewee beforehand. Most people will permit recording, but a few will refuse (because it makes them feel uncomfortable or intimidated). You should, of course, respect their wishes. Using a hidden device is unethical.

Conducting an Interview

Here are some tips on how to conduct an interview.

Start in a friendly, relaxed manner.   Before you begin your questions, you need to establish rapport. You can express appreciation ("Thanks for letting me come by to talk to you today") and sincerely make complimentary remarks (about the pictures on the wall, the person's organization, etc.). Every person enjoys compliments—it's human nature. Try to read the person's body language—does your source seem relaxed or hurried? Feedback will help you decide whether to plunge quickly into the subject of the interview.

Get biographical information.   Since the person you are interviewing is one of your sources, you need to be able to tell your audience later why he or she is an authority on your subject. If you have not been able to get background information in advance, the early part of the interview is a good time to get it because it continues the building of rapport. You could say, for example, "Where did you get your doctorate?" or "How long have you been working on this issue?"

Ask both prepared and spontaneous questions.   Earlier we noted that you should decide ahead of time exactly what questions you want to ask. There are two types of questions that can be prepared in advance: closed and open-ended.

closed question
a question requiring only a short, specific response.

Closed questions require only yes or no responses or short, factual answers. Examples: "Do Democrats outnumber Republicans in this state?" "What percentage of registered voters actually voted in the last presidential election?" Closed questions are effective in getting specific data.

open-ended question
a question that permits a broad range of responses.

Open-ended questions give the interviewee a wide latitude for responding. For example, "How do you feel about negative political ads?" The advantage of such a broad question is that the interviewee can choose the points he or she wishes to emphasize—points about which it may not have occurred to you to ask. The disadvantage is that such questions may allow an interviewee to wander off the subject into irrelevant side issues.

There are two types of questions that cannot be prepared in advance and may need to be asked spontaneously during the interview: clarifying and follow-up.

clarifying question
a question designed to clear up confusion.

Clarifying questions are used when you are confused about what the person means. Ask a question like "Could you explain that a little more?" or say "Correct me if I'm wrong, but what I think you're saying is . . ." Don't shy away from asking clarifying questions because you are afraid of showing your ignorance. Remember that you are there to interview the person precisely because you are "ignorant" in his or her area of expertise. So ask about any point that you don't understand. The interviewee will appreciate it and respect you more.

Follow-up questions are designed to encourage the interviewee to elaborate on what he or she has been saying—to continue a story or to add to a comment. Here are some examples: "What happened next?" "Were you upset about what happened?" "Could you give me some examples of what you're talking about?"

follow-up question
a question designed
to stimulate
elaboration.

Make the interview more like a conversation than an interrogation. Be natural and spontaneous, and follow the flow of conversation. Don't act as if you must plow through your list of questions item by item. Simply check off the questions as they are answered. Toward the end of the interview, ask those questions that still have not been covered. Also, the person may bring up surprising aspects of your topic that you have not thought about; this should inspire you to ask spontaneous follow-up questions.

Ask about other sources and visual aids. Interviewees may be able to tell you about other people you can interview, and they may point you to other sources that you were unaware of. They may even be willing to lend or give you visual aids that you can use in your speech.

Ask if you've omitted any questions. When you have gone through all the prepared questions, ask the interviewee if there are any items that you have failed to ask about. You may find that you have inadvertently overlooked some important matters.

End the interview on time. Respect the amount of time that was granted when you set up your appointment; if you were allotted 20 minutes, stay no more than 20 minutes—unless, of course, the interviewee invites you to stay longer.

Ask for permission to contact again. Ask your source if it is okay for you to contact them with follow-up questions, or if you need clarifications. Doing so will keep the door open for a continuing dialogue, and may even grant you easier access to that person in the future (for example, the source may give you his or her cell phone number). As you leave, be sure to thank the person again.

Following Up

After you leave the interview, you have three important tasks.

Promptly expand your notes. Immediately after the interview, go through your notes and expand them (by turning words and phrases into complete sentences) while the conversation is fresh in your mind. If you wait two weeks to go over your notes, they will be stale and you may have to puzzle over your scribbling or you may forget what a particular phrase means.

Evaluate your information. Evaluate your notes to see if you got exactly what you were looking for. If you are confused on any points or find that you need more information on a particular item, call or e-mail the interviewee and ask for help. This should not be a source of embarrassment for you—it shows that you care enough about the subject and the interviewee to get the information exactly right.

Write a thank-you note. A brief note, either in an e-mail or a traditional card, thanking the interviewee is a classy finale. If possible, mention some of the interviewee's points that you will likely use in your speech.

Saving Key Information

You should systematically save the key information that you find. Being organized will allow you to craft your speech more efficiently and will also help you avoid plagiarizing and attributing information to incorrect sources. Below are some tips to help you manage your material.

Printouts and Photocopies

If you make printouts of websites and photocopies of articles and book pages, analyze them carefully to extract the most important details and to plan any necessary follow-up research. Use a highlighter to spotlight information that supports your topic so that you can quickly review the main points of your sources later. On each separate document, be sure to identify the author, publication or website, publication date, and page numbers in case your papers get disorganized. Storing your printouts and photocopies in labeled folders can help keep you organized.

If you're unable to print digital sources, copy and paste the text to a Word document and highlight key information there. Include the publication information as you would on a printout or photocopy, and label your document clearly.

Notes

There are two types of notations you should make: bibliography citations and notes of key ideas. These notes do not have to be handwritten, of course. You can create the equivalent on your computer, tablet, or smartphone.

Bibliography Citations

As you gather materials, record the names of books and articles that seem promising. These citations will help you locate materials and will come in handy later when you put together the bibliography for your speech. In addition, if you need to consult a book or an article again for clarification or amplification of facts, the data on your citation should help you find it quickly. Figure 3 shows two sample bibliography citations.

Tips for Your Career

TIP 1

Develop a Filing System for Important Ideas

Do you have a stockpile of key ideas that you will be able to use after you start your postcollege career? If not, start building one today. To succeed in any career, you must have information available on short notice, so a bank of information will come in handy when it's time to write a report or prepare a presentation. Managers and colleagues will be impressed by the wealth of relevant information at your fingertips.

A two-part system tends to work best:

1. *Computer files for materials you find online.* Store relevant text files and screenshots in labeled folders, and bookmark important websites. You can create subdirectories within the file folders and bookmark folders with obvious names (for example, TAX LAW for information on tax laws in your field).

2. *File folders for clippings, printouts, and articles.* For each folder, use a sticky note as a label (this makes it easier to discard a topic that is no longer of interest). Include notes that you take during presentations and interviews. Since many of your instructors are experts in their fields, you may want to file lecture notes from some of your college classes.

Author, title, publication, date, page numbers	Semuels, Alana. "Moving to Mars." The Atlantic Nov. 2015: 28-30.
Personal comment	[Do other scientists believe that Mars has lots of underground water?]

Library call number	TL799M3.P48
Author, title, publisher, and date of publication	Petranek, Stephen. How We'll Live on Mars. Simon & Schuster, 2015.
Personal comment	[See p. 5 on why travel to Mars is an "insurance policy" for humans.]

Figure 3
Sample Bibliography Citations for a Book and a Magazine Article

Make a bibliography notation for every book or article that you think might be helpful. You may end up with more sources than you have time to consult, but it is better to have too many sources than not enough. Leave space on each citation for personal comments, which can help you evaluate which sources are most likely to yield good information.

Table 2 shows how to format the most common citations, using the style guidelines of either the Modern Language Association (MLA) or the American Psychological Association (APA). Find out if your instructor has a preference.

Notes of Key Ideas

As you read through books and articles, make notes of key ideas. Put a subject heading at the top of each note, as shown in Figure 4. These headings will be valuable when you finish making your notes because they will help you group the notes into related batches. Identify each note with the author's name. There is no need to write down full bibliographical information, because those details are already on your bibliography citations.

In making notes, follow these steps:

- Quickly read through the material to see if there is anything worth noting.

- If there is, reread the material, this time very carefully.

- Try to summarize the key points in a few simple sentences. Your task is to interpret, evaluate, and boil down ideas, not convey a text verbatim.

Table 2   **How to Cite Sources**

Book with one author	MLA	Wilcox, Christie. *Venomous: How Earth's Deadliest Creatures Mastered Biochemistry.* Scientific American/FSG Books, 2016.
	APA	Wilcox, C. (2016). *Venomous: How earth's deadliest creatures mastered biochemistry.* Scientific American/FSG Books.
Book with two authors	MLA	Fairgrieve, Duncan, and Richard S. Goldberg. *Product Liability.* 3rd ed., Oxford UP, 2016.
	APA	Fairgrieve, D., & Goldberg, R.S. (2016). *Product liability* (3rd ed.). Oxford University Press.
E-book	MLA	Lilla, Mark. *The Shipwrecked Mind.* Kindle ed., New York Review of Books, 2016.
	APA	Lilla, M. (2016). *The shipwrecked mind.* New York Review of Books.
Magazine article	MLA	Gladwell, Malcolm. "Thresholds of Violence." *The New Yorker,* 19 Oct. 2015, pp. 30–38.
	APA	Gladwell, M. (2015, October 19). Thresholds of violence. *The New Yorker,* 30–38.
Scholarly journal article	MLA	Simmons, Cameron P. "A Candidate Dengue Fever Vaccine Walks a Tightrope." *The New England Journal of Medicine*, vol. 373, 2015, pp. 1263–64.
	APA	Simmons, C.P. (2015). A candidate dengue fever vaccine walks a tightrope. *New England Journal of Medicine,* 373, 1263–1264.
Web document	MLA	Rosner, Hillary. "The Bug That's Eating the Woods." *National Geographic*, 24 Apr. 2015, ngm.nationalgeographic.com/2015/04/pine-beetles /rosner-text.
	APA	Rosner, H. (2015, April 24). The bug that's eating the woods. *National Geographic.* http://ngm.nationalgeographic.com/2015/04/pine-beetles /rosner-text
E-mail	MLA	Hernandez, Maria. "Installing a Modem and a Router." Message to Susan Jackson, 6 Apr. 2015.
	APA	Personal communications are cited as in-text citations only, in APA style.
Interview	MLA	Strickland, Melanie. Personal interview. 7 Oct. 2015.
	APA	Personal interviews are cited as in-text citations only, in APA style.
DVD, film, or video recording	MLA	*Rick Steves' Europe.* PBS, 2016.
	APA	PBS Documentaries. (2016). *Rick Steves' Europe* [DVD]. PBS.

Note: For situations not covered here, you can visit MLA and APA style guides on the Internet.

- While striving for brevity, make sure that you put summarized information in a coherent form. If you jot down a phrase like "anorexia–Cheerios," and then wait five days before organizing your notes, you may forget the meaning of that note. Write out a coherent sentence such as this: "One anorexic woman bragged about eating nothing but Cheerios—one Cheerio a day."

Subject heading	*Habitation on Mars*
Author and page number	*Semuels, p. 30*
Summary of author's information	*Humans could live in underground caverns that would protect from solar radiation and dust storms and keep the temperature constant.*

Figure 4
Sample Note for an Article Summary

- Occasionally, you will find an arresting phrase or a short, vivid sentence that you want to convey to your listeners in the form of a direct quotation. Be sure to put quotation marks around such passages in your notes. Don't use too many direct quotations in your notes, however, because you may end up copying large blocks of text without proper evaluation and condensation.

- Take more notes than you probably will need. It is better to have too much raw material than not enough.

- You can add personal comments at the end of a note to provide ideas on how to use the note or how to connect it to other notes. You also can express a personal reaction, such as "Sounds implausible—check other sources." Use square brackets or some other device to distinguish your own comments from the text that you are summarizing.

- Use a separate note for each idea. This will make it easy to sort your notes by subject headings.

In the chapter on evaluating information, we will turn our attention to how to assess the information that you have gathered.

Resources for Review and Skill Building

Summary

Sound research goes beyond a simple Google search. Before beginning your research, develop a specific purpose statement for your speech, and then devise a detailed research plan. Start early and follow your plan systematically. In finding materials for your speeches, you can draw from three major resources—libraries, the Internet, and field research.

Libraries are good resources because they often have material that is unavailable elsewhere. Libraries provide access to a plethora of mainstream publications and databases that you can use to find highly vetted sources, such as scholarly journals. However, the most valuable resource in any library is the reference librarian, who is a specialist in locating information. Don't be shy about asking the librarian for help!

The Internet can yield an overwhelming number of search results. Using advanced search techniques can help you find valuable information. Search tools include search engines, online groups and forums, blogs, and question-and-answer sites.

Field research—gathering information firsthand—can yield up-to-date and anecdotal information. You might rely upon your own observations and experiences, or you can interview knowledgeable people on your campus or in your community.

To prepare for an interview, do extensive research on the topic and then draw up a list of questions to ask. Conduct the interview in a relaxed, conversational manner. You also can conduct interviews electronically via e-mail or social networks like Facebook.

To save information, create a filing system using printouts, index cards, or a computer. On all notes of key ideas, put a subject heading at the top and have only one idea per note. These notes can later be arranged systematically as you organize and outline your material.

Key Terms

abstract, *95*

blog, *97*

citation, *95*

clarifying question, *100*

closed question, *100*

field research, *97*

follow-up question, *101*

full text, *95*

interlibrary loan, *95*

open-ended question, *100*

reference librarian, *93*

search engine, *95*

scholarly journal, *94*

Review Questions

1. What role should your specific purpose statement play in the research stage of preparation?

2. How can using the library aid you in your research?

3. Why do you have to be careful with content in mainstream news publications?

4. What distinguishes scholarly journals from other types of research?

5. How can you narrow your Google search results to information desired?

6. Which kinds of blogs are most useful to a researcher?

7. How can you conduct a survey to aid in speech preparation?

8. For finding an expert for a face-to-face interview, where is a good place to start?

9. What is the advantage of using a recorder in an interview?

10. What steps should you take after an interview is completed?

Building Critical-Thinking Skills

1. Any person of any age can host a website on any subject and include anything he or she desires. From the viewpoint of a researcher, what are the advantages and disadvantages of this wide-open system?

2. If you use a search engine to find information about literature in the fantasy genre, and you enter the keyword "fantasy," what kind of irrelevant websites are you likely to find in your list of results?

3. For a speech on medieval armor, which would provide better information—books or websites? Defend your answer.

4. If you want a smartphone video of your interview with an expert, what would be the advantage of having a friend make the recording?

5. How do you save key information? What are the pros and cons of your method?

Building Teamwork Skills

1. In a group, choose a topic about which everyone would like to know more. Then brainstorm at least 15 questions that could be asked in an interview with an expert to elicit the most important information about the subject.

2. Working in a group, discuss which approach—Internet or traditional library resources (books, magazines, etc.)— would be superior for finding answers to these research questions: (a) What are the causes of the Israeli–Palestinian conflict? (b) How many people were killed in house fires last year in the United States? (c) How effective are flu shots? (d) What was the impact of the Black Death on European civilization? (e) What is the highest-grossing film of all time?

Examining Your Ethics

Answer: C. An ethical speaker will give a report that is fair and accurate, even if giving the specialists' assessment might seem to weaken her argument.

End Notes

1. Kathy Herrlich, Research and Instruction Department, Northeastern University, "Search Tips," Northeastern University Library website, www.lib.neu.edu/online_research/help/search_tips (accessed October 18, 2015).

2. Stephen Petranek, *How We'll Live on Mars* (New York: Simon & Schuster/TED, 2015), p. 3.

3. Associated Press, "Vanderbilt Medical Students Eat on $1 per Meal," https://oklahoman.com/article/feed/123239/vanderbilt-medical-students-eat-on-1-per-meal (accessed December 11, 2015)

4. Frederick Forsyth, quoted in "Writing Bytes," *New York Times Book Review*, November 3, 2013, p. 13.

Evaluating Information

OUTLINE

Being an Honest Investigator

Finding Trustworthy Information

Applying Critical-Thinking Skills

Analyzing Internet Sites

OBJECTIVES

After studying this chapter, you should be able to

1. Explain the criteria for trustworthy information.
2. Utilize critical-thinking skills to reject claims based solely on anecdotes, testimonials, and opinions.
3. Understand how to interpret polls and recognize the fallibility of experts.
4. Know how to scrutinize Internet sites for signs of bias and deception.

WHEN TAYLOR SWIFT released her single "Me" in 2019, thousands of Swift fans posted a screenshot of them listening to the song with the hashtag "#mebucks" on Twitter and Instagram, and waited for a coupon from Starbucks.[1]

Sadly, the free coffee never came. Despite an official-looking ad and hundreds of people indicating that it worked for them, it was an Internet hoax—"fake news"—and Starbucks was forced to address several disappointed customers.

"Fake news" has been a term that has risen to prominence over the past decade. But what is "fake news"? The phrase implies media reports ("news") that are false ("fake"). The term has existed in the American lexicon for decades. One of the most famous accounts of "fake news" happened on October 30, 1938, when an audio adaptation of *The War of the Worlds* was broadcast over radio, causing panic among some listeners who thought New York City was under a real alien attack.[2]

Ironically, not all "fake news" is untrue. In recent years, the phrase has taken on a secondary meaning, specifically by politicians around the world. *Merriam Webster* states that the term is often used "to describe stories which [are] seen as damaging

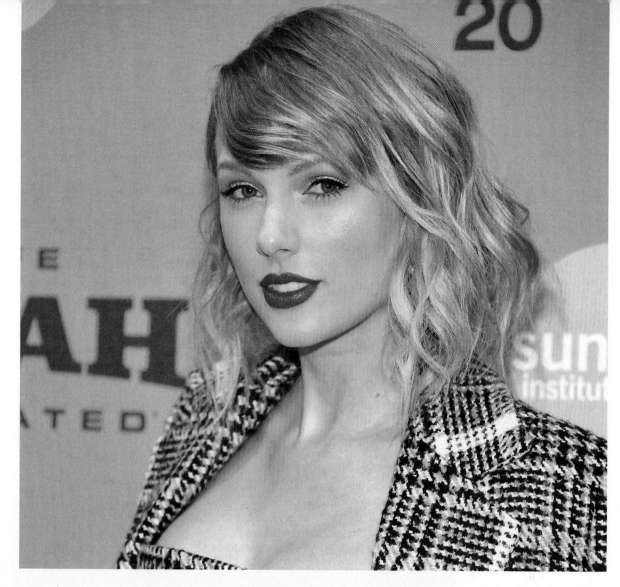

to an agency, entity, or person."[3] Interestingly, this new definition has no relationship to a story's authenticity. A media account may be completely accurate, but still be labeled as "fake news" by the person it is criticizing. Much of the content labeled "fake news" by politicians today falls into this secondary definition of the term.

However, as demonstrated by the thousands of #mebucks posts, genuine "fake news" can spread rapidly, especially on social media. And it's not just limited to made-up stories about a free cup of Joe with your Taylor Swift song. An analysis of Facebook users showed that during the 2016 presidential election, "fake news" stories regarding the candidates were shared more than 8.7 million times.[4]

In public speaking, we often rely on media accounts to reinforce our main points. In this chapter, we will look at how to evaluate information to determine what is reliable and disregard what may be fake.

Being an Honest Investigator

Despite critical coverage often labeled "fake news," national media outlets continue to produce journalism critical of powerful leaders. How can this information be trustworthy? Respected journalists strive to be honest investigators, with their primary obligation being to the truth and their primary loyalty to citizens.[5] Likewise, speakers—who have a captive audience for a specific amount of time—have a responsibility to be honest investigators, presenting truthful information to their audience.

Conscientious, ethical speakers share two characteristics:

1. *They are willing to work hard.* Avoiding intellectual laziness, they dig for all relevant facts and refuse to rely on opinions, hearsay, and first impressions.

2. *They are intellectually honest.* Once they know the facts, they analyze them objectively and draw reasonable conclusions—even if it means admitting that their original idea is erroneous. They are more interested in finding and sharing truth than in clinging to a cherished cause or winning an argument.

Conscientious, ethical speakers adjust long-held perceptions when confronted with overwhelming evidence to the contrary. A speaker's commitment is to deliver information that is rooted in fact, not in anecdotes and hearsay.

For example, many coaches use a story about basketball player Michael Jordan to emphasize traits like persistence and dedication. They recount the story of how, as a first-year student, Jordan was cut from his high school basketball team. According to this legend, Jordan used that disappointment as motivation to improve his game, eventually becoming one of the greatest basketball players in history.

It is a story that has transcended athletics, becoming an incredible tale about hard work and overcoming adversity. However, that story is not true. Like all first-year basketball players at his high school in 1978, Jordan was automatically placed on the junior varsity team.[6] He was never cut from a team.

Knowing the facts, ethical speakers would no longer use this story, even if they have used it in the past.

Finding Trustworthy Information

As you examine information you have collected for a speech, your task is to determine which items are valuable and which are are not. But how do you separate the accurate from the inaccurate? To be considered trustworthy, information should be factual, reliable, well-supported, current, verifiable, fair, and comprehensive.

1. **Is the information factual?**

   Every day we encounter information that is presented as fact, but is actually rooted in opinions or anecdotes. Often the person or organization communicating such information has a vested interest in promoting it. Consider the Michael Jordan myth described earlier in this chapter. The story that he was cut from his high school team was actually perpetuated by Jordan himself to promote his personal brand. Finding the facts often requires thorough research, checking the information against the remaining six criteria.

2. **Is the information reliable?**

   The sheer quantity of information available online can be overwhelming. But not all that you discover in an Internet search originates with a reliable source. For example, a Google search using the term "Iraq War" yields more than 278 million results! Among the top results is a *Wikipedia* entry. But is *Wikipedia* a reliable source? According to its own definition, the information in *Wikipedia* is "written collaboratively by largely anonymous volunteers who write without pay."[7] Although *Wikipedia* helps you locate information quickly, you should not assume that its sources are reliable.

Reliable research comes from sources that are honest and authoritative. Other top results for "Iraq War" include links from *Encyclopedia Britannica*, *History,* and *Time*. These well-established publications are written and edited by professionals and have a dependable track record of documenting history.

One way to determine if a source is reliable is to consider what is at stake if the source presents information that is inaccurate. If *Wikipedia* gets information wrong, there are no consequences. The information will likely be corrected by another user, and *Wikipedia*'s reputation as a collaborative online encyclopedia remains intact. However, if *Britannica, History,* or *Time* get their facts wrong, a writer or editor will be held accountable and the publication's reputation as a reliable source will be damaged.

3. **Is the information well-supported?**

"Because I said so!" This argument may work for a parent to a child, but it does not suffice as evidence to back up a claim or research. Evidence is at the root of trustworthy information. Anecdotal information can be used to help illustrate a point, but honest investigators ground their speeches in facts.

With so much information available around the clock, it is easy to rely on anecdotes and hearsay. For example, many believe that crime is increasing in the United States. It is easy to understand why one would believe this disturbing trend. On Internet news sites, social media, alerts on cell phones, and TV news, Americans are bombarded with reports of violent crime. However, the facts tell a much different story. FBI statistics show that violent crime rates have dramatically *decreased* in the United States over the decades, from 611.0 (crimes per 100,000 people) in 1997 to 386.3 in 2016.[8]

Just because people hear more about crime than they did in the past does not mean that there is more crime. By referencing well-supported information, an honest investigator can debunk widely believed, yet untrue claims.

4. **Is the information current?**

Trustworthy information is usually the most up-to-date information.

Throughout history, people afflicted with the skin condition leprosy were quarantined into "leper colonies," for fear that the disease was highly contagious, and even deadly.[9] However, as more scientific research was conducted and antibiotics to combat leprosy were developed, leprosy became treatable and its spread dissipated. In 2000, the World Health Organization declared leprosy to be eradicated as a public health problem.[10]

Yet this disease retains a harsh stigma that can be misused to stoke irrational fear. If giving an informative speech on leprosy, an honest investigator might highlight the historical significance of the disease, but would rely on more recent research to emphasize how modern medicine has largely eradicated the condition.

5. **Is the information verifiable?**

Even the best-planned scientific research can have its limitations. For this reason, sound scientific research must be able to be reproduced or replicated, meaning that another researcher should be able to produce the same results using the parameters of the original study.[11] When searching for trustworthy information, it is important to find more than one source that confirms the information.

6. **Is the information fair?**

"Three leading independent research organizations" conducted surveys of more than 113,000 doctors and found that most medical practitioners smoke Camel cigarettes . . . and this statistic is an 'actual fact.' Furthermore, smoking Camels has led to "not one single case of throat irritation."[12]

Such claims seem ridiculous today and would be quickly dismissed by students. But in the early to mid-1900s, consumers were inundated by advertisements from tobacco companies making such claims. The information wasn't limited to just advertisements. When repeated studies found links between smoking and lung cancer, the leading tobacco companies funded research to show there was no relationship between the habit and the disease.[13] Although one may accurately convey information from these studies, they are merely spreading misinformation.

When finding trustworthy information, it's important to understand where the information is coming from. To determine whether information is fair, consider the following questions:

- Does the source have an agenda?
- Who is funding the research?
- Where was the information reported?
- Is the information presented as propaganda or as fact?

7. **Is the information comprehensive?**

A 2014 study in the *Annals of Internal Medicine* found that eating less saturated fat does not lower a person's risk for heart disease.[14] This finding was highly publicized, leading a *New York Times* columnist to proclaim, "Butter Is Back"[15] and a *Time* cover story saying, "Eat Butter."[16] The stories put the study in context, but the headlines sent shockwaves throughout the medical community, with many doctors and scientists questioning how the results were being misinterpreted.[17] Although the study did not find a correlation between butter and heart disease, it did not conclude that butter has no negative health effects. A more comprehensive look at the study would reveal the true nature of the study.

An honest investigator includes all the relevant data, and does not selectively choose elements of data that do not paint the whole picture.

Courtesy of R. J. Reynolds Tobacco Company; Blank Archives /Hulton Archive/Getty images

Applying Critical-Thinking Skills

To be a savvy consumer of information, you must develop critical-thinking skills—the ability to evaluate evidence with fairness and intellectual rigor. You need *healthy* skepticism, which is not sour negativity that rejects everything—something that plagues conspiracy theorists. Rather, have an open-minded inquiry that asks probing questions: "What is the source of this information?" "How do I know this is true?" "Could this source be biased?"

Critical thinkers go beyond the obvious. They dive deep for underlying truth.

The following are some critical-thinking techniques to help you identify false information and confirm the facts.

Recognize Dubious Claims

Some claims are compelling because they seem to be based on common sense. But look more closely and you could see major flaws.

Reject claims based solely on anecdotes.   Anecdotes can be helpful in speeches when illustrating a point. Personal anecdotes can be especially powerful. For example, in a speech about the dangers of playing high school football, a speaker might recount a time he suffered a concussion while playing football in high school. However, on its own, the speaker's story is not enough to showcase the dangers of playing high school football. The speaker's experience is not the same as everyone's experience—many people have played high school football and have never suffered a concussion.

Anecdotes should be used only as a launchpad to trustworthy information. In the above example, after recounting his personal story a speaker might say, "I'm not alone. According to a study by Boston University, 21 percent of high school football players' brains evaluated suffered a concussion."[18]

Likewise, using external anecdotes can be helpful in speeches, but can be misleading—and even dangerous—if used as the main source for information. An anti-vaccination movement in the United States was popularized when celebrity Jenny McCarthy claimed in 2007 that her son's autism was caused by him receiving a measles-mumps-rubella (MMR) vaccine. McCarthy made this claim, citing her "mommy instinct" as proof, on several popular TV programs at the time that were watched by more than 15 million viewers.[19] However, repeated studies by the Centers for Disease Control and Prevention (CDC) show no link between the MMR vaccine and autism.[20]

Despite the scientific evidence, McCarthy's anecdote was repeated by other celebrities and fueled an anti-vaccination movement, leading to a reduction in the number of parents not vaccinating their children in the immediate years that followed (from 92.3 percent in 2007 to a 10-year low of 90 percent in 2009).[21] What followed was a dramatic increase in measles cases over the next decade, with more than 1,000 cases reported in 2019 (compared with 63 cases in 2010) for a disease that was previously eradicated in the United States.[22]

Rightly used, anecdotes can add interest to your speech. But when anecdotes are the sole proof, the results can not only be misleading, but also dangerous.

Reject claims based solely on opinions.   Avoid being swayed by the strongly held **opinions** of your sources. Advocates who believe passionately in their ideas are often highly persuasive and charismatic, winning people over with their sincerity and burning conviction. But unless your sources' opinions are supported by solid evidence, they are worthless. Everyone is entitled to his or her opinion, but opinions are not facts.

opinion
a conclusion or judgment that remains open to dispute but seems true to one's own mind.

Find More Than One Source

There are countless sources available on any given topic, often with contradicting information. For example, a Google search using the phrase "Should I spank my child?" nets more than 6 million results. Within the first 10 results is one titled "Do Not Spank Your Children," and below it, another titled "8 Reasons to Spank Your Kids."

Table 1   **Source Comparison on the Research Subject "Should I Spank My Child?"**

	Psychology Today	madamenoire.com
Factual?	Yes. The article contains information from multiple sources utilizing information from respected research journals.	No. It's clear the article is merely the author's opinion.
Reliable?	Yes. *Psychology Today* is a well-respected publication.	No. The website is unknown and is filled with similar stories based solely on opinion.
Well-supported?	Yes. Multiple sources are cited in the article supporting the author's claim.	No. There are no sources supporting the author's premise.
Current?	Yes. The article is dated September 24, 2018.	No. The article is dated February 8, 2011.
Verifiable?	Yes. The information comes from research studies, and even includes links to the research.	No. The author gives no supporting data, and offers only one or two sentences on each reason.
Fair?	Yes. Although its premise is soundly stated in the title, the conclusion is based on the results of sound research.	Yes. The author doesn't appear to have a hidden agenda; the article is not judgmental and even suggests utilizing other discipline methods before spanking.
Comprehensive?	Yes. The article incorporates multiple studies.	No. Each bullet point is followed by two or three sentences of nonattributed opinions.

If you're giving a speech on disciplining children, should you include both of these sources? Here's where some critical-thinking skills come into play. As noted earlier, there are seven criteria to follow when finding trustworthy information. Let's examine these two search results according to the criteria (see Table 1).

The "Do Not Spank Your Children" result links to an article published by *Psychology Today*.[23] The article, dated September 24, 2018, focuses on the results of a study published July/August 2018 in the journal *American Psychologist*. The study—and this article—concludes that spanking children is ineffective and harmful to the child, resulting in behavioral and mental health problems. The article provides links to other websites that discuss alternative discipline techniques, as well as the study and another research study on spanking.

The "8 Reasons to Spank Your Kids" result links to an article published on madamenoire.com.[24] The article, dated February 8, 2011, is a personal account from the author. The author does not provide any external research to support her premise, but does include a link to the author's blog, *Politically Unapologetic*.

Based on our criteria for finding trustworthy information, the first article is overwhelmingly more reliable. However, one source is still not enough. Scanning the search results nets several other articles that fulfill the trustworthy information criteria, including results from *NBC News*,[25] *The Atlantic*,[26] and the American Academy of Pediatrics.[27]

Examine Opposing Viewpoints

Some research topics are naturally one-sided. For example, if you are researching for a speech on "finding a cure for breast cancer," you're unlikely to find articles *against* finding a cure for breast cancer. And there's no need to conduct opposition research when your topic is one-sided.

However, many topics have two or more sides, and it is important to examine the opposing side of the issue for which you are advocating. For example, in the vaccines/autism example cited earlier, it can be helpful to know how the anti-vaccination movement was started. With a little research on the opposing side, you will find that much of the anti-vaccination movement is rooted in a 1998 study published in the respected British medical journal, *The Lancet.* The study, conducted by Andrew Wakefield and 12 of his colleagues, reported a link between the MMR vaccine and autism.[28] Almost immediately after the study was published, similar studies refuted the link, and it was eventually discovered that the researchers were funded by a movement opposed to vaccination: the researchers cherry-picked data to get the outcome they desired, and the study made false claims.[29] In 2010, *The Lancet* retracted the study. As any reputable research journal would do, it did not delete the study from its history, but rather labeled it as "retracted."

Knowing this fact can be very helpful if you're conducting a speech on the importance of vaccinations. You might include this information in your speech, or at a minimum, you would be prepared to counter an anti-vaccination argument in the question-and-answer period.

As noted earlier, being an honest investigator requires an obligation to the truth. Without examining all sides of an issue, this obligation cannot be fulfilled.

Be Cautious When Using Polls

Every major poll showed Hillary Clinton would defeat Donald Trump in the 2016 presidential election. So when Trump pulled off the upset, many became skeptical of polling. However, most 2016 presidential election polls were correct! How can this be? The mistake was in how political pundits interpreted the polls, not in the polls themselves.

Political news site Real Clear Politics averaged the 11 most recent polls before Election Day showing Clinton with 45.5 percent of the vote and Trump with 42.2 percent, a difference of 2.3 percent.[30] In the final popular vote, Clinton received 48.2 percent of the vote and Trump 46.1 percent, a difference of 2.1 percent. The polls were within two-tenths of a percent of being completely accurate!

Of course, American presidential elections are not decided by popular vote, but rather by the Electoral College. This fact essentially renders national polls meaningless and puts the focus on individual state polls. Most major polling organizations produced polls showing Clinton with the lead in several "battleground states." For example, the last CNN/ORC poll produced before Election Day showed Clinton with 49 percent support among "registered voters" in Pennsylvania, while Trump had 46 percent.[31] Trump ended up winning Pennsylvania with 48.2 percent to Clinton's 47.5 percent. So what went wrong?

Again, the problem was with the pundits and not the polls. Every poll has a **margin of error**—the number of percentage points at which survey results may vary. In the CNN/ORC Pennsylvania poll, the margin of error was +/– 3 points, meaning that the pollsters recognized that Clinton could get as much as 52 percent and as little as 46 percent, while Trump could get as much as 49 percent and as as little as 43 percent. The final Pennsylvania vote (Trump 48.2 percent, Clinton 47.5 percent) was within the margin of error of the CNN/ORC poll.

margin of error
a statistic expressing the amount of random sampling error in a survey's results.

In addition to considering margin of error, it's important to recognize potential bias by applying the critical-thinking skills discussed earlier. Reputable pollsters will be up front about their polling techniques, provide a reasonable margin of error, and publish the results along with the exact wording of the questions.

As a tornado approaches a highway overpass, it creates a dangerous wind tunnel.

©Ingram Publishing/ SuperStock; Don Farrall/Getty Images

Recognize the Fallibility of Experts

Experts can be a good source of information, but don't assume they are infallible. Every year experts are proven wrong in one way or another. For many years, for example, some experts on tornado safety have given this advice: if you are caught by a tornado, seek shelter under a highway overpass. But this advice is bad, and it has cost dozens of lives. The National Weather Service says that hiding under an overpass is one of the *worst* things you can do because the overpass becomes a dangerous wind tunnel.[32]

Some experts have a PhD or an MD and are affiliated with a university or a medical facility, so they must be trustworthy, right? Unfortunately, there are unreliable, deceptive people in every field. Likewise, many groups with official-sounding names often produce data intended to promote a particular viewpoint. The data may be accurate, but care must be taken in interpreting the results. Approach information with healthy skepticism and utilize the seven steps for "finding trustworthy information" to ensure you are finding the best possible information available.

Analyzing Internet Sites

Information on the Internet ranges from extremely useful to dangerously inaccurate. By applying the critical-thinking skills described in the previous section, one can filter out much of the inaccurate information. Remember, information should be factual, reliable, well-supported, current, verifiable, fair, and comprehensive. Don't be swayed by widespread dissemination. Just because thousands of people reposted a photo of a shark swimming on a flooded highway does not mean that a shark was actually on a highway. Websites, just like photos, can be easily manipulated to look accurate and reliable. In addition to using critical-thinking skills, consider who is behind the posted information and when in doubt, verify the information against other websites.

Tips for Your Career

Be Willing to Challenge What Is Shared in Social Media

Before social media, few people had the ability to spread disinformation so quickly to mass audiences. However, as evidenced with the Taylor Swift example in this chapter's introduction, anyone with a social media account now has that potential power.

For example, a photo of a shark swimming on a highway continuously pops up in various social media feeds whenever a natural disaster results in the flooding of a coastal roadway. Of course, the photo is not real; it was manipulated by merging two old photographs. After Hurricane Harvey in 2017, a little-known Scottish journalist tweeted the photo with the caption, "Believe it or not, this is a shark on the freeway in Houston, Texas." Within 18 hours, the tweet was retweeted 88,000 times.

The journalist later said he was testing how fast a fake photo would spread, later tweeting, "When America is this easy to troll with #FakeNews we should all be worried."

Be skeptical of information presented as fact in social media posts. Apply critical-thinking skills and verify information before hitting that "retweet" or "share" button. Even better, if you find the information is false, share what you have discovered, with a link to the source.

Although on the surface it may seem harmless to retweet a seemingly innocent photo, by doing so you are perpetuating the spread of fake news. Furthermore, potential employers may examine your social media accounts, and several examples of spreading misinformation may jeopardize your chances of working for that organization.

Source: Brian Koerber, "The History behind That Fake Photo of a Shark Swimming on a Highway," Mashable, https://mashable.com /2017/09/14/shark-on-flooded-highway-hoax-history/ (accessed November 15, 2019).

Jason Michael/Twitter, Inc.

Investigate Sponsors and Authors

Who is behind a website? Are the owners and writers honest and unbiased? To help you evaluate a site, use these strategies.

Look for Author Credentials

Is the author of a website qualified to write authoritatively on the subject at hand? Look for some mention of his or her credentials or achievements. If none are listed, look for an e-mail address and send a message like this: "Could you please tell me about your qualifications and experience on this subject?" If the author is affiliated with a professional organization or has written other materials on the subject, it should be easy for you to verify.

Get Background Information on Sponsors

Who is funding or sponsoring a website? If the site does not display this information on the opening screen, sometimes you can get details on other pages of the site (such as "About Us"). Or, if there is an e-mail address, you can send a message requesting background information.

Table 2
Top-Level Domains

Original	
.com	commercial (business)
.org	nonprofit organization
.net	networks
.gov	government nonmilitary organization
.mil	U.S. military branches
.edu	educational and research institutions
Additional	
.biz	businesses
.info	informational
.name	individuals

Try googling the website and evaluating what supporters and opponents of the website are saying about it.

Examine Internet Domain Names

An Internet address is known as a domain name. The suffix at the end of the name signifies the "top-level domain," indicating whether the address belongs to a business, an educational institution, or one of the other broad categories shown in Table 2. These top-level domains can give you clues about a source's objectivity and motivations.

Commercial websites (.com) are the most unpredictable. Although many commercial websites are used to promote specific brands or companies and are up front about who it represents, some sites can be unpredictable. For a few bucks anyone can purchase a domain name if it is available. For example, cnn.com is a well-known news website, and is the fourth most visited news website in the world.[33] However, over the years several cnn.com clone websites have come and gone, for example, cnn-channel.com, tv-cnn.com, and breaking-cnn.com. At times, these websites purported to have major breaking news stories, but all of them were proved false.

Most ".edu" sites are reserved for educational institutions, but that does not mean all the information on the site is reliable. Some university professors preach easily debunked ideas, using their school's ".edu" account. For example, Dr. Arthur R. Butz of Northwestern University has been repudiated by most of his colleagues for his assertion that the Holocaust—the extermination of millions of Jews and many others in Europe by the Nazis—never happened.[34]

We also should be cautious when evaluating other noncommercial domains. For example, nonprofit organizations (.org) are often reliable sources (recognizing the inherent bias of the organization), but again, anyone with a few bucks can purchase a ".org" website.

Look for Country of Origin

Gathering information from throughout the world can be rewarding. If you are researching ways to combat soil erosion and you find a website on an innovative program in Costa Rica, you have broadened your knowledge base.

Beware, however, of using such material incorrectly. Suppose you come across an appealing website that lists major prescription drugs and the conditions they treat. If you notice that the page originates in another country, you would be wise to use the information carefully, if at all. Other countries have different trade names and different rules on which drugs are permissible. A prescription drug that is available in a developing nation may not be FDA-approved for the United States.

Most websites display an address or give some indication of the place of origin. For those that do not, you will have to look for clues:

1. **Investigate place names that do not sound familiar.** If you are looking for articles on criminal law and you find a website about legal cases in New South Wales, find out just where New South Wales is located. When you discover that it is a state in Australia, explore whether the information applies to your topic.

2. **Be aware of international country abbreviations.** Websites from many countries include two-letter abbreviations. For example, www.cite-sciences.fr is the address for a French science site.

You can find a list of international abbreviations by typing "Internet top-level domains" into a search engine.

Below are a few abbreviations that are sometimes misinterpreted:

- **ca** stands for Canada, not California (which is **ca.us**).
- **ch** stands for Confederation Helvetica (Switzerland), not China (which is **cn**).
- **co** stands for Colombia, not Colorado (which is **co.us**).
- **de** stands for Deutschland (Germany), not Denmark (which is **dn**).
- **za** stands for South Africa, not Zambia (which is **zm**).

Check the Date

Make sure you use recent sources. Most websites will give the date on which the information was created or updated. This information can usually be found at the bottom of the web page or in the byline if it is a news story.

If no date is given, don't use the site's information without confirming it on other sites. In some cases, the date will indicate whether the author is still interested in the subject and still making an effort to keep the research and material fresh.

Look for Verifications

To find good information and avoid the bad, consult websites that evaluate information, such as these:

- Snopes.com is the leading source of corrections for myths and misconceptions spread on the Internet and social media.
- Factcheck.org is a nonprofit website that focuses on combatting "fake news," specifically in the political arena.
- TruthOrFiction.org dispels rumors and disputed "facts," with a special focus on mistruths spread on social media.

You can also ask librarians and faculty members on your campus for their ideas on how to find reliable websites on your speech topic. Many university library websites have guides to evaluating Web pages. In addition to your own school's library website, you can use a search engine to find valuable guides through other university libraries.

Resources for Review and Skill Building

Summary

When you evaluate material, look for high-quality information that is factual, reliable, well-supported, current, verifiable, fair, and comprehensive.

Apply healthy skepticism and utilize critical-thinking skills when evaluating data. Reject claims that are based solely on anecdotes, testimonials, or opinions. Don't use just one source, because it might turn out to be wrong. Examine opposing viewpoints in an effort to find truth and to be able to respond to possible listener objections.

Understand how to interpret polls and recognize that polls are merely a snapshot in time, not intended to be a predictor of an outcome.

Recognize the fallibility of experts. Don't assume that affiliation with a prestigious university is assurance of credibility.

Apply critical-thinking skills when evaluating websites. Understand the different website extensions and what they mean. Investigate site sponsors and authors to see if they are legitimate authorities on their subject matter.

Key Terms

margin of error, *115*

opinion, *113*

Review Questions

1. What are the characteristics of trustworthy information?

2. What is anecdotal evidence? Why does it fail to prove an assertion?

3. How do opinions differ from facts?

4. What makes information reliable?

5. Why should more than one source be consulted?

6. Should you ignore opposing viewpoints?

7. Why are polls often unreliable?

8. What are the domain names for commercial, nonprofit, and educational websites?

Building Critical-Thinking Skills

1. Imagine a website called www.superamazingskin.com that touts a miracle drug that banishes acne. The drug is praised on the website by a man identified as Roger Taschereau, MD. You are trying to decide whether to recommend the product in a speech you are preparing. What is your evaluation of the website up to this point? What additional steps should you take before recommending the drug?

2. In a TV commercial, a tennis star claims that a certain herbal supplement increases one's stamina. Should consumers be skeptical? Defend your answer.

3. A recent *ABC News* poll says that 65 percent of Americans approve of spanking children. The school board is using this statistic to support a proposal to add corporal punishment to the local high school. Is this poll correct? Should the poll's results be used to defend corporal punishment in the public school?
    Is there better information the school board should be using? Defend your answer with research.

Building Teamwork Skills

1. Can a person find relief from pain by attaching tiny magnets to an injured area? In a group, discuss how to find reliable information on "biomagnetic therapy," which has grown in popularity in recent years. Rank the sources below from (probably) most reliable to (probably) least reliable. Discuss why some of these sources are likely to be more reliable than others.

   a. A website devoted to debunking the claims of alternative medicine

   b. A website that sells magnets and is operated by a self-styled "alternative healer" who claims that a magnetic mask placed on one's face can cure head colds

   c. A brochure by a corporation that sells over $1.5 billion worth of magnetic materials each year

   d. A recently published scholarly book, with reference notes, by a biology professor at the University of Washington

   e. An endorsement of magnets by a professional baseball pitcher who places them on his pitching arm

   f. An e-mail interview this week with Edward McFarland, MD, head of sports medicine at Johns Hopkins University, who has studied biomagnetics

2. Working in a group, compile a list of current information sources used by you and other group members (for example, *ABC News, USA Today, The Daily Show,* Facebook pages, *The Huffington Post*). Next, place these sources into three categories: very reliable, fairly reliable, and not reliable. Justify your evaluation.

End Notes

1. Kate Taylor, "Starbucks Is Battling Fake Viral Ads Promising Free Drinks to People Who Stream Taylor Swift and Lady Gaga Songs," *Business Insider,* August 26, 2019, www.businessinsider.com/taylor-swift -starbucks-deal-hoax-2019-4.

2. Brad Schwartz, *Broadcast Hysteria: Orson Welles's War of the Worlds and the Art of Fake News.* (New York: Farrar, Straus and Giroux, 2015).

3. *Merriam Webster,* "The Real Story of 'Fake News'," www.merriam-webster.com/words-at-play/the-real-story -of-fake-news.

4. Craig Silverman, "This Analysis Shows How Viral Fake Election News Stories Outperformed Real News on Facebook," November 16, 2016, www.buzzfeednews .com/article/craigsilverman/viral-fake-election-news -outperformed-real-news-on-facebook#.jepaXOx1m.

5. Bill Kovach and Tom Rosenstiel, *The Elements of Journalism: What Newspeople Should Know and the Public Should Expect,* 3rd ed. (New York: Three Rivers Press, 2014).

6. Samantha Grossman, "A Myth Debunked: Was Michael Jordan Really Cut From His High-School Team?," *Time,* January 16, 2012, https://newsfeed.time.com /2012/01/16/a-myth-debunked-was-michael-jordan-really -cut-from-his-high-school-team/.

7. *Wikipedia,* "Wikipedia: About," https://en.wikipedia.org /wiki/Wikipedia:About (accessed November 15, 2019).

8. FBI Universal Crime Reporting, "Crime in the United States," https://ucr.fbi.gov/crime-in-the-u.s/2016/crime-in -the-u.s.-2016/topic-pages/tables/table-1 (accessed November 15, 2019).

9. S. Jarcho, "Medical Numismatic Notes IX. Coins of the Leper Colony at Culion and of the Philippine Health Service," *Bulletin of the New York Academy of Medicine,* https:// europepmc.org/backend/ptpmcrender.fcgi?accid=PMC180 6917&blobtype=pdf (accessed November 15, 2019).

10. World Health Organization, "Leprosy," www.who.int /news-room/fact-sheets/detail/leprosy (accessed November 15, 2019).

11. National Research Council, *Scientific Research in Education* (Washington, DC: National Academies Press, 2002), https://doi.org/10.17226/10236.

12. Martha N. Gardner and Allan M. Brandt, "The Doctor's Choice Is America's Choice: The Physician in U.S. Cigarette Advertisements, 1930–1953," *American Journal of Public Health,* www.ncbi.nlm.nih.gov/pmc/articles /PMC1470496/ (accessed November 15, 2019).

13. Lisa M. Bero, "Tobacco Industry Manipulation of Research," *Public Health Chronicles,* www.ncbi.nlm .nih.gov/pmc/articles/PMC1497700/pdf/15842123.pdf (accessed November 15, 2019).

14. R. Chowdhury, S. Warnakula, S. Kunutsor, et al., "Association of Dietary, Circulating, and Supplement Fatty Acids with Coronary Risk: A Systematic Review and

Meta-analysis," *Annals of Internal Medicine,* 160 (2014), pp. 398–406, https://doi.org/10.7326/M13-1788.

15. Mark Bittman, "Butter Is Back," *The New York Times,* www.nytimes.com/2014/03/26/opinion/bittman-butter-is-back.html (accessed November 15, 2019).

16. "Eat Butter," *Time,* June 27, 2014.

17. Kit Stolz, "How to Confuse the Media and Public: Butter Them Up," USC Annenberg Center for Health Journalism, www.centerforhealthjournalism.org/2014/07/03/how-confuse-media-and-public-butter-them (accessed November 15, 2019).

18. Barbara Moran, "CTE Found in 99 percent of Former NFL Players Studied," *The Brink,* www.bu.edu/articles/2017/cte-former-nfl-players/ (accessed November 15, 2019).

19. Karin Roberts, "When It Comes to Vaccines, Celebrities Often Call the Shots," *NBC News,* www.nbcnews.com/health/health-care/when-it-comes-vaccines-celebrities-often-call-shots-n925156 (accessed November 15, 2019).

20. Centers for Disease Control and Prevention, "Vaccines Do Not Cause Autism," www.cdc.gov/vaccinesafety/concerns/autism.html (accessed November 15, 2019).

21. Centers for Disease Control and Prevention, "Table 66: Vaccination Coverage for Selected Diseases," www.cdc.gov/nchs/data/hus/2017/066.pdf (accessed November 15, 2019).

22. Centers for Disease Control and Prevention, "Measles Cases and Outbreaks," www.cdc.gov/measles/cases-outbreaks.html (accessed November 15, 2019).

23. Arash Emamzadeh, "Do Not Spank Your Children: Research on Usefulness and Psychological Consequences of Spanking Is Reviewed," *Psychology Today,* www.psychologytoday.com/us/blog/finding-new-home/201809/do-not-spank-your-children (accessed November 25, 2019).

24. LaShaun Williams, "8 Reasons to Spank Your Kids," https://madamenoire.com/40373/8-reasons-to-spank-your-kids/ (accessed November 15, 2019).

25. Maggie Fox, "Here's What Spanking Does to Kids. None of It Is Good, Doctors Say," NBC News, www.nbcnews.com/health/health-news/here-s-what-spanking-does-kids-none-it-good-doctors-n931306 (accessed November 15, 2019).

26. Joe Pinsker, "Spanking Is Still Really Common and Really Bad for Kids," *The Atlantic,* www.theatlantic.com/family/archive/2018/11/spanking-kids-effective/574978/ (accessed November 15, 2019).

27. American Academy of Pediatrics, "What's the Best Way to Discipline My Child?," www.healthychildren.org/English/family-life/family-dynamics/communication-discipline/Pages/Disciplining-Your-Child.aspx (accessed November 15, 2019).

28. Andrew Wakefield and 12 others, "RETRACTED: Ideal-Lymphoid-Nodular Hyperplasia, Non-specific Colitis, and Pervasive Developmental Disorder in Children," *The Lancet,* February 28, 1998, pp. 637–41.

29. Sathyanarayana Rao and Chittaranjan Andrade, "The MMR Vaccine and Autism: Sensation, Refutation, Retraction, and Fraud," National Institute of Health, www.ncbi.nlm.nih.gov/pmc/articles/PMC3136032/ (accessed November 15, 2019).

30. Real Clear Politics, 2016 Presidential Election Polls, www.realclearpolitics.com/epolls/2016/president/us/general_election_trump_vs_clinton_vs_johnson_vs_stein-5952.html#polls (accessed November 15, 2019).

31. CNN/ORC International Poll, 2016 Presidential Election— Pennsylvania, http://i2.cdn.turner.com/cnn/2016/images/11/02/relpa2.pdf (accessed November 15, 2019).

32. National Weather Service, "Severe Weather Safety and Survival," www.weather.gov/oun/safety-severe-roadsafety (accessed November 15, 2019).

33. eBiz, "Top 15 Most Popular News Websites," September 2019, www.ebizmba.com/articles/news-websites (accessed December 10, 2019).

34. Scott Jaschik, "A Holocaust Denier Resurfaces," Inside Higher Ed, www.insidehighered.com/news/2006/02/08/butz (accessed January11, 2016).

Supporting Your Ideas and Avoiding Plagiarism

OUTLINE

Reasons for Using Support Materials

Types of Support Materials

Avoiding Plagiarism

Sample Speech with Commentary

OBJECTIVES

After studying this chapter, you should be able to

1. Explain why support materials are needed in a speech.
2. Describe nine types of support materials: definitions, vivid images, examples, narratives, comparisons, contrasts, analogies, testimonies, and statistics.
3. Discuss the use and abuse of statistics in speeches.
4. Avoid plagiarism and improper use of copyrighted materials.
5. Give proper credit to sources.

CAN FOOTBALL FANS literally cause the earth to shake? Yes, asserted student speaker Anthony Carino in an informative speech in his public speaking class.

At first his instructor was disbelieving—until Carino gave more details. In a football playoff game in their home stadium, the Seattle Seahawks clinched a victory over the New Orleans Saints when Marshawn Lynch ran 67 yards for a touchdown. This caused a crowd of 66,336 in the stadium to cheer, jump, and stomp so vigorously that the stands shook and the earth trembled.

John Vidale, a geophysicist at the University of Washington's Pacific Northwest Seismic Network, said that vibrations—the equivalent of a small earthquake (magnitude 1 or 2)—were detected by a nearby seismometer at 4:43 P.M., the precise moment when Lynch reached the end zone for his touchdown. For the next 30 seconds, the seismometer recorded "moderate shaking," said Vidale. No damages were reported.[1]

Seattle Seahawks fans are known for being boisterous, but could they set off an earthquake?

Kevin Terrell/AP Images

Carino's instructor abandoned his disbelief because Carino backed up his assertion with support materials, including testimony from a reputable expert (the geophysicist), statistics, and diagrams.

When you are a speaker, you can make assertions, but you can't expect your audience to believe you unless you back up your statements with solid, credible support. In this chapter we will look at nine popular types of support material.

support materials
elements that illustrate
or substantiate a point.

Reasons for Using Support Materials

Support materials enable you to move from general and abstract concepts, which are often hard for audiences to understand and remember, to specific and concrete details, which are more easily grasped. Support materials add spice and flavor to a speech, but they are more than just seasonings. They are basic nourishment that is essential to the success of a speech. Let's look at five reasons why support materials are so important.

To Develop and Illustrate Ideas

In a speech about the abundance of plastic litter, a speaker might show photos of the "Great Pacific Garbage Patch," noting that the largest landfill in the world is actually not on land, but in the northern Pacific Ocean.

The speaker may cite several statistics to convey the magnitude of the problem of plastic litter: 20 billion pounds of plastic end up in the ocean each year, plastic constitutes 90 percent of all trash floating in the ocean, and in some areas of the ocean, plastic outnumbers fish by a six-to-one ratio.[2] However, a photo of a "plastic island" really illustrates the mundane statistics.

To Clarify Ideas

Helping the listener make sense of your ideas is one of the main reasons for using support material. In the above example, a speaker might note the reason why plastic litter is the dominant form of litter in the ocean by comparing the length of time needed for various materials, including plastic, to decompose.

Table 1 illustrates that single-use plastic bottles can take centuries to decompose, which explains why the litter hangs around as it gathers in the ocean.

Table 1   **Length of Time Needed for Decomposition of Various Products**

Paper towel	2–4 weeks
Paper bag	1 month
Newspaper	6 weeks
Apple core	2 months
Milk carton	3 months
Plywood	1–3 years
Cigarette butt	1–5 years
Plastic bag	10–20 years
Tin can	50 years
Aluminum can	80–200 years
Plastic bottle	450 years

Source: Fahzy Abdul-Rahman, "Reduce, Reuse, Recycle: Alternatives for Waste Management," College of Agricultural, Consumer and Environmental Sciences, New Mexico State University, https://aces.nmsu.edu/pubs/_g/G314/welcome.html (accessed January 2, 2020).

To Make a Speech More Interesting

One way to make a speech more interesting is to find support materials that make the abstract more comprehensible. For example, in noting the size of the Great Pacific Garbage Patch, a speaker might compare the land mass of the floating litter to the size of Texas . . . times two!

Better than any statistic, this analogy, as reported in the *Los Angeles Times,*[3] demonstrates the degree of the problem of ocean litter.

To Help Listeners Remember Key Ideas

Even the best-researched speeches can leave the listener wondering why the speech was relevant to them. As noted in the chapter on selecting topic, purpose, and central idea, the central idea is the message you want listeners to remember from your speech. Sometimes there may be other ideas you want your listeners to take away, perhaps so they can apply it to their own lives.

In speaking about the abundance of plastic litter in the ocean, a speaker might want listeners to know there is something they can do to help solve the problem—such as using reusable shopping bags. Noting that the typical reusable bag has the life span of 700 plastic bags, the speaker might display seven reusable bags, identify seven people in the audience, and note how each of them can virtually "pick up" 700 plastic bags from the ocean just by using the reusable bag in place of plastic.

To Help Prove a Point

If you want to prove an assertion, you must have evidence. To help alleviate the amount of plastic consumption, some municipalities have banned the use of plastic bags at grocery stores. But the bans alone do not prove a point about plastic waste reduction. As noted in the chapter on evaluating information, trustworthy information is needed to help prove a point. According to *Scientific American,* a year after San Jose, California, banned plastic shopping bags, the city saw a 60 percent reduction of plastic litter in creeks and rivers.[4]

If advocating for methods to reduce plastic litter, that statistic will help bring the point home.

Types of Support Materials

In this chapter, we will look at *verbal* support materials, reserving *visual* supports for the chapter on presentation aids. The cardinal rule of using verbal supports is that they must be relevant: they must develop, explain, illustrate, or reinforce your message. They should not be thrown in just to enliven a speech.

Let's look at nine popular types of verbal support: definition, vivid image, example, narrative, comparison, contrast, analogy, testimony, and statistics.

Definition

One of the biggest obstacles to successful communication is the assumption that your listeners define words and phrases the same way you do. If you are speaking on vegetarianism, it is not enough to say, "I'm in favor of the vegetarian diet." Exactly what do you mean by the term? Some vegetarians eat fish, while others avoid all types of meat. You need to give listeners your **definition** of the term so that they can know precisely what you are supporting. And you should also clarify how the vegetarian diet (as you define it) differs from the vegan diet, which is similar but more restrictive.

definition
a statement of the meaning of a word or phrase.

Avoid using formal dictionary definitions. Instead, use informal definitions that can be easily understood by the audience. Here is an instructive case: *awesome* is defined by the *Merriam-Webster Dictionary* as "inspiring awe." However, the term is widely used in language for less than awe-inspiring situations—"That hamburger was *awesome!*" According to the Online Etymology Dictionary, the origin of the word dates back to the 1590s and means "profoundly reverential." *Profound* means "intellectual depth" and *reverence* means "to stand in awe, respect or honor." So was that hamburger really so good that it impacted you to your intellectual core, and that you stand in honor of it? Likely no. But that solar eclipse that momentarily turned day into night, confusing plants and animals that rely on the patterns of the sun—that was truly *awesome*.

Such a definition does more than help the listeners understand the term—it also helps them remember it.

Vivid Image

vivid image
a description that evokes a lifelike picture within the mind of the listener.

Images are often thought of as photos or artistic renderings. However, **vivid images** are word pictures that are created by describing objects, animals, people, places, or situations. Many writers do an excellent job creating vivid images, describing complex scenes through their words. For example, here is the opening of a story written by journalist Dave Rice for the *San Diego Reader*.[5]

> It's just before 8:00 on a cool December morning.
>
> A crowd of about 30 people has gathered at the edge of a short pier on the north end of Seaport Village. A light breeze blows in off San Diego Bay, carrying the scent of freshly caught fish and live crustaceans being unloaded into ice-packed display tables and water-filled tanks.
>
> "Forty-eight through at the open. We're down from last week," mutters Pete Halmay, a 74-year-old sea-urchin diver and one of the local fishermen who have toiled for years to get the Tuna Harbor Dockside Market up and running.
>
> Still, customers continue to roll in as the morning progresses, perusing tables of iced whole and filleted tuna, rockfish, cod, swordfish, and tanks filled with live crabs and sea urchin along with a display of stacked cans of locally caught tuna, which is shipped to Seattle for canning since no local facilities exist in what was, as late as the 1960s, the tuna capital of the world.

This description makes the market come to life, even for those who have never been to a fish market. The author appeals to all senses: sight (San Diego Bay, ice-packed display tables), smell (scent of freshly caught fish), hearing (the talk of the fishermen), feeling (the cool December breeze), and taste (filleted tuna, rockfish, crabs).

To make your description come alive in the minds of your listeners, you must use *specific details*. Instead of merely saying, "The dessert tasted good," say, "The crunchy pretzels were coated with a soft, white yogurt icing, giving a delicious blend of sweetness and saltiness in each smooth, yet crispy bite."

Example

example
an instance that serves to illustrate a point.

An **example** is an instance or a fact that illustrates a statement or backs up a generalization. In a speech about the Asian culture, you might note how Asian culture is tremendously diverse, as the region includes widely known Asian countries such as China, Japan, and Vietnam, as well as Middle Eastern countries such as Syria, Iran, and Iraq. These examples of Asian culture illustrate your point about the diversity of Asian culture.

Examples do not have to be relegated to your words. In some instances, it might be beneficial to use physical examples. In a speech about nonverbal communication, you might ask audience members to shake hands with the person next to them, and explain how some believe that a firm handshake displays confidence, but a too-firm handshake can be seen as threatening and a too-limp handshake can be seen as lacking self-esteem.

How many examples do you need to develop a point? In some cases, one example is sufficient; other situations might require a series of examples. Ask yourself, "If I were those people sitting out there, how many examples would I need in order to understand, remember, or be convinced?"

Narrative

One of the most powerful of all support materials is a **narrative**, which is a story that explains or illustrates a message. Narratives are audience favorites, lingering in the mind long after a speech has ended.

> At one time the most popular athlete in the world—the only athlete to ever be named an All-Star in both the NFL and MLB—he was now standing in the batter's box for the first time in two years. It had been a long recovery from a gruesome injury of which no professional athlete had ever come back. It was two years of pain—the physical pain of a grueling rehab, and the emotional pain of losing his mother to cancer. But this was the moment he was waiting for. This was his chance to silence all critics and show he could still play ball. This was the chance to fulfill a promise he made to his mother before her death—that he would play again and dedicate his first at bat to her. Pinch hitting for the Chicago White Sox in the bottom of the sixth inning against the New York Yankees, Bo Jackson connected on the second pitch from Neal Heaton, launching it deep into the right-field bleachers as a sellout crowd of more than 42,000 cheered him on. That moment not only fulfilled a promise to himself and his mother, but it also marked a medical milestone for athletes—and since Bo Jackson, dozens of professional athletes have played again after hip replacement surgery.

The above narrative contains all the elements of a typical narrative arc—the technique used by authors: the setup, tension, climax, and resolution. The above narrative could be used in a speech about Bo Jackson, hip replacement surgery, or the importance of rehabilitation. Regardless of the speech topic, the narrative is truly memorable.

People *love* stories, and even a sleepy or distracted member of the audience finds it hard to resist listening. As with all support materials, narratives must be relevant to your message. Never tell a story, no matter how spellbinding, if it fails to explain, illustrate, or reinforce your key ideas.

While the preceding story is factual, there are occasions when you may want to use a **hypothetical narrative**, that is, an imaginary situation.

> You're driving on the highway and you hear a ding from your phone. You know you're not supposed to text and drive, but what could be the harm of checking one message? You glance down to unlock your phone, and notice the funny message from your friend. You decide to start typing a snarky reply, and the next thing you remember is waking up in an ambulance. Thank goodness you're alive! But as your try to subtly move your fingers and toes, you overhear the medics talking and realize there was another person in the accident. The person you crashed into did not make it.

narrative
a story that illustrates a point.

hypothetical narrative
imaginary story related to help listeners visualize a potential situation.

This hypothetical scenario dramatically demonstrates the potential impact of texting-and-driving.

Comparison and Contrast

comparison
showing how two or more items are alike.

Sometimes the best way to explain a thing or a concept is to make a **comparison**—that is, show how it resembles something else:

> Stretching more than 586,000 square miles, Alaska is by far the largest state in the United States. How big is Alaska? It's about one-fifth the size of the contiguous 48 states and larger than the area of California, Texas, and Montana, *combined*. If you placed a cutout of Alaska (including its islands) on a map of the United States, it would stretch north-to-south from Minnesota to Texas and east-to-west from South Carolina to California.

By giving a comparison, the speaker enhanced the audience's appreciation of the sheer size of Alaska.

contrast
showing how two or more items are different.

While a comparison shows how things are similar, a **contrast** shows how they are different:

> There are many conservation efforts underway to protect turtles, whose populations are declining due to increasingly polluted waters and disappearing islands that serve as breeding grounds. But some areas are trying to tamp down the spread of one particular turtle breed. The red-eared slider, the inspiration for the *Teenage Mutant Ninja Turtles*, rose to prominence as household pets in the 1990s as the cartoon characters become popular. However, many parents were ignorant of the turtle's 30-year life span, the aggressive nature of the turtles, and the weekly maintenance required to maintain a clean turtle habitat. Many red-eared sliders were released into the wild. This dominant turtle species upset the natural ecosystems where they were released, killing off other turtle breeds and consuming food once reserved for other animals. As a result the sale of the once-popular pet was banned in several areas, including the state of Florida.

Contrasting turtle conservation efforts with how a certain breed of turtle became a public nuisance brings better understanding of humans' impact on wildlife.

Analogy

analogy
resemblance in some respects between things that are otherwise dissimilar.

A special type of comparison is the **analogy**, which explains a concept or an object by likening it to something that is—at first glance—quite different.

How do analogies differ from ordinary comparisons? While ordinary comparisons show similarities between two things of the same category, analogies show similarities between two things of different categories:

> At the Tennessee Aquarium in Chattanooga, there is an exhibit titled "Turtles: Nature's Living Sculptures—Architecture in Bone." Turtle shells are displayed alongside illustrations of masterpieces of architecture—Gothic cathedrals, arches, buttresses, geodesic domes, and keystones. You can easily see that turtles and architectural wonders employ the same principles of design and the strength to withstand massive weights without being crushed.

An analogy tries to show that what is true in one case is true in another. Another type of analogy compares two unrelated things to show how a similar desirable result can be achieved:

> Cramming for a test the night before is like trying to bake a cake faster by raising the oven temperature from 350 to 550 degrees. It just won't work.

Testimony

Just like the court uses witnesses to give their **testimony**, either because they witnessed the event in question or because they are experts in a field related to the case, speakers should use testimony to back up assertions made in speeches.

The main advantage of using testimony is that it gives you instant credibility. Quoting an expert is a way of saying, "I'm not the only one who has this idea; it has the backing of a leading authority on the subject."

testimony
statement by a knowledgeable person, used by a speaker to explain or bolster a point.

How to Use Testimony

There are three ways to use testimony:

1. **Quote verbatim.** Sometimes it is effective to quote a source word for word. For example, if speaking about the importance of a free press in American democracy, one might quote Thomas Jefferson:

   Were it left to me to decide whether we should have a government without newspapers or newspapers without a government, I should not hesitate a moment to prefer the latter.[6]

   Quoting Jefferson—a founder of the United States—is effective because it takes the argument out of the present day and refers back to the founding principles of the country. Reciting his quote word-for-word leaves no room for misinterpretation; paraphrasing would have weakened its use as testimony.

   quote verbatim
   to cite the exact words used by a source.

2. **Summarize.** When a statement is long, quoting it verbatim can bore the audience. It may be best to summarize any quotation that is more than one or two sentences. For example, earlier in Jefferson's 1787 letter, he wrote:

   The people are the only censors of their governors: and even their errors will tend to keep these to the true principles of their institution. To punish these errors too severely would be to suppress the only safeguard of the public liberty. The way to prevent these irregular interpositions of the people is to give them full information of their affairs thro' the channel of the public papers, & to contrive that those papers should penetrate the whole mass of the people.

   The above quote is very wordy and listeners might get lost in its use of eighteenth-century English. To summarize this statement, a speaker might say:

   Jefferson thought so highly of newspapers that he believed them to be the safeguard of democracy, reporting the government's actions to citizens.

   summarize
   to give the substance of a statement in condensed form.

3. **Paraphrase.** If a quotation has archaic or technical language or is laced with jargon, consider paraphrasing it. In summarizing, you are trying to sum up in a sentence or two the entire meaning of the text. When paraphrasing, you are rephrasing the text to make it more understandable. In paraphrasing the third sentence of the Jefferson letter, you might say:

   Newspapers should be allowed to report on the government without censorship so all citizens can get information on government affairs.

   paraphrase
   to restate material, using different words.

Ethical Considerations

Here are some guidelines for using testimony in an ethical and responsible manner.

Be fair. Context is critical when providing testimony. For example, when only a portion of a quote is presented—meaning that it is presented outside the context of the complete

Tips for Your Career

Give Listeners Bonus Material

Imagine that you want to persuade an audience to rescue animals by adopting them, and you have been allotted 15 minutes to speak. You abide by the time limits, but you have to omit a couple of powerful video clips. What can you do?

Situations like this happen frequently. You have lots of good support materials but not enough time to fit them in. The solution is to provide bonus materials at the end of your presentation so that participants can examine them later. Provide links to YouTube videos, a paper with a list of resources, or access to a Google or Dropbox drive for more information.

For example, if you are giving a speech on adopting animals, you might give your audience a handout listing local shelters and information on how to adopt a pet. You might also prompt them to e-mail you if desired so you can grant them access to a Google drive with the forms needed to complete an adoption.

Golden Pixels LLC/Shutterstock

statement from which it derives—its meaning can easily be misunderstood. If a teacher said to you, "If you don't study for this test, you are going to fail," it would be misleading, not mention unethical, to quote the teacher as saying, "You are going to fail."

Use testimony from unbiased sources.   Ethical speakers avoid using sources that are biased. Suppose you are researching the question of universal health care, and you come across statements by two "experts" who are on the payroll of pharmaceutical companies. Could you expect such sources to be unbiased? Of course not. Reject such "evidence" and look instead for statements by people who have no vested interest in the issue.

State the credentials of your source.   If you quote a famous person, such as Abraham Lincoln or Steve Jobs, you don't need to give any background information about the person. But for authorities who are not well-known, be sure to give some biographical data to establish their credibility. For example, you might say, "Jack Smithson, who spent 25 years as a research scientist for NASA, says that . . ."

Statistics

statistics
numerical facts assembled to present significant information about a subject.

Statistics are numerical ways of expressing information. Consider the following example, which makes use of a plethora of statistics:

> If you drive between Indianapolis and Chicago on I-65, you'll be driving through Meadow Lake Wind Farm, one of the largest tracts of wind turbines in the world. The 144-square-mile farm contains 353 turbines and comprises 92,000 acres. That's larger than the entire island of Manhattan, and twice the size of Washington, DC.

The energy produced by wind farms is important in the fight against climate change. According to researchers at Yale, energy produced by wind has a carbon footprint of 20 grams of carbon dioxide per kilowatt hour. In comparison, the cleanest natural gas plants produce more than 400 grams of carbon dioxide per kilowatt hour, and the cleanest coal plants generate 800 grams of carbon dioxide per kilowatt hour.[7]

Don't care about climate change? Well how about money? According to the Institute for Energy Economics and Financial Analysis, coal energy costs the consumer up to $143 per megawatt hour, natural gas can cost as much as $74, and wind tops out at $56.[8] With the average American household consuming 10 megawatts of electricity each year, those relying on wind energy are saving $870 annually over coal users and $180 over natural gas users.

As this example illustrates, statistics don't have to be dry and boring. By comparing statistics to things widely understood, statistics can be made interesting. And by personalizing statistics, in this case showing how much people can save, seemingly abstract statistics can become relevant to your audience.

Statistics can be especially effective in persuading an audience to accept a particular point. Shoni Schimmel, one of the first Native American women to play for a professional basketball team, tries to educate the public about Native Americans. To dispel stereotypes and show that they are not all alike, she uses statistics. She tells her audience that there are more than 560 federally recognized Native tribes in the United States, "with each one different from the rest." She drives the point of her statistic home with personal, unique narratives about growing up in a middle-class home on the Umatilla Reservation in Oregon.

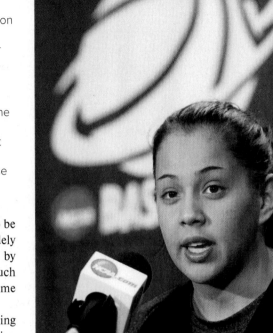

Shoni Schimmel, one of the first Native Americans to play for the WNBA, tries to educate the public about Native Americans.

Sue Ogrocki/AP Images

Understanding Statistics

Although statistics can provide powerful support for ideas, they also can be easily misused, either willfully or through carelessness or ignorance. Unfortunately, there is much truth in the old statement "You can prove anything with statistics." To understand how statistics are used (and abused), let's look at several of the more popular varieties: averages (mean, median, and mode), percentages, and correlations.

Averages.   The most popular kind of statistic is the **average**. It can provide interesting views of a subject, as when one speaker pointed out, "On an average day, 24 mail carriers in the United States receive animal bites." Giving the average in a case like this is much more compelling than simply stating the annual total.

average
a single value that represents the general significance of a set of unequal values.

Though averages seem like straightforward pieces of statistical data, there are pitfalls: most people are unaware that there are actually three kinds of averages: the mean, the median, and the mode. To understand these terms, consider Figure 1, which shows three ways for figuring the average age of recent winners of Oscars (Academy Awards) for Best Actress.

Figure 1
**Understanding
Averages**

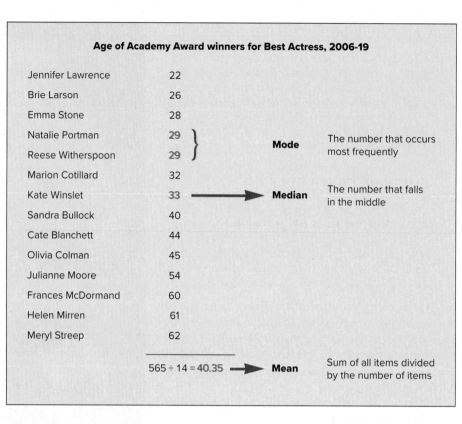

Age of Academy Award winners for Best Actress, 2006-19

Jennifer Lawrence	22		
Brie Larson	26		
Emma Stone	28		
Natalie Portman	29 ⎫ **Mode**	The number that occurs most frequently
Reese Witherspoon	29 ⎭	
Marion Cotillard	32		
Kate Winslet	33 → **Median**	The number that falls in the middle
Sandra Bullock	40		
Cate Blanchett	44		
Olivia Colman	45		
Julianne Moore	54		
Frances McDormand	60		
Helen Mirren	61		
Meryl Streep	62		

$565 \div 14 = 40.35$ → **Mean**   Sum of all items divided by the number of items

mean
in a set of numbers, the sum of all figures divided by the number of figures.

median
the number that falls in the middle of a numerical ranking.

mode
the figure that appears most frequently in a set of figures.

The **mean**, which is what most people use when they are asked to compute an average, is derived by adding all the ages (for a total of 565) and dividing by the number of actresses (14). This makes the mean age 40.35.

The **median** is derived by listing the numerals, ranging from highest to lowest (or lowest to highest), and then locating the numeral that falls in the middle. (*Memory aid:* Just as the median is the strip in the *middle* of a highway, the median is the *middle* number.) In this case, 33 is precisely in the middle, so it is our median. Our example has an *odd* number of figures, which makes it easy to find the median; when you have an *even* number of figures, the median is defined as the number halfway between the median pair.

The **mode** is simply the number that occurs most frequently: in this case, 29.

As a researcher, you need to know the meanings of these three terms, but as an ethical speaker, you should restrict your use of the word *average* to the mean because that is what most people think of as the average. For the other two types of averages, simply explain them in context without using the word *average*. Regarding Figure 1, for example, you could say, "The age that appears most often on this list is 29." For the median, it would help your audience if you said, "Ages range from 22 to 62, with 33 falling in the middle."

percentage
a rate or proportion per hundred.

Percentages.   Giving a **percentage** (a portion of 100) can be a useful way to make a point. For example, suppose you find that 2 percent of the employees in a company have physical disabilities, and yet only 1 percent of the parking spaces have been designated for employees with disabilities. With these figures, you can make a good argument for increasing the number of spaces for employees with disabilities.

Unfortunately, percentages can be misleading. A television commercial might say, "Eighty percent of the doctors interviewed said they recommend Feel Good pills for their patients." How many doctors were involved? If only 10 doctors were interviewed, and 8 of them gave the endorsement, the commercial is accurate (8 out of 10 amounts to 80 percent) but misleading because you will likely expect that a larger number of doctors were interviewed.

Correlations.   The term **correlation** refers to the degree of relationship between two sets of data.

correlation
the degree of relative correspondence between two sets of data.

Suppose your professor has the IQ scores and grade-point averages for you and 20 of your friends. When she compares the two sets of data, she finds that for most of you, the higher the IQ, the higher the grade-point average. She can now state that there is a high correlation between the two sets of data. This should be no surprise: for most people in our society, the higher the IQ, the greater the level of academic achievement they experience. Statisticians would say that IQ scores and grade-point averages are highly correlated.

Now let's suppose that your professor compares the IQ scores with the shoe sizes of you and your friends. Will she find that the larger the foot, the higher the IQ? No, of course not. There is absolutely no pattern to observe—no correspondence between foot size and intelligence. In the language of statisticians, there is no correlation at all.

Correlation is a handy statistical device because it can help us predict probable outcomes for individuals. For example, because a high correlation is known to exist between exercising regularly and longevity, medical experts can predict that a person who runs regularly is likely to live longer than someone who doesn't exercise.

However, while correlation can be a highly effective way to interpret data, it is often misunderstood and misused by people who think that it proves a cause-and-effect relationship. *Correlation does not equal causation.* Just because two sets of data are correlated, we cannot conclude that one causes the other. For example, a widely publicized 2002 study by the National Weight Control Registry correlated eating breakfast with successful weight loss.[9] Many media reports mistakenly reported that the study found that eating breakfast can help one lose weight. But that is not what the study found. It merely found that many who eat breakfast are also successful at losing weight. It did not control for various factors, including what they ate for breakfast, their workout habits, and what they ate the rest of the day. For a study to show causation, it would have to control for these—and many other—variables, including the age, gender, and overall health of the study's participants.

Guidelines for Using Statistics

Here are some guidelines to consider when you are evaluating statistics for possible use in a speech.

Use statistics fairly.   A health blogger informed Internet readers of a fact that seemed disturbing: the air that airlines pump into an airplane cabin isn't pure oxygen. "It's mixed with nitrogen, sometimes almost at 50%." Horrors! Travelers are subjected to adulterated air! It's awful—until we consider that the natural proportion of nitrogen in the atmosphere is 78 percent. No problem, after all. The blogger used a true piece of information but left an erroneous impression.[10]

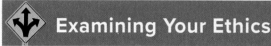

Examining Your Ethics

Fact 1: In contrast to the 1970s, Americans today consume 25 percent more vegetables and fruits.

Fact 2: Potatoes account for 30 percent of the vegetables, usually as chips or fries.

Which one of the following is the best way to present these facts in a speech?

A. Americans today eat 25 percent more vegetables and fruits than they did in the 1970s. Potatoes account for 30 percent of the vegetables.

B. Americans eat 25 percent more vegetables and fruits than they did in the 1970s, but this is not as heartening as it sounds. Some 30 percent of the vegetables are potatoes, usually chips or fries, which of course are heavy in fat.

C. Americans today eat 25 percent more vegetables and fruits than they did in the 1970s.

For the answer, see the last page of this chapter.

Use statistics sparingly.   A long recital of hard-to-digest statistics is difficult for an audience to absorb:

Poor:	According to the U.S. Census Bureau, based on the population over five years old, 230,947,071 Americans speak English at home, and 60,577,020 speak a different language at home. Of the latter number, 37,579,787 speak Spanish, 2,882,497 speak Chinese, and 1,594,413 speak Tagalog.
Better:	According to the U.S. Census Bureau, 79 percent of Americans speak English at home and almost 13 percent speak Spanish. The remaining 8 percent speak other languages.

The statistics in the first version might work in a written essay, but in a speech they would be hard for the audience to follow. The second version, streamlined and simple, would be easier for the audience to hear and digest.

Round off long numbers.   In print, a long number is no problem, but in a speech, it is hard for the listener to absorb. A rounded-off number is easy to say and easy for the audience to grasp.

Poor:	In the last presidential election, 136,669,276 Americans voted.
Better:	In the last presidential election, more than 136 million Americans voted.

Translate your statistics into vivid, meaningful language.   If you have a statistic that would be meaningless to most listeners or difficult for them to visualize, translate it into simple, down-to-earth language.

A 6-mile-long asteroid struck Earth 66 million years ago. That's an asteroid the size of 106 football fields!

Relate statistics to familiar objects.   One way to make statistics dramatic is to relate them to something familiar. English astronomer Fred Hoyle once made the point that outer space isn't as remote as many people think. Instead of using dry statistics, he created a startling image that everyone could relate to: "It's only an hour's drive away if your car could go straight upward."[11]

Avoiding Plagiarism

plagiarism
stealing the ideas or words of another and passing them off as one's own.

To enrich a speech, you can use materials (such as examples, stories, and statistics) from many different sources. As you do, though, take care to avoid **plagiarism**, which means taking someone else's words, ideas, or images and pretending they are your own.

You will never be in danger of committing plagiarism if you do two things: (1) give credit to your sources and (2) use borrowed materials in an ethical, responsible way—not mindlessly copying or unacceptably para-phrasing, as explained in this section.[12]

Plagiarism is theft. It is unethical and in some cases illegal (if a copyright is infringed). It is a lazy avoidance of work. It plunders the hard work done by others, and it risks breaking a bond of trust that should exist between speakers and listeners.

Most listeners assume that a speech is the speaker's own creation, and when they find out otherwise, they feel deceived and angry. Here is an example:

Examining Your Ethics

Stealing written words and passing them off as your own in a spoken presentation is which of the following:

A. A greater offense than using them in a printed document
B. Equally as wrong as using them in a printed document
C. A lesser offense than using them in a printed document

For the answer, see the last page of this chapter.

> Philip Baker resigned as dean of the University of Alberta's medical school after admitting that he had plagiarized large portions of a speech at a graduation banquet. He had appropriated a famous address by surgeon Atul Gawande that had been delivered at Stanford University a year before and disseminated widely on the Internet.

As Baker delivered his speech, some students recognized the plagiarism, got out their smartphones, found the original speech online, and followed along as he gave Gawande's speech word-for-word.

One of the students who had used her smartphone to track the speech, medical school graduate Sarah Fung, told a newspaper later that the incident showed a profound lack of respect for the students and the university.[13] If caught, a plagiarist suffers humiliation and sometimes a penalty, such as failing a class or losing a job.

Types of Plagiarism

The Department of English at Penn State University cites three major types of plagiarism: wholesale copying, cut and paste, and unacceptable paraphrase. [14]

Wholesale Copying

If you copy an entire work or a section of a work, making no changes or just a few minor tweaks, you are guilty of blatant theft. But what if you give credit to the original source—does this make the copying acceptable? No, because you have stolen the author's manner of expression, choice of words, and way of organizing the material.

Imagine a speaker who finds an article about the Galapagos Islands on the Smithsonian Institution's website, downloads it, and uses virtually the entire article as her speech. Even if she gives credit by saying, "I derived my information from the Smithsonian Institution," she is still guilty of plagiarism.

Other examples of wholesale copying are (1) buying a speech from a website that sells papers and speeches to students and (2) persuading a friend to create a speech for you. If you engage in these kinds of cheating, you are doing more than behaving unethically—you are cheating yourself of the learning experience that can be gained by preparing your own speech.

There is one exception to the no-copy rule: if you give credit, you may copy a brief quotation. For example, you might say, "In the words of humorist Erma Bombeck, 'Anybody who watches three games of football in a row should be declared brain dead.'"[15] This can enliven your presentation.

Cut and Paste

Samuel (we'll call him) is a lazy researcher. He sits in front of his computer and searches online to get material for his next speech. He snags a piece of information from one website and copies it into a document. Then, directly underneath, he pastes another snippet from another website, and so on, until he has "created" a speech. Samuel has done his work mechanically, with no real thinking, no synthesis of ideas, no creativity, and no originality. He has committed "cut and paste" plagiarism by copying bits and pieces of material from several sources and stringing them together to make a speech. Even though he is stealing fragments instead of a whole document, it is still wrong because he is passing off the work of others as his own.

"Cut and paste" is not only unethical—it is sometimes counterproductive. Listeners don't want a collection of miscellaneous fragments. They would prefer a summary and evaluation of what you have discovered.

Some students defend their "cut and paste" activities by pointing out that they give credit for each piece of information. That's a good thing, but they need to go further—they need to make the information and the style of presenting it their own.

Unacceptable Paraphrase

Paraphrasing—taking someone's material and restating it in your own words—is a legitimate way to report what others have said (if you give credit). But you must put the material into your own way of speaking. If you just replace a few words—for instance, *freedom* for *liberty*—this still constitutes plagiarism because you retain the overall organization of ideas and the basic sentence structure of the original document. See Table 2 for an example of a bad paraphrase and a good one.

Examining Your Ethics

Steve, an executive at an advertising agency, is preparing a presentation on how a client can sell more vacuum cleaners. While gathering ideas, he interviews a colleague named Bob, who suggests a brilliant strategy for boosting sales. Steve likes the strategy so much that he uses it in his presentation, leaving the impression that it was his own idea. He makes no mention of Bob. Which of the following statements is correct?

A. Steve should have given full credit to his colleague Bob in the presentation.
B. There was no need for Steve to reveal his source because the audience was interested in the idea itself, not the identity of the creator.
C. Steve had no obligation to reveal whose idea it was, since the idea came from a colleague working for the same company, and all ideas should be shared among colleagues.

For the answer, see the last page of this chapter.

Table 2   **How to Paraphrase without Plagiarizing**

ORIGINAL:

"Dogs catch our yawns. Just as happens between humans, dog subjects who saw someone yawning themselves began uncontrollably yawning in the next few minutes. Chimpanzees are the only other species we know of for whom yawning is contagious."

—Alexandra Horowitz, *Inside of a Dog: What Dogs See, Smell and Know* (New York: Scribner, 2010), p. 280.

UNACCEPTABLE PARAPHRASE:	**COMMENTS:**
"Dogs imitate our yawns. In the same way that humans yawn, dogs who see someone yawning will yawn uncontrollably very soon. Chimps are the only other type of animals that we know about who yawn contagiously."	This is too close to the original. The speaker fails to speak in his own language and style, and he fails to give credit to Alexandra Horowitz.

ACCEPTABLE PARAPHRASE:	**COMMENTS:**
"Alexandra Horowitz, in her book *Inside of a Dog*, says that humans, dogs, and chimpanzees are the only species that yawn after seeing someone else yawn. For example, if a dog sees you yawn, it will yawn within the next few minutes."	The speaker restates—in his own way of speaking—Horowitz's ideas, and he is careful to give her credit.

Giving Credit to Sources

Always tell your audience where you got your information. This is important for three reasons: (1) You protect yourself from accusations of plagiarism. (2) You satisfy listeners' curiosity about the origin of your material. (3) You demonstrate that you are an ethical researcher who wants to give credit where credit is due.

To look at the steps leading up to your speech, let's discuss a hypothetical scenario:

You are preparing a speech on how to invest money in the stock market. In your outline, you list all your sources. Here is an example of one entry:

Becket, Michael. *How the Stock Market Works.* Kogan Page, 2012.

In the speech itself, you don't need to state the complete citation in the format printed above. To do so would clutter your remarks with too many distracting details. Simply say, "In a book titled *How the Stock Market Works,* Michael Becket, the small-business editor of London's *Daily Telegraph,* says . . ."

Some students wonder, if you don't need to say the complete citation in the speech, why bother putting it in the outline? There are three reasons: (1) Your instructor will want to see it. (2) You need it for yourself if you have to go back to your sources for further investigation. (3) At the end of your speech, some listeners may ask for the complete data so that they can pursue your topic further.

There are five ways to share your sources with an audience. For classroom speeches, consult your instructor for guidance on which method he or she prefers. For career and community speeches, you can use any of these techniques, or even combine them.

1. **Give credit as you go through your speech.** When citing a source, use an **oral footnote** (which is the equivalent of a footnote in a written document); for example, you could say, "According to the *CBS Evening News* of March 15 of this year . . ." and "In the words of Thomas Jefferson . . ." (For more examples, see Table 3.)

   oral footnote
   a spoken citation of the source of one's material.

   Oral footnotes do more than just give credit: they also bolster your credibility. You are saying, in effect, "I didn't pull this information out of thin air; I derived it from someone who is an authority on the subject."

   When you are quoting verbatim, use "oral" quotation marks, such as "To quote Albert Einstein . . ." or "In the words of Jane Austen . . ." This is smoother than saying "Quote" at the beginning of a statement and "Unquote" at the end. Use a slight pause to signal that you have finished quoting.

   An effective technique is to hold up your note with the quotation so that listeners can see that you are reading word-for-word.

Table 3   **Sample Oral Footnotes**

Interview	"Two weeks ago, when I interviewed Dr. Jennifer Wang, head of the pediatrics unit at Memorial Hospital, she emphasized that all children should be vaccinated for measles."
Website	"According to the Honeymoon section of About.com, the most popular honeymoon travel destination—by far—is Hawaii."
News media	"On NBC's *Today Show* in February of this year, career counselor Zack Manchester discussed two keys to a successful job interview: wear the right outfit and maintain good eye contact."
Book	"In his recent book, *Last of the Dinosaurs,* dinosaur expert Thom Holmes says that evidence has been mounting that the mass extinction of most species of dinosaurs was caused by the collision of a large asteroid with Earth."

Tips for Your Career

Be Specific When Citing Internet Sources

"I got my information from the Internet."

That is a common statement by many speakers in business and professional settings. It is worthless—like saying, "I got my information from people."

Instead, when you speak to colleagues, say something like this: "My information on TV's depiction of women comes from an article by Sue Naegle, president of the cable TV network HBO. The article was posted on HBO's website."

Another big mistake occurs when speechmakers cite a search engine (usually Google) as their source. Google is *not* a source—it's a delivery system. Giving credit to Google is like citing the U.S. Postal Service as the source of medical information mailed to you by the American Medical Association. Don't even mention Google. Instead say, "My information about cancer medications comes from Dr. Nancy H. Nielson, who provided a detailed report on the website of the American Medical Association."

2. **Give global credit in the introduction.** After they grab their listeners' attention in the opening of a speech, some speakers like to provide an overview of all the resources they will be using in the body of the speech. For example, "All of my information in this speech comes from the book *Wind Power* by energy researcher Paul Gipe, an article in *National Geographic* published in April of this year, and a recent e-mail interview with Cristina Archer of Stanford University, one of the world's top experts in alternative energy."

3. **Display a slide or a poster listing your sources.** If you use this technique, you should not show complete citations (as you would in a handout, discussed below). Rather, you should have condensed versions of the bibliography information (to reduce text). Using the example we discussed earlier, you could condense book information like this:

   > *How the Stock Market Works*
   > by Michael Becket

4. **Provide listeners with a handout listing sources.** A complete list of your sources with full bibliography details can help listeners evaluate the credibility of your message. Your handout should be distributed at the end of a speech so that it does not distract the audience from focusing on your remarks.

5. **Display all books, articles, and materials.** For speeches that discuss visual objects, consider showcasing your materials on a table at the front of the room, and inviting listeners to view the materials after the speech.

Using Copyrighted Material

Copyright is the ownership of intellectual property, such as songs, books, articles, photos, videos, websites, and computer software. A copyright can be held by the author or by the sponsoring company, and it is protected by U.S. and international laws. Except for some special situations (discussed below), it is illegal to use copyrighted material unless you get permission (and in some cases pay a fee).

This photo of the 1919 Chicago "Black Sox" is in the public domain, meaning that it is owned by the community at large.

Chicago Tribune

Anyone who uses copyrighted material improperly can be charged with **copyright infringement.** If convicted, a person can be forced to pay a fine, and in some cases serve prison time.

A copyright notice is usually attached to a product, but it is not required. In other words, an item such as a photo on the Internet is owned by the copyright holder *even if there is no copyright notice attached.* Likewise, you own the copyright for photos you have taken on your phone, art you created, and even papers you have written.

How can you use copyrighted material and stay within the limits of law? The answer depends on the setting for your speech or presentation, as discussed below.

1. **Classroom speeches.** Good news for students: You don't need to worry about copyright in a classroom speech because you are engaged in a nonprofit, educational activity, which is exempt from legal restrictions. This means you can use anything—photos, videos, music, poems, and so on—without worrying about whether you are violating the law.

2. **Career and community speeches.** Outside of the classroom, different rules apply. Before you can use copyrighted materials in a presentation or in handouts, you must get permission to do so (and in some cases pay a fee)—unless an item falls under one of these three exceptions: public domain, fair use, and royalty-free.

Public Domain

Anything published or created more than 95 years ago is no longer protected by copyright and is said to be "in the **public domain**," which means you are free to use it however you please. If, for example, you are doing a speech on the 1919 Chicago "Black Sox" scandal, you can freely use any photos published of the team, without violating the law.

Any publication of the *federal* (not state) government is not copyrighted and can be used freely. Thus, a U.S. Department of Agriculture booklet on avoiding food

copyright infringement
unauthorized use of legally protected material.

public domain
what is owned by the community at large; unprotected by patent or copyright.

poisoning can be reproduced and distributed without your needing to get permission or pay a fee.

Fair Use

fair use
allowable and reasonable exceptions to copyright rules.

A loophole in copyright laws—called the **fair use** doctrine—was created to enable scholars, writers, and public speakers to disseminate information without having to spend enormous amounts of time getting permission for every item used. The fair use doctrine allows you to use small amounts of material if you meet *all three* of the following tests.[16]

1. You use only a small and relatively insignificant portion of a copyrighted work.

2. Your purpose is primarily educational, rather than commercial.

3. You do not cause economic harm to the copyrighted work.

Two notes of caution: (1) Fair use does not remove the need to cite your sources. You still should give credit. (2) A common mistake is to think that if you take a copyrighted work and make some changes here and there, it is no longer protected by copyright law and becomes your property. That is wrong. If you take the transcript of a speech, change some words, rewrite some sentences, and modify the visual aids, the speech is still not yours. If you download a photo of a movie star and manipulate it on Photoshop, the photo still does not belong to you, even if you give the proper credit.

Royalty-Free Material

Although copyright violations are typically not a concern for classroom speeches, it can be a prominent issue in other student work, especially when that work is being published and/or recorded. A mistake some students make is republishing photos they found on the Internet, or using copyrighted music for video production pieces, and thinking it's acceptable by simply putting a note "Music/Photo courtesy of . . ." There was no courtesy involved! Even if it was due to ignorance, that student stole copyrighted material and is liable to be sued.

royalty-free
devoid of restrictions or fees.

To avoid fees and legal uncertainties, many speakers, writers, and editors buy artwork (such as drawings and photos) and multimedia works (such as music, sound effects, and videos) that are **royalty-free**—that is, free of restrictions and fees. When you pay for a royalty-free product, you are buying the right to use it in a publication, speech, or video production without having to ask permission or pay anything extra.

There are also some royalty-free materials available for free online in the Creative Commons. For example, unsplash.com provides royalty-free photos to users, with instructions on each photo on who should receive the photo credit.

Sample Speech with Commentary

To see how support materials can be used, let's look at a speech by student speaker Brian Snowden. A commentary alongside the transcript points out the types of support materials that are used. (*Note:* The speaker delivered this speech in a conversational manner, looking at the audience most of the time and glancing occasionally at brief notes. What you see below is the transcript of what he said. In other words, he did *not* write out the speech and read it aloud—a method that would have been ineffective with his audience.)

No Laughing Matter

COMMENTARY

SPEECH

[The speaker begins by displaying the photo in Figure 2.]

I like clowns—I always have—so I was surprised when I heard a report on NBC TV news about several hospitals in the United States and Europe that have banned clowns from performing in children's wards. Their reason? They say that many kids are frightened by clowns—some of the kids have even developed a phobia.

Figure 2

To grab attention and set a mood, the speaker displays a photo, a type of support that will be discussed in the chapter on presentation aids. For the benefit of any members of the audience who speak English as a second language, the photo quickly specifies which of several definitions of "clown" is being used.

izusek/Getty images

Brian Snowden gives a **definition** of coulrophobia.

This news was intriguing to me, so I decided to do some research. I discovered that the hospitals were right: there are many children and even some adults who are afraid of clowns. If the fear is extreme, it is called coulrophobia or clown phobia. Coulrophobia has been in existence for hundreds of years, but it was relatively rare until recent times. Now it is widespread among children throughout the world. What has caused this upsurge? How many people are affected? How are professional clowns coping with the problem? These are the questions I would like to answer today.

Examples of movies are given.

The number one reason for the upsurge in coulrophobia is the depiction of evil clowns in movies and TV shows. Most researchers say that the epidemic began in November 1990. That's when ABC aired Stephen King's *It* as a miniseries. I should say, in all fairness, there have been other movies that depict evil clowns, including *Killer Klowns from Outer Space, The Nightmare Before Christmas,* and *Clownhouse.* But Stephen King gets most of the blame because his clown, Pennywise, terrified millions of children.

A **vivid image** helps the audience grasp the full horror of the clown.

To describe Pennywise, I am going to paraphrase the words of Juliet Bennett-Rylah, who wrote an article in *Spry* magazine entitled "Stephen King Ruined the Circus." Pennywise, she says, is a clown with flashing zombie eyes and razor teeth. He is terrifying—white-faced and bald-headed except for two shocks of red hair. His makeup forms angry brows and a huge, red mouth. His voice is the deathbed mumblings of an old man with a throat full of tar. Worst of all, he murders children.

A **narrative,** or story, shows how troubling the phobia can be.

After seeing the show as a child, Bennett-Rylah had nightmares for many weeks, and she had trouble sleeping. The phobia persisted for years. When her best friend gave her a tiny clown doll as a present three years later, she wanted to throw it away, but her father told her it would be rude to throw a gift into the garbage. So she buried it in the back yard. Whenever the circus came to town, she would be invited to attend, but she would vigorously shake her head. Whenever a show about a clown came on the TV in the living room, she would leave the room.

An **analogy** is useful to help listeners comprehend the mind of a child.

To help you understand why clowns are so disturbing to some children, let me give you an analogy. Imagine how you would react if you were traveling in a rural area and you came across a village where all the inhabitants were extraterrestrial aliens with scaly green skin and gigantic eyes. In the minds of some children, clowns are strange, alien creatures.

Statistics show the extent of the problem.

How widespread is the fear of clowns? Several researchers, including Dr. Penny Curtis of the University of Sheffield in England, have estimated that about 40 percent of children are afraid of clowns. Their fears range from mild to the extreme level, coulrophobia. What about adults? Some adults still have the coulrophobia that originated in childhood. *Psychology Today* magazine says that eight percent of adults suffer from a phobia, and coulrophobia is one of the most common phobias.

A **narrative** gives a good view of adult phobia.

Adults with coulrophobia get little sympathy from other adults, and sometimes they are made fun of. On an Internet discussion forum on phobias, a man in California wrote that in his office, his co-workers knew of his intense fear of clowns. One day they put a clown doll in a chair in his office. He was terrified, and he left

A **comparison** is made to fear of snakes.

The speaker relates a **narrative** that also shows a **contrast** between being a clown before the Stephen King movie and being a clown today.

Citing **testimony** from a professional clown gives credibility to the speaker's remarks.

More **testimony** gives a **contrast** between the nineteenth century and today.

In his closing, Snowden makes a **contrast** between the present and the future.

work for the day. The next day he removed the chair, and replaced it with a new one. By the way, if you understand phobias, you will realize that what the co-workers did is not humorous—it's cruel. It's like tossing a snake into the lap of someone who is afraid of snakes.

Is coulrophobia having an impact on the world of clowns? I could not find any data on whether the number of clowns has decreased, but I did find some reports of clowns who are no longer finding any joy in clowning.

For the past 23 years, Jim Jelinske dressed as a clown whenever he gave anti-bullying presentations in schools in Dubuque, Iowa. He enjoyed being "Jelly the Clown." He enjoyed putting on full clown makeup and attaching a red nose. But he recently quit being a clown. He still makes his presentations, but he no longer appears as Jelly the Clown. He told a reporter for the *Dubuque Telegraph Herald* that "it wasn't fun anymore" because of the "rising tide of clown fear." He said that Stephen King's horror movie caused a "whole different atmosphere for clowns."

While Jelinske has put away his clown costume, many other clowns are continuing to perform, and some of them make an effort to avoid frightening children. Peggy Williams, a clown with the Barnum & Bailey circus, is quoted in *The Washington Post* as saying, "A child who is afraid of clowns has been introduced to them out of context too quickly." She says a clown needs to keep a respectful distance and not let parents force a child into "getting too close too soon."

Some clowns try to soften their faces and costumes. Beth Byrd, a professional clown, told the *Kansas City Star* that traditional clown makeup was created in response to the primitive lighting in three-ring circuses in the nineteenth century. The exaggerated features were necessary in order for the clown to be seen. Nowadays that is not necessary. She says she downplays makeup and costume. "My mouth is my real mouth," she says, "and I paint my own nose. Children must be able to see that you're human."

To summarize what we've covered, fear of clowns is no laughing matter, especially if it develops into clown phobia. An epidemic of clown phobia was ignited by movies and TV shows in the 1990s, and the effects are being reinforced today, with the recent reboot of the "It" franchise.

We can only hope that in the future, instead of seeing horrible clown-monsters created by Stephen King and others, children will encounter happy, friendly clowns who will bring a smile to their faces and joy to their hearts.

Resources for Review and Skill Building

Summary

Verbal support materials are vital to the success of a speech. They develop, illustrate, and clarify ideas; they make a speech more interesting and meaningful; and they can help prove an assertion.

Some of the more popular types of verbal supports are (1) *definition,* which helps make sure that your listeners understand key terms as you intend them to be understood; (2) *vivid image,* which is a word picture that helps listeners visualize concepts; (3) *example,* which is an instance that illustrates a statement; (4) *narrative,* which is a story that amplifies your message; (5) *comparison,* which shows how two or more things are alike; (6) *contrast,* which shows how two or more things are different; (7) *analogy,* which explains a concept by likening it to something that seems different; (8) *testimony,* which provides input from experts; and (9) *statistics,* which are numerical ways of conveying information.

Of all these types, the narrative (or story) is the favorite of most audiences. People love to hear stories and are more likely to remember them than most other parts of your speech. As with all support materials, you must make sure that a narrative explains, illustrates, or reinforces the message of your speech. Telling a story that is irrelevant to the subject is not appropriate in informative and persuasive speaking.

Statistics such as averages, percentages, and correlations can be useful in a speech, but you must be careful to use them accurately and fairly. Make them as interesting and as meaningful as possible.

When borrowing information for a speech, be careful to avoid plagiarism—taking someone else's words, images, or other content and using them as your own creation. Plagiarism is unethical, whether it involves wholesale copying of an entire work, cutting and pasting together bits and pieces from several different sources, or inappropriate paraphrasing. You can avoid plagiarism if you are careful to summarize information in your own words, and if you give credit to your sources.

A related ethical and legal issue is copyright infringement. Don't use copyrighted material outside of the classroom unless you get permission from the copyright holder or unless the material falls into one of three categories: public domain, fair use, and royalty-free.

Key Terms

analogy, *130*

average, *133*

comparison, *130*

contrast, *130*

copyright infringement, *141*

correlation, *135*

definition, *127*

example, *128*

fair use, *142*

hypothetical narrative, *129*

mean, *134*

median, *134*

mode, *134*

narrative, *129*

oral footnote *139*

paraphrase, *131*

percentage, *134*

plagiarism, *136*

public domain, *141*

quote verbatim, *131*

royalty-free, *142*

statistics, *132*

summarize, *131*

support materials, *126*

testimony, *131*

vivid image, *128*

Review Questions

1. List five reasons why support materials are important in a speech.

2. Why are informal definitions usually superior to dictionary definitions in a speech?

3. What must speakers use to make vivid images successful?

4. How many examples are needed to develop a point?

5. What term is used to refer to a story about an imaginary situation?

6. What is the difference between a comparison and a contrast?

7. A speaker who likens worrying to rocking in a rocking chair is using which kind of support material?

8. What is the main advantage of using testimony in a speech?

9. Why should statistics be used sparingly?

10. How can you avoid plagiarism in a speech?

11. Define *fair use.*

Building Critical-Thinking Skills

1. At a beach on the Atlantic Ocean, whenever ice cream sales increase, the number of drownings increases. In other words, there is a strong correlation between ice cream sales and drownings. Does the correlation prove that ice cream contributes to drownings? Explain your answer.

2. In a speech on weird stunts, a speaker paraphrased an analogy created by *New York Times* columnist Janet Maslin: "Texting with your toes is like climbing Mt. Everest in house slippers—impressive but not necessary." Why are these words considered an analogy instead of a comparison?

3. In two or three sentences, give an informal definition (not a dictionary definition) of one of these terms:
   a. Friendship
   b. Pizzazz
   c. Ideal pet

Building Teamwork Skills

1. In a group, choose several focal points (such as music and food preferences) and analyze how group members compare and contrast with one another. In what way are group members most alike and most unalike?

2. Working in a group, analyze these statistics. Discuss why they can be technically accurate but still misleading.
   a. "Last year 37 people were killed by automobile airbags."
   b. "Three out of four doctors surveyed said that margarine is healthier for the heart than butter."
   c. "Studies show that children with longer arms are better at solving math problems than children with shorter arms."
   d. "College-educated people drink 90 percent of all bottled mineral water sold in the United States, so we can say that a high correlation exists between an advanced educational level and consumption of mineral water."
   e. "The average American parents last year named their daughter Isabella and their son Jacob."

Examining Your Ethics

Ethics Box 1 Answer: B. A speaker should present all of the facts and point out their significance. Answers A and C are accurate statements, but they fail to give the full picture so therefore are misleading.

Ethics Box 2 Answer: B. It is an equally serious offense to steal someone else's words in a spoken presentation as it is in a printed document, as evidenced by the number of public speakers who lose their jobs for plagiarizing.

Ethics Box 3 Answer: A. An ethical researcher should always give credit where it is due. If you're not sure, ask yourself, "How would I feel if I came up with a great idea and someone else took credit for it?"

End Notes

1. Sandi Doughton and Danny O'Neil, "Seahawks Fans' Frenzy Felt by Seismometer," *The Seattle Times,* www.seattletimes.com (accessed November 4, 2015).

2. Jacob Silverman, "Why Is the World's Biggest Landfill in the Pacific Ocean?," https://science.howstuffworks.com /environmental/earth/oceanography/great-pacific -garbage-patch.htm (accessed January 2, 2020).

3. Kenneth R. Weiss, "Altered Oceans: Plague of Plastic Chokes the Seas," *Los Angeles Times,* www.latimes.com /world/la-me-ocean2aug02-story.html (accessed January 2, 2020).

4. "Do Plastic Bag Bans Work?," *Scientific American,* www .scientificamerican.com/article/do-plastic-bag-bans-work/ (accessed January 2, 2020).

5. Dave Rice, "Where to Buy Really Fresh Fish," *San Diego Reader,* www.sandiegoreader.com/news/2016/jan/06 /feature-where-buy-really-fresh-fish/# (accessed January 18, 2020).

6. Thomas Jefferson, *The Works, Vol. 5. Correspondence 1786–1789,* Online Library of Liberty, https://oll .libertyfund.org/quotes/302 (accessed January 20, 2020).

7. Philip Warburg, "An Introduction to the State of Wind Power in the U.S.," Yale Climate Connections, www .yaleclimateconnections.org/2019/10/an-introduction-to -the-state-of-wind-power-in-the-u-s/ (accessed January 20, 2020).

8. Elizabeth Weise, "On World Environment Day, Everything You Know about Energy in the U.S. Might Be Wrong," *USA Today,* www.usatoday.com/story /news/2019/06/04/climate-change-coal-now-more -expensive-than-wind-solar-energy/1277637001/ (accessed January 20, 2020).

9. Nicholas Gerbis, "10 Correlations That Are Not Causations," *How Stuff Works,* https://science .howstuffworks.com/innovation/science-questions/10 -correlations-that-are-not-causations8.htm (accessed January 20, 2020).

10. Jordan Ellenberg, "How Not to Be Misled by Data," *The Wall Street Journal,* www.wsj.com (accessed January 4, 2016).

11. Fred Hoyle, "Sayings of the Week," *The Observer,* September 9, 1979.

12. The Modern Language Association of America, *MLA Style Manual and Guide to Scholarly Publishing,* 3rd ed. (New York: The Modern Language Association of America, 2008), pp. 165–67; Diana Hacker and Nancy Sommers, *A Writer's Reference,* 8th ed. (Boston: Bedford/ St. Martin's, 2015), pp. 17–27.

13. Codi Wilson, "Medical Dean's Convocation Speech Angers U of A Students," *Edmonton Journal,* www .pressreader.com/canada/edmonton-journal/20110613 /textview (accessed January 20, 2020); Sarah Boesveld, "University of Alberta Medical School Dean Resigns after Plagiarizing Speech," *National Post,* https:// nationalpost.com/news/canada/university-of-alberta -medical-school-dean-resigns-after-plagiarizing-speech (accessed January 20, 2020).

14. Department of English, "Plagiarism Policy," Penn State University, http://english.la.psu.edu/undergraduate /plagiarism-policy (accessed January 20, 2020).

15. "Erma Bombeck," The Quotations Page, www .quotationspage.com/quotes/Erma_Bombeck/ (accessed January 20, 2020).

16. "Copyright Information and Education," University of Minnesota Libraries, www.lib.umn.edu/copyright (accessed January 20, 2020).

Presentation Aids

OUTLINE

Advantages of Visual Aids

Types of Visual Aids

Presentation Software

Media for Visual Aids

Preparing Visual Aids

Presenting Visual Aids

Communicating in Other Channels

OBJECTIVES

After studying this chapter, you should be able to

1. Explain seven advantages of using visual aids in a speech.
2. Describe the types of visual aids.
3. Describe the media for visual aids.
4. Prepare appropriate visual aids.
5. Present visual aids effectively.
6. Communicate in channels other than visual.

IN HER SENIOR YEAR at Illinois State University, Jillian Jones, a student nurse and a member of Army ROTC, gave a demonstration to her Army comrades on how to perform emergency medical procedures. She used a sophisticated dummy to simulate real-world patient care.

Jones encouraged audience members to practice what she taught them by touching and "treating" the dummy patient. This technique is a good example of the power of presentation aids. Imagine how difficult it would have been for Jones to describe and demonstrate medical procedures without using the dummy. Aids not only help an audience to understand key points, but they also make a presentation more interesting and exciting.[1]

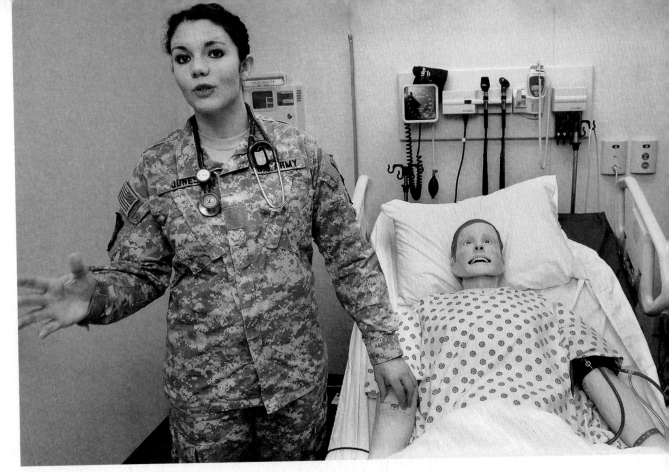

A dummy patient helps Jillian Jones teach medical procedures.

Lori Ann Cook-Neisler/AP Images

Presentation aids can be conveyed in six channels of communication—vision, hearing, smell, taste, touch, and physical activity. (Jones used vision, hearing, touch, and physical activity.) We will cover all six channels in this chapter, but our primary focus will be on visual aids, because they are the most widely used. The typical attitude of audiences is "Don't just tell me—show me."

Advantages of Visual Aids

While *verbal* supports (discussed in the chapter on supporting your ideas and avoiding plagiarism) are important for explaining and illustrating your ideas, you should also use *visual* support. Let's examine some reasons for using visual aids.

1. **Visual aids can make ideas clear and understandable.** Your listeners can quickly grasp how to jump-start a car if you display a drawing that shows where to connect battery cables.

2. **Visual aids can make a speech more interesting and emotional.** In a speech on hospital architecture, an architect showed color slides of beautiful gardens integrated into the design of healing centers and viewable from patients' windows. The slides added a lively element to a technical subject. A visual aid can also add an emotional impact to the speech that would be difficult to evoke otherwise. For example, the famous Depression-era photo of a woman with her children in the Dust Bowl makes the audience feel the heartbreak of poverty better than most descriptions.

3. **Visual aids can help an audience remember facts and details.** Research shows that oral information alone is not as effective as oral information coupled with visual aids.[2] Imagine that you give the same speech on how to create a spreadsheet on a computer to two different groups. To the first group, you use only words; to the second group, you use words plus visuals. If the audiences are tested a week later, the second group will score far higher in comprehension.[3]

4. **Visual aids can make long, complicated explanations unnecessary.** In medical schools, professors use close-up slides and videos to teach surgical procedures. The visuals show exactly where and how to make an incision, sparing the professor from having to give a tedious verbal explanation.

5. **Visual aids can help prove a point.** If a prosecutor shows the jury a surveillance video in which the defendant is seen robbing a store, the jury can be easily convinced of the defendant's guilt.

6. **Visual aids can add to your credibility.** Researchers have found that presenters who use good visual aids are rated by listeners as more persuasive and credible than presenters who use no visuals. *But a note of warning:* If listeners think that visual aids are poor, their confidence in the speaker declines. In other words, if you can't use a good visual, don't use any at all.[4]

7. **Visual aids enhance communication with people who speak English as a second language.** As more and more audiences include professionals and businesspeople from other countries, international students, immigrants, and others whose command of English is imperfect, visual aids have become a crucial way to overcome language limitations.

Dorothea Lange's famous Depression-era photo "Migrant Mother," could help an audience understand the pain and struggle of a life lived in poverty.

Source: Library of Congress Prints and Photographs Division [LC-DIG-fsa-8b29516]

Types of Visual Aids

In this section, we will look at various types of visual aids. As you select aids for your speeches, be flexible. Linda Larson, former public speaking instructor at Mesa Community College, advised her students to think of "tools" instead of "visual aids." In various jobs, not every tool works. For example, not every job needs a hammer. In a particular speech, a PowerPoint slide may be the wrong tool, while a handout may be the perfect tool.

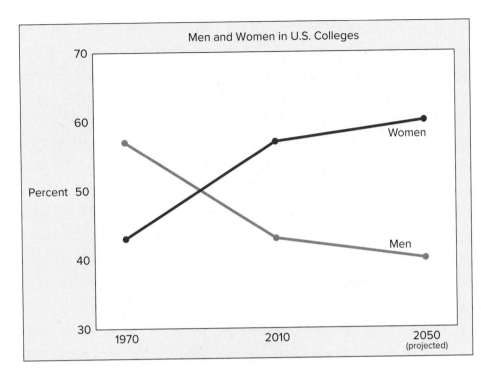

Figure 1

Sample Line Graph

In 1970 in the United States, 43 percent of college students were women and 57 percent were men. Today women have surpassed men, and by 2050, it is expected that women will make up 60 percent of all college students, while men fall to 40 percent.

On the Internet, you can find graphs, tables, drawings, photos, videos, and animations on a vast variety of subjects. Keep in mind that copyright restrictions do not apply to these items when used in classroom speeches because you are engaged in noncommercial, educational, one-time use of materials. For many business and professional presentations, however, you need to seek permission. Regardless, you should always cite and reference your visuals to give credit to the original creators.

Graphs

Graphs help audiences understand and retain statistical data. The **line graph,** which is widely used in textbooks, uses a horizontal and a vertical scale to show trends and the relationship between two variables, such as percent and years in Figure 1.

A **bar graph** consists of horizontal or vertical bars that contrast two or more variables, as in Figure 2. A bar graph can effectively display a great deal of data in a clear, easily comprehended manner.

A **pie graph** is a circle representing 100 percent that is divided into segments of various sizes (see Figure 3). A pie graph used in a speech should have no more than 7 or 8 wedges. (If necessary, several small segments can be lumped together into an "all others" category.) If you see a 20-piece pie graph in your research, resist the temptation to use it in a speech. While such a graph is fine in a book because readers can scrutinize it as long as they wish, it would be difficult for audiences to decipher during a presentation.

Of all graphs, a **pictorial graph** is perhaps the easiest to read. Pictorial graphs use symbols or pictures that are directly related to the quantities they represent, which creates a visual that can be grasped instantly. Figure 4 is an example of a pictorial graph.

line graph
a visual consisting of lines (charted on a grid) that show trends.

bar graph
a visual that contrasts two or more sets of data by means of parallel rectangles of varying lengths.

pie graph
a circle showing a given whole that is divided into component wedges.

pictorial graph
a visual that dramatizes statistical data by means of pictorial forms.

Figure 2

Sample Bar Graph

This bar graph shows that the life span of the average American has increased over the centuries and is expected to become even longer in future centuries, according to the U.S. Centers for Disease Control and Prevention.

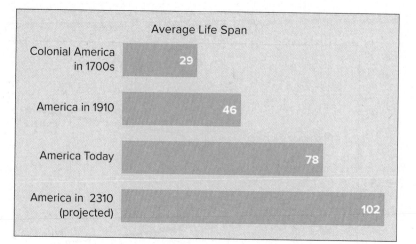

Average Life Span

Colonial America in 1700s: 29
America in 1910: 46
America Today: 78
America in 2310 (projected): 102

Figure 3

Sample Pie Graph

A study of low-wage workers in New York City, Chicago, and Los Angeles showed that 68 percent of workers experienced at least one pay-related violation, or "wage theft," by their employer in the previous week.[5]

Percentage of Low-Wage Workers Experiencing a Pay-Related Violation ("Wage Theft") in the Previous Work Week

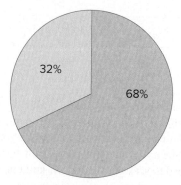

32%   68%

☐ Experienced one pay-related violation in the previous work week
☐ Did not experience one pay-related violation in previous work week

Figure 4

Sample Pictorial Graph

When the speaker explains that each image represents five billion dollars, the audience can quickly visualize the drastic change in wealth held by the world's richest American.[6]

Wealth of the Richest American

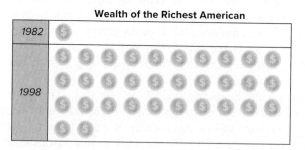

1982
1998

Tables

table

numbers or words arranged systematically in rows and columns.

Tables present information in rows and columns. Figure 5 shows how easy it can be to understand a table. By making the first column represent rank, the second column represent girls' names, and the third column represent boys' names, you can read across the rows to see the five most popular baby names for both boys and girls.

Most Popular Baby Names, Last Five Years		
Rank	**Girl**	**Boy**
1	Emma	Noah
2	Olivia	Liam
3	Sophia	Mason
4	Isabella	Jacob
5	Ava	William

Figure 5

Sample Table

A table is an effective type of information chart. This table shows the most popular names chosen for girls and boys in the United States in a recent five-year period.

Note of caution: Most instructors dislike a speech that is nothing more than a recitation of a lengthy list. For example, a list of 42 lucrative careers is a lazy way of creating a speech because there is no analysis of the data. A better speech would focus on a more narrow set of careers, explain why those careers are in demand, and discuss the ongoing prospects for people in those careers.

Drawings and Photos

Drawings are helpful visual aids because they can illustrate points that would be difficult to explain in words or that photographs cannot capture. One kind of drawing that is highly effective is a map. By sketching a map yourself (either by hand or using a computer program), you can include only those features that are pertinent to your speech. If you were speaking about the major rivers of America, for example, you could outline the boundaries of the United States and then draw heavy blue lines for the rivers, leaving out extraneous details, such as cities. Figure 6 shows a map of the United States that visually reflects the most populated states where half of all Americans live.

Because photographs have a high degree of realism, they are excellent for providing information and proving points. Lawyers, for example, often use photographs of the scene of an accident to argue a case. Photographs can also be used to evoke an emotional response from your audience, thus gaining their attention and delivering the full force of your point. Figure 7, for example, shows a dramatic image of people fleeing a hurricane. A photograph like this would be helpful during a speech informing your audience about how to prepare for natural disasters, or a speech persuading your audience to donate to a charity that aids victims of natural disasters. In a speech, you should not use a photograph unless it can be enlarged so that everyone can see it clearly.

Video and Animation

With video, you can transport your audience to any corner of the world. To give listeners a glimpse of the rich spectacle of Mexican weddings, student speaker Victor Treviño showed a video of ritual, music, and dance at the wedding celebration of his sister in Guadalajara.

Figure 6

Sample Map

This map illustrates that half of all Americans live in just nine states. From highest to lowest population, they are (1) California, (2) Texas, (3) Florida, (4) New York, (5) Illinois, (6) Pennsylvania, (7) Ohio, (8) Georgia, and (9) North Carolina.

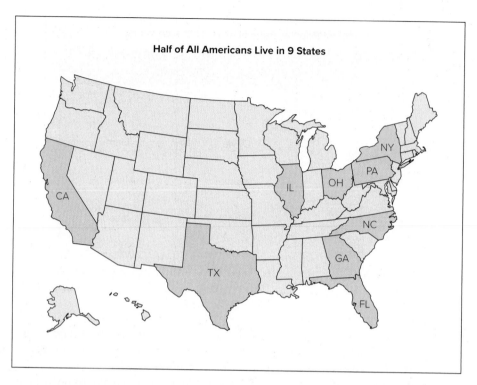

Half of All Americans Live in 9 States

Figure 7

Sample Photograph

This image demonstrates the power of photos to convey information and emotion. It shows men in Key West, Florida, holding on to one another as they struggle to escape from a hurricane that killed hundreds of people as it swept through the Caribbean.

Dave Martin/AP Images

If you make a video of an interview as part of your research, you may be able to use some excerpts in your speech. Student speaker Adrienne Shields interviewed a bank official on how crooks steal from ATMs. In her speech, Shields played brief video segments of the official as he demonstrated the machine's vulnerabilities. The video was much more effective than a verbal description alone.

Many speakers use clips from commercial videos and online sources such as You-Tube. A video clip should be brief—usually no more than 20 seconds in length—so that the voice of the speaker in the video doesn't overtake your voice as the live presenter in the room. Additionally, the clip should not contain material that might offend any audience member. Avoid choosing a clip that has only a weak connection to your topic. (One student played an amusing YouTube clip on canine misadventures, but it was irrelevant to his topic—spaying and neutering pets.)

Animation, or a sequence of drawings such as diagrams or cartoons, can be used in a PowerPoint presentation or video to clarify points. In courtroom trials, for example, lawyers often use animated drawings to re-create a car accident and help the jury understand what happened.

Audio and video special effects are available in presentation software like PowerPoint and Prezi and can sometimes be used effectively. However, be aware that effects must be used carefully. Misused effects, or too many effects, can be distracting for your audience. If your listeners become irritated by frequent screen wipes, zooms, and sounds, they will be less receptive to your message.

Objects and Models

Three-dimensional objects make good visual aids, provided they are large enough for everyone in the audience to see. You could display items like a blood-pressure gauge, a hibachi, handmade pottery, mountain-climbing equipment, or musical instruments.

A model is a representation of an object. One speaker used take-apart models of pyramids to discuss how the ancient Egyptians probably built them. Another speaker displayed two made-to-scale plastic models—one of an adult human and the other of an Argentinosaurus (one of the largest known dinosaurs). The human was minuscule in comparison, helping audience members get a sense of the enormous size of the dinosaur. One advantage of a model is that you can move it around. If you have a model of the human spine, for example, you could manipulate it to demonstrate pressure points and the causes of back pain.

Yourself and Volunteers

Using yourself as a visual aid, you can demonstrate physical activities, such as yoga positions, judo holds, karate chops, stretching exercises, relaxation techniques, ballet steps, and tennis strokes. You can also don historical costumes, scuba-diving equipment, or operating room attire. For example, one student came to class dressed as a clown to give a speech on her part-time job at children's birthday parties. The costume and makeup created interest in the speech and illustrated how she presented herself to children. In another example, a nursing student used relevant medical dress to demonstrate proper donning and doffing techniques, which are important for maintaining a sterile environment. Because it can be distracting to your audience, do not wear a costume unless it is truly relevant to the key points of your speech.

Volunteers can also enhance some speeches. You could use a friend, for example, to illustrate self-defense methods. Your friend could pose as an attacker, and then you as the presenter could demonstrate how to protect yourself. (For a classroom speech, be sure to get permission from your instructor before using a volunteer.)

Make sure you line up volunteers far in advance of speech day and, if necessary, practice with them to make sure they perform smoothly. Have substitutes lined up in case the scheduled volunteers fail to appear. Give instructions to volunteers in advance so that they know when to stand, when to sit, and so on. You don't want your volunteers to become a distraction by standing around when they are not needed.

Tips for Your Career

Never Let Visuals Substitute for a Speech

Because visual aids are so powerful, some speakers let them dominate a speech. The visuals become the real show, with the speaker acting as a mere technician. It is easy for this to happen, especially if you have some dazzling slides or a spectacular video. The punch and glitz of the visuals can make you feel inadequate, and you may think you ought to step aside and let the graphics take command.

This attitude is misguided. For example, someone who once gave a presentation on photography techniques used part of a *National Geographic* video to illustrate his point. He assumed that his listeners would prefer a slick, professional video to his own words, so he let the video take up most of the time. The speaker's only contributions were the few comments he made at the end. Later, several listeners recommended that the speaker talk more and use less video, because the video was less helpful than the remarks. The video was unable to slow down, explain difficult concepts, and sense whether the audience was absorbing key information.

People can see well-made video productions on TV or online at any hour of the day, but a speech has a dimension that video lacks—a living, breathing human engaged in the stimulating act of direct communication, who can provide immediate feedback in the question-and-answer period.

Presentation Software

In classroom and career settings, speakers often present their material on a screen, using images, text, videos, animations, and sounds. To see samples of how presentation aids are being used today, go to TED.com or search YouTube for "TED talks," which are videos of presentations from TED (Technology, Entertainment, Design) conferences. One good example is called "Know Your Worth, and Then Ask for It," by Casey Brown; it can be found easily by typing the title in a search engine.

Types of Software

linear
a sequence that proceeds from beginning to end.

To prepare your material, use presentation software, which is available in two different types:

Linear.   Programs like PowerPoint and Keynote use slides that follow a straight line—first slide, second slide, and so on.

non-linear
an overall map that permits zooming in and out.

Non-linear.   Programs like Prezi don't use slides. Instead, they use a broad canvas on which you place your material. You can zoom in and out of one element at a time, and you can pan across the canvas.

Some presenters prefer linear methods, while others prefer the non-linear approach. You can try them out and decide for yourself. (For classroom speeches, your instructor may require one or the other.)

Additionally, there are tools available online that will help you create professional-looking graphics that you can print out or insert in your presentation slides. Two examples are Venngage (an infographic maker) and Canva (an online graphic design tool with templates). You can find them, and others, using a search engine.

PowerPoint Slides

Microsoft PowerPoint is a presentation program that permits you to create and show slides containing artwork, text information, graphs, charts, animations, and audiovisuals.

Use a PowerPoint slide when you need to illustrate, explain, or enhance a key point in your speech. Make each slide attractive and simple. Choose graphics whenever possible, and use only small amounts of text.

The Basic Steps

To get maximum benefit from PowerPoint, take these steps:

1. **Create your outline before you even think about using PowerPoint.** Your slides should *not* be your speech. In other words, don't collect a bunch of photos and then give a speech that just adds narration to the photos. PowerPoint slides should be aids—helpers—for the key ideas that you have already created in your outline.

2. **Look at your outline and ask, "Do I need visuals to highlight or explain any of my key points?"** Some points will not need visuals, but others may require them so that the audience will understand and remember what you are trying to say.

3. **For points that need visual support, decide which type of visual would be most effective.** Options include photos, drawings, graphs, charts, lists of key ideas, or other visuals discussed in this chapter.

4. **Create your PowerPoint presentation slides.** Each slide should be succinct, informative, and appealing. If you need help making your PowerPoint, try using the Goodwill Community Foundation tutorial on its website.

5. **Practice in the room where you will be presenting.** Rehearse with all of the equipment several times so that you don't fumble during the actual speech. If possible, have a friend give a critique. Check your slides from the back row. If any words or graphics are hard to see, revise them before speech day.

6. **Give your speech, making sure that you—not the slides—are the dominant presence in the room.** Some speakers let PowerPoint become the "star of the show" and stand shyly in the shadows, stare at the screen, and narrate what appears on the slides. They are letting technology upstage a live, dynamic human being. You can avoid this mistake by boldly seizing your role as the primary communicator. Stand as close as possible to your listeners, and try to stay connected to them. Keep the room partially lit so that the audience can see your face. Focus all of your energy on reaching the listeners. Look at them—not the screen.

The Basic Steps in Action

Let's take another look at the steps we just discussed and use them in a scenario.

Step 1: Create your outline before you even think about using PowerPoint.

Your speech will be devoted to telling listeners how they can avoid becoming victims of identity theft, a crime in which personal information is stolen and used to defraud the victim. You create your outline with carefully selected main points and support material.

Step 2: Look at your outline and ask, "Do I need visuals to highlight or explain any of my key points?"

You see three ideas that can use some visual support to help the audience remember them. For our scenario, let's focus on just one. You plan to warn listeners that they should *never* carry a Social Security card in their wallet because if the card is stolen, it can be used to buy a car or open a credit-card account at their expense. You decide that a dramatic visual would help drive home the point.

Step 3: For points that need visual support, decide which type of visual would be most effective.

To avoid overloading your slide, you decide to use just nine words ("Never Carry Your Social Security Card in Your Wallet"), emphasizing the words "Never Carry." Additional words are unneeded because you will supply all the details orally. Though not essential, a photo would brighten the slide and make it more interesting, so you search on the Internet and find a photo of a woman with a wallet.

Step 4: Create your slides.

In the PowerPoint program, you create a simple, readable slide with the photo and the key words. The result is shown in Figure 8.

Step 5: Practice in the room where you will be presenting.

A week before your speech, you go to the classroom and run through several rehearsals, using all the equipment until you are proficient with it. A friend sits in the back row and gives you a critique. She suggests that one slide needs larger print for visibility. Later, you revise the slide.

Step 6: Give your speech, making sure that you—not the slides—are the dominant presence in the room.

You stay at center stage throughout your speech, focusing your attention and energy on the audience. Because you have only a few slides, the screen at the front of the room stays blank most of the time. When you display a slide, you continue to look at the audience. After discussing it, you blank the screen (press "B" on a keyboard or "A/V Mute" on a remote control) until you are ready to discuss the next slide.

Problems and Solutions

Imagine sitting in the audience as a speaker displays a text-heavy, boring PowerPoint slide. He reads every word to you. Now imagine one hour of seeing 25 more slides just like the first one, and all of them are read to you. By the end of the presentation, you are weary and irritated.

This torment is known in the business and professional world as "death by Power-Point." According to *IndustryWeek,* "PowerPoint presentations have drugged more people than all the sleeping pills in history."[7]

The problem is not the PowerPoint software—it's the speakers. Why do they inflict so much misery? One reason is that they are *self-centered* instead of *audience-centered*.

If you focus primarily on yourself and your own convenience, PowerPoint seems like an easy way to create a speech. All you have to do is dump your information onto slides and read the material aloud. You don't even have to look at your audience.

If you are audience-centered, on the other hand, you will ask yourself, "How can I help my listeners understand and remember my key points?" If you decide that Power-Point can help you reach your goal, you will make sure that your slides are interesting and easy to grasp. During the presentation, instead of hiding behind the technology, you will occupy center stage. You will look directly at your listeners and stay connected to them.

Below are six rules to help you avoid inflicting death by PowerPoint.

Rule 1: Don't assume you need PowerPoint

Problem

It is a mistake to think that every presentation should have PowerPoint. Consider a student who has compelling stories to tell about the Mafia. If she uses a slide like the one in Figure 9, she undermines the emotional intensity of her speech.

Figure 9
An Unnecessary Slide

The Mafia
- Bribery
- Murder
- Extortion

Figure 10
Rosanna Scopelliti Delivers Her Speech without a PowerPoint Slide

Maurizio Lagana/Getty Images

Solution

In Figure 10, Rosanna Scopelliti is speaking at a college in Italy, urging students to work for the defeat of the Mafia, which murdered her father, a judge. She uses no PowerPoint. Instead, she paints pictures with words—vivid images more powerful than PowerPoint slides like the one in Figure 9.

Rule 2: Choose images over text (when possible)

Problem

Text is sometimes needed on a slide, but not in this case. When instructor Jan Caldwell sees a slide like Figure 11, she thinks, "I feel conflicted. Do you want me to read your slide or listen to you?"[8]

Solution

Display a photo (like Figure 12) while sharing your information orally. Mark Maloney, a member of a Toastmasters public speaking club in Midlothian, Virginia, uses mostly photos in his slides. "I try to stick with one word or phrase per slide and let the pictures—and my mouth—do the talking."[9]

You can find beautiful, royalty-free (or very affordable) images online at websites like Creative Commons, Pixabay, or 123RF.

Rule 3: Use text sparingly

Problem

While images are preferable to text, sometimes you may need to use words on the screen. But you make a mistake if you display large blocks of text, which are boring and fatiguing (as shown in Figure 13).

Favorite Color

- A survey throughout the world found that a majority of people picked blue as their favorite color.
- The earth is mostly blue, with the sky and the water, and the color blue goes with everything.

Figure 11
Unnecessary Text on a Slide That Would Be Read Word for Word

You make a second mistake if you read the text aloud—a common practice that some people consider a form of torture.

Solution

In the "solution" slide (Figure 14), text is okay because you want to help listeners remember the key points. Only a small amount of text is needed because you will elaborate with spoken words.

What about all the empty space on this slide? Is that bad? Not necessarily. The space makes the key words stand out—and it makes the slide more inviting to the eye. But, the empty space could also be filled with a relevant image that complements the text.

Figure 12
An Image Complements the Speaker's Words

Olga Danylenko/Shutterstock

Figure 13
A Text-Heavy Slide

Prevent a Cold
You can avoid getting a cold if you exercise every day, make sure to wash your hands with soap and water many times a day, and don't touch your face because cold viruses enter the body through eyes, nose, and mouth.

Figure 14
An Easy-to-Read Slide
with Limited Text

Prevent a Cold

1. Exercise regularly

2. Wash hands often

3. Don't touch face

Figure 15
A Slide with Busy
Formatting

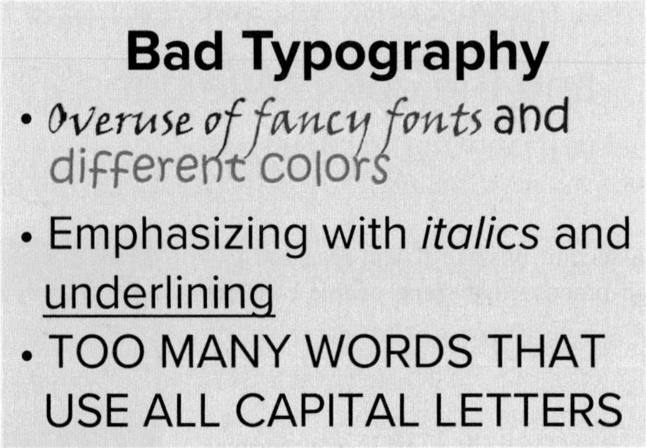

Bad Typography

- *Overuse of fancy fonts* and different colors
- Emphasizing with *italics* and <u>underlining</u>
- TOO MANY WORDS THAT USE ALL CAPITAL LETTERS

Rule 4: Format text for easy reading

Problem

The slide in Figure 15 hinders easy reading because (1) it uses too many different type-faces and colors, (2) it emphasizes with italics and underlining, and (3) it has too many words in all capital letters.

Solution

Choose a typeface that is simple and easy to read, and avoid a lot of different colors, as shown in Figure 16. To emphasize a word or phrase, use bold print, but avoid italics and underlining (which may be fine for printed material but impede readability on-screen). Use words in all capital letters only for headings—excessive use is tiring to the eyes and hard to read.

Figure 16
A Well-Formatted Slide
with a Single Font

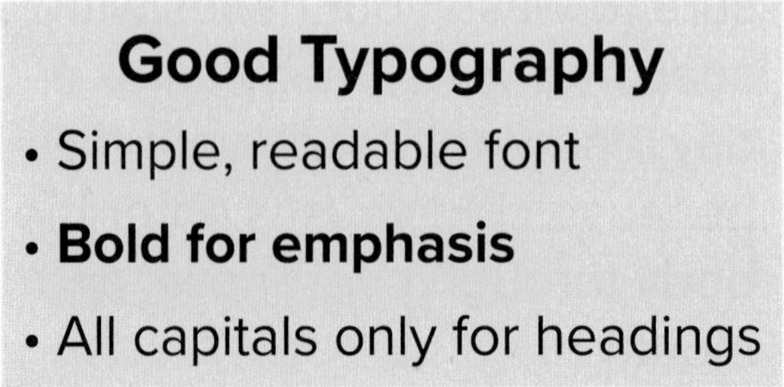

Good Typography

- Simple, readable font
- **Bold for emphasis**
- All capitals only for headings

Figure 17
A Slide with a
Distracting Template

Burke/Triolo Productions/Getty
Images

Rule 5: Choose templates carefully

Problem

The template in Figure 17 is busy and distracting. For a speech on cold-weather ailments, the green theme is inappropriate, evoking summer, not winter.

Other mistakes include (1) the dull photo, (2) that there are more words than necessary, and (3) that the green text is superimposed over a similarly colored background, making the words difficult to read.

Solution

Use a template that has a simple, attractive design, as shown in Figure 18. PowerPoint has a number of built-in templates for you to use, and other templates can be found by typing "PowerPoint templates" into a search engine. To find built-in PowerPoint templates, open the program and navigate to the "Design" tab. Using the ribbon bar at the top of the page, look through the thumbnails for a clean design that complements your presentation.

Figure 18
A Slide with a Simple,
Attractive Template

gosphotodesign/Shutterstock

Figure 19
A slide with too many images creates visual clutter.

©Hamilton Gregory

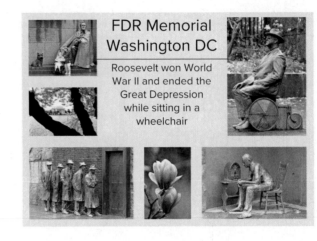

Instead of inserting a ho-hum photo, the speaker found an engaging image of a woman enjoying the warmth from a cup of hot tea. This helps make the point that hot liquid promotes healing and is comforting. The speaker also shortened the text and made it a contrasting color to the background, making it easy to read.

In some work environments, or at some conferences, you may be required to use a specific template that fits with the organization's branding. Ask your marketing department or conference planners for a standard template.

Rule 6: Avoid visual clutter

Problem

Figure 19 has too many small images. Your listeners might fail to follow what you are saying because their eyes are roving over the slide.

Some speakers try to solve the problem by using a "build"—displaying the first element, then adding the second, and so on. Though this is an improvement, you still end up with visual clutter.

Solution

Create six slides, one for each image. (Figure 20 shows one of the six.) As a result, each image will be large, and it will be the focus of attention.

Does this approach add to the length of the presentation? No. Showing six simple slides should take no more time than showing one cluttered slide.

Since most information should be provided orally, the speaker could say, "This slide shows a visitor in a wheelchair posing for a photo at the famous FDR memorial in Washington, DC. The FDR statue is a top attraction for persons with mobility impairments who admire Roosevelt for the great deeds he performed while sitting in a wheelchair."

Media for Visual Aids

The types of visual aids we have discussed in this chapter—charts, graphs, and so on—can be conveyed to the audience through a variety of media.

Figure 20
**A Slide Focusing on a
Single Image**

©Hamilton Gregory

Multimedia Projectors

Multimedia projectors can project a large array of audiovisuals—text slides, photos, draw-ings, animations, video clips, and DVDs—onto a screen. They are usually linked to desk-top or laptop computers, but some units need only a memory card or USB flash drive. It is essential that you familiarize yourself with the multimedia projector prior to your presentation, so technical issues do not delay your speech.

Depending on the brightness of the screen and the strength of the machine's projec-tion, you may need to dim the lights in a room, especially if you want to convey the full richness of a photo or a video.

Boards

Two types of presentation boards are whiteboards (well-known for their multicolored, "dry erase" markers) and chalkboards. Either type of board makes a good tool for visual aids if you have complex drawings that require frequent insertions and erasures—for example, if you are diagramming plays for a soccer team. A board can also be useful to develop a visual in real time—for example, to work out a math problem for your audience.

Boards have some disadvantages. If you put your visual—a graph, say—on a board during your speech, you have to turn your back to the audience; while you're drawing, their attention drifts away from you, and you may find it hard to regain it. Would it be a good idea to put your graph on the board before the speech begins? No, because the audience would be distracted by it; they would scrutinize it before you are ready to talk about it. (It would do no good to say, "Don't pay any attention to this until I get to it." Such a request would make the graph all the more interesting—and therefore distracting.) There is one possible solution: cover the part of the board on which you have written. But this can be awkward. You would have to find something large enough to do the job without being distracting. Another problem is that speakers preceding you might also be planning to use the board, and they might have to erase your visual aid.

Because of the limitations of boards, some instructors forbid their use in a class-room speech, so be sure to find out your instructor's policy.

Figure 21
Effective Use of a Poster

In a speech on organ donation, Jessica Melore of Branchburg, New Jersey, says she would have died if she had not received a heart donation from the young woman pictured in the poster—Shannon Eckert of Mechanicsburg, Pennsylvania—who lost her life in a car crash.

Douglas Bovitt/Courier-Postl/ AP Images

Posters

You can put many kinds of visual aids—such as graphs, drawings, and charts—on posters. Figure 21 shows the effective use of a poster.

In the age of PowerPoint, posters are not outdated—they are widely used. In courtrooms, for example, many attorneys prefer posters to PowerPoint because posters can be placed on easels and kept on display for long periods, enabling jury members to glance at them whenever they need to refresh their memories. In some cases, jurors are allowed to take the posters into the deliberation room. (Normally you shouldn't keep posters on display after you've discussed them, but this situation is an exception to the rule.)

Make sure there is a reliable place to put your posters. If you prop them against a chalkboard or tape them to a wall, they may fall to the floor during the middle of the speech. Using thumbtacks might work if a cork board or some other suitable place for tacking is available. One technique is to pile your posters on a desk and hold them up one at a time, being sure to hold them steady. Another method is to put your poster on an easel (which your school's audiovisual department may be able to provide). Even with an easel, however, some posters tend to curl and resist standing up straight. To prevent this, tape a second poster board or a piece of cardboard to the back of your poster. (*Tip:* An even better solution to the problem of curling is to buy poster stocks that are sturdier than the standard stock sold at drugstores. Office-supply and craft stores have foam boards. Though more expensive than standard poster stock, these materials will not sag or curl.)

Like all visuals, posters must be large enough to view throughout the room. Make sure that your poster is an appropriate size, and that any text on the poster is large enough to be read by people sitting in the back. Additionally, putting just one image on the poster is better than using multiple smaller images, which can cause clutter and distract from the impact of the visual.

Flip Charts

flip chart
a large pad of paper consisting of blank sheets (hinged at the top) that can be flipped over to present information sequentially.

A **flip chart** is a giant writing pad with pages that are glued or wired together at the top. It can be mounted on an easel. When you are through with each page, you can tear it off or flip it over the back of the easel. Some flip charts have pages that can be stuck to a wall after they are torn off, as well.

You can prepare the visuals on each page in advance, or you can "halfway" prepare them—that is, lightly pencil in your sheets at home; then during the speech, with a heavy marker, trace over the lines. With some flip charts, the paper may be so thin that ink will seep to the next page, so you may need to leave a blank page between each two drawn-on sheets.

Be aware that some instructors disapprove of student speakers writing on a flip chart during a speech, so check with your instructor before using one.

Handouts

Despite the availability of high-tech tools, one of the most popular formats used in business and professional presentations is the paper **handout.** It is easy to explain the enduring popularity of handouts: they are easy to prepare, can be updated quickly at the last moment, and provide a permanent document that listeners can take with them when they leave a presentation.

Giving listeners text-heavy handouts during a speech is a sure way to lose them.

Loginova Elena/Shutterstock

Though handouts are popular, they are often misused. I have witnessed the following fiasco dozens of times: A presenter distributes stacks of handouts at the beginning of a talk. While he or she discusses each handout, the room is filled with the sound of rustling papers as the listeners race ahead, reading material the presenter has not yet reached and ignoring or only half-listening to what he or she is saying. (Some speakers try to solve this problem by imploring the audience to stay with them and not read ahead, but this is futile; humans are naturally curious, and they cannot resist reading.)

Because listeners study the pages instead of paying attention to the speaker, handouts are banned in some public speaking classes. Even if your instructor permits them, they are usually unsuitable during a classroom speech because distributing them eats up time and creates a distraction.

handout
material distributed to an audience as part of a speaker's presentation.

The best use of handouts—especially lengthy, complex documents—is to give them *after* the question-and-answer period so that listeners can take them for further study and review. (For classroom speeches, check with your instructor; he or she may prefer that you wait until the end of the class period; if you give out material at the end of your speech, students might read it instead of listening to the next speaker.)

One exception to the preceding advice is that for informal presentations in career and community settings, it is permissible to distribute a handout during a presentation if it is short and simple—a one-page document with an easy-to-understand graphic or a *small* amount of text. In such situations, follow these guidelines: (1) Never distribute a handout until you are ready to talk about it—a premature handout grows stale. (2) Avoid talking about a handout while you are distributing copies. Wait until every listener has a copy before you start your explanation.

Visual Presenters

A **visual presenter,** also known as a document camera or ELMO (the name of a leading manufacturer), is a camera mounted on a stand and pointed at a platform below. What the camera sees is shown on a monitor or projected onto a screen by means of a digital projector. Visual presenters can show two-dimensional items such as photos and diagrams, and they also can show three-dimensional objects such as jewelry. A zoom feature permits very small items, such as a coin, to be enlarged for easy viewing.

visual presenter
a device capable of producing images of both two- and three-dimensional objects.

Preparing Visual Aids

Here are some guidelines for planning and creating your visual aids.

Choose Visuals That Truly Support Your Speech

Before using a visual, ask yourself this question: Will it help clarify or illustrate an important idea in my speech? If the honest answer is no, discard it. Your job is not to dazzle people with pretty colors on a screen or to impress them with your creative artwork. A beautiful drawing of an airplane in flight, for example, would not contribute much to a speech on touring the castles of Europe.

Prepare and Practice Far in Advance

Practice using your visuals as you rehearse your speech. If you will be using unfamiliar equipment, rehearsals will help prevent fumbling or faltering during your speech.

Unless you've planned it out carefully, don't create a visual—such as a diagram on a whiteboard—while you are actually giving your speech: few people can write or draw effectively while speaking to an audience. Make them far in advance so that they are not sloppy and unpolished.

Choose the Appropriate Number of Visuals

A common mistake is to display a large number of boring slides. For this reason, some speech coaches recommend that you use only three or four slides in a speech. Some supervisors forbid employees from using more than three. Although such rules might improve some speeches, they are too rigid to apply to all. The best rule is this: use a visual whenever it can make a key point more interesting, understandable, and memorable. Some speeches (such as a eulogy) may need no visuals at all. Some may need only one, while others may need more than a dozen.

Before speech day, practice in front of classmates or colleagues and ask their advice on which visuals, if any, should be eliminated.

While deciding how many visuals to use, here is an important consideration: when listeners complain about too many visuals, they are usually referring to slides or posters that are densely packed with text. They rarely complain about the number of visuals if all of them are exciting, easy-to-grasp photos and illustrations.

Make Visual Aids Simple and Clear

Make each visual aid so simple that your listeners can quickly grasp its meaning—either at a glance or after minimal explanation by you. Avoid complexity. Too much information can confuse or overwhelm the listeners.

Sometimes you might see a wonderful graphic in a book. Will it translate into a wonderful graphic in a speech? Not necessarily. Some visual aids in books are jam-packed with fascinating details; they are suitable in a book because the reader has ample time to analyze them, but they're too complex for a speech.

In visuals such as graphs, make all labels horizontal. (In a textbook, many labels are vertical because readers of a book can turn the visual sideways, but listeners should not be forced to twist their necks to read vertical lettering.) You do not need to label every part of your visual since you are there to explain the aid.

If you are displaying a multidimensional object, be sure to turn it during your talk so that everyone can see all sides of it.

Aim for Back-Row Comprehension

A common mistake is to use graphics that are difficult or impossible for everyone in the audience to see. The solution is to design every visual aid for the back row. *If all lettering and details cannot be seen easily and comfortably by a person in the rear of the room, don't use the visual.* Here are some guidelines:

Make letters, numbers, and graphics much larger than you think necessary. Be on the safe side. People rarely complain about visuals being too large.

Make enlargements. You can magnify a too-small visual by using visual presenters, PowerPoint slides, or posters. Here are some of the easiest options:

- If an object is too small for an audience to see in person, take a close-up picture with your digital or smartphone camera and show the photograph on a large screen through PowerPoint, or have a print shop, like Staples or FedEx Office, turn it into a poster.

- To turn a printed photo or drawing into a PowerPoint slide, you can scan the item to your computer, converting it to a digital file. If you do not have a scanner, try visiting the media center on your campus or a print shop in your community. You may also be able to take a picture of the photo or drawing with a digital camera or smartphone to digitize the image, but be sure the quality of the final image is high, with no shadows or glares.

- If your digital image is too small, try using an online image editor to enlarge it without losing the quality. (Enter "online image editor" into a search engine to find websites that allow you to change the sizes of images for free.)

Test the visibility of your visuals. Before the day of your speech, go to the room where you will be speaking, display your visual aid in the front of the room, and sit in the back row to determine whether you can see it clearly. (Even better, have a friend sit in the back row to offer feedback.) If your visual cannot be seen with crystal clearness from the back row, discard it and create another (or simply don't use one).

Use Colors Carefully

To enliven visual aids, use color—but use it carefully. Here are two important issues to consider:

1. Color-blindness is an inherited condition that makes it impossible to see colors the way most people do. Few women are color-blind, but about 8 percent of men have some degree of color-blindness. While there are several varieties of the condition, the most common is red-green, which means a difficulty or inability to distinguish red and green when they are next to each other. If you put red letters on a green background (or green on top of red), a person with red-green color-blindness probably could not read the text. The best advice is to avoid placing red and green close together on a visual aid.[10] See Figure 22 for an example of an image that does not show careful color usage.

2. For all people, whether or not they are color-blind, the color combination that is clearest and most readable is dark text on a light-colored background. One of the safest choices is black on light yellow, with red for emphasis. What about using white text on top of black or dark-blue backgrounds? Although this color scheme is dramatic, it can cause eye fatigue, so it should be used rarely if at all.

The founder of Facebook, Mark Zuckerberg, who is red-green color-blind, chose blue and white for Facebook's icon because he can see those colors clearly.

Rvlsoft/Shutterstock

Presenting Visual Aids

Here are some tips for using visual aids effectively in your speeches.

Choose the Best Time to Show Visuals

Many speakers undermine their speech's effectiveness by showing visual aids at inappropriate times. Here are several guidelines.

Don't display a visual before your speech begins.   If visual aids are in plain sight before you start, you deprive your speech of an element of drama and freshness. There are exceptions, of course, such as when you must set up items for a demonstration on a table in front of the room.

Display a visual whenever the audience needs help understanding a point.   One speaker gave a talk on rock formations in caves but waited until the end to show photos illustrating his points. During the body of the speech, listeners were mystified and frustrated: What do these rock formations look like? Though he ultimately showed pictures, his listeners would have experienced a much greater understanding of the subject matter if he had displayed the images as he went along.

If listener comprehension is unharmed, it is acceptable to delay visuals.   In some cases, you may want to withhold a visual or a demonstration to build suspense. In a speech on how to use Taekwondo martial arts techniques to break objects, student speaker Lee Wentz stood in front of a cement block as he spoke, waiting until the end to demonstrate the actual breaking of the block with one hand. This built suspense as the audience wondered whether he would succeed, which made his accomplishment even more exciting to the audience.

Never Circulate Visual Aids among Audience Members

Some people try to solve the problem of a too-small visual aid (such as a piece of jewelry) by passing it around the room, but this is a mistake. People will look at the visual instead of listening to the speaker, and there's likely to be distraction, perhaps even whispered comments, as it is being passed from one person to another. Some speakers walk from listener to listener to give each person a close-up view of the visual aid. This is also a poor technique because the listeners who are not seeing the visual may become bored or distracted, and they may start whispering comments to their friends. Moreover, the listeners who are looking at the aid may ask questions that mean nothing to the audience members who have not seen it yet. In a case like this, the speaker can easily lose the audience's attention and interest.

One way to solve the problem of a too-small object is to leave it in the front of the room and invite the audience to see it *after* the speech or at the end of class. This strategy is acceptable unless listeners need to see the aid during your speech to understand what you are talking about. In this case, the best solution is to create an enlarged image of the object to display during the speech and then permit listeners to take a look at the real object after the speech.

Tips for Your Career

Ask a Friend to Assist You

For speeches that you give on the job or in the community, you may want to ask a friend to assist you. Here are some of the ways in which an assistant can be useful:

1. An assistant can help you set up and operate audiovisual equipment, turn lights off and on, or search for a missing extension cord. Such assistance will free you to concentrate on getting your message across to the audience.

2. If you are speaking to strangers, the presence of your friend can give you a psychological boost—you have an "ally" in the room.

3. An assistant may be able to handle any distractions or emergencies that arise. If, for example, a group of people start a loud conversation right outside the room in which you are speaking, the assistant can open the door and whisper a request for silence.

4. Your assistant can stand or sit in the back of the room while you are speaking and give you advice with hand signals on which the two of you have agreed in advance. For example, you can create unique signals for the following advice:

   - "Slow down—you're talking too fast."
   - "Speak louder—I can barely hear you."
   - "You're looking at your notes too much."
   - "You've reached the time limit—wrap things up and sit down."

5. An assistant can give you a critique of your speech afterward so that you can learn from any mistakes you have made. Sometimes the assistant can mingle with the audience in the hall after your speech and find out how listeners responded to the presentation so that you can learn about your strengths and weaknesses.

When they need to show steps in a process, some speakers invite the audience to come to the front of the room and gather around a table. One speaker did this so that everyone could see him making garnishes out of vegetables (he transformed a tomato into a "rose"). If you are considering this approach, here are three guidelines: (1) Use the technique only with small audiences. (2) Make sure no listeners with disabilities are excluded from participating. (3) Get your instructor's permission before trying this in a classroom speech.

Remove Physical Barriers

Right before a speech, move any objects or furniture that might block the view of some audience members. If you're using equipment such as a projector, make sure it doesn't obstruct anyone's vision. If, despite your best efforts, some audience members will be blocked from seeing your visuals, ask them (before you start your introduction) to shift their chairs or move to a different part of the room.

Make Sure Listeners Get Maximum Benefit from Visuals

Don't rush through your visuals. A common mistake is for speakers to display a visual for a moment and then remove it from view. To these speakers, the visual is simple and obvious (they have seen it so many times, they are tired of it), but they should realize that it is brand-new to the listeners, who need time to study and absorb the contents.

Discuss each visual aid. But, you might say, can't listeners see and figure it out for themselves? In some cases, that is true, but by discussing each visual as you display it, you guarantee that listeners stay in step with you. As the speaker, it's your responsibility to make sure that listeners understand the relevance of the visual.

Examining Your Ethics

In a speech on how violent criminals should be treated, a speaker used PowerPoint to show a grisly photo of a victim who had been hacked and dismembered by a vicious attacker. The speaker wanted to shock his listeners and make them pay attention to a serious problem, but some listeners were repulsed and nauseated. Which of these statements do you support?

A. The speaker should be commended for having the courage to force the audience to look squarely at a real social problem.

B. The speaker should have shown the photo but advised the audience beforehand, "If anyone is squeamish about seeing bloody body parts, close your eyes until I tell you to open them."

C. The speaker should have made his points with words, omitting a grisly photo that was certain to offend and upset some audience members.

For the answer, see the last page of this chapter.

For a complex visual, don't wave your hand in the general direction of the aid and assume that the audience will know which feature you are referring to. Be precise. Point to the specific part that you are discussing with your finger, a pen, or an extendable pointer. To avoid twisting your body, use the hand closer to the aid.

Don't Let Visuals Distract from Your Message

Visuals should never distract your audience from what you are saying. Here are some tips.

Show one visual at a time. If you display five posters on a chalk tray simultaneously, your listeners will scrutinize the fourth poster while you are talking about the first. To keep the eyes and minds of your listeners focused on you and your remarks, show a visual, discuss it fully, put it away, and then display your next visual. There is one exception to this rule: if you have a visual aid that can provide a simple, undistracting backdrop or evoke a mood, you may leave it on display during the entire speech. One speaker kept a bouquet of flowers on the front table throughout her speech on gardening; the flowers provided a pleasing complement to her remarks.

Blank the screen. If you have an interval between PowerPoint slides, blank the screen by pressing "B" on your keyboard or "A/V Mute" on the remote control for the projector.

Be careful using animals or children as visuals. The use of pets or kids as visual aids can be risky, and should be approached with caution. Ask yourself, is the pet or child especially relevant to your speech? Will the pet or child make a very strong impact on your audience? Can you guarantee the cooperation of the pet or child? If the answer to any of these questions is no, find a safer alternative visual aid. One student speaker brought her ferret to class to demonstrate that they make excellent pets. The trouble was that critter made noise and acted up, causing the audience to laugh at its antics rather than listen to her speech. Additionally, some members of your audience may have pet-related allergies, so surveying your audience in advance will help you avoid accidentally causing a sneezing fit—or worse—during the speech.

However, a well-coached child or a well-trained pet can be a valuable visual aid. A nursing student may use a child to demonstrate a head-to-toe assessment on a pediatric patient, for example. If you decide to use a pet or child as a visual aid, make sure to get permission from your instructor first, because they may not allow pets or children in the classroom.

Don't Talk to Your Visual Aid

Many speakers are so intent on explaining a visual aid that they spend most of their time talking to it instead of to the audience. You should stand next to your aid and face the audience during most of your discussion. Look at the aid only in two situations:

1. When you introduce it, look at it for several seconds—this is long enough to draw the listeners' attention toward it.

2. Whenever you want to direct the audience's attention to a particular segment, look at the aid for one or two seconds as you point out the special feature.

Use Progressive Revelation

Whenever possible, use **progressive revelation**—that is, reveal only one part or item at a time until all elements are visible. If, for example, you are discussing three sections of a sculpture, you can keep the entire piece covered at the beginning, and then unveil one section at a time when you are ready to discuss it. Progressive revelation creates suspense, making the listeners curious about what comes next, and it prevents them from reading or studying ahead of you. A variation of this technique, called the "build," is used in PowerPoint to reveal parts of a slide—for example, a pie chart can be shown one piece at a time until all pieces make up the pie. Likewise, the animation tool in PowerPoint can be used to display bullet points one at a time, only revealing the next one when you are ready to speak about it.

progressive revelation
piece-by-piece unveiling of a visual.

Plan for Emergencies

With visual aids, there is always a chance of a foul-up, so you should plan carefully how you will handle any problems that might arise. Before you use any electronic media, speak with your instructor or the program chairperson to make arrangements (for darkening the room, getting an extension cord, and so on). Always check out the location of your speech in advance. Is there an electrical outlet nearby? If not, can you get an extension cord? Can the room be darkened for PowerPoint slides? Is there a place to put your posters? Is there a whiteboard or a chalkboard?

Be prepared for the unexpected, such as the sudden malfunctioning of a computer or a multimedia projector. Some disasters can be mitigated by planning ahead. For example, you can have paper copies of your PowerPoint slides for quick distribution. If equipment breaks down and cannot be fixed quickly, continue with your speech as best you can. Try to keep your poise and sense of humor.

Presenting Visuals in Online Presentations

For your job, community event, or online course, you may need to use visuals as part of a **synchronous,** or real-time, web-based presentation. The organization sponsoring the presentation may use a common web conferencing tool, such as Zoom, WebEx, Adobe Connect, or GoToMeeting, to deliver your performance. While each tool is slightly different, all of them allow you to share your screen, so participants can see the desktop of your computer, or share documents that you created in advance, like a PowerPoint presentation. Some may also include a virtual whiteboard, which you can use to write or draw a diagram for your audience. Make sure that you discuss the capabilities of the platform being used with the organization well in advance of the meeting.

synchronous
existing or occurring at the same time; frequently used to refer to online meetings that happen in real time.

Some general tips for presenting visuals in online presentations include the following:

1. Make sure to discuss the capabilities of the web conferencing platform with your contact at the organization sponsoring the presentation in advance of the speech.

2. Prepare and load all documents prior to the meeting start. Some platforms may require that your visuals are in a certain format, like PDF, prior to uploading them, so be sure to convert them as necessary.

3. Make sure to close any windows that you will not be using prior to sharing your desktop with your audience. You don't want an embarrassing e-mail or instant message to pop up for your audience to see! Further, you should clean up the documents on your desktop and change your background image to present yourself in an orderly, professional manner to your audience.

4. Find out if you are going to be in control of the meeting space, or if you will have to rely on another "host" to scroll through a document or advance your PowerPoint slide. That way, you can rehearse the use of the visuals and/or develop a signal to let the person hosting the meeting know that he or she can progress through your visual.

5. Some presentations may be broadcast over social media using tools like Facebook Live. In these cases, make sure that you coordinate with the individual broadcasting the speech so that he or she can properly capture your visuals for your audience to view.

Communicating in Other Channels

While the visual channel of communication is powerful, don't overlook other channels—hearing, taste, smell, touch, and physical activity—which can be effective avenues for reaching your audience.

Hearing

In almost all presentations, the sense of hearing is paramount, since you use your voice to convey words and meaning. In addition, you can supply audio aids. For example, to accompany a visual presentation on dolphins, marine biologist Jennifer Novak played an audio clip of the clicks, whistles, and other sounds that dolphins use to communicate with one another.

The Internet has a rich variety of audio sources. For example, National Public Radio (npr.org) provides audio clips and podcasts that you can download to a computer, phone, or other smart device and play during a presentation. It's also possible to insert audio clips into PowerPoint presentations. NPR downloads include the following:

- Music and comments by the Latin jazz drummer Poncho Sanchez
- Interviews with ex-smokers who share their secrets for quitting the habit
- The lilting sounds of Irish accents in Dublin

Taste and Smell

Known as the chemical senses, taste and smell are closely related channels. Floral designer Charlene Worley gave a speech on how flowers provide not only messages of love and consolation but also medicine and food. At the end of her talk, she invited the audience to sniff a bouquet she had created. She also appealed to the sense of taste by serving crackers on which she had spread jam made from violets.

In culinary demonstrations, smelling a savory dish as it is prepared can stimulate appetite and interest, and tasting it can help the audience decide whether it is worthwhile.

Many business and professional presentations are held in rooms with a side table that provides beverages and snacks. This courtesy is more than simply satisfying people's hunger and thirst. Experienced presenters have discovered that the aroma of fresh coffee and the savor of tasty food can put an audience in a receptive mood and make it easier to inform or persuade. For example, many real estate agents know that the smell of coffee evokes childhood memories of a pleasant home where breakfast is being prepared, so they arrange to have a pot of coffee brewing as they enter a house with a client to help make the house seem like a home.

Touch and Physical Activity

Wishing to disprove the notion that snakes have slimy skin, herpetologist Jeanne Goldberg invited listeners to come forward and stroke the nonpoisonous king snake she was holding. Many listeners were surprised to find the skin dry and firm, with a texture like glass beads tightly strung together.

For learning new skills, the sense of touch is often coupled with physical activity. You need touch and muscular movement to apply first aid, draw a map, or perform a card trick. To persuade people to buy a product, some presenters give an audience hands-on experience. For example, one laptop computer sold well because sales representatives put laptops in front of listeners and invited them to try out the keyboard's pleasing responsiveness. In some situations, presenters provide physical activity by passing out pads and pens and inviting listeners to take notes during the presentation.

A culinary class taught by a Nepalese chef involves seeing, hearing, smelling, tasting, touching, and physical activity.

sam100/Shutterstock

Using Multiple Channels

How many channels should you use? Some speeches (such as inspirational talks) do not require a variety of channels, but in many situations (such as teaching new material), the more you can use, the greater the likelihood that your listeners will understand and remember the information.[11]

In some cases, you can appeal to all the major channels in a single presentation. For example, in a culinary class, students can *see* the process as it is demonstrated, *hear* the explanations, *smell* the aromas, *taste* the delicacies, and use *touch* and *physical activity* as they practice making a dish.

Resources for Review and Skill Building

Summary

Presentation aids—which can involve vision, hearing, smell, taste, touch, and physical activity—enrich and enliven a speech. The most popular type, visual aids, can make your ideas clear and understandable; make your speech more interesting and memorable; help an audience remember facts and details; make long, complicated explanations unnecessary; help prove a point; add to your credibility; and enhance communication with people who speak English as a second language.

The major types of visual aids include graphs, tables, drawings, photos, videos, animations, objects, models, yourself, and volunteers.

Presentation software comes in two varieties—linear (like PowerPoint and Keynote) and non-linear (like Prezi). The

most popular program, PowerPoint, can put listeners to sleep unless a speaker creates engaging slides that have attractive graphics and avoid excessive text and visual clutter.

Visual aids can be conveyed to the audience through various media: multimedia projectors, boards, posters, flip charts, handouts, and visual presenters.

There are six guidelines for preparing visual aids: (1) Choose visual aids that truly support your speech. (2) Prepare and practice far in advance. (3) Choose the appropriate number of visuals. (4) Make your aids as simple and clear as possible. (5) Aim for comprehension by everyone, including the people in the back row. (6) Use colors carefully, taking color-blindness into consideration.

There are eight tips for presenting visual aids: (1) Decide on the best time to show visuals. (2) Never circulate a visual aid among audience members. (3) Remove physical barriers so that everyone has an unimpeded view. (4) Make sure listeners get the maximum benefit from each visual. (5) Make sure the aids don't distract from your message. (6) Don't talk to your aids. (7) Use progressive revelation. (8) Plan how you would handle equipment failure.

Although visuals are the most popular form of presentation aids, the other channels of communication—hearing, taste, smell, touch, and physical activity—can be quite effective. Whenever possible, use several channels to maximize listener understanding and retention.

Key Terms

bar graph, *153*	linear, *158*	progressive revelation, *175*
flip chart, *168*	non-linear, *158*	synchronous, *175*
handout, *169*	pictorial graph, *153*	table, *154*
line graph, *153*	pie graph, *153*	visual presenter, *169*

Review Questions

1. List at least six types of visual aids.

2. Is it legal to use graphics from the Internet in a student speech in the classroom? Explain your answer.

3. What are the worst mistakes that plague PowerPoint slides?

4. List at least five media for presenting visual aids.

5. The text recommends that you "aim for back-row comprehension." What does this mean, and why is the advice necessary?

6. How can speakers test the visibility of their visuals?

7. For the benefit of people with the most common form of color-blindness, which colors should never be placed next to or overlaying each other in visual aids?

8. Is it always a mistake for a speaker to wait until the conclusion of a presentation to show a visual or perform a demonstration? Explain your answer.

9. Why would it be a mistake to circulate a small photograph during your speech?

10. What is progressive revelation?

Building Critical-Thinking Skills

1. "Some pictures may be worth a thousand words, but a picture of a thousand words isn't worth much," said the late corporate executive Don Keough. Explain what this means in terms of oral presentations.

2. At one website devoted to communication, public speakers are advised to distribute thought-provoking handouts at the beginning of a speech so that "if members of the audience get bored during the speech, they will have something interesting to read." Do you agree with this advice? Defend your position.

3. A traditional, printed photograph is too small for an audience to see clearly. How would you make a photograph large enough to display?

Building Teamwork Skills

1. Working in a group, create a scenario in which a sales representative gives a presentation that involves at least four of the six channels of communication.

2. In a group, create an outdoor sign that violates the guidelines of this chapter. Then, create a new sign that corrects all the mistakes.

Examining Your Ethics

Answer: C. Visual aids can be used to gain an emotional response from listeners, but it is unfair and insensitive to subject listeners to a visual that is offensive or nauseating. This could also cause some audience members to stop listening to the message.

End Notes

1. Jillian Jones, telephone interview, September 14, 2015; Constance Bourg, "Visual Storytelling: Seeing Is Believing," Brand Stories, www.brandstories.net (accessed November 17, 2015).

2. Linda M. Tapp, "A Picture Is Worth a Thousand Words," American Society of Safety Engineers, onepetro.org (accessed November 17, 2015).

3. Hamilton Gregory, Experiment using two groups of 40 students each.

4. Rune Pettersson, *Information Design: An Introduction* (Amsterdam, The Netherlands: John Benjamins, 2002), pp. 103–04; Stephen Petrina, *Advanced Teaching Methods for the Technology Classroom* (Hershey, PA: Idea Group, 2006), pp. 12–13.

5. A. Bernhardt, R. Milkman, N. Theodore, et al., *Broken Laws, Unprotected Workers: Violations of Employment and Labor Laws in America's Cities,* 2015, https://s27147.pcdn.co/wp-content/uploads/2015/03/BrokenLawsReport2009.pdf.

6. Inequality.org, "Wealth Inequality in the United States," n.d., https://inequality.org/facts/wealth-inequality/.

7. Lance Secretan, "Spirit at Work—Inspirational Teaching," *IndustryWeek,* December 21, 2004, www.industryweek.com (accessed November 17, 2015).

8. Jan Caldwell, public speaking instructor, Asheville-Buncombe Technical Community College, e-mail interview, January 30, 2012.

9. Mark Maloney, "What Advice Do You Have for Creating Slideshows?," *Toastmaster,* July 2014, p. 8.

10. Hannah Alvarez, "A Guide to Color, UX, and Conversion Rates," User Testing, www.usertesting.com (accessed November 12, 2015); "Colour Blindness," *Biology Online,* www.biology-online.org (accessed November 12, 2015).

11. E. Michael Smith, MD, Department of Psychiatry and Behavioral Sciences, University of Oklahoma Health Services Center, e-mail interview, June 3, 2008; Martin Lindstrom, *Brand Sense: Sensory Secrets behind the Stuff We Buy* (New York: Free Press, 2010), p. 8.

The Body of the Speech

OUTLINE

OBJECTIVES

After studying this chapter, you should be able to

1. Explain the importance of skillfully organizing the body of the speech.

2. Create the body of a speech by using a central idea to develop main points.

3. Identify and use five patterns of organization: chronological, spatial, cause–effect, problem–solution, and topical.

4. Identify and use four types of transitional devices: bridges, internal summaries, signposts, and spotlights.

5. Simplify the process of organizing speech material.

WHEN INVITED TO COLLEGE CAMPUSES, Mexican actor Gael García Bernal does not give speeches about his acting career. Instead, he talks about something he feels passionate about—the plight of refugees from Syria. Bernal is a global ambassador for Oxfam, an international confederation of 17 organizations working in 94 countries worldwide to find solutions to poverty and injustice. He has visited refugee camps in the Middle East and has raised funds for medicine, food, and clothing for displaced Syrians.

In his speeches, he organizes his material in a problem–solution pattern, which means that he devotes the first half of his talk to the explanation of a problem, and the second half to outlining the solution to the problem.[1]

Gael García Bernal uses the problem–solution pattern to organize his speeches.

Chris Pizzello/Invision/AP Images

Using a pattern to organize a speech is a good way to make sure that your material is clear, logical, and—most importantly—understandable to the audience. In this chapter, we will discuss some of the most popular and effective patterns of organization.

Before proceeding, let's look at where we stand in the speech-preparation process. In previous chapters, we discussed finding and developing materials such as statistics, examples, and visual aids. Now our task is to organize. We must take all our materials—our bricks and mortar—and put them together to build a solid, coherent structure. This chapter will focus on organizing the body of a speech, and future chapters will focus on creating introductions and conclusions, as well as putting all the parts together to outline the speech.

The Importance of Organization

A well-organized speech has vast advantages over a poorly organized one:

1. **A well-organized speech is easier to understand.** Wesley J. Smith, a former judge at a small-claims court in Los Angeles, says, "The most effective cases I heard involved people who presented their side of the issue as if they were telling a story. Their cases were organized logically, with a beginning, a middle, and an end. That not only kept my interest but helped me quickly understand the issues."[2]

2. **A well-organized speech is easier for the audience to remember.** In an experiment with a list of endangered species, one group of students memorized list A in Figure 1 and another group memorized list B. When tested two weeks later, the students who had learned list A recalled 56 percent of the terms, while the students who had learned list B recalled 81 percent.[3]

   List A is difficult to remember because the animals are listed in random order. List B is easier to remember because items are grouped in meaningful clusters (mammals, birds, reptiles, and fish). In a good speech, you should apply the same principle: group your ideas in meaningful clusters that are easy to comprehend and recall.

3. **A well-organized speech is more likely to be believed.** Studies show that if you present a poorly organized speech, your listeners will find you less believable at the end than they did at the beginning of the speech.[4] If your speech is well organized, however, you will come across as someone who is in full command of the facts, and therefore believable.

Creating the Body

A speech works best if it is divided into three well-developed sections: introduction, body, and conclusion. Does this mean that you should begin by working on the introduction? Not necessarily. Many experienced speakers find it easier to prepare the body first and then prepare the introduction. If you stop to think about it, this makes sense: How can you write an introduction before you know what you will say in the body?

Figure 1

A List of Endangered Species Shown in Two Formats

Because it is organized in logical clusters, list B is easier to memorize and retain than list A.

List A	List B	
Indian python	**Mammals**	
Cheetah		
Great white shark	Polar bear	Gorilla
Gorilla	Cheetah	Gray wolf
Hawksbill turtle		
Hawaiian crow	**Birds**	
Gray wolf		
California condor	California condor	Hawaiian crow
Common sturgeon	Shore plover	Whooping crane
Polar bear		
Whooping crane	**Reptiles**	
Giant catfish	American crocodile	Indian python
Shore plover	Hawksbill turtle	Painted terrapin
Painted terrapin		
Cutthroat trout	**Fish**	
American crocodile	Giant catfish	Cutthroat trout
	Great white shark	Common sturgeon

Let's look at a good technique for creating the body.

Start with your *specific purpose,* which is the goal of your speech, and your *central idea,* which is the key concept that you want to get across to your audience. (If you are unsure about these terms, please review the chapter on selecting topic, purpose, and central idea before proceeding in this chapter.)

Suppose you hear a news report about a charity that has been ripping off donors, and you decide to devote your next speech to charity fraud. After reading articles and conducting interviews, you come up with the following purpose statement:

Specific Purpose: To persuade my audience to be cautious in donating to charity

Next, ask yourself, "What is my essential message? What big idea do I want to leave in the minds of my listeners?" The answer is your central idea. Here is one possibility:

Central Idea: Before donating to a charity, make sure it is legitimate.

This central idea is your speech boiled down to one sentence. It is what you want your listeners to remember if they forget everything else.

The next step is to ask yourself this question: "How can I get my audience to understand and accept my central idea?"

The best way to get the central idea across to your audience is to develop and drive home a few **main points** that are based on the central idea. In our charities example, here are three main points that could be made:

main points
key assertions made by a speaker to develop his or her central idea.

I. Some charities give only a tiny sum of money to people in need.

II. These charities channel most of their money to salaries and gifts for staff members.

III. Potential donors should look for warnings posted on the Internet by watchdog groups that monitor charities.

The first and second main points focus on the problem (charity rip-offs), and the third main point provides a solution (investigation on the Internet).

By themselves the main points are not sufficient. Listeners would want more information, so you need to develop each main point with support materials such as narratives, examples, and statistics. For instance, if your listeners heard the first main point, that some charities give only a small amount of money to the people they supposedly serve, they might say, "Well, okay, can you give some examples?" Here are a couple of examples you could use:

• *The New York Times* reported that one man set up a charity to help wounded veterans, raising more than $168 million in two years. But he gave only 25 percent to help vets.[5]

• *The Washington Post* reported that four cancer charities were accused by the Federal Trade Commission of scamming donors out of $187 million.[6]

For the second main point, you could describe the lavish lifestyles of the owners of rip-off charities. For the third main point, you could discuss websites that post lists of fraudulent charities. At the end of your speech, you could give all listeners a handout containing the web addresses so that they could pursue their own investigations later.

To see an overview of the process we have just discussed, take a look at Figure 2, which shows the key elements of a speech aimed at persuading listeners to eat fish frequently. The specific purpose leads to the central idea, which is sustained by two main points. The main points are not likely to be believed by the audience unless they are supported by solid information such as statistics and testimony from experts. For example, the speaker could cite clinical tests by reliable medical researchers that demonstrate the value of omega-3 acids (found in fish) for the brain and the heart.

Figure 2
Speech preparation should start with a specific purpose and a central idea. Then the central idea is developed by two or three (or occasionally four) main points, which in turn are strengthened by a variety of support materials, such as examples and statistics.

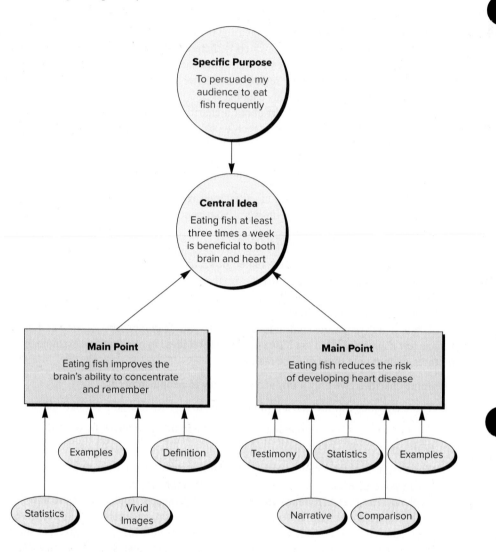

Devising Main Points

"Do I need more than one main point?" some students ask. Yes. If you have only one main point to develop your central idea, you have a weak structure, like a bridge that has only one pillar to hold it up. If you provide only one main point, your listeners have only *one* reason to believe your central idea. If you give them two or three main points, you multiply your chances of convincing them.

"How many main points should I have?" you may be asking. To answer this and other questions, let's examine some guidelines for refining main points.

Limit the Number of Main Points

A common mistake of public speakers is to cram too many points into a speech. They do this because they are approaching the speech from their own viewpoint and not from the viewpoint of the listeners. If you ask yourself, "How much information can I squeeze into the five minutes allotted?," you are approaching the speech from your own viewpoint. To approach the speech from the audience's viewpoint, you should ask, "How much information can the audience comfortably pay attention to, understand, and remember?"

Audiences simply cannot absorb too much new information. You should know this from your own experience; you can probably recall many speakers (including some teachers) who overwhelmed you with a barrage of ideas, facts, and figures. Don't be reluctant to cut and trim your material.

Exactly how many main points should you have? In a short speech (5 to 10 minutes), you should limit yourself to two or three (or occasionally four) main points. That is as much as an audience can absorb. In a longer speech, you could have as many as five main points, but most experienced speakers cover only two or three, regardless of the length of their speech.

Restrict Each Main Point to a Single Idea

Each main point should focus on just one idea. Consider the following:

Poor:	I. Driverless cars can be used to deliver food to people with disabilities, and they can reduce drunk driving accidents.
Better:	I. Driverless cars can be used to deliver food to people with disabilities.
	II. Driverless cars can reduce drunk driving accidents.

The first set makes the mistake of covering two issues; the second set splits the material into two distinct points.

Avoid Announcements

Rather than simply announcing a topic, each main point should make an assertion, or a forthright declaration of the idea that you want to convey. Imagine that you write the following:

Poor: I'll talk about hot-dog headaches.

What about it? What's your point? You have done nothing but announce your topic.

Better: Sodium nitrites contained in hot dogs cause many people to suffer headaches.

Now you have made a point—a clear assertion of what you want to convey to your audience.

Customize Points for Each Audience

As you play with ideas in your search for main points, ask yourself, "What main points would work best with this particular audience?" If you tailor your speech to each audience's needs and desires, you may end up using different main points with different audiences.

Let's say you plan to give speeches in your community aimed at persuading people to take up nature photography as a hobby. If you talk to a group of college students, you can anticipate that they will raise the objection that photography is too expensive. So you create a main point—"Photography is not out of reach for people with modest incomes"—and devote a good portion of your speech to giving specific examples and prices. If, however, you speak to an audience of wealthy individuals who could easily afford any kind of camera, this point may be unnecessary.

Another potential main point is that nature photography teaches a person to see the world with fresh eyes—to find "splendor in the grass," the visual glories that abound in nature for those who develop keen perception. This would be a good point to make with an audience of urban dwellers who rarely explore the outdoors. But if your audience is a birdwatchers' society, this point is probably unnecessary; these people have already trained their eyes to detect nature's nuances.

Having 3 main points is better than having 10.

iCreative3D/Shutterstock

Tips for Your Career

Test and Verify Your Material

A software "techie" was assigned by his company to give a sales presentation to an audience of potential clients. He was told to "show the audience how our software can help people in their industry."

He spoke for 30 minutes, and at the end, he was blistered by scornful comments from his listeners. "You have given us examples of how your software can help people at banks," one listener said. "Don't you know that we are healthcare professionals and everything you have told us is worthless to us?"

To avoid mistakes like this, it's a good idea to test the relevance, strength, and accuracy of your speech in advance. Here are four techniques:

- Before a presentation, go over the highlights with some of your future listeners to determine if your content is helpful for this particular audience. If the "techie" had done so, he would have avoided a big blunder.

- Do an "expert check." Discuss your material with someone who is knowledgeable about your subject, so that he or she can point out any errors or omissions.

- Try out your material on friends or relatives. Victoria Vance, a hospital nutritionist who gives talks in her community on diet and nutrition, tests her ideas with her husband and teenage children at the dinner table. "I tell them, 'I'm going to give a speech at a high school next week. Here's what I plan to say.' Then I casually tell them the main points of my speech. Occasionally one of the kids will break in with something like, 'But,

Do an "expert check" by asking a knowledgeable person if what you are planning to say in your presentation is accurate.

Pressmaster/Shutterstock

Mom, are you saying that *all* fast food is bad for you?' That tells me the places in the speech where I need to add some more explanations or examples."

- For each main point, think of the typical people who will be in your audience and ask yourself, "How will they react to this?" Then, shape your material accordingly. If your imaginary listeners say, "How do you know this is true?," give the name and credentials of the expert from whom you derived your material. If they ask, "What do you mean by that?," give them an explanation. If they say, "Who cares?," show them the importance of your subject.

Use Parallel Language Whenever Possible

parallel language
equivalent grammatical forms to express equivalent ideas.

Parallel language means that you use the same grammatical forms throughout a sentence or a paragraph. Read the following sentence aloud: "Joe enjoys hunting, fishing, and to camp." There is nothing wrong with the sentence grammatically, but it doesn't sound as pleasant to the ear as this version: "Joe enjoys hunting, fishing, and camping." Rather than the discord of *-ing, -ing,* plus *to,* our ears prefer the rhythm of *-ing, -ing, -ing,* as in the second sentence.

Suppose that you started with the following:

Specific Purpose:	To persuade my audience to swim for exercise
Central Idea:	Swimming is an ideal exercise because it reduces nervous tension, is not known to cause injuries, and builds endurance.

Now decide which of the following sets of main points would be more effective:

First Set: I. You can work off a lot of nervous tension while swimming.

II. Muscle and bone injuries, common with other
sports, are not a problem with swimming.

III. Swimming builds endurance.

Second Set: I. Swimming reduces nervous tension.

II. Swimming does not typically cause muscle and
bone injuries.

III. Swimming builds endurance.

The second set is preferable because it follows a parallel grammatical form throughout (the noun *swimming* followed by a verb). This consistent arrangement may not be practical in every speech, but you should strive for parallelism whenever possible.

Organizing Main Points

Main points should be organized in a logical, easy-to-follow pattern. Five of the most popular patterns used by speakers are chronological, spatial, cause–effect, problem–solution, and topical.

Chronological Pattern

In the **chronological pattern**, you arrange your main points in a *time* sequence—what occurs first, what occurs second, and so on. If, for example, you are describing a process, you can use the chronological pattern to show the step-by-step progression. For an illustration, see Figure 3.

The chronological pattern is a logical choice for a speech dealing with periods of time in history. If, for example, you were speaking on the history of immigration in the United States, you could divide your subject into centuries, from the seventeenth to the twenty-first.

If you were speaking on the life of a person, you might divide your speech according to the stages of life, as in the following example:

Specific Purpose: To inform my listeners of the heroism of Harriet Tubman, a
leading nineteenth-century abolitionist

Central Idea: Harriet Tubman was a courageous woman who escaped from
slavery and then returned to the South to rescue others.

Main Points:

(Childhood)   I. Born a slave on a plantation in Maryland, Tubman suffered
many whippings while growing up.

(Youth)   II. She escaped to freedom by using the Underground Railroad.

(Adulthood)   III. Wearing various disguises, Tubman smuggled over 300 slaves
to safe havens from 1850 to 1860.

Just as parallel lines are pleasing to the eye, parallel language is pleasing to the ear.

Hamilton Gregory

chronological pattern an arrangement of information in a time sequence.

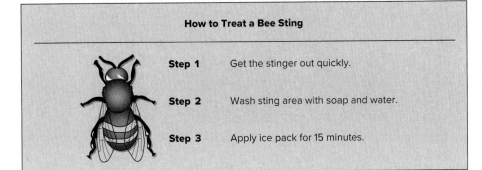

How to Treat a Bee Sting

Step 1	Get the stinger out quickly.
Step 2	Wash sting area with soap and water.
Step 3	Apply ice pack for 15 minutes.

Figure 3
Chronological Pattern
The process of treating a bee sting is a chronological pattern (or time sequence)—what to do first, second, and third.

Spatial Pattern

In the **spatial pattern**, you organize items according to the way in which they relate to each other in *physical space*—top to bottom, left to right, north to south, inside to outside, and so on. If you were speaking on the solar system, for example, you could discuss the Sun first, then move outward in space to Mercury, Venus, Earth, Mars, and so on. Here is an example in which the speaker divides a car into space-related sections:

Specific Purpose: To tell my audience how to inspect a used car before deciding whether to buy it

Central Idea: If you examine a used car carefully and critically, you can avoid buying a "lemon."

Main Points: I. Inspect the condition of the car's body.

II. Inspect the condition of the car's motor.

III. Inspect the condition of the car's interior.

For an example of the spatial pattern as used from top to bottom, see Figure 4.

Cause–Effect Pattern

In some speeches, you are concerned with why something happens or happened—a cause-effect relationship. For example, some people refuse to ride in elevators because they have an inordinate fear of closed spaces. Their claustrophobia is the *cause* and their refusal to ride in elevators is the *effect*. For an illustration of a **cause–effect pattern** in a speech, see Figure 5.

Sometimes it is more effective to start with the effects and then analyze the causes, as in this case:

Specific Purpose: To explain to my listeners why many people are unable to get bank loans for a new car or house

Figure 4
Spatial Pattern

For a discussion of the architectural features of the Eiffel Tower, a speaker could use the spatial (physical space) pattern, progressing from top to bottom or from bottom to top.

WDG Photo/Shutterstock

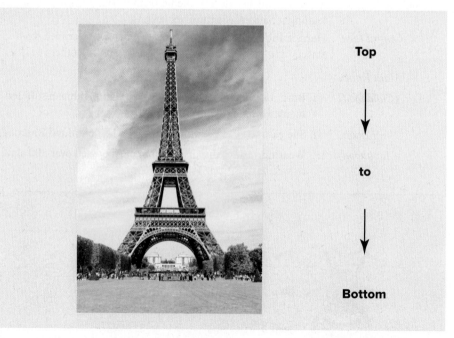

Top

to

Bottom

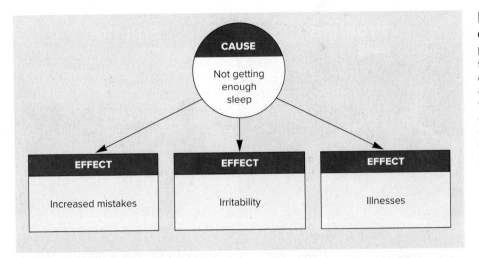

Figure 5
Cause–Effect Pattern
For a speech about insuf-
ficient sleep, a speaker
could show a cause–
effect relationship where
the cause is not getting
enough sleep, and the
effects are increased
mistakes, irritability, and
illness.

Central Idea: If you are denied a loan for a new car or house, it could be because you have been incorrectly branded as a poor credit risk by credit-rating companies.

Main Points:

(Effect)   I. Many people are barred from getting loans for a new car or house without ever knowing the reason.

(Cause)   II. The credit-rating companies that keep computerized files on 90 percent of Americans frequently make mistakes without the consumer ever knowing.

In this case, putting the effect first is a good strategy because it makes the listeners receptive to the rest of the speech—they are curious to know what caused the situation.

Problem–Solution Pattern

A much-used device for persuasive speeches is the **problem–solution pattern**, which divides a speech into two main sections: a problem and its solution. Here is an example:

Specific Purpose: To persuade my audience to support "pet therapy" for lonely older adults in nursing homes

Central Idea: Contact with a pet can decrease the loneliness and improve the physical and emotional health of older adults in nursing homes.

Main Points:

(Problem)   I. Many older adults in nursing homes are lonely and depressed—emotional states that harm their physical health.

(Solution)   II. Researchers have discovered that contact with a pet improves the older adult's physical and emotional health.

This pattern has the advantage of simplicity. You convince the listeners that a particular problem exists, and then you tell them how it can be solved. See Figure 6 for another example.

Topical Pattern

In the **topical pattern**, you divide your central idea into components or categories, using logic and common sense as your guides.

problem–solution pattern
an arrangement of material that explores a problem and then offers a solution.

topical pattern
a division of a topic into components, types, or reasons.

Figure 6
Problem–Solution Pattern

A speech on how to feel good mentally and physically could discuss a problem (depression and stress) and offer a solution (exercise).

Ingram Publishing/Getty Images

Thus, a speech on the symphonic orchestra could be divided into three sections: string instruments, wind instruments, and percussion instruments. A speech on job interviews could be divided into three types of interviews: personal, group, and online. See Figure 7 for another example.

Here is a portion of an outline that illustrates the topical pattern:

Specific Purpose: To inform my audience of the two kinds of sleep that all people experience

Central Idea: The two kinds of sleep that all people experience at alternating times during the night are NREM (non-rapid-eye-movement) sleep and REM (rapid-eye-movement) sleep.

Main Points: I. NREM (non-rapid-eye-movement) sleep is the period in which a person does very little dreaming.

II. REM (rapid-eye-movement) sleep is the period in which a person usually dreams.

Figure 7
Topical Pattern

A speech on typefaces could be divided into three major styles. Serif letters have small embellishments, such as lines projecting from the main stroke of a letter, while sans-serif letters have no embellishments. Script letters simulate fancy handwriting.

A variation of the topical pattern is sometimes called the **statement-of-reasons pattern**. The speaker subdivides an idea by showing reasons for it, as in the following example:

Specific Purpose:	To persuade my listeners that telephone companies should use alternatives to cellular phone towers
Central Idea:	Telephone companies should be required to place their cellular antennas on buildings and trees rather than on freestanding towers.

Main Points:

(First Reason)	I. Cellular phone towers are huge and ugly.
(Second Reason)	II. Cellular telephone antennas work as effectively on church steeples, tall trees, and high buildings as they do on freestanding towers.
(Third Reason)	III. Steeples, trees, and buildings are available for use because many churches, landowners, and businesses desire the fees that telephone companies pay for antenna placement.

Note of caution: Some students make the mistake of thinking that the topical pattern is a formless bag into which anything can be dumped. Though you have a great deal of liberty to organize your points in whatever order you choose, you still must apply logic—for example, by arranging your points from least important to most important, or separating your material into three major subdivisions.

statement-of-reasons pattern
a variation of the topical pattern in which a speaker gives reasons for an idea.

Selecting Support Materials

In the preceding sections, we concentrated on main points, but main points by themselves are not enough for the body of a speech. You also need support materials—such as examples, narratives, testimony, and statistics—to develop and amplify your main points. As discussed in the chapter on supporting your ideas and avoiding plagiarism, support materials help your audience understand and remember main points.

To see how support materials can be developed for main points, let's take a look at an outline of the body of a speech by student speaker Chris Wolffram, who uses the statement-of-reasons pattern to explain why we should support raising the minimum driving age to 20.[7] The introduction and the conclusion for this speech are printed in the chapter on introductions and conclusions.

Should teenagers be allowed to drive?

Dmitry Kalinovsky/123RF

Take Teenagers Off the Road

COMMENTARY	SPEECH

SPEECH

General Purpose: To persuade

Specific Purpose: To persuade my audience to support a raise in driving age from 16 to 20 years old

Central Idea: Teenagers are the age group with the highest vehicular accident rate. We should raise the driving age to 20 to reduce the rate of vehicular accidents and fatalities for young drivers.

BODY

I. Teenagers are evaluated as risky on the road, both from medical and economic perspectives.

     A. Research shows that the human brain doesn't fully develop until a person's mid-twenties.

> The author appeals to strong sources, including researchers and medical centers.

         1. This finding was reported by Dr. Jesús Pujol and a team of researchers in 1993.

         2. The University of Rochester Medical Center (n.d.) explains that while adults think with their pre-frontal cortex, which governs rational thought, teenagers think with their amygdala, which is the emotional center of the brain.

     B. Rental and insurance companies view teenagers as a higher risk on the road.

         1. Many of us have experienced difficulty trying to rent a car under the age of 25, because rental companies view younger drivers as a risk, regardless of whether they are licensed.

         2. According to the Rocky Mountain Insurance Information Association (n.d.), insurance companies frequently charge higher rates for younger drivers; they note that "The highest insurance rates are paid by any male driver under the age of 25" (para. 10).

(*Transition:* Because teenagers' brains aren't fully developed, they are more susceptible to distractions behind the wheel.)

II. Teenagers face a number of distractions as they drive, which often lead to accidents and even death.

     A. How many of us in this room have been distracted while driving, or felt pressured to check our phones while on the road?

> The speaker uses a rhetorical question to connect the content with the audience.

     B. According to the AAA Foundation for Traffic Safety (2017), the most common distractions that result in an accident by a teenager include interacting with one or more passengers (15%); using a cell phone (12%); looking at something in the vehicle (10%); looking at something outside the vehicle (9%); singing/moving to music (8%); grooming (6%); and reaching for an object (6%).

C. Because teenagers are even more susceptible to these distractions than adults, we should raise the driving age to 20 to keep teenagers off the road.

(*Transition:* Additionally, teenagers are susceptible to drunk driving, which can be exceptionally deadly.)

III. Drunk driving claims a high number of teenage lives.
   A. People of all ages are at increased risk of injury or death when driving drunk.
      1. In total, over 10,000 people die each year due to drunk driving accidents (National Highway Traffic Safety Administration, n.d.).
      2. When someone is driving with a blood alcohol content over .08, the legal limit in every U.S. state, they will experience a decreased ability to concentrate, short-term memory loss, difficulty controlling speed, reduced ability to process information (such as turn signal detection), and impaired perception (National Highway Traffic Safety Administration, n.d.).
   B. For teens, the peer pressure to drink and drive combined with poor and inexperienced decision making lead to a very dangerous situation.
      1. According to the Centers for Disease Control and Prevention (CDC) (2012), "Young drivers (ages 16–20) are 17 times more likely to die in a crash when they have a blood alcohol concentration of .08% than when they have not been drinking" (para. 3).
      2. Additionally, one in five teen drivers who were involved in a crash resulting in a fatality in 2010 had some alcohol in their system (CDC, 2012).

> The speaker uses statistics to support his point.

REFERENCES

AAA. (2015, March 25). *Distraction and teen crashes: Worse than we thought*. https://newsr oom.aaa.com/2015/03/distraction-teen-crashes-even-worse-thought/

AAA Foundation for Traffic Safety. (2017). *Rates of motor vehicle crashes, injuries and deaths in relation to driver age, United States, 2014–2015*. https://aaafoundation.org/rates-motor-vehicle-crashes-injuries-deaths-relation-driver-age-united-states-2014-2015/

Centers for Disease Control and Prevention. (2012). *Teen drinking and driving: A dangerous mix*. https://www.cdc.gov/vitalsigns/teendrinkinganddriving/index.html

Halsey III, A. (2016, October 12). Car crashes remain leading cause of death for teens, but fatalities drop by almost half in a decade. *The Washington Post*. https://www.washingtonpost.com/local/trafficandcommuting/car-crashes-remain-leading-cause-of-death-for-teens-but-fatalities-drop-by-almost-half-in-a-decade/2016/10/11/9d190a82-8fb3-11e6-9c85-ac42097b8cc0_story.html

Pujol, J., Vendrell, P., Junqué, C., Martí-Vilalta, J. L., & Capdevila, A. (1993). When does human brain development end? Evidence of corpus callosum growth up to adulthood. *Annals of Neurology, 34*(1), 71–75. https://doi.org/10.1002/ana.410340113

Rocky Mountain Insurance Information Association. (n.d.). *Teens shopping for auto insurance*. http://www.rmiia.org/auto/teens/Buying_Auto_Insurance.asp

United States Department of Transportation, National Highway Traffic Safety Administration. (n.d.). *Drunk driving*. https://www.nhtsa.gov/risky-driving/drunk-driving

University of Rochester Medical Center. (n.d.). *Understanding the teen brain*. https://www.urmc.rochester.edu/encyclopedia/content.aspx?ContentTypeID=1&ContentID=3051

If possible, distribute your supporting materials evenly. In other words, don't put all your support under point I and leave nothing to bolster point II. This does not mean, however, that you should mechanically place the same number of supporting points under every main point. You have to consider *quality* as well as *quantity*. A single powerful anecdote may be all that is required to illustrate one point, whereas five minor supports may be needed for another point.

When you are trying to decide how many supporting points to place underneath a main point, use this rule of thumb: have enough supporting points to adequately explain or bolster the main point, but not so many that you become tedious and repetitious.

Supplying Transitions

transition
an expression that links ideas and shows the relationship between them.

Words, phrases, or sentences that show logical connections between ideas or thoughts are called **transitions**. They help the listeners stay with you as you move from one part of your speech to the next. To get an idea of how transitions work, take a look at the following two paragraphs. The first has no transitions.

Poor: Olive oil is used extensively in Mediterranean cooking. It never became popular in Latin America. Olive trees can grow in Mexico and coastal regions of South America. The colonial rulers in Spain did not want anyone competing against Spain's farmers. They banned the production of olive oil in Latin America. The oil had to be imported. It was very expensive.

Now let's add transitions (shown in bold print):

Better: Olive oil is used extensively in Mediterranean cooking. **However,** it never became popular in Latin America. Olive trees can grow in Mexico and coastal regions of South America, **but** the colonial rulers in Spain did not want anyone competing against Spain's farmers, **so** they banned the production of olive oil in Latin America. The oil had to be imported **and therefore** was very expensive.

The transitions make the second paragraph superior because they illustrate the connection from one point to the next.

In a speech, transitions clarify the relationship between your ideas, thereby making them easy to comprehend. They serve as signals to help the listeners follow your train of thought. Here is a sampling of the many transitional words or phrases in the English language:

- To signal addition: *and, also, furthermore, moreover, in addition*
- To signal time: *soon, then, later, afterward, meanwhile*
- To signal contrast: *however, but, yet, nevertheless, instead, meanwhile, although*
- To signal examples: *for example, to illustrate, for instance*
- To signal conclusions: *in summary, therefore, consequently, as a result*
- To signal concession: *although it is true that, of course, granted*

In public speaking, special types of transitions can be employed to help your listener follow your remarks. Let us look at four of them: bridges, internal summaries, signposts, and spotlights.

Bridges

In crossing a bridge, a person goes from one piece of land to another. In a speech, the speaker can build **bridges** to explain to listeners what they are leaving behind, and where they are about to go.

bridge
a transitional device that links what went before with the next part of a speech.

Imagine that you had the following as your first main point in a speech on workplace violence:

I. Violence in the workplace has increased in recent years.

You give examples and statistics to back up this point, and now you are ready for your second main point:

II. Workplace violence can be reduced if managers and employees are trained in conflict resolution.

How can you go from point I to point II? You could simply finish with point I and begin point II, but that would be too abrupt. It would fail to give the listeners time to change mental gears. Use a bridge to smoothly refer back to the first main point at the same time you are pointing forward to the second:

> Although workplace violence has increased dramatically, the situation is not hopeless. There is a way to reduce the number of incidents—a way that has proven successful in many companies throughout the world.

This is a successful bridge because it smoothly and gracefully takes your listeners from point I to point II. It also stimulates their curiosity about the next part of the speech.

Internal Summaries

At the end of a baseball game, announcers always give a summary of the game. But during the game itself, they occasionally give a summary of what has taken place up to the present moment ("We're in the middle of the fifth inning; Detroit is leading Milwaukee 4 to 3 on a grand-slam homer by . . ."). Though this summary is designed primarily for the viewers who have tuned in late, it is also appreciated by the fans who have been watching the entire game because it gives them a feeling of security and confidence—a sense of knowing the "main facts." You can achieve the same effect in a speech. During

In a speech, a bridge takes listeners smoothly from one idea to another.

JohannesS/Shutterstock

the body of a speech, when you finish an important section, you may want to spend a few moments summarizing your ideas so that they are clear, understood, and retained by your audience as you move into your next point. This device, called an **internal summary**, is especially helpful if you have been discussing ideas that are complicated or abstract. An internal summary can be combined with a bridge to make an excellent transition, as follows:

> [*Internal summary*] By now I hope I've convinced you that all animal bites should be reported to a doctor or health official immediately because of the possibility of rabies. [*Bridge*] While you're waiting for an ambulance or for an examination by a doctor, there is one other important thing you should do.

internal summary
a concise review of material covered during the body of a speech.

Signposts

signpost
an explicit statement of the place that a speaker has reached.

Just as signposts on a road tell motorists their location, **signposts** in a speech tell listeners where they are or where they are headed. If you give a speech on how to treat a cold, you could say, "Here are three things you should do the next time you catch a cold." Then the audience would find it easy to follow your points if you said, "First, you should . . . Second, you should . . . Third, you should . . ." Using these signposts is much more effective than linking your points by saying, "Also . . ." or "Another point is . . ."

Spotlights

spotlight
a device that alerts listeners to important points.

Spotlights are transitional devices that alert the listeners that something important will soon appear. Here are some examples:

- Now we come to the most important thing I have to tell you.
- What I'm going to explain now will help you understand the rest of the speech.
- If you take with you only one idea from this speech . . .

Spotlights can build anticipation: "And now I come to an idea that can mean extra money in your pocket . . ."; "If you want to feel healthier and happier, listen to the advice of Dr. Julia Brunswick . . ."

When you choose transitional devices, remember that your listeners are totally unfamiliar with your speech, so try to put yourself in their shoes at each juncture. Ask yourself, "How can I lead the listener from one point to another in a way that is logical and smooth?"

Simplifying the Process

Organizing bits and pieces of material into a coherent, logical speech can be a difficult task, but it can be simplified if you use the following method:

1. **Survey all your material.** Bring together and examine your personal observations, interview notes, research notes, and visual aids.

2. **Choose an organizational method.** Three options are recommended:

   - **Computer entries.** Most word processing programs permit split screens, so that you can have notes in one window and an outline in another, making it easy to look over your notes and transform them into items for your outline.

   - **Sticky notes.** This method uses file folders of different colors, with a different-colored folder for each major part of the speech. Sticky notes are placed inside the folders so they can be seen in order at a glance when the folder is opened.

- **Index cards.** This method is similar to the sticky notes, except that index cards are used. The cards can be kept together by a rubber band or stored in a file folder.

All three options give you flexibility. You can easily move items around, add extra material, and delete unimportant points. Items can be spread out in full view—computer entries on a screen, sticky notes in file folders, and index cards on a table-top. This procedure lets you see the "big picture"—the overall architecture of your speech.

3. **Limit each note to just one idea.** To make the method work effectively, *you must use a separate computer entry, sticky note, or index card for each point.* This will make it easy to move items around.

4. **Experiment with different sequences.** Try several ways of arranging your material until you find a good sequence, a smooth flow that will be easy for the audience to follow. Business trainers Laurie Schloff and Marcia Yudkin use the card system, but their advice can be applied to computer entries and sticky notes as well:

> Sit in a comfortable chair and shuffle those ideas, asking yourself questions like, "What if I start with this, and move on to this, then this . . . ?" You're looking for a smooth, natural flow from each point to the next. Some sort of sequence will eventually emerge from this exercise. Don't get perturbed if you end up with extra cards that refuse to fit in; any leftover material might be perfect for the question-and-answer period after your speech, or for another presentation.[8]

5. **Transfer your material to a formal outline.** Once you have your information arranged, it's a good idea to transfer it to a formal outline as a way to gain control over it and to test its strength and continuity. Your instructor may have a required format for the outline. If not, I suggest you use the format shown in the chapter on outlining the speech.

Resources for Review and Skill Building

Summary

A well-organized speech is more understandable, credible, and memorable than a poorly organized one.

The body of the speech should be organized with two or three (occasionally four) main points that develop the central idea of the speech. There are four guidelines for main points: (1) Restrict each main point to a single idea. (2) Avoid announcements. (3) Customize points for each audience. (4) Use parallel language whenever possible.

Arrange the main points in a logical pattern, such as *chronological,* in which main points are placed in a time sequence; *spatial,* in which items are arranged in terms of physical space; *cause-effect,* in which causes and effects are juxtaposed; *problem-solution,* in which a problem is explained and a solution is offered; or *topical,* in which a central idea is divided into components.

Next, select support materials to back up the main points, and then supply transitions to help the listeners stay with you as you move from one part of your speech to the next. Common types of transitions are bridges, internal summaries, signposts, and spotlights.

To simplify the task of organizing material, use one of these three options: computer entries, sticky notes, or index cards. Put one item on each computer entry, sticky note, or index card so that you can easily add, delete, and rearrange your material.

Key Terms

bridge, *195*

cause–effect pattern, *188*

chronological pattern, *187*

internal summary, *196*

main points, *183*

parallel language, *186*

problem–solution pattern, *189*

signpost, *196*

spatial pattern, *188*

spotlight, *196*

statement-of-reasons pattern, *191*

topical pattern, *189*

transition, *194*

Review Questions

1. How many main points should you have in a speech?

2. How many ideas should be represented in each main point?

3. What is meant by the advice to "customize points for each audience"?

4. Which pattern of organization would be best suited for a speech on the solar system?

5. Which pattern of organization would be ideal for a speech on food contamination and how the problem can be corrected?

6. Which pattern of organization would be best suited for a speech on the three major reasons why businesses declare bankruptcy?

7. Why are transitions important in a speech?

8. In terms of speech organization, what is an internal summary?

9. Describe the transitional device called *bridge*.

10. Describe the transitional device called *spotlight*.

Building Critical-Thinking Skills

1. Which organizational pattern is used in the following outline?

   Specific Purpose: To inform my listeners how to sound-proof a room

   Central Idea: A room can be insulated so that sounds do not penetrate.

   Main Points:

   (Top)   I. The ceiling can be covered by acoustic tile and a tapestry to block sounds from above.

   (Middle)   II. The walls can be covered with ceiling-to-floor tapestries (and heavy, lined drapes for windows) to block noise from outside.

   (Bottom)   III. The floor can be covered with acoustic padding and wall-to-wall carpet to block sounds from below.

2. Which organizational pattern is used in the following outline?

   Specific Purpose: To tell my listeners how to revive a person who is in danger of drowning

   Central Idea: To revive a person who is in danger of drowning, you should follow three simple procedures.

   Main Points:

   (First)   I. Lay the victim on his or her back and tilt the head back so that the chin juts upward.

   (Second)   II. Give mouth-to-mouth resuscitation until the victim breathes regularly again.

   (Third)   III. Place the victim on his or her stomach with the head facing sideways.

3. Most public speaking experts recommend that you use complete sentences to create your central idea and main points. Why do you think this advice is given?

4. Which pattern would a speaker probably choose for a speech on how society's obsession with thinness has led to unhealthy weight-loss methods and eating disorders?

5. In a speech, transitions must be more prominent than they are in a book. Why?

Building Teamwork Skills

1. Working in a group, examine the following scrambled statements and decide which is the central idea and which are the main points. (One item below is a central idea and the other two are main points to develop the central idea.) Discuss what kinds of support materials would be needed under each main point.
   a. Many U.S. companies that have instituted the 30-hour workweek report higher job satisfaction and performance with no loss of profits.
   b. A 6-hour day/30-hour workweek should be the standard for full-time employees in the United States.
   c. All Western European countries have fewer working hours than the United States.

2. In a group, discuss which organizational pattern would be most effective for each of the following speech topics:
   a. Why most fatal car accidents occur
   b. Three types of working dogs
   c. How to gift wrap a present
   d. Stalking—and what can be done to stop it
   e. A giant redwood tree

Examining Your Ethics

Answer: A. It is okay to change the pattern of organization while you are still creating your speech. B is unethical because failing to report findings in your own words is a form of plagiarism; and C is a bad strategy.

End Notes

1. Gael García Bernal, telephone interview, January 9, 2015.

2. Wesley J. Smith, attorney, Los Angeles, e-mail interview, September 10, 2007.

3. Hamilton Gregory, Experiment that replicates numerous psychologists' studies that reach the same conclusion.

4. Miriam J. Metzger, Andrew J. Flanagin, Keren Eyal, Daisy R. Lemus, and Robert M. McCann (all from University of California, Santa Barbara), "Credibility for the 21st Century: Integrating Perspectives on Source, Message, and Media Credibility in the Contemporary Media Environment," *Communication Yearbook,* 27 (Mahwah, NJ: Erlbaum, 2003), p. 302.

5. "An Intolerable Fraud" [Editorial], *The New York Times,* www.nytimes.com (accessed November 25, 2015).

6. Ariana Eunjung Cha, "Cancer Charities Scam," *The Washington Post,* www.washingtonpost.com (accessed January 7, 2016).

7. Jane E. Brody, "Health 'Facts' You Only Thought You Knew," *The New York Times,* www.nytimes.com (accessed November 25, 2015); John Wendle, "The Things We Put in Our Ears May or May Not Hurt Us," Columbia News Services, jscms.jrn.columbia.edu (accessed November 25, 2015); Laura Lee, *100 Most Dangerous Things in Everyday Life and What You Can Do about Them* (Sydney: Murdoch Books, 2004), p. 50; "Giants Linebacker Injures His Ear," *The New York Times,* www.nytimes.com (accessed November 25, 2015); "February Farewells," "The Lugubrious Log," http://deathtodeath.blogspot.com (accessed November 25, 2015).

8. Laurie Schloff and Marcia Yudkin, *Smart Speaking* (Boston: Podium Publishing, 2011), p. 111.

CHAPTER 1

Introductions and Conclusions

OBJECTIVES

After studying this chapter, you should be able to

1. Formulate effective attention material for the introductions of your speeches.
2. Formulate effective orienting material for the introductions of your speeches.
3. Create effective conclusions for your speeches.

COURTROOM BATTLES ARE LIKE DRAMAS, with three distinct parts:

- Beginning (opening statement)
- Middle (examination of evidence)
- End (closing argument)

While all three parts are important, most attorneys say that their opening and closing statements to the jury usually determine whether they win or lose a case.[1] "When you first talk to the jury, you've got to make a favorable impression and win their empathy immediately," says Michelle Roberts, a defense attorney in Washington, DC. Later, near the end of the trial, "your closing argument must be powerful and persuasive."[2]

In speeches outside the courtroom, the stakes are rarely so high: no one will be forced to go to prison or pay a million dollars in damages if the introduction and the conclusion are weak. Nevertheless, these two parts have great importance. If

you don't have a lively introduction, you can lose your audience. "People have remote controls in their heads today," says business executive Myrna Marofsky. "If you don't catch their interest, they just click you off."[3] And a conclusion that is weak or clumsy can mar the effectiveness of what otherwise might have been a good speech.

Attorney Erlinda Ocampo Johnson argues a case in a courtroom in Santa Fe, New Mexico. For most attorneys, their opening and closing remarks to a jury often determine whether they win or lose a case.

Introductions

The introduction to your speech has two main goals: first, to capture and hold your audience's attention and interest, and second, to prepare your audience intellectually and psychologically for the body of the speech. Let's examine each goal in greater detail.

Gain Attention and Interest

If you were sitting in an audience, would you want to listen to a speech that begins with "I'd like to talk to you today about household appliances"?

The subject sounds dull. You might say to yourself, "Who cares?" and let your attention drift to something else.

Now imagine that you were sitting in the audience when student speaker Giancarlo Bruno began a speech with these words:

> Did you know that clothes dryers cause 15,000 home fires in the United States every year? Often a fire results from the buildup of lint that blocks the flow of air. You can avoid the problem by cleaning the lint trap every time you use your dryer.[4]

Bruno used alarming statistics as an attention-grabber, immediately engaging his audience in a speech on appliances as fire hazards.

An attention-grabber is needed because of an unfortunate fact: audiences don't automatically give every speaker their full, respectful attention. As you begin a speech, you may find that some listeners are engaged in whispered conversations with their neighbors. Or, you may notice that your listeners are are looking at you but their minds are far away, floating in a daydream or enmeshed in a personal problem. So, your task is clear: grab their attention when you start talking.

But grabbing their attention is not enough. Your introduction must also make listeners want to hear the rest of your speech. Some speakers grab attention by telling a joke, but a joke does not create interest in the rest of the speech. Bruno's provocative opener made the typical listener want to learn more about protecting a home from fire.

attention material
the part of the introduction designed to capture audience interest.

"Grabbers," or **attention material**, should always be the first part of your introduction. Let's examine some of the more common varieties. Sometimes two or more types of attention material can be combined to create a more compelling introduction.

Relate a Story

Telling a story is one of the most effective ways to begin a speech because people love to listen to narrative accounts. Student speaker Tisha Clements began a speech with this story:

> A few years ago, my husband and I were sitting at a concert. About 45 minutes into the concert, I noticed my husband sweating profusely and he couldn't sit still. We decided to go to the Emergency Room to get him checked out. While sitting in the waiting room, he said he was hurting all over and his heart felt as if it were going to jump out of his chest. When he finally was examined by the doctors and nurses, they couldn't find anything, but they ran several tests. A few days later, the doctor called and diagnosed him with anxiety disorder.

Clements spent the rest of her speech explaining the causes and treatments for anxiety attacks. As Clements demonstrates, a story should always provide an easy and natural entry into the rest of the speech.

As an alternative to a true story, you can use a **hypothetical illustration**, as demonstrated by a student speaker who created the following fictional account:

> Imagine that tomorrow you become a victim of identity theft. A criminal steals your Social Security number, your bank account and credit-card numbers, and all of your personal information, such as your full name, date of birth, names of parents, schools attended, medical records, and so on. The criminal withdraws all the money you have in your bank accounts and runs up big debts on your credit card. Then he goes one step further. He commits crimes while using your name. Now you are faced with the enormous challenge of clearing your name and correcting erroneous information. This will drain you of money, time, and energy. And it will make you angry, scared, and depressed.

In the rest of the speech, the student explained how members of the audience could take steps to protect themselves from identity theft. Note that while hypothetical illustrations can be effective attention-grabbers, as an ethical speaker you must ensure that your introductory stories are based in reality and not fallacies (instances of faulty reasoning based on poor logic). Different types of fallacies are discussed in chapter 17.

hypothetical illustration
an imaginary scenario that illuminates a point.

Ask a Question

Asking a question can be an effective way to intrigue your listeners and encourage them to think about your subject matter as you discuss it. There are two kinds of questions that you can use as attention material: the rhetorical question and the overt-response question.

With a **rhetorical question**, you don't want or expect the listeners to answer overtly by raising their hands or responding out loud. Instead, you want to trigger their curiosity by challenging them to think about your topic. For example, you could open your speech with the following question:

> With powerful radio signals being beamed into outer space at this very moment, is there any realistic chance that we human beings will establish radio contact with other civilizations in the universe during our lifetime?

Not only does such a question catch the attention of the listeners, but it also makes them want to hear more. It entices them to listen to your speech for the answer to the question.

rhetorical question
a question asked solely to stimulate interest and not to elicit a reply.

With an **overt-response question**, you want the audience members to reply by raising their hands or answering out loud. For example, student speaker Meredith Bollinger began a speech by asking the following question:

> There is only one Olympic sport in which men and women compete against each other head to head in direct confrontation. Which sport am I talking about?

overt-response question
a question asked to elicit a direct, immediate reply.

One listener guessed water polo—wrong. Another guessed softball—wrong. Another guessed synchronized swimming—wrong. Finally, Bollinger gave the correct answer: equestrian (horseback) competition. See Figure 1 for another example of an overt-response question.

Here are some pitfalls to avoid when asking questions.

Avoid questions that can fizzle. One student began a speech by asking, "How many of you are familiar with Snapchat?" Everyone raised a hand, so the speaker looked foolish as he continued, "Today I'd like to inform you about what Snapchat is." Before you choose a question, imagine the answers you might get from the audience. Could they cause embarrassment or awkwardness?

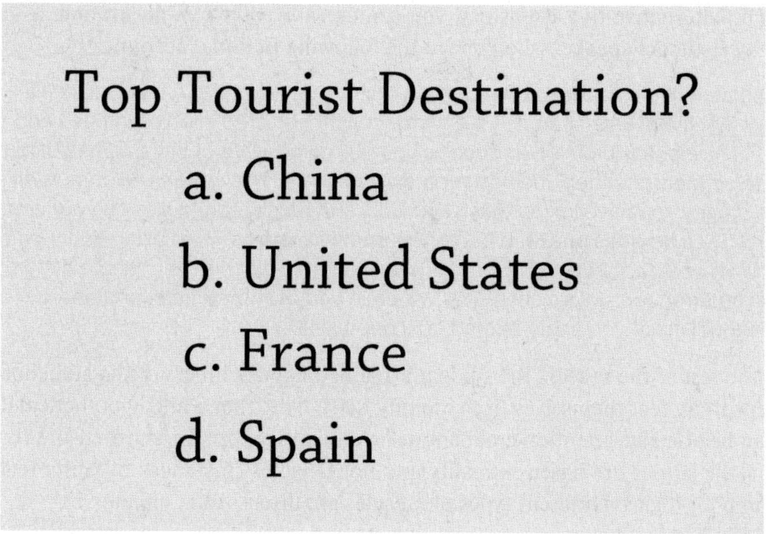

Figure 1
The overt-response
question on this
PowerPoint slide grabbed
the audience's atten-
tion before the speaker
revealed that the world's
most visited country is
France, according to
the UN World Tourism
Organization.

© Hamilton Gregory

Top Tourist Destination?
a. China
b. United States
c. France
d. Spain

Figure 1
The overt-response question on this PowerPoint slide grabbed the audience's attention before the speaker revealed that the world's most visited country is France, according to the UN World Tourism Organization.

© Hamilton Gregory

When you ask questions, don't drag out the suspense.   If listeners are forced to guess and guess until the right answer is found, they may become exasperated, wishing that the speaker would get to the point.

Never ask embarrassing or personal questions.   Avoid questions like, "How many of you have ever tried cocaine?" or "How many of you use an underarm deodorant every day?" An audience would rightfully resent such questions as intrusions into their private lives.

Never divide your audience into opposing camps by asking "loaded" questions.   An example of a loaded question is, "How many of you are smart enough to realize that capital punishment is an absolute necessity in a society based on law and order?" By phrasing your question in this way, you insult those who disagree with you.

When asking overt-response questions, don't expect universal participation.   With some overt-response questions, you can try to get every member of the audience to participate, but this can be very risky, especially if you poll the audience in this way: "How many of you favor the death penalty? Raise your hands. Okay, now, how many of you are opposed to the death penalty? Okay, thanks. How many of you are undecided or unsure?" What if 3 people raised their hands for the first question, 5 for the second question, 10 for the third—but the remaining 67 people never raised their hands? This is a common problem, and it results in major embarrassment for the speaker. Sometimes audiences are in a passive or even grumpy mood; this is especially true with "captive" audiences—that is, audiences that are required (at work or at school) to listen to a speech. In such a case, refrain from asking questions that require the participation of the entire audience.

Make sure the audience understands whether you are asking a rhetorical question or an overt-response question.   If you ask, "How long will Americans continue to tolerate shoddy products?," the audience knows you are not expecting someone to answer "Five years." It is clearly a rhetorical question. But suppose you ask, "How many of you have ever gone swimming in the ocean?" The listeners may be confused about whether you want them to raise their hands. Make it clear. If you want a show of hands, say so at the beginning: "I'd like to see a show of hands, please. How many of you have ever gone swimming in the ocean?" Alerting

them in advance not only helps them know what you want but also makes them pay special attention to the question, since they know that you are expecting them to respond.

Make a Provocative Statement

An opening remark that shocks, surprises, or intrigues your listeners can certainly grab attention. (Just make sure the statement is not one that would offend or alienate the audience.) Student speaker Vanessa Sullivan began a speech on human cloning with this statement:

> I have seen a human clone with my own eyes. And so have you.

Then she explained:

> Richard Lewontin, professor of biology at Harvard University, says that about 30 human genetic clones appear every day in the United States. You and I know them as identical twins. Dr. Lewontin says that "identical twins are genetically more identical than a cloned organism is to its donor."[5]

Sullivan went on to argue that despite important ethical problems, cloning is not as far from human experience as many people think.

Cite a Quotation

A quotation can provide a lively beginning for a speech. In a speech on showing respect, student speaker Blake Painter began with this opening statement:

> The American poet Maya Angelou once said, "If you have only one smile in you, give it to the people you love. Don't be surly at home, then go out in the street and start grinning 'Good morning' at total strangers."

Quotations usually work best when they are short. Don't use a quotation that is so long that the listeners lose track of where the quotation ends and your remarks begin. The best way to indicate that you have finished quoting is to pause at the end of the quotation. The pause acts as an oral punctuation device, signaling the end of one thought and the beginning of another.

Arouse Curiosity

An effective attention-getter is one that piques the curiosity of the audience. Brenda Johnson, a chef, began a speech with the following statement:

> I am addicted to a drug. I have been addicted to it for many years now. I feel like I need it to make it through the day. If I don't get this drug, my head aches. I'm nervous, irritable, and I begin to tremble. It's true—I am addicted.

Having aroused the curiosity of her listeners, Johnson continued:

> I am addicted to caffeine. Most people don't realize that caffeine is a drug—and that it is very addictive. It is present not only in coffee and tea and soft drinks but also in many legal drugs such as weight-control pills and pain relievers.

Johnson spent the rest of the speech giving details about caffeine and how listeners could reduce their intake.

Provide a Visual Aid or Demonstration

Any of the visual aids we discussed in the chapter on presentation aids could be used to introduce a speech, but you must be sure that while the aids get the audience's attention, they also are relevant to the main points of your speech. One student showed

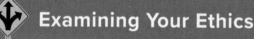

Examining Your Ethics

Bert is preparing a classroom speech about an urban street artist who is famous for his graffiti. To grab the audience's attention, he is thinking about using a shocking opener—a desecrated cross, which Bert thinks is a perfect example of the artist's innovative technique. Should Bert show the image?

A. No, he should choose an image that would be unlikely to offend the audience.

B. He should show the image without explanation and allow audience members to form their own opinions about the artist's work.

C. He should show the image, but warn listeners that it might be offensive to some people, and ask them to try to stay open-minded and focus on the artist's technique instead of the subject matter.

For the answer, see the last page of this chapter.

slides of sunbathers on a beach to begin a talk on sharks. Though there was a logical link (sometimes sunbathers who go into the water must worry about sharks), the connection was too weak to justify using these particular slides. In a case like this, it would be better to show a slide of a ferocious shark while describing a shark attack.

A demonstration can make an effective opener. Working with a friend, one student gave a demonstration of how to fight off an attacker, and then talked about martial arts. If you want to give a demonstration, get permission from your instructor beforehand. *One note of caution:* Never do anything that might upset the listeners. For example, for a speech on spiders, pulling tarantulas out of a box and letting them walk about would upset some people and make them unreceptive to your message.

Give an Incentive to Listen

At the beginning of a speech, many listeners have an attitude that can be summed up in these two questions: "What's in it for me?" and "Why should I pay attention to this speech?" Such people need to be given an incentive to listen to the entire speech. So, whenever possible, state explicitly why the listeners will benefit by hearing you out. It is not enough to simply say, "My speech is very important." You must *show* them how your topic relates to their personal lives and their own best interests. If, for example, you were giving a talk on cardiopulmonary resuscitation (CPR), you could say, "All of you may someday have a friend or loved one collapse from a heart attack right in front of your eyes. If you know CPR, you might be able to save that person's life." Now each person in the audience sees clearly that your speech is important to his or her personal life.

orienting material
the part of the introduction that gives listeners the information they need to fully understand and believe the rest of the speech.

Orient the Audience

Once you have won the interest of your listeners through your attention material, you should go into the second part of your introduction, the **orienting material**. Orienting material provides listeners with a clear sense of what your speech is about, and any other information that the audience may need in order to understand and absorb your ideas. The orienting material is a road map that makes it easy for the listeners to stay with you on the journey of your speech, and not get lost and confused.

The orienting material does more than prepare the listeners intellectually for your speech; it also prepares them psychologically. It reassures them that you are well-prepared, purposeful, and considerate of their needs and interests. It shows them you are someone they can trust.

The three most common ways to orient the audience are to (1) give background information, (2) establish your credibility, and (3) preview the body of the speech. They are listed in this order because number 3 is usually delivered last, as a prelude to the body.

If you tell listeners you will explain how to avoid food poisoning, they have an incentive to listen carefully.

Klaus Vedfelt/Getty images

Tips for Your Career

Use an "Icebreaker" to Start Off a Community Speech

Many speakers at business and professional meetings start off by saying something like this: "I'm glad to have a chance to speak to you today." They are giving an *icebreaker*—a polite little prologue to "break the ice" before getting into their speech.

In outline form, here is how an introduction with an icebreaker would look:

    i. Icebreaker

    ii. Attention Material

    iii. Orienting Material

When you give speeches in the community, an icebreaker is helpful because it eases your nervous tension and lets the audience get accustomed to your voice. You don't need an icebreaker for classroom speeches because your audience has already settled down and is ready to listen.

"Hello. How are you?" as an icebreaker sounds too breezy, and it leaves a question as to whether the speaker wants the audience to roar a response like "Fine, thank you!" It is much better to say, "I appreciate the opportunity to speak to you tonight." This icebreaker doesn't confuse the audience, and you can continue with your introduction easily from there.

In addition to expressing appreciation for the invitation to speak, you can include a thank-you to the person who introduced you, or a reference to the occasion (for example, "I'm delighted to take part in the celebration of Martin Luther King's birthday").

A note of caution: An icebreaker should be very brief—just a sentence or two. If you are too slow getting into the attention material of your introduction, you may cause some listeners to tune you out.

Do you need all three audience orientation options for every speech? For classroom speeches, follow your instructor's guidelines. For some career speeches, you may not need the first two. The best advice is to use an option if it will promote audience understanding and acceptance of your speech.

Give Background Information

Part of your orienting material can be devoted to giving background information—definitions, explanations, and so on—to help your listeners understand your speech. In a speech on the Boston-to-Washington megalopolis, Vandana Shastri used her orienting material to define the term:

> A megalopolis is a region made up of several cities and their suburbs that sprawl into each other. The biggest megalopolis in the United States is a densely populated, 500-mile-long corridor that starts in Boston and goes southward through Connecticut, New York City, northern New Jersey, Philadelphia, Wilmington (Delaware), Baltimore, and then ends in the Washington, DC, suburbs of northern Virginia.

Sometimes it helps the audience if you explain the boundaries of your speech. For example, suppose that you are giving a speech promoting the idea that returning to work and school will help save an economy struggling with the consequences of the Covid pandemic. If you are not careful, many people in your audience will reject your argument immediately by saying to themselves, "Return to work! In the middle of a deadly pandemic? Why should I, or anyone, risk health for the sake of an economy?" In your orienting material, you can head off such objections by saying, "In this speech, I will talk about ways we can keep the economy healthy during this time of Covid-19. I'm not talking about people risking their lives. Until a vaccine is developed, society should be seeking new ways to work and learn remotely." By showing the boundaries of your subject, you increase the chances that the audience will listen with open minds.

In a speech on taking good photos, revealing your experience as a semi-pro photographer enhances your credibility.

Borysevych.com/Shutterstock

credibility
audience perception of a speaker as believable, trustworthy, and competent.

Establish Your Credibility

No one expects you to be the world's authority on your subject, but you can increase your audience's chances of accepting your ideas if you establish your **credibility**—that is, give some credentials or reasons why you are qualified to speak on the subject. When student speaker Randy Stepp talked about how to escape a burning building, he enhanced his credibility by mentioning that he was a volunteer firefighter in a rural community and had fought many fires.

Some people shy away from giving their credentials or background because they think that doing so makes them seem boastful and arrogant. This concern is unfounded if you provide facts about yourself in a modest, tactful manner. In other words, if you are speaking on air pollution, say something like, "I'm a chemist and I've analyzed in my lab the content of the air that we breathe in this community" instead of "I'm a professional chemist, so I know more about air pollution than anybody else in this room."

For information that does not come from your personal experience, you could cite your sources in the orienting material. For example, one speaker said, "The information I am giving you today comes from a book by Eric Klinenberg titled *Climate Change and the Future of Cities.*"

Note: Mentioning your sources in the orienting material is just one of two options for citing sources. You can also reveal the sources throughout your speech as you give information from them. Before choosing an option, find out your instructor's preference.

In some speeches, you should tell the audience your connection to the topic—that is, why you are speaking on that particular subject. For example, you could say, "I am speaking on defective automobile tires because my sister was seriously hurt in an accident that was caused by faulty tires."

Confess any conflict of interest or bias. You might say, for example, "I urge you to use *Consumer Reports* for product evaluations because I think it's the most trustworthy source. However, I should tell you that I get paid for being one of their advisers."

preview
a preliminary look at the highlights of a speech.

Preview the Body of the Speech

Have you ever had trouble listening to a speech or lecture because the information seemed jumbled and disconnected and you couldn't grasp the significance of what was being said? The speaker can help avoid this problem by giving the listeners a **preview** of the body of the speech. A preview is like a map that gives you the lay of the land as you travel. Arrows placed on top of the map can help you stay on course and not get lost. Your instructor may have specific requirements for what you must put in your preview. Unless he or she advises you otherwise, I recommend that you include your central idea, your main points, or both.

1. **State the central idea.** Your audience can listen intelligently to your speech if you stress your central idea in the orienting material. For example, you could say, "Acid rain is killing all the trees on our highest peaks in the East. To prove this, I will provide evidence from leading scientists." Occasionally, in special situations, it is best to withhold divulging your central idea until late in the speech. (See the chapter on persuasive strategies for more on this technique.)

   In a speech on losing weight, Mary E. McNair, a nurse, stated her central idea in this way:

   Fad and crash diets can actually backfire, causing a person to gain more weight in the long run than was originally lost.

This helped the audience members listen with "the right set of ears." They knew to pay attention to what she had to say about the counterproductive effects of fad and crash diets.

2. **State the main points.** In most speeches, listeners appreciate being given a brief preview of your main points. For example, Barbara LeBlanc outlined her main points for her speech on alternative energy:

> I believe that passive-solar heating should be used in every home for two reasons: First, it's easy to adapt your house to passive solar. Second, the energy from passive solar is absolutely free. Let me explain what I'm talking about.

By stating the main points, LeBlanc not only helped the audience members listen intelligently, but also gave them an incentive to listen by mentioning the possibility of saving money.

Giving a preview by stating the central idea and the main points reassures the listeners that you are not going to ramble. In other words, you give the audience a message that says, loud and clear, "I'm well-prepared. I know exactly what I'm going to say. I'm not going to waste your time."

Guidelines for Introductions

Here are some points to keep in mind for introductions.

1. **Don't prepare your introduction first.** When you prepare a speech, it's usually best to complete the body of the speech and *then* work on your introduction. Once you have developed your main points, you are in a stronger position to decide how to introduce them.

2. **Make your introduction simple and easy to follow, but avoid making it too brief.** Your audience needs time to get into the groove of your speech. If the introduction is too short, it may go by too fast for the listeners to absorb. That is why effective joke tellers stretch out their introduction to give the listeners time to get "into" the joke.

   If the idea of stretching out an introduction sounds wrong to you, it is probably because you have been taught in English classes to write concisely. While it is an error in a writing class to stretch out essays, it can be valuable to do so with a speech's introduction that might otherwise be too abrupt for an audience.

   A note of caution: Don't let this tip cause you to go to the opposite extreme—being tedious and long-winded. Be brief, but not too brief. If you are unsure about whether you have achieved a happy medium, deliver your speech to relatives or friends and then ask them if they thought your introduction was too long or too short.

3. **Make sure that your introduction has a direct and obvious tie-in with the body of the speech.** A common mistake is for speakers to give an introduction that has a weak or dubious link with the rest of the speech. This kind of introduction can be annoying and confusing to the listeners.

4. **Never apologize.** You weaken your speech and hurt your credibility if you say things like "I didn't have much time to prepare," "This may be too technical for you," or "I'm sorry I didn't draw a diagram."

Like a map on a smartphone, a preview in a speech gives a panoramic view of the subject and provides directions to the goal.

Alexey Boldin/Shutterstock

Conclusions

When movies are made, the producers spend a lot of time and energy on getting a "perfect" ending because they know that if the ending is unsatisfying, the viewers will tend to downgrade the film as a whole. As with the movies, the ending of a speech can either add to or subtract from the audience's opinion of the entire speech. It is worthwhile, therefore, to spend a lot of time working on your conclusion.

In your conclusion, you should do three important things: (1) signal the end of the speech to satisfy the audience's psychological need for a sense of completion, (2) summarize the key ideas of the speech, and (3) reinforce the central idea with a clincher. Let us discuss these points in greater detail.

Signal the End

Imagine that you are listening to your favorite song on your smartphone and letting your mind float freely with the music. Then suddenly, before the song is finished, the battery goes out. You missed only the last 10 seconds of the song, but you feel annoyed. Why? Because most people need to experience a sense of completion.

In listening to a speech, we have the same need for a sense of finality. We don't like an abrupt halt—we like to hear a conclusion that is psychologically satisfying.

To give listeners a satisfying finale, provide signals that the end is approaching. These signals can be verbal, nonverbal, or both.

Verbal signals.   You can openly announce that you are coming to your conclusion by saying, "So, in conclusion, I'd like to say . . . ," "Let me end by saying . . . ," or "Let me remind you of the three major points I've explained today."

Nonverbal signals.   Two nonverbal cues are subtle but important: (1) say your conclusion with a tone of dramatic finality and (2) subtly intensify your facial expression and gestures. These cues should come naturally to you, since you have seen numerous speakers use them in your lifetime. If you feel unsure of yourself, practice your conclusion in front of a mirror or, better yet, in front of a friend (who can give you feedback). You can also record your rehearsal on your smartphone or video camera and play it back to see whether you have the appropriate tone of finality in your voice.

Summarize Key Ideas

Because listening is often a difficult mental task, some people in the audience might get drowsy or inattentive toward the end of your speech. But when you signal that you are about to finish, listeners usually perk up. If they know they can rest soon, they are better able to stay alert for a few more minutes. Like runners near the finish line, they can bring forth an extra burst of energy.

This mental alertness of your listeners gives you a good opportunity to drive home your message one more time. One of the best ways to do this is to summarize your key ideas. There is a formula for giving a speech that has been around for over 100 years. Sometimes it is attributed to a spellbinding country preacher, sometimes to a savvy Irish politician. The true originator will probably never be known, but the formula is worth heeding:

Tell 'em what you're going to tell 'em.

Tell 'em.

Then tell 'em what you told 'em.

The first sentence refers to the introduction, the second to the body, and the third to a summary in the conclusion. The summary gives you a chance to restate the central idea, the main points, or both.

If you are like a lot of people, you may say, "Why do I need to repeat my message? Isn't this overkill?" Actually, the answer is no, because research shows that restating your main points increases the likelihood that the listeners will remember them.[6] Unlike in an essay or paper, your listeners can't go back and reread the important information they may have missed, so it's all the more important to drive your main points home in your speech.

A summary should be brief, as in this recap of the body of a speech about avoiding food poisoning:

> So remember the most important ways to avoid food poisoning at a restaurant: Always order the most popular items on the menu because they sell quickly and aren't sitting around in the fridge for days. If you are served an undercooked meat or egg product, send it back for further cooking and always ask for a new plate.

Listeners don't mind hearing this kind of information again; it helps them retain it.

Reinforce the Central Idea with a Clincher

In addition to providing a summary, close your speech with a **clincher** that reinforces the central idea—a finale that drives home the main theme of your entire speech.

Use a clincher that is memorable and leaves a lasting impression with the listener. You can find clinchers by using some of the techniques mentioned earlier in this chapter for the introduction (such as a rhetorical question or a visual aid), or by using some of the following techniques.

clincher
a final statement in a speech that drives home the key concept of the speech.

Cite a Quotation

A good quotation can dramatize and reinforce a speaker's central idea. After urging her audience always to buckle seat belts, one speaker closed her speech with the following:

> I would like to close with a quotation from Laura Valdez, an emergency medicine technician in California, who said, "I have driven my ambulance to hundreds of traffic accidents. I have found many people already dead, but I have yet to unbuckle the seat belt of a dead person."

Richard Kern closed his speech on why citizens should fight social ills rather than succumb to despair with a quotation:

> Let me leave you with the words of Eleanor Roosevelt: "It is better to light one candle than to curse the darkness."

Eye contact is important at the end of your speech, so if you use a quotation, practice it so that you can say it while looking at the audience, without using your notes.

Issue an Appeal or a Challenge

In a persuasive speech, you can end by making an appeal or issuing a challenge to the audience. If you are trying to persuade your listeners to donate blood, you can end by saying the following:

> Next week the bloodmobile will be on campus. I call upon each of you to spend a few minutes donating your blood so that others may live.

One speaker tried to convince her audience to make out a will, and in her conclusion she issued a challenge:

> The simple task of writing a will can protect your family and give you peace of mind. It is a sad fact that three out of four Americans will die without a will. Are you going to be one of them? I hope not. Why don't you write your will before you go to bed tonight?

Give an Illustration

An illustration is a popular way to reinforce the central idea of a speech. In a speech urging classmates to avoid Internet gambling, one student speaker concluded with a true story:

> In his entire life, college senior Mark Scott had never gambled until one night, when he got an e-mail that said, "Congratulations, Mark. You won $100." Scott was intrigued, and he clicked on the gambling site and began playing blackjack. After an hour, $175 of his money was gone. Three months later, he had run up a $9,000 gambling debt on his credit card.

Refer to the Introduction

Using the conclusion to hearken back to something said in the introduction is an effective way to wrap up your speech.

In a speech on pet therapy, student speaker Jake Harland used the photo in Figure 2 in his introduction and again in his conclusion. He began by saying, "This puppy was one of 15 homeless dogs brought into George Mason University Law School to see if students would like to play with them to relieve stress during final exams. At the end of my speech, I'll tell you what happened to this puppy." During the body of the speech, he explained that the law school wanted to show students that playing with a pet was a better way to reduce stress and depression than overeating or drinking. At the end of the speech, Harland showed the photo again and said, "The student in this picture, Julie Dewberry, and her classmates ended up keeping all 15 dogs for a week, and later—after

Figure 2
Stress Relief

Linda Davidson/The
Washington Post/Getty Images

exams—they reported that the dogs had helped them to relax and take breaks from studying. By the way, all of the dogs were adopted, some by students."

Guidelines for Conclusions

There are four pitfalls to avoid in conclusions.

1. **Don't drag out the ending.** Some speakers fail to prepare a conclusion in advance. When they reach what should be the end of their remarks, they cannot think of a graceful way to wrap things up, so they keep on talking. Other speakers signal the end of their speech (by saying something like "So, in closing, let me say . . ."), but then they drone on and on. This gives false hope to the listeners. When they see that the speaker is not keeping the promise, they feel deceived and become restless.

2. **Don't end weakly.** If you close with a statement such as "I guess that's about all I've got to say," and your voice is nonchalant and unenthusiastic, you encourage your listeners to downgrade your entire speech. End with confidence.

3. **Don't end apologetically.** There is no need to say, "That just about does it. I'm sorry I didn't have more time to prepare . . . ," or "That's it, folks. I guess I should have looked up more facts on . . ." Apologies make you look incompetent. Besides, some people may not have noticed anything wrong with your speech or your delivery; you may have done better than you realized, so why apologize?

4. **Never bring in new main points.** It is okay to use fresh material in your conclusion; in fact, it is a good idea to do so, as long as the material does not constitute a new main point. Let's say you have given your audience three well-explained techniques for losing weight. It would be a mistake to end by saying, "Oh, yes, and another technique is . . ." This would drag out your speech. On the other hand, it would be acceptable to end with a brief comment about the 10 pounds you lost because you used the techniques discussed in the body of the speech.

Sample Introduction and Conclusion

In the chapter on body of the speech, we looked at the body of a speech on raising the driving age. Now let's see how Chris Wolffram developed an introduction and a conclusion for his speech.

Take Teenagers Off the Road

COMMENTARY	SPEECH

	General Purpose:	To persuade
	Specific Purpose:	To persuade my audience to support a raise in driving age from 16 to 20 years old
	Central Idea:	Teenagers are the age group with the highest vehicular accident rate. We should raise the driving age to 20 to reduce the rate of vehicular accidents and fatalities for young drivers.

(continued)

INTRODUCTION

I. Attention Material

A. Do you know the leading cause of death for teenagers? It is not cancer, or heart disease, or domestic violence, or gun-related accidents.

B. Actually, the number one cause of for teenagers has long been vehicular accidents (Hasley III, 2016).

C. Further, according to the AAA Foundation for Traffic Safety (2017), 16- to 19-year-olds accounted for 2,162 crashes for every 100 million miles driven in 2014–2015, whereas 20- to 24-year-olds accounted for 572.

D. I know many in this room have kids, and while the number of teenage fatalities has declined in recent years (Hasley III, 2016), not a single parent should have to bury his or her child, especially for something so preventable as an accident in a car.

II. Orienting Material

A. To help solve this crisis, I propose that we raise the driving age to 20 years old.

B. Why raise the age to 20? First, we will consider the brain development of teenagers; second, we will discuss the various types of distractions a teen faces behind the wheel; and third, we will talk about the impact of drunk driving on teenagers.

CONCLUSION

I. Summary

A. As we wrap up, I want you to remember a few important points.

B. The leading cause for death among teenagers is motor vehicle accidents.

C. Because teenagers' brains are still early in their development, and because they are especially susceptible to distracted and drunk driving, we should raise the driving age to 20 years old.

II. Clincher

A. So, we can sit back and let thousands of our children die each year due to preventable vehicular accidents.

B. Or we can address this with urgency and be the voice for our children—and for those who no longer have a voice of their own.

The speaker opens with a question that is designed to capture the listeners' attention. He also uses some shocking statistics to draw in the audience.

To give listeners a clear road map of his speech, the speaker states his central idea and main points.

The body of the speech, which appears in the chapter on the body of the speech, uses the statement-of-reasons pattern.

The speaker gives a brief summary of the key information in the speech.

The speaker closes with a strong appeal to the listeners' emotions.

Resources for Review and Skill Building

Summary

Much of the success of a speech depends on how well the speaker handles the introduction and the conclusion. The introduction consists of two parts: attention material, which gains listeners' attention and interest, and orienting material, which gives the audience members the information they need to listen intelligently to the rest of the speech.

For attention material, you can use one or more of the following techniques: tell a story, ask a question, make a provocative statement, cite a quotation, arouse curiosity, provide a visual aid or demonstration, and provide the audience with an incentive to listen.

For orienting material, you have three options: give background information, such as definitions; establish your credibility on your topic; and preview the body of the speech (by stating the central idea, the main points, or both).

The introduction should have a direct and obvious tie-in with the body of the speech. Avoid apologies and a too-brief introduction.

The conclusion of your speech should signal the end, summarize your key ideas, and reinforce the central idea with a clincher. A clincher may be an appeal or a challenge, an illustration, a reference to the introduction, or any of the techniques mentioned for attention material (such as a rhetorical question).

Avoid conclusions that are weak, apologetic, or drawn-out. While fresh material may be used, never bring in new main points.

Key Terms

attention material, *202*

clincher, *211*

credibility, *208*

hypothetical illustration, *203*

orienting material, *206*

overt-response question, *203*

preview, *208*

rhetorical question, *203*

Review Questions

1. Why is it necessary to have attention material at the beginning of a speech?

2. What is a rhetorical question?

3. What is an overt-response question?

4. How can you give listeners an incentive to listen to a speech?

5. What is the purpose of the orienting material in the speech introduction?

6. What is credibility?

7. In what way does a preview of main points reassure the audience?

8. Why is it a mistake to end a speech abruptly?

9. Why should you restate your main points in the conclusion?

10. What is a clincher?

Building Critical-Thinking Skills

1. What advice would you give a speaker who says in the introduction, "This speech may be too technical for you"?

2. Create a rhetorical question concerning the destruction of the Central American rain forest.

3. If you are uncertain how much background information is needed by the audience, what is the best way to find out?

4. Although introductions and conclusions are both important, describe a situation where the introduction is more important than the conclusion. Then, describe a situation where the conclusion is more important.

Building Teamwork Skills

1. In a group, brainstorm possible attention-getters to intro-
    duce speeches on the following:

    a. World famine
    b. Burglar alarm systems
    c. Vacationing in Italy
    d. Overcoming fatigue
    e. Finding an honest car repair shop

2. Working in a group, discuss how listeners react when
    they hear speakers make these apologies:

    a. "I didn't have much time to prepare."
    b. "I'm not much of a speaker."
    c. "I know this is a boring topic."
    d. "I had wanted to show you some PowerPoint slides."
    e. "That last speech is a tough act to follow."
    f. "I hate public speaking."
    g. "I'm really nervous."

Examining Your Ethics

Answer: A. While grabbing attention is a good technique, the
speaker should choose a different image—one that does not
shock and disrespect any listener. Showing a desecrated cross
would put some listeners out of a receptive frame of mind.

End Notes

1. "Opening Statements, Burdens of Proof," National Parale-
    gal College, nationalparalegal.edu (accessed December 3,
    2015); Matthew J. Smith, Esq., "Preparing Your Closing
    Argument," Smith, Rolfes & Skavdahl Company, www
    .smithrolfes.com (accessed December 3, 2015).

2. Michelle Roberts, Washington, DC, attorney, telephone
    interview, May 19, 2000.

3. Myrna Marofsky, president, ProGroup, e-mail interview,
    September 22, 2008.

4. The student's material was derived from "Safety Tips from
    Portland Fire & Rescue's Prevention Division," www
    .portlandoregon.gov (accessed October 8, 2015).

5. Sullivan derived her material from R. C. Lewontin, "The
    Confusion over Cloning," *New York Review of Books*,
    www.nybooks.com (accessed December 7, 2015).

6. Ingemar Svantesson, *Learning Maps and Memory Skills*,
    3rd ed. (London: Kogan Page, 2004), p. 90.

Outlining the Speech

OBJECTIVES

After studying this chapter, you should be able to

1. Explain the importance of developing an outline for a speech.
2. Create a coherent outline for a speech.
3. Create effective speaking notes based on your outline.

IMAGINE HIRING A BUILDER to construct a two-story house like the one pictured here. When you move in, you discover that he forgot to create a staircase between the first floor and the second floor.

Such a blunder might be hard to imagine, but it actually happened in 1926 in Palm Beach, Florida. A homebuilder named Addison Mizner forgot to include a staircase in a home built for George S. Rasmussen. Mizner tried to rectify his mistake by placing stairs on the outside of the house, but this forced the Rasmussen family to put on raincoats when they needed to go upstairs or downstairs on rainy days.[1]

Mizner never would have made such a mistake had he created and adhered to a detailed architectural blueprint showing the exact placement and dimensions of all components of the house.

If you build a two-story house like this, how can you avoid Addison Mizner's mistake of failing to include a staircase?

karamysh/Shutterstock

In public speaking, the equivalent of a blueprint is an outline, which can be used to make sure that all parts are included and that they fit together harmoniously. Many speakers say that an outline helps them organize their thoughts into a logical sequence and see which points are irrelevant, improperly placed, or poorly developed. It also helps them stay on message and prevents them from rambling.[2]

Outlining is the culmination of the process we began describing many chapters ago—the process of gaining control of our subject matter. Up to this point, we have talked about formulating objectives and then organizing them in the body, introduction, and conclusion of your speech. Now we will discuss how to put all these elements together in outline form.

Guidelines for Outlining

Instead of using an outline, why not just write out the entire speech? For one thing, a word-for-word script would create a sea of material that might overwhelm you. Even worse, you might be tempted to read the script, a method that could put the audience to sleep.

An outline is better than a script because it shows the basic structure of your ideas in a streamlined form. It also helps you see the relationship between ideas.

In essence, outlining is a commonsense way of arranging information in a logical pattern. The Federal Bureau of Investigation's Crime Index, for example, can be broken down into two broad categories:

FBI Crime Index

I. Violent crimes
II. Property crimes

We could then break down each category into specific types of crimes:

I. Violent crimes

   A. Murder

   B. Rape

   C. Robbery

   D. Aggravated assault

II. Property crimes

   A. Burglary

   B. Larceny-theft

   C. Motor vehicle theft

   D. Arson

If we wanted to, we could divide items A, B, C, and D into subcategories. For example, we could break down murder into categories of weapons used, with one category for guns, one for knives, and so on.

To understand how an outline fits into the overall process of developing a speech, take a look at Figure 1. This flowchart shows your next three steps: First, create an outline; second, use the outline to prepare speaking notes; and third, use the speaking notes to deliver the speech. The first two steps will be covered in this chapter; the third step, delivering the speech, will be discussed in the chapter on delivering the speech. (For classroom speeches, your instructor may have different guidelines. You should, of course, follow his or her rules.)

Choose an Outline Format

The two most popular formats for outlines are the *topic outline* and the *complete-sentence outline*. Find out if your instructor prefers or requires one or the other. Some instructors and professional speakers recommend using both methods—the topic format in the early stages of preparation (when you are struggling to impose order on your material) and the complete-sentence format in the later stages (when you are refining and polishing your ideas).

Outline

Step 1 Create an Outline

This is a slice from a student's outline. An outline is the basic structure of a speaker's ideas in streamlined form. It is not a word-for-word script. A detailed outline (like this one) is used only for preparation. It is not taken to the lectern.

> I. Avoid choosing the wrong dog.
> A. Never buy on a whim.
> B. Research to find the right breed for you.
> C. Get to know a dog before adoption.

Speaker's notes

Step 2 Prepare Speaking Notes

The speaker prepares brief notes—derived from his outline—to be used in practicing and delivering the speech. These notes contain only a few key words—just enough to jog his memory. By using brief notes instead of his outline, he avoids the mistake of reading a speech.

> I. Wrong dog
> A. Never -- whim
> B. Research
> C. Get to know

Speaker's actual words

Step 3 Deliver the Speech

When he delivers the speech, the speaker talks in a natural, conversational manner, glancing at his note cards occasionally to remind himself of his next point.

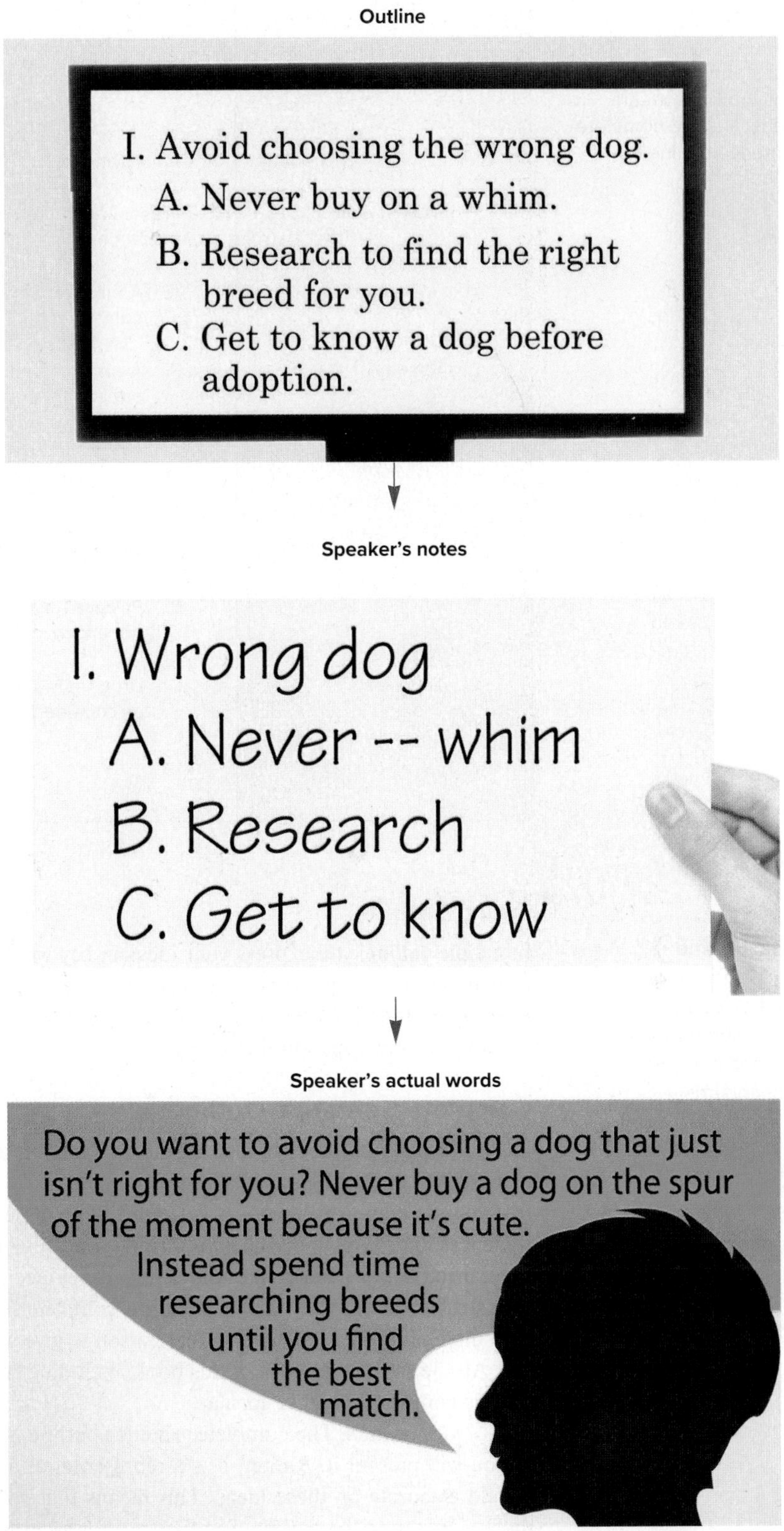

> Do you want to avoid choosing a dog that just isn't right for you? Never buy a dog on the spur of the moment because it's cute. Instead spend time researching breeds until you find the best match.

Figure 1

The outline-to-speech process has three steps.

Maria Gritsai/Alamy Stock Photo; vipman/Shutterstock; Petr Vaclavek/Shutterstock

Figure 2

Some speakers use both forms of outlines: the topic outline for early drafts, and the complete-sentence outline for refinements.

Topic Outline	Complete-Sentence Outline
Pre-employment Screening	Pre-employment Screening
I. Presenting self	I. Presenting yourself to a potential employer gives you a chance to highlight your qualifications for a job.
A. Job interview	A. A job interview can show your enthusiasm and commitment.
B. Résumé	B. A résumé summarizes your experience, education, and skills.
II. Testing	II. Testing is used by employers to eliminate unqualified or high-risk applicants.
A. Skills tests	A. Skills tests determine if you have the aptitudes and abilities needed for the job.
B. Physical exams	B. Physical exams determine whether your health will allow you to fulfill the duties of the job.
C. Drug tests	C. Drug tests screen for illegal substances such as cocaine and marijuana.

Topic Outline

topic outline
a systematic arrangement of ideas, using words and phrases for headings and subheadings.

In a **topic outline**, you express your ideas in key words or phrases. The advantage of this format is that it is quicker and easier to prepare than a complete-sentence outline. The FBI Crime Index outline shown earlier in this chapter is a topic outline. For another example, see the topic outline in Figure 2.

Complete-Sentence Outline

complete-sentence outline
a systematic arrangement of ideas, using complete sentences for headings and subheadings.

In the **complete-sentence outline**, all your main points and subpoints are expressed in complete sentences (see Figure 2). Unless your instructor tells you otherwise, we recommend that you use complete sentences for your final outline. Here is why: (1) Writing complete sentences forces you to clarify and sharpen your thinking. You are able to go beyond fuzzy, generalized notions and create whole, fully developed ideas. (2) If another person (such as an instructor) helps you with your outline, complete sentences will be easier to understand than mere phrases, thus enabling that person to give you the best possible critique.

All the sample outlines in this book, including the one featured later in this chapter, use the complete-sentence format.

Note of caution: The complete-sentence outline is not your speech written out exactly as you will present it. Rather, it is a representation of your key ideas; the actual speech should elaborate on these ideas. This means that your actual speech will contain many more words than the outline. See Figure 1 for an example.

Use Standard Subdivisions

In the standard system of subdividing, you mark your main points with roman numerals (**I, II, III,** etc.); indent the next level of supporting materials underneath and mark them with capital letters (**A, B, C,** etc.); then use Arabic numerals (1, 2, 3); then lowercase letters (a, b, c); and if you need to go further, use parentheses with numbers and letters. Here is the standard format:

   I. Major division

  II. Major division

      A. First-level subdivision

      B. First-level subdivision

         1. Second-level subdivision

         2. Second-level subdivision

            a. Third-level subdivision

            b. Third-level subdivision

               (1) Fourth-level subdivision

               (2) Fourth-level subdivision

      C. First-level subdivision

Notice that each time you subdivide a point, you indent. For most speeches, you will not need to use as many subdivisions as illustrated here.

Avoid Single Subdivisions

Each heading should have at least two subdivisions or none at all. In other words, for every heading marked "A," there should be at least a "B." For every "1" there should be a "2." The reason is obvious: how can you divide something and end up with only one part? If you divide an orange, you must end up with at least two pieces. If you end up with only one, you have not really divided the orange. One problem that arises is how to show on an outline a single example for a particular point. Below is the *wrong* way to handle the problem:

      A. Many counterfeiters are turning to items other than paper money.

         1. Counterfeit credit cards now outnumber counterfeit bills.

      B. . . .

This is wrong because item "A" cannot logically be divided into just one piece. There are two ways to correct the problem. One way is simply to eliminate the single item and combine it with the sentence above it:

      A. Many counterfeiters are turning to items other than paper money: counterfeit credit cards now outnumber counterfeit bills.

      B. . . .

Another way to handle the problem is not to number the item but simply to identify it in the outline as "example":

      A. Many counterfeiters are turning to items other than paper money. Example: Counterfeit credit cards now outnumber counterfeit bills.

      B. . . .

TIP 1

Tips for Your Career

When No Time Limit Is Set, Speak Briefly

We have discussed why you should never exceed your time limit, but what should you do when no time limit is set? The best advice is this: Be brief. Keep it short.

How brief should you be?

- For a short presentation, aim for 5 to 7 minutes—a popular length, especially when several presenters are scheduled to speak.

- For longer speeches, aim for 18 minutes. By rule, 18 minutes is the limit for world-famous TED Talks, sponsored by TED (Technology, Entertainment, Design) Conferences. Chris Anderson, the current curator of TED Talks, says that 18 minutes is

"a natural human attention span . . . You can listen to something serious that long without getting bored or exhausted."

Whenever you are in doubt about length, remember that it is better to err on the side of brevity. If, when you finish a speech, the listeners are still hungering for more wisdom from you, no harm is done. They will probably invite you to come back and speak again. But if you speak so long that they become bored, weary, and sleepy, they will resent you for wasting their time.

Source: Charlie Rose, "TED Talks," CBS News, www.cbsnews.com (accessed December 11, 2015).

Parts of the Outline

The parts of the outline discussed below are keyed to the sample outline presented in the next section. Your instructor may have requirements for your outline that deviate somewhat from the description in these pages. (See Figure 3 for a schematic overview of a typical outline.)

1. **Title.** Your outline should have a title, but you *will not actually say it in your speech.* In other words, don't begin your speech by saying, "How to Lose Weight Permanently" or "The title of my speech is 'How to Lose Weight Permanently.'"

   If you should not say the title, why even have one? For classroom speeches, your instructor may want you to write one simply to give you experience in devising titles. For some out-of-class speeches, a title may be requested so that your speech can be publicized in advance. A catchy title might entice people to come to hear you.

   Your title should be brief and descriptive. That is, it should provide a clear idea of what your speech is about. For example, "The Increase in Cheerleader Injuries" is a short and helpful preview of the speech topic. If you want an attractive, catchy title, you can use a colorful phrase coupled with a descriptive subtitle—"Nothing to Cheer About: The Increase in Cheerleader Injuries." Here are some other examples:

   - Czech It Out! Why You Should Visit Prague
   - Are You Being Ripped Off? How to Find an Honest Mechanic
   - Ouch! What to Do When a Bee Stings You
   - SuperStore: The Rise of Walmart

2. **Purposes and central idea.** Having your general purpose, specific purpose, and central idea listed on your outline will help you focus the main points and supporting materials.

3. **Introduction and conclusion.** The introduction and the conclusion are so vitally important in a speech that they deserve special attention and care. Both sections should have their own numbering sequence in the outline, independent of the body of the speech.

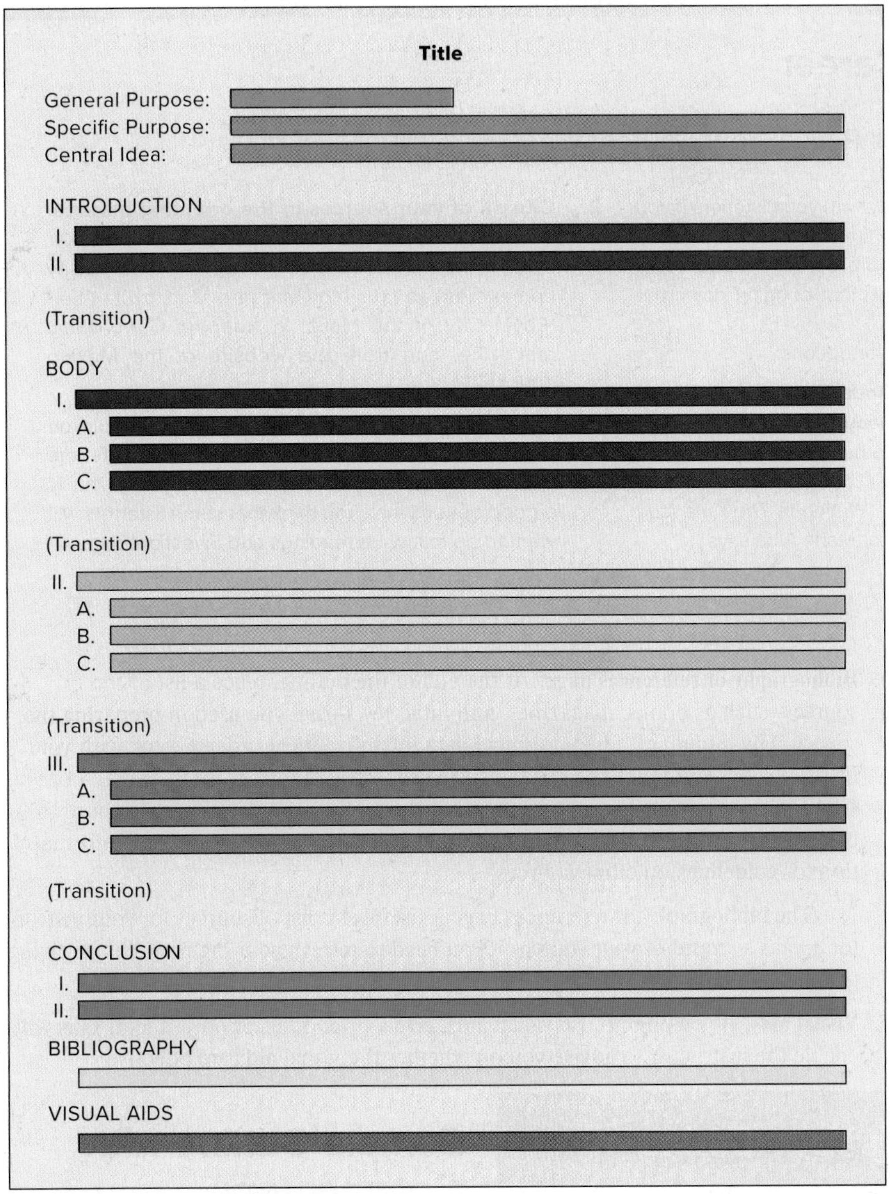

Figure 3
An Overview of a Typical Outline Although this outline shows three main points, a speech may have two or occasionally four.

4. **Body.** In the body of the outline, each main point should be identified by roman numerals. The body has its own numbering sequence, independent of the introduction and conclusion. In other words, the first main point of the body is given roman numeral I.

5. **Transitions.** The transitional devices we discussed in the chapter on the body of the speech should be inserted in the outline at appropriate places. They are labeled and placed in parentheses, but they are not included in the numbering system of the outline.

   While transitional devices should be placed wherever they are needed to help the listener, make sure you have them in at least three crucial places: (1) between the introduction and the body of the speech, (2) between the main points, and (3) between the body of the speech and the conclusion.

Tips for Your Career

Decide How You Will Reveal Your Sources

You strengthen your credibility with your listeners if you tell them where you got your information, but it would be boring if you read your bibliography aloud. How, then, can you cite sources without bogging down the speech?

Here are the most popular options:

1. **Reveal the key data about your sources as you proceed through the body of your speech.** You could preface new points by saying something like "According to an article in the latest issue of *Scientific American* . . ." or "Writing in *The American Journal of Nursing,* Doctor Marie Alba says . . ."

2. **Cite all of your sources in the orienting material of the introduction.** For example, one speaker said, "The information I am giving you today comes from an article by Margaret Zackowitz titled 'Royal City of the Maya' in *National Geographic* magazine, and from the website of the Mexico Tourism Board."

3. **List sources on a handout.** The handout should be provided at the end of the speech so that listeners will not be distracted while you are speaking. This is a good option when you think that some listeners will want to do follow-up readings and investigations.

6. **Bibliography or references page.** At the end of the outline, place a list of the sources—such as books, magazines, and interviews—that you used in preparing the speech. Give standard bibliographical data in alphabetical order. Check with your instructor to see if he or she wants you to use a special format, such as MLA or APA style. Also, your instructor may want the bibliography or references page to be on a separate page. Otherwise, see Table 1 in the chapter on locating information for guidelines on citing sources.

   The bibliography or references page is useful as a list of sources for your instructor *and* as a record of your sources if you need to refresh your memory before giving the speech again.

7. **Visual aids.** If you plan to use visual aids, give a brief description of them. This will enable the instructor to advise you on whether the visual aids are effective.

Examining Your Ethics

An organization of cancer survivors advertised an upcoming speech by an oncologist. The title of the speech was "A Cure for Cancer." Unsurprisingly, the title drew a big crowd for the doctor's presentation. But if listeners were hoping for an announcement of a cure, they were disappointed; the doctor discussed research possibilities that *might* someday prove to be effective in fighting cancer. What would have been a more ethical title for the speech?

A. How to Beat Cancer
B. Exciting New Developments in Cancer Treatment
C. Looking to the Future: Possible Cancer Cures

For the answer, see the last page of this chapter.

Sample Outline with Commentary

Below is an outline for a speech called "Not as Healthy as They Sound" by Jeffrey Omura. A transcript of the speech is printed at the end of this chapter.

Although the following outline uses the complete-sentence format, your instructor may prefer that you create a topic outline (discussed earlier in this chapter). To create a topic outline, use the same system as here except write words or phrases instead of full sentences.

The speaker's outline uses the topical pattern, dividing the subject into two types of foods.

Not as Healthy as They Sound

COMMENTARY

SPEECH

General Purpose: To inform

Specific Purpose: To inform my audience of some foods that are not as healthy as they sound

Central Idea: Some healthy-sounding foods are not as high in nutritional value as you might think.

Purposes and central idea should appear at the top of the outline to help the speaker stay on target.

INTRODUCTION

I. Attention Material

The introduction has its own label and numbering sequence.

A. At a coffee shop, you try to choose between a chocolate donut with sprinkles and a corn muffin. (Show photo.) [See Figure 4.]

B. You decide on the corn muffin because it's healthier, but is it?

The speaker grabs attention by describing an interesting choice.

C. The donut has 270 calories, while the corn muffin has 510 ("Food Fight," 7).

1. You need 2,000 calories per day, so the corn muffin provides about one-quarter of your daily needs.

2. Also the corn muffin has a great deal more fat than the donut.

D. Over 12 people who were interviewed said the corn muffin was healthier.

II. Orienting Material

A preview lets listeners know what the speech will cover.

A. Let's look at some other foods that are not as healthy as they sound.

B. My goal is not to dictate a diet, but simply to inform you of some interesting facts.

Transitions are placed in parentheses and are not part of the numbering system.

(*Transition:* Let's start with vegetables.)

270   510

Figure 4
A corn muffin has far more calories than a chocolate donut.

Bryan Solomon/Shutterstock; Anton Prado Photo/ Shutterstock

(continued)

BODY

> Roman numerals are used for main points.

I. Vegetables can be nutritious, but often they are loaded with extra fat and calories.
   A. A salad with tomatoes, lettuce, cucumbers, and other veggies can be okay if you add a modest amount of low-fat dressing.
      1. But some people choose a salad at a fast-food restaurant because they think it's healthier than a burger. (Show slide.) [See Figure 5.]
      2. One fast-food chain sells a Spicy Chicken Caesar Salad with 750 calories, while its quarter-pound hamburger has 470 calories ("New Law").
      3. A salad becomes high in calories and fat if it's topped with cheese, bacon, croutons, spicy chicken strips, and a large quantity of high-fat dressing.

> Under each main point, subpoints are marked with capital letters.

   B. Potato chips are high in fat, so veggie chips sound healthier.
      1. Veggie chips are not more nutritious than potato chips, says Patricia Chuey of Vancouver, Canada, a nutritionist and author of *Simply Great Food*.

> Sub-subpoints are marked with Arabic numerals (1, 2, 3).

      2. They are high in fat and calories.
      3. They have almost none of the nutritional value of real vegetables.
   C. A veggie sandwich sounds healthy, but beware.
      1. It's not all that healthy if you order the Veggie Supreme sub at one fast-food chain.

> Each level of subordination is shown by indention.

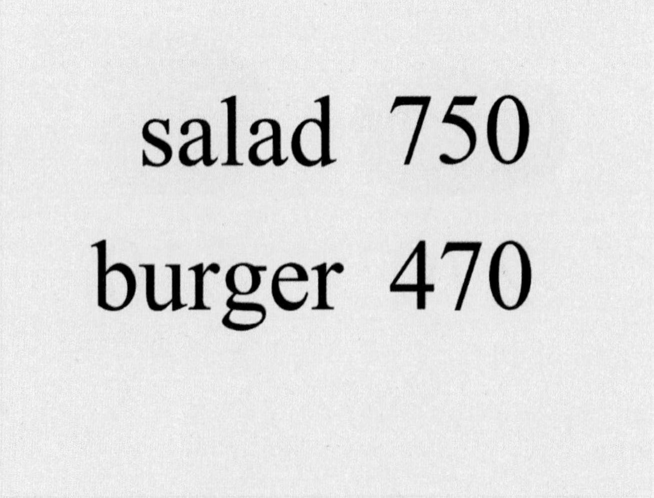

      2. The Veggie Supreme was rated as the Worst "Healthy" Sandwich in America (Zinczenko).
      3. It has 1,106 calories and 56 grams of fat, surpassing the calories and fat in two Big Macs from McDonald's.
      4. The sub is a foot long, contains three different kinds of cheese, and is covered in oil.
      5. Of course, you can avoid the extra fat and calories if you ask the restaurant to skip the cheese and oil.

Figure 5
At a fast-food restaurant, a salad can have more calories than a hamburger.

salad 750

burger 470

Figure 6
Commercial granola bars
are far different from
homemade ones.
Igor Dutina/Shutterstock

(*Transition:* Let's look at our second category of foods.)

II. Nuts, fruits, and dairy products can be nutritious, but sometimes they have surprisingly high amounts of fat and calories.

   A. Granola bars would seem to be a super-healthy food. (Show photo.) [See Figure 6.]
   1. They contain nuts, dried fruits, and whole oats.
   2. They can be very healthy if you make your own granola bars at home.
   3. But commercial granola bars have lots of sugar and syrup.
   4. "They're basically cookies masquerading around as health food," says Jayne Hurley, a senior nutritionist with the Center for Science in the Public Interest.

   B. Yogurt-covered raisins sound like a healthy combination.
   1. By themselves, raisins and yogurt are good foods, says Rosie Schwartz, a dietitian in Toronto, Canada.
   2. But commercial yogurt-covered raisins are deceptive.
   3. The "yogurt" coating is not real yogurt, but a high-calorie combination of sugar, oil, and some dried milk.
   4. One cup of yogurt-covered raisins has 750 calories, more calories than in two slices of homemade chocolate cake with chocolate frosting.

   C. Combining two healthy foods—yogurt and fruit—sounds healthy.
   1. Yogurt is a nutritious food, and fruit contains essential vitamins and minerals.
   2. So wouldn't it be healthy to buy a container of yogurt that has fruit on the bottom?
   3. But Schwartz says it's not real fruit on the bottom.
      a. It's actually fruit jam loaded with sugar.
      b. One serving can contain as many as 28 grams of sugar.
      c. That's more sugar than in a cup of vanilla ice cream.

(*Transition:* Let's review.)

Transitions are needed between main points.

Complete sentences are used to make sure all material is clear and well-developed.

Even though complete sentences are used, this outline is not a script to be read aloud. It is just a skeleton of key points. In the speech itself, the speaker expands on the points, using additional words in a conversational-style delivery.

Audiences like to know the source of information—in this case, an expert.

The final transition prepares the audience for the conclusion.

(continued)

The conclusion has its own label and numbering system.	**CONCLUSION** I. Summary A. Some foods are not as healthy as they sound.
The speaker summarizes the main points.	B. They include corn muffins, some fast-food salads, veggie chips, the Veggie Supreme sub, granola bars, yogurt-covered raisins, and yogurt with fruit on the bottom. II. Clincher
A graceful ending is achieved by referring to the dramatic question asked at the beginning of the speech.	A. Rather than dictate, I have just given information. B. I'll bet all of you will remember that you don't save calories by choosing a corn muffin over a chocolate donut.

The conclusion has its own label and numbering system.

CONCLUSION

I. Summary
- A. Some foods are not as healthy as they sound.

The speaker summarizes the main points.

- B. They include corn muffins, some fast-food salads, veggie chips, the Veggie Supreme sub, granola bars, yogurt-covered raisins, and yogurt with fruit on the bottom.

II. Clincher

A graceful ending is achieved by referring to the dramatic question asked at the beginning of the speech.

- A. Rather than dictate, I have just given information.
- B. I'll bet all of you will remember that you don't save calories by choosing a corn muffin over a chocolate donut.

WORKS CITED

The works-cited list includes all sources used to prepare the speech.

Chuey, Patricia. "Re: Interview about *Simply Great Foods*." Received by Jeffrey Omura, 14 July 2011.

"Food Fight." *Consumer Reports*, Mar. 2008: 7.

Sources are listed alphabetically.

Hurley, Jayne. "Granola Bars." Center for Science in the Public Interest Online, 21 Feb. 2011, https://cspinet.org/tip/10-common-food-goofs.

"New Law Requires Big Restaurant Chains to Provide Nutritional Facts." KGET-TV, Bakersfield, CA, 14 July 2011.

The MLA format shown here is explained in the chapter on locating information, along with another format, APA.

Schwartz, Rosie. "Re: Questions for Speech on Healthy Foods." Received by Jeffrey Omura, 13 July 2011.

Zinczenko, David. *Eat This, Not That!* Rodale, 2012.

VISUAL AIDS

Visual aids should be listed so that the instructor can give guidance.

Two PowerPoint slides comparing calories.
One photo of granola bars.

Speaking Notes

After you have devised an outline, what do you do with it? Do you use it to practice your speech? No. Do you take it with you to the lectern to assist you in the delivery of your speech? No. You use the outline only for *organizing* your ideas. When it comes to *practicing* and then *delivering* the speech, you should use brief **speaking notes** that are based on the outline.

Speaking from brief notes is a good technique because it enables you to look at your audience most of the time, occasionally glancing down to pick up your next point. It encourages you to speak naturally and conversationally.

speaking notes
brief reminders of the points a speaker plans to cover during a speech.

How about using no notes at all? Would that be even better? No, without notes, you might forget important points, and you might fail to present your ideas in a logical, easy-to-follow sequence.

Notes bolster your sense of security. Even if you are in full command of the content of your speech, you feel more confident and self-assured knowing that you have notes as a safety net to rescue you if your mind goes blank and you fail to recall your next point.

Some people have the idea that using notes is a sign of mental weakness or a lack of self-confidence, but this belief is unfounded. Most good speakers use them without losing the respect of an audience. After all, your notes represent a kind of compliment to your listeners. They show that you care enough about the occasion to spend time getting your best thoughts together in a coherent form. The kind of speaker that audiences *do* look down on is the windbag who stands up without notes and rambles on and on without tying things together.

Guidelines for Preparing Notes

As you read these guidelines, you may want to refer to the sample speaking notes in Figure 7.

- Make indentations in your speaking notes that correspond to those in your outline. This will reinforce the structure of the speech in your mind. Some speakers use checkboxes and dashes to signal points; others use the same numbering system that they used in their outline.

- Use only one side of a sheet of paper or note card because you might forget to turn over the paper or card.

- Write down only the minimum number of words or phrases necessary to trigger your memory. If you have too many words written down, you may overlook some key ideas, or you may spend too much time looking at the notes instead of at the audience. Exceptions to this rule are long quotations or statistics that you need to write out in full for the sake of accuracy.

Cues remind the speaker to look at the audience and speak slowly during the introduction.

For reminders, red ink is effective.

Each card is numbered so that if the speaker accidentally drops or scrambles the cards, they can be put back into order very easily.

Only a few key words are used to jog the speaker's memory.

Figure 7
Here are samples of note cards for the speech about foods that sound healthy. Only the first two cards are shown.

Card 1:
Introduction   ①

LOOK AT AUDIENCE
SLOW!

☐ Donut?
☐ Corn muffin?

SLIDE

☐ Muffin healthier?

Card 2:   ②

☐ Consumer Reports
  - Donut, 270
  - Muffin, 510
  -2,000 calories

PAUSE

- Write words in large letters that are neat and legible so that you have no trouble seeing them when you glance down during a speech.
- Include cues for effective delivery, such as "SHOW SLIDE" and "PAUSE" (see the sample notes in Figure 7). Write them in a bright color so that they stand out. Some speakers find it helpful to use a variety of coded colors on their notes—for example, black for main points, green for support materials, blue for transitions, and red for delivery cues.
- Use the same set of notes during your speech that you used while rehearsing, so you are thoroughly familiar with the location of items on your prompts. An experienced speaker once made the mistake of writing out new note cards prior to giving his speech, because the notes he practiced with had so many editing marks that he felt they would be a distraction. This turned out to be a mistake, because the notes were so new that some of the key words failed to trigger his memory quickly, causing him to falter at several points. He should have stayed with the original notes. Even though they were filled with arrows and insertions and deletions, he knew them intimately, and had a strong mental picture of where each point was located on the cards. The new notes, in contrast, had not yet "burned" their image into his mind.
- Don't put your notes on the lectern in advance of your speech. A custodian might think they are trash and toss them out, or a previous speaker might accidentally scoop them up and walk off with them.

Options for Notes

Your instructor may require you to use one particular kind of note system, but if you have a choice, consider using one of these four popular methods.

Option 1: Use Note Cards

Your speaking notes can be put on note cards, as shown in Figure 7.

Note cards (especially the 3″ × 5″ size) are compact and rather inconspicuous, and they are easy to hold (especially if there is no lectern on which to place notes). The small size of the card forces you to write just a few key words rather than long sentences that you might be tempted to read aloud verbatim. If you use cards, be sure to number each one in case you drop or scramble them and need to reassemble them quickly.

Option 2: Use a Full Sheet of Paper

If you use a full sheet of paper, you can have the notes for your entire speech spread out in front of you. There are, however, several disadvantages: (1) Because a whole sheet of paper is a large writing surface, many speakers give in to the temptation to put down an overabundance of notes. This hurts them when speaking because they end up spending too much time looking at their notes and too little time making eye contact with the audience. (2) A full sheet of paper can cause a speaker's eyes to glide over key points, because the "map" of the speech is so large. (3) If a sheet is brought to the room rolled up, it can curl up on the lectern, making it uncooperative and difficult to read. (4) If a sheet is handheld because no lectern is available, it tends to shake and rustle, distracting listeners.

If you have access to a lectern, you can use several 8.5″ × 11″ sheets in a clever way: put notes only on the top one-third of a sheet, leaving the bottom two-thirds blank. This will help your eye contact because you can glance at your notes without having to bow your head to see notes at the bottom of the page.

A final tip: To avoid the distraction of turning a page over when you have finished with it, simply slide it to the other side of the lectern.

Option 3: Use Visual Aids as Prompts

A popular technique is to use your visual aids (such as PowerPoint slides or posters) as the equivalent of note cards. The visuals jog your memory on what to say next, and they give you the freedom to walk around the room instead of staying behind a lectern.

If you use this strategy, avoid using a visual aid that is primarily a cue for yourself and has no value for the audience. In other words, design a visual aid for audience enlightenment, not for speaker convenience. Take a look at the notes in Figure 7. They are fine on note cards, but if they were displayed on a slide, they would be confusing and inappropriate for the audience.

Option 4: Use Electronic Devices

If your instructor approves, you can put your notes on a smartphone or tablet. Just make sure that you limit yourself to brief notes, not the full text of your speech.

These options do not have to be used exclusively. They can be combined. For example, you could use note cards for part of a speech and visuals as prompts for another part.

Using one full sheet of paper for his notes, Chicago Bears running back Matt Forte gives a speech to a high school in Chicago.

Barry Brecheisen/AP Images

Controlling Your Material

While preparing your outline, don't let your material become like an octopus whose tentacles ensnare you and tie you up. You must control your material, rather than letting your material control you. Here are four things you can do to make sure that you stay in control.

1. **Revise your outline and speaking notes whenever they need alterations.** Some students mistakenly view an outline as a device that plants their feet in concrete; once they have written an outline, they think that they are stuck with it—even if they want to make changes. An outline should be treated as a flexible aid that can be altered as you see fit.

2. **Test your outline.** One of the reasons for creating an outline is to *test* your material to see if it is well-organized, logical, and sufficient. Here are some questions that you should ask yourself as you analyze your outline (in your career, you can ask colleagues to critique your outline using the same questions):

   • Does the introduction provoke interest and give sufficient orienting material?
   • Do I preview the central idea and/or main points?
   • Do the main points explain or prove my central idea?
   • Are the main points organized logically?
   • Is there enough support material for each main point? Is there too much?
   • Do I have smooth transitions between introduction and body, between main points, and between body and conclusion?

- Have I eliminated extraneous material that doesn't truly relate to my central idea?
- Does my conclusion summarize the main points and reinforce the central idea?
- Is my conclusion strong and effective?

3. **Revise for continuity.** Often an outline looks good on paper, but when you make your speaking notes and start practicing, you find that some parts are disharmonious, clumsy, or illogical. A speech needs a graceful flow, carrying the audience smoothly from one point to another. If your speech lacks this smooth flow, alter the outline and speaking notes until you achieve a continuity with which you are comfortable. (If you practice in front of friends, ask them to point out parts that are awkward or confusing.)

4. **Make deletions if you are in danger of exceeding your time limit.** After you make your speaking notes, practice delivering your speech while timing yourself. If the speech exceeds the time limit (set by your instructor or by the people who invited you to speak), go back to your outline and speaking notes and trim them. Deleting material can be painful, especially if you have worked hard to get a particular example or statistic. But it *must* be done, even if you exceed the limit by only several minutes.

Sample Speech as Presented

Earlier we examined the outline and sample notes for Jeffrey Omura's speech about foods that are not as healthy as they seem at first glance. A transcript of the speech as it was delivered is printed below. Notice that the wording of the actual speech is not identical to that of the outline, because Omura delivers the speech extemporaneously, guided by brief speaking notes.

Not as Healthy as They Sound

You go into a coffee shop, and you decide to buy a pastry to go with your coffee. [*Speaker shows the slide in Figure 4*] At first you're attracted to the chocolate donut with sprinkles, but then you decide to go with the corn muffin because you figure it must be a lot healthier. But is it?

According to *Consumer Reports* magazine, the donut has 270 calories, while the corn muffin has almost twice as many—510. The average person needs about 2,000 calories per day, so the corn muffin gives you almost one-quarter of your daily allotment. The corn muffin also has a lot more fat than the donut.

I asked over a dozen people which they thought was healthier. Everyone said the corn muffin. It does sound healthy, doesn't it? Today I'd like to show you some other foods that aren't as healthy as you might think. By the way, I'm not trying to tell you what you should eat. I just want to inform you about some surprising facts. Let's start with vegetables, which by themselves are very nutritious, but they're often served in ways that add a lot of extra fat and calories. Consider a salad with vegetables like tomatoes, lettuce, cucumbers. It can be healthy if you put a single serving of low-fat dressing on it. But the problem is, some people go into a fast-food restaurant and they order the salad because they think it's going to be healthier than the burger.

[*Speaker shows the slide in Figure 5*]

A TV station in Bakersfield, California, KGET—they report that one fast-food chain sells a Spicy Chicken Caesar Salad with 750 calories, compared to the quarter-pound hamburger, which has 470 calories. What some people don't know is that a salad can become high in calories and fat if you add extra things like cheese, bacon, croutons, spicy chicken strips, and a large quantity of high-fat dressing.

You may have heard about potato chips being loaded with fat and contributing to the increased rate of obesity. So let's say you're in a grocery store and you see a bag of veggie chips. What could be unhealthy about that? Didn't your mother always say, "Eat your veggies?" Well, let's check with Patricia Chuey of Vancouver, Canada. She's a nutritionist and author of *Simply Great Food.* She says veggie chips are no more nutritious than potato chips. They're loaded with fat and they're high in calories. And they contain almost none of the nutritional value of real vegetables.

Well, how about a veggie sandwich? It can be healthy if you make it at home. But it's not as healthy if you get the Veggie Supreme sub at one national fast-food chain. A best-selling book *Eat This, Not That!* rated the Veggie Supreme as the Worst "Healthy" Sandwich in America. It has 1,106 calories and 56 grams of fat—more calories and more fat than you'd get in two Big Macs. The problem is, the foot-long sub comes with three different kinds of cheese, and it's covered in oil. By the way, in a case like this, you can avoid the extra fat and calories if you just ask the restaurant to skip the cheese and oil.

Now let's turn to nuts, fruits, and dairy products. As with vegetables, they can be very nutritious, but sometimes they, too, have unexpected high amounts of fat and calories.

Consider granola bars. [*Speaker shows the slide in Figure 6*] They sound so wholesome and nutritious. They include nuts, dried fruits, and whole oats. Nutrition experts say that if you make your own granola bars,

they can make a good healthy snack. But Jayne Hurley, a senior nutritionist with the Center for Science in the Public Interest, says that commercial granola bars you see in stores are loaded with sugar and syrup. She says, quote, "They're basically cookies masquerading around as health food."

Next we come to yogurt-covered raisins. What could be unhealthy about that combination? Rosie Schwartz, a dietitian in Toronto, Canada—she says that raisins by themselves are fine, and yogurt by itself is fine. But she says commercial yogurt-covered raisins—they're not what you think. The so-called yogurt coating is different from the yogurt you buy in the dairy section of your store. The coating is mostly sugar, oil, and some dried milk—and it's loaded with calories. One cup of yogurt-covered raisins has 750 calories—that's more calories than you'll find in two typical slices of homemade chocolate cake with chocolate frosting.

What would happen if you mixed two healthy foods together—like yogurt and fruit? Yogurt is a nutritious, calcium-rich snack. Fruit contains essential vitamins and minerals. So how about buying containers of yogurt that have fruit on the bottom? Sounds even better than the ordinary yogurt, doesn't it? But Schwartz says it's not real fruit on the bottom. It's fruit jam loaded with sugar. One serving can contain as many as 28 grams of sugar. That's more sugar than you'll find in a cup of vanilla ice cream.

Let's summarize. I've tried to show you that many foods are not as nutritious as you might think—corn muffins, some fast-food salads, veggie chips, the Veggie Supreme sub, granola bars, yogurt-covered raisins, and yogurt with fruit-on-the-bottom.

As I said in the beginning, I'm not trying to tell you what you should eat. But at least now you know you're not saving calories if you go with the corn muffin instead of the chocolate donut.

For three additional complete outlines and transcripts of speeches, see the samples at the end of the chapters on speaking to inform, speaking to persuade, and persuasive strategies.

Resources for Review and Skill Building

Summary

An outline is as important to a speechmaker as a blueprint is to a builder: the outline provides a detailed plan to help the speaker organize his or her thoughts into a logical sequence and to make sure nothing important is left out.

Two popular types are the topic outline, which uses words and phrases for headings, and the complete-sentence outline, which uses entirely written-out headings. Some speakers use both forms: the topic outline for early drafts and the complete-sentence outline for refinements.

The parts of the outline include the title, general purpose, specific purpose, central idea, introduction, body, conclusion, transitions, bibliography, and visual aids.

After you complete your outline, prepare speaking notes based on it. You have four options: note cards, a full sheet of paper, speaking notes displayed as a visual aid, or an electronic device. Whichever you choose, avoid writing too many words because when you use notes in a speech, you want to be able to glance down quickly and retrieve just enough words to jog your memory.

Through all these stages, control your material by revising your outline and speaking notes whenever they need alterations. Test the strength of your outline, and revise for continuity—a smooth, logical flow from one part to another. Finally, make deletions if you are in danger of exceeding your time limit.

Key Terms

complete-sentence outline, *222*   speaking notes, *230*   topic outline, *222*

Review Questions

1. Why is an outline recommended for all speeches?

2. What is a topic outline?

3. What are the advantages of using complete sentences in an outline?

4. Why should each subdivision of an outline have at least two parts?

5. What are the parts of an outline?

6. Why should you have a title for your outline if it should not be spoken in the speech?

7. What are the advantages of using cards for speaking notes?

8. What are the disadvantages of using a full sheet of paper for speaking notes?

9. What are the advantages of using visual aids as speaking prompts?

10. You are advised to "revise for continuity" while practicing your speech. What does this mean?

Building Critical-Thinking Skills

1. Sort out the following items and place them into a coherent topic outline. In addition to a title, the scrambled list includes three main points, with three subpoints under each: Museums, Visa, Clothes, Activities, Passport, Beaches, Studying Abroad, Airplane tickets, Computer, Travel documents, Restaurants, Photographs, Packing.

2. For an outline on different foods, which major headings would you create?

3. If you practice in front of friends, why is it better to say, "Tell me the parts that need improvement," instead of "Tell me if you like this"?

4. Transform the topic outline in the next column into a complete-sentence outline. Create a central idea for the outline.

Research

I. Library

   A. Printed material

   B. Electronic databases

   C. Audiovisuals

II. Personal

   A. Experiences

   B. Interviews

   C. Surveys

Building Teamwork Skills

1. Working in a group, create a central idea and a topic outline for one of the following topics. Put each item on a separate index card or piece of paper so that the group can experiment with different sequences. Your outline should have at least three main points, each of which should have at least three subpoints.

   a. Natural disasters
   b. Fast food
   c. Leisure-time activities
   d. Good health

2. In a group, create a *complete-sentence outline* on how to study effectively. Include a central idea, at least three main points, and at least four subpoints under each main point.

Examining Your Ethics

Answer: C. This title makes it clear that the treatments are not available now but may be possible in the future. Choice A is unethical because it makes it seem like the oncologist will give a step-by-step method of curing cancer. And B makes it sound like the speech will explain new treatments that will be available soon.

End Notes

1. Bill Bryson, *At Home: A Short History of Private Life* (New York: Doubleday, 2010), p. 234.

2. Hans Friedrich Ebel, Claus Bliefert, and William E. Russey, *The Art of Scientific Writing* (New York: Wiley, 2004), pp. 88–89.

Design Credits: (sound waves) Jamie Farrant/Getty Images; (road sign) Last Resort/Getty Images

Wording the Speech

OBJECTIVES

After studying this chapter, you should be able to

1. Explain the importance of choosing words that are appropriate for the audience and the occasion.
2. Use words that are clear, accurate, and vivid.
3. Describe the significant differences between oral and written language.

A KNUCKLEBALL IS a rare pitch in baseball, and it is feared and detested by hitters. Because of the complicated way the ball is gripped and hurled, it bobs and weaves, dancing about as it crosses home plate. Former American League umpire Ron Luciano explains why a knuckleball is so rare: "Pitchers can't control it, hitters can't hit it, catchers can't catch it, coaches can't coach it, and most pitchers can't learn it. It's the perfect pitch."[1]

R.A. Dickey is one of the few pitchers in modern times to master the art of throwing a knuckleball effectively. In recent years, while playing for the New York Mets and the Toronto Blue Jays, he has been one of the most successful pitchers in the major leagues. Trying to hit a knuckleball, he says, "is like trying to hit a butterfly in a typhoon."[2]

This image of a butterfly in a typhoon is an artful use of words, an example of the vivid language Dickey uses in his speeches and interviews. In this chapter, we will look at how you, too, can use the power of language to enhance and illustrate your message.

Pitcher R.A. Dickey describes his famous knuckleball to students at Lipscomb University in Nashville, Tennessee.

Mark Humphrey/AP Images

The Power of Words

If you witnessed a car crash, could you appear in court and give an accurate report of what you saw? Before you answer, consider this:

Courtroom lawyers have discovered that they can influence eyewitness testimony simply by choosing certain words when they ask questions. To demonstrate how this technique works, psychologist Elizabeth Loftus showed a group of people a video depicting a two-car accident. After the video, some of the viewers were asked, "About how fast were the cars going when they *smashed* into each other?" Other viewers were asked the same question except that the word *smashed* was replaced by the word *hit*. Viewers who were asked the *smashed* question, in contrast to the *hit* viewers, gave a much higher estimate of speed, and a week later, they were more likely to state that there was broken glass at the accident scene, even though no broken glass was shown in the videotape. Why? Because *smash* suggests higher speed and greater destruction than *hit*. Thus, a single word can distort our memory of what we have seen with our own eyes.[3]

The power of words is used by advertisers and retailers, as these research items show:

- Advertising agencies have learned that sales of a product can be increased if ads contain any of these words: *new, quick, easy, improved, now, suddenly, amazing,* and *introducing*.[4]

- Until a few decades ago, the toothfish was considered a "trash" fish—unfit for family meals. But when Lee Lantz, an American fish merchant, renamed it "Chilean sea bass" despite it actually being a type of cod that is rarely found off the coast of Chile, it became hugely popular and one of the most expensive items in restaurants.[5]

This little word has the power to boost sales significantly.

Hamilton Gregory

Can mere words have such power? Yes, but we shouldn't call words "mere." As writer C. J. Ducasse says, "To speak of 'mere words' is much like speaking of 'mere dynamite.' "[6] The comparison is apt. If dynamite is used responsibly, it can clear a rockslide on a highway; if used irresponsibly, it can maim and kill.

In public speaking, if powerful "dynamite" words are used responsibly, they can keep listeners awake and interested, but if used irresponsibly, they can deceive audiences, distort facts, and dynamite the truth. And if "dynamite" words are used too often, they lose their power. For example, every four years presidential candidates and political commentators will declare that year's election as "the most important election in history," or some variation of that statement.[7]

Obviously, there can only be one "most important" election in a lifetime. But that does not stop people from making the "dynamite" statement every election. That phrase has likely lost its power with many voters. Ethical speakers use words responsibly—not as clever devices of deception or exaggeration, but as vivid portraits of truth.

Finding the Right Words

The difference between the right word and the almost right word, Mark Twain once observed, is the difference between lightning . . . and the lightning bug. The truth of Twain's remark can be seen in the following historical vignette: One of President Franklin D. Roosevelt's most famous speeches was his address to Congress asking for a declaration of war against Japan in the aftermath of the Japanese attack on the American fleet at Pearl Harbor. As written by an assistant, the speech began this way:

> December 7, 1941: A date which will live in world history.

Before speaking, Roosevelt crossed out the words *world history* and substituted the word *infamy.* Here is what he ended up saying:

> December 7, 1941: A date which will live in infamy.

This has become one of the most famous sentences in American history, along with such memorable statements as "Give me liberty or give me death!" And yet, if Roosevelt had used the original sentence, it never would have become celebrated. Why? Because *infamy*—a pungent word tinged with evil and anger—was the right description for the occasion; *world history*—dull and unemotional—was merely "almost right." Lightning . . . and the lightning bug.

In choosing words for your speeches, your goal should not be to select the most beautiful or the most sophisticated, but to use the *right* words for the *right* audience. In the Emmy Award–winning Amazon Prime show *The Marvelous Mrs. Maisel,* the main character—Miriam "Midge" Maisel— discovers her talent of performing standup comedy in the 1950s, a time when the comic circuit was almost exclusively male. Her raunchy brand of humor is a huge hit with unsuspecting audiences in comedy clubs. But when she gives a speech at a friend's wedding and launches into her R-rated routine, the crowd is mortified and Midge ends up humiliating herself and her friend.

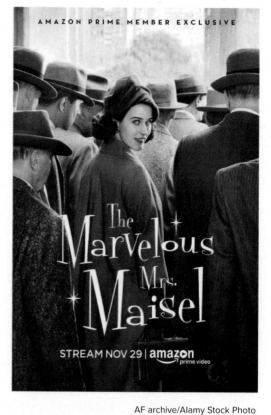

AF archive/Alamy Stock Photo

As you analyze your audience before a speech, ask yourself, "How can I best express my ideas so that the audience will understand and accept them?" Words that may be ideal for one audience may be unsuitable for another, as Mrs. Maisel found out.

While considering your audience, you also should use words that are suitable for the *occasion.* If you speak at a fund-raiser, your words should be uplifting and encouraging; at a funeral, solemn and respectful; at a political rally, rousing and emotional.

Using Appropriate Words

Never make political, religious, racial, ethnic, or gender references that might alienate anyone in your audience. Ask yourself, "Is there any chance that what I'm planning to say will offend someone in the audience?" If you have any doubt whether a word is appropriate, don't use it. Some might call this political correctness, but it's really about respecting your audience. You want your audience to listen to what you have to say. Even if it is done inadvertently, offending someone during your speech is a sure-fire way to lose the attention of your audience.

Use Gender-Neutral Terms

In using occupational terms, stay away from language that reflects **gender-biased stereotypes**, such as *male nurse* instead of *nurse*, and *female soldier* instead of *soldier.* See Table 1 for some other examples.

gender-biased stereotype generalization that assigns roles or characteristics to people on the basis of gender.

Table 1   **Gender-Neutral Alternatives**

Original	Preferred Form
fireman	firefighter
policeman	police officer
chairman	chair, chairperson
cameraman	camera operator
mailman	mail carrier
man-made	artificial
craftsman	artisan
foreman	supervisor

Avoid Gender-Biased Pronoun Usage

For centuries the masculine pronouns *he, his,* and *him* were used in the English language to designate an individual when gender was immaterial. In a sentence such as "Every driver should buckle *his* seat belt before *he* starts the engine," the pronouns *his* and *he* were understood to refer to drivers in general, both male and female.

Tips for Your Career

He/She/They

Fortune 500 company Virgin Group made headlines in 2019 when company founder Sir Richard Branson encouraged company employees to include their preferred gender pronouns in their Virgin Group e-mail signatures.

"At Virgin, we believe that everyone, regardless of sexual orientation or gender identity, should have the right to be who they are, wherever they are. It's important to our people, their families, our business partners and customers," Branson wrote in a blog post.

Although some may scoff at this move, Virgin Group's decision represents a growing trend in business and society. Earlier in 2019, Merriam-Webster updated its dictionary to include the singular use of *they* "to refer to a single person whose gender identity is nonbinary." In 2017 the *AP Stylebook*—the style guide used by media professionals—declared the singular use of *they* acceptable for people who identify as nonbinary.

The move to have employees identify preferred gender pronouns may seem like a politically motivated decision, but Jamie Wareham notes in *Forbes* that it makes business sense to adopt such policies: "With only seconds to make the impression in your email to get a response—or a follow on your socials—showing your pronouns could be the difference between the click that you need."

Recognizing gender-preferred pronouns shows respect to all people, and makes it clear how an individual wants to be recognized. "Getting someone's pronoun right can feel like a very small gesture, but it can mean the world," Branson wrote.

Sources: Jessica Stillman, "Virgin Just Added Gender Pronouns to Email Signatures. Should Your Company Do the Same?," *Inc.*, www.inc.com/jessica-stillman/virgin-just-added-gender -pronouns-to-email-signatures-should-your-company-do-same .html (accessed February 9, 2020); Jamie Wareham, "Should You Put Pronouns in Email signatures and Social Media Bios?," *Forbes*, www.forbes.com/sites/jamiewareham/2020/12/30 /should-you-put-pronouns-in-email-signatures-and-social-media -bios/#4d82d9f96320 (accessed February 9, 2020).

TIP 1

Today, rather than having a gender pronoun assigned by the writer or speaker, sub-jects are given the autonomy to choose their own identity: *he/him* for those identifying as male, *she/her* for those identifying as female, or *they/their* for those identifying as nonbinary.

Determining what pronouns to use can be confusing when speaking in generalities. There are two ways to avoid this problem and be inclusive of all listeners:

1. **Use plural pronouns.** Say simply, "All drivers should buckle *their* seat belts before *they* start the engine." This alternative has the advantage of being simple, while including everyone.

2. **Use** the **pronoun** *you*. For example, "Whenever *you* get behind the wheel, *you* should buckle *your* seat belt before starting *your* engine." For speeches, this is almost always the best of the alternatives—it's simple and direct.

Using Words Accurately

To use words accurately, you need to be sensitive to two types of meanings—denotations and connotations—and you need to use correct grammar.

Use Precise Denotations

The **denotation** of a word is the thing or idea to which it refers—in other words, its diction-ary definition. For example, the denotation of *chair* is a piece of furniture on which one person may sit.

denotation
the thing or idea to which a word refers.

Try to use denotations precisely, bearing in mind the following cautions:

Be aware that some words have more than one denotation (in the minds of the public). The word *inflammable,* for example, is defined in dictionaries as "capable of burning quickly," but because of the prefix *in-* (which usually means "non") many people think that it means "not flammable." To be on the safe side, avoid using *inflammable* and instead use these words: *flammable* and *nonflammable.*

Take care with words that have different denotations to different people. What does *middle age* mean? Some people who are 30 say that it starts at 40, and some who are 40 say that it starts at 50. If middle age is an important concept in a speech, define the age span you mean by the term.

Be certain of the denotation. Some words are often misused by speakers, who may end up unintentionally insulting someone by their wrong application of the word. For example, someone who is famous at his or her craft might be mistakenly described as *notorious*. But *notorious* means "being famous or well known, typically for some bad qual-ity or deed."

Control Connotations

The **connotation** of a word is the emotional meaning that is associated with it. The words *economical, frugal,* and *cheap* are synonyms; they have the same denotation, but the con-notations are different: *economical* has a positive connotation, *frugal* is neutral, and *cheap* has negative overtones. Connotations often change over time. For example, the word *political* was once synonymous with "public sphere," but now it implies "calculating" or "partisan."[8]

connotation
the emotional over-tones of a word that go beyond a dictionary definition.

As a listener and as a speaker, you should be aware of how connotations express the attitude of the person using the words. For example, if giving a speech about the president of the United States, the words used to describe the presi-dent have very different connotations. A positive connotation would be calling the president a *national leader*. A neutral connotation would be the term *commander in chief*. A negative connotation would be identifying the president as a *politician*. All three are accurate terms to describe the president, but all carry very different connotations.

Connotations can make a difference in persuasive campaigns. For years, environmentalists tried to save swamps from being filled in and built on; they were often unsuccessful until they began to use the synonym *wetlands*. *Swamp* evokes the image of a worthless quagmire filled with creepy, crawly creatures, while *wetland* suggests a watery wilderness of exotic birds and plants. Likewise, fringe groups often hijack popular terms to promote an extreme agenda. For example, the term *patriot* means "a person who vigorously supports his or her country and is prepared to defend it against enemies." Military personnel are the ultimate patriots, putting their lives on the line for the sake of their country. However, hate groups in the United States have used the term *patriot* to defend white nationalism. The white supremacist group Patriot Front even has the term *patriot* in its name.

In exploring connotations, you don't have to rely solely on your own judgment. Check out a website like Thesaurus.com to explore synonyms and get a feel for how positive, negative, or neutral they are. Typing a word followed by "synonyms" into a search engine will also generate a brief list of synonyms. Another trick is to type the word followed by "connotation" to see what the term may imply.

Use Correct Grammar

If you are like most people, you grew up speaking the way your family and friends did. For example, Americans have different ways of describing a carbonated sugary drink. Generally, people on the East and West Coasts refer to the drink as *soda*, people in the Midwest call it *pop*, and people in the Southeast call it *Coke*.

Putting aside regional terms and dialects, there are generally agreed-upon rules of grammar that individuals must follow if they hope to progress in their career. For example, using the term *ain't* in conversation or speaking in slang may be looked upon negatively by potential employers.

Are they judging others unfairly? Of course, but many people associate poor grammar with a lack of education and even low intelligence. They will seldom come right out and tell you that your grammar is incorrect. A boss, for example, may feel awkward about telling an employee his or her grammar is unacceptable. So the employee is never told the real reason why he or she is being denied a promotion.

Achieving Clarity

To be clear in the words you use, you must first be clear in your thinking. Think about a word before you use it. Ask yourself, will it be clear to someone who is new to my subject? In this section, we will examine how you can achieve clarity by using words that are simple, concrete, and precise.

Use Simple Words

A speechwriter for President Franklin D. Roosevelt once wrote, "We are endeavoring to construct a more inclusive society." President Roosevelt changed the wording to, "We're going to make a country in which no one is left out."[9] Roosevelt knew that although big words are sometimes needed to convey a precise meaning, a good communicator will choose simple words whenever possible.

But what if you want to convey a complex idea? Don't you need complex language—big words and weighty phrases? No. If you examine great works of literature, you will see that profound thoughts can be expressed easily and beautifully by simple words. Some of the greatest pieces of literature in the English language—the King James Bible and Shakespeare's works—use simple words to convey big ideas. For example, in Hamlet's famous soliloquy ("To be or not to be . . .") 205 of the 261 words are of one syllable. Citing an American literary classic, Abraham Lincoln's Second Inaugural Address ("With malice toward none . . ."), William Zinsser writes, "Of the 701 words in [the address], 505 are words of one syllable and 122 are words of two syllables."[10]

Big words are often used by pretentious speakers, who want to impress the audience with their intelligence, while simple words are preferred by audience-centered speakers, who want to make sure their ideas are clear. Here is an example of the contrasting styles:

Pretentious Speaker: From time immemorial, human beings have used their tongues to apply salivary secretions to heal a contusion, and medical researchers have ascertained that the procedure may indeed be efficacious.

Audience-Centered Speaker: Licking a wound—a technique used by humans for centuries—may actually promote healing, according to medical researchers.

Use Concrete Words

Concrete words name or describe things that the listeners can see, smell, hear, taste, and touch—for example, *balloon, flower, gunshot, pizza,* and *desk*. They differ from **abstract words**, which refer to intangible ideas, qualities, or classes of things—for example, *democracy, mercy,* and *science*. While a certain amount of abstract language is necessary in a speech, you should try to keep it to a minimum. Whenever possible, choose concrete language because it is more specific and vivid, and therefore more likely to be remembered by your audience. Concrete words help you create the mental images that you want to convey to your listeners. See Table 2 for some examples.

concrete words words that name persons and things that we can know by our five senses.

abstract words words that name qualities, concepts, relationships, acts, conditions, and ideas.

Table 2   **Abstract to Concrete Language**

Abstract	Concrete
She is wealthy.	She makes $600,000 a year, has a winter home in San Diego and a summer home in Switzerland, and owns four sports cars.
It was a stormy day.	The sky was gray and gloomy, and the cold, moist wind stung my face.
Rattlesnakes are scary.	Its beady eyes staring at you without ever blinking, a rattlesnake can slither through the brush without making a sound—until it suddenly coils and makes its terrible buzzing rattle.

Use Precise Words

The most commonly quoted authority in America is "they," as in the following sentences:

They say that too much salt is bad for you.

They say that listening to loud music is not dangerous, as long as you don't feel any pain in your ears.

Instead of a vague "they," provide a precise source. For the first sentence, find reliable sources: "Researchers at Johns Hopkins University have found that too much salt in one's diet can cause . . ." For the second sentence, if you try to find who "they" are, you may discover that loud sound can cause permanent damage to one's hearing even if the noise is at a level that is not painful. The mysterious "they" can be wrong.

Two kinds of words—doublespeak and misused jargon—rob a speech of precision.

Beware of Doublespeak

When some federal and state legislators raise taxes, they don't refer to their action as "raising taxes." To do so might anger taxpayers. Instead they say they voted for "revenue enhancement."

doublespeak
language that is designed to confuse or to be misunderstood.

"Revenue enhancement" is an example of **doublespeak**, language that is deliberately misleading, evasive, meaningless, or inflated. Two of the most popular types of doublespeak are euphemisms and inflated language.

euphemism
a mild, indirect, or vague word used in place of one that is harsh, blunt, or offensive.

Euphemisms.   These are pleasant, mild, or inoffensive terms that are used to avoid expressing a harsh or unpleasant reality. If a public official talks about *regulated organic nutrients* and says that the stuff *exceeds the odor threshold,* would you know that he is talking about sewage sludge and admitting that it stinks?[11]

Euphemisms are not always undesirable. Sometimes we use euphemisms to soften blunt reality as a way of showing respect for others. For example, imagine that you have a friend who chose to end the life of a very sick and suffering pet dog. If you say, "I'm sorry you decided to have the vet kill your dog," your friend might be hurt by your unsparing language. But if you use a euphemism and say, "I'm sorry your dog had to be put to sleep," you are showing kindness and a concern for your friend's feelings. And there is no deception—your friend knows exactly what you mean.[12]

However, when a euphemism is used to deceive, it becomes doublespeak. Here are some examples:

- The Internal Revenue Service reported that in one recent year its overloaded phone system had 8.8 million "courtesy disconnects." This doesn't sound so bad until you learn that the euphemism refers to the fact that the IRS hung up on taxpayers calling for help 8.8 million times.[13]

- Businesses don't like to say that they have fired employees or laid them off. When one company laid off thousands of employees, it noted that it had taken action to reach its "synergy-related head-count adjustment goal."[14]

⬥ Examining Your Ethics

A United Airlines pilot spilled coffee all over his plane's communications equipment, causing navigation problems and forcing him to make an emergency landing in Toronto. An airline spokesperson referred to the incident as "a communications incident." Which of the following would have been the most ethical explanation by the airline?

A. "One of our pilots spilled coffee on equipment, causing navigation problems and forcing an emergency landing in Toronto."

B. "One of our pilots experienced issues with the airplane communications system and chose to make an emergency landing in Toronto."

C. "Because of an accident with onboard liquids, one of our pilots was forced to make an emergency landing in Toronto."

For the answer, see the last page of this chapter.

While some euphemisms can be deciphered, others are confusing. If a physician spoke of a *negative patient care outcome,* would you know that the term means death?[15]

Euphemisms can be harmful. Some food companies don't want to list sugar on a product's list of ingredients, so they use the term *evaporated cane juice.* Don Barrett, a lawyer in Mississippi, says that such deception is not a harmless crime: "To diabetics and some other people, sugar is just as deadly as poison."[16]

The best advice is this: use euphemisms if tact and kindness require them; avoid them if they serve to deceive or confuse.

Inflated language. This kind of doublespeak is designed to make the ordinary seem extraordinary. The following examples show uses of inflated language:

- A used car is advertised as a *pre-owned car.*
- A seafood restaurant calls its servers *seafood specialists.*
- A pizza chain calls its drivers *delivery ambassadors.*

Some inflated language seems harmless. If garbage collectors prefer to be called *sanitation engineers,* so what? But the problem arises when inflated language causes misunderstanding and confusion. For example, a national pet store chain calls its employees *pet counselors.* This term implies that the employee has some sort of expertise in veterinary counseling and can give professional advice to pet owners regarding care for their furry friends. However, these *pet counselors* are merely customer service agents with no formal training in veterinary medicine or counseling.

Avoid inflated terms unless it is clearly understood and preferred by your audience.

inflated language
words designed to puff up the importance of the person or thing being described.

Don't Misuse Jargon

If a physician refers to a heart attack as an "acute myocardial infarction," she is using **jargon**, the specialized language of a group or a profession. Jargon is acceptable if all your listeners share your specialty. But if some listeners are outside your field, either avoid specialized terms or define them.

Some speakers use jargon unconsciously. Because they use certain words at work every day, they fail to realize that people outside their field may be unaware of the words' meanings. A journalist might give a speech about conducting research in the *morgue,* leaving listeners confused as to why one would conduct research around a bunch of cadavers. But the journalist was referring to the *news morgue* located in many newsrooms that keeps records of all things published.

Jargon can especially be confusing with sports terms. After professional road-racing cyclist Lance Armstrong performed effectively during a day in the Tour de France competition, he told reporters, "There was no chain on the bike." What? It turns out that he didn't mean what he seemed to say. Unknown to most people outside cycling, the expression is used by riders to describe what it feels like when everything seems easy.[17]

Jargon is especially baffling to listeners who speak English as a second language. When you are speaking to these listeners, omit jargon or—if it is necessary to use a specialized term—explain it in concrete terms.

jargon
the technical language of a group or profession.

Using Vivid Language

"The best speaker," according to an Egyptian proverb, "is one who can turn the ear into an eye." How can one perform such magic? By using vivid language, such as imagery, metaphors, and similes.

Imagery

imagery
words that evoke mental pictures or images.

You can bring an abstract idea to life by using **imagery**—precise, descriptive words that create images. One of the most famous political speeches of the twenty-first century was delivered by then Illinois state senator Barack Obama at the 2004 Democratic National Convention:

> Well, I say to them tonight, there's not a liberal America and a conservative America—there's the United States of America. There's not a Black America and white America and Latino America and Asian America; there's the United States of America. The pundits like to slice-and-dice our country into Red States and Blue States; Red States for Republicans, Blue States for Democrats. But I've got news for them, too. We worship an awesome God in the Blue States, and we don't like federal agents poking around our libraries in the Red States. We coach Little League in the Blue States and have gay friends in the Red States. There are patriots who opposed the war in Iraq and patriots who supported it. We are one people, all of us pledging allegiance to the stars and stripes, all of us defending the United States of America.[18]

Spencer Platt/Staff/Getty images

Obama used imagery to break stereotypes often placed upon people living in different sections of the country. These images built upon each other to ultimately show how the country is more united than divided. For Obama, this speech was so successful that it catapulted his status as a relative unknown in national politics to becoming a future president.

Metaphors and Similes

metaphor
a comparison implying similarity between two things.

Two devices that are especially effective for creating mental pictures are metaphors and similes. A **metaphor** is a figure of speech in which a word or a phrase that ordinarily describes one thing is used to describe another to suggest a resemblance. Athletes frequently use metaphors, comparing sports to war and the game to a battle. But metaphors can be used in non-sports speeches, too. For example, in a speech about Navy ships, a speaker might say, "Enemy submarines were sharks that prowled the sea for prey." Comparing submarines and sharks creates a metaphor that is vivid and powerful. A metaphor is a shortcut that lets us pack a great deal of meaning into just a few words.

simile
a comparison, using *like* or as, of otherwise dissimilar things.

A **simile** is the same as a metaphor, except that the comparison between two things is made with the word *like* or *as*. For example, American novelist Marjorie Kinnan Rawlings wrote, "The water made a sound like kittens lapping."

Here are some other examples of the effective use of metaphors and similes:

- A panic attack is like the brakes going out while driving a speeding car. You know you're skidding off the road, but you have no way of stopping.

- I'm a glorified taxi driver for my household: drop one kid off at baseball practice, another kid to dance rehearsal, and the other kid to a birthday party. And I don't even get a tip!

- As the storm intensified, the clasps of thunder shook the earth like a meteor crashing to the ground.

Beware of using a **mixed metaphor**, which occurs when a speaker combines two metaphors that don't logically go together. For example, if you say, "He stepped up to the plate and grabbed the bull by the horns," you are switching jarringly from a baseball image to a rodeo image.

One of the most famous examples of a mixed metaphor in the English language was uttered in the Irish Parliament by Boyle Roche in 1790: "Mr. Speaker, I smell a rat. I see him floating in the air. But mark me, sir, I will nip him in the bud."[19]

Avoid **clichés**, which are trite, worn-out words or phrases. Here are some examples: *better late than never, last but not least, raining cats and dogs, at the crack of dawn,* and *throw caution to the wind.* Clichés are evidence of lazy writing/speaking, because they are simply recycling old phrases. Be more clever. Eliminate clichés by trying to find fresh, lively alternatives. Instead of saying, "His tie *stuck out like a sore thumb,*" say something like "His tie was as out-of-place as a comedian at a funeral."

mixed metaphor
incongruously combined metaphors.

cliché
an overused word or phrase.

Using Rhetorical Devices

Rhetorical devices are artful arrangements of words to make one's remarks more interesting and memorable. Four of the most popular devices are alliteration, antithesis, parallel structure, and repetition.

Alliteration

Alliteration is the use of successive words that begin with the same consonant sound. We must love alliteration because our culture is filled with examples—in popular expressions (baby boomers), advertising slogans ("so soft and silky"), product names (Coca-Cola), TV shows (*Mad Men*), computer games (Leisure Suit Larry in the Land of the Lounge Lizards), sports events (Final Four), and names (Peter Pan).

Used sparingly, alliterative phrases can add sparkle to a speech. For example you might say, "We need to help the hungry and homeless survivors of the tornado." But excessive use of alliteration can make you look silly: "I detest the puny political pygmies who pontificate piously about pure piffle."

alliteration
repetition of the beginning sounds of words.

Antithesis

An **antithesis** is a rhetorical device in which sharply contrasting ideas are juxtaposed in a balanced structure, as in "He has cold hands, but a warm heart." The balance and the contrast emphasize the ideas and make the sentence memorable.

The device has been used in great historical speeches, including President John F. Kennedy's famous words, "Ask not what your country can do for you—ask what you can do for your country." It also can be used in your speeches, with phrasing such as the following:

antithesis
balanced juxtaposition of two contrasting ideas.

- "We want action, but they give us words."
- "They call it an eyesore. I call it home."
- "They don't care about people, but they do care about possessions."

Tips for Your Career

Explore Rhetorical Devices

Have you ever used a polysyndeton in a speech?

A *polysyndeton* is the repetition, in quick succession, of several conjunctions (such as *and, or, nor, but*) that are unnecessary but give a dramatic rhythm to a spoken sentence. For example, an operations manager might assure her colleagues, "We will be even more efficient this year. That's because compared to other companies, we have better employees *and* faster software *and* a stronger infrastructure, *and* the largest warehouse in the business." You can say the sentence without all those conjunctions, but you would lose a great deal of power.

A polysyndeton is just one of dozens of rhetorical devices. Search for "rhetorical devices" online to find lists of devices and their meanings. You can also search for specific rhetorical devices on YouTube to explore clips taken from speeches, sermons, movies, songs, and so on.

Most of the devices were originally identified and labeled by teachers of rhetoric in ancient Greece and Rome. They have esoteric names such as *epanalepsis* (the repetition of a word or phrase at the end of a statement that was originally said at the beginning the statement), but don't be put off. If you familiarize yourself with rhetorical devices and listen to audio examples, you will realize that the techniques are easy to use and can enrich your own speeches.

Parallel Structure and Repetition

parallel structure
equivalent grammatical forms used to express ideas of equal importance.

You can make your language memorable by taking advantage of rhythmic patterns. One such pattern is **parallel structure**—the repetition of a grammatical structure. Words, phrases, or clauses are arranged in parallel form, as in these examples:

We want a government...	of the people, by the people, for the people.
We need parents who will...	praise honest efforts, punish bad behavior, and ignore inconsequential acts.

repetition
repeating words or phrases for emotional effect.

Another effective rhythmic technique is **repetition** of words and phrases, as in the remark "This proposal is crazy, crazy, crazy."

When repetition and parallel structure are combined, the result can give emphasis to ideas while being pleasant to the ear.

I try to be a good dad, but oftentimes I fail.

I try to be a good dad, but sometimes I lose my kids in the grocery store.

I try to be a good dad, but sometimes I accidentally cuss in front of them.

I try to be a good dad, but sometimes I pretend I'm asleep when they're asking me questions.

I try to be a good dad, but oftentimes I fail.

Oral versus Written Language

One of the biggest mistakes some speakers make is to treat oral language in a speech as having the same requirements as written language. While the two forms of communication are similar, oral language requires more elaboration and repetition than written language. In an essay, you can write something like this:

As an environmental prophet, Susan Jameson is a canary, not a cuckoo.

That succinct sentence is excellent in an essay. The reader can study it at leisure if the meaning does not pop up immediately. But in a speech, a listener needs elaboration, such as this:

> As an environmental prophet, Susan Jameson is a canary, not a cuckoo. We can trust her to be reliable. She's like the canaries that coal miners used to take into mines to detect poisonous gases. If the canaries died, the miners knew they needed to rush to safety. Like a canary, Jameson can reliably tell us when the environment is in danger. She is not a cuckoo—a bird that sings false warnings.

In addition to expanding material, a speaker must often use pauses and give vocal emphasis to certain words. For example, consider this concise sentence by author James Thurber: "Do not look back in anger, or forward in fear, but around in awareness." This sentence is perfectly written, but in oral communication, it is too compact to be easily retained. When used in a speech, it would be better to expand and dramatize it, giving emphasis to three key words: "As James Thurber advises: [*Pause*] Do not look *back* in anger [*Pause*] . . . Do not look *forward* in fear [*Pause*] . . . Instead, look *around* in awareness." The pauses let the words sink in.

In oral communication, you need to repeat key ideas. *In oral communication, you need to repeat key ideas.* You can use the exact same words, but if possible, change the wording—not only for the sake of variety, but also to increase your chances of reaching different segments of your audience. One set of words might work well for some listeners, while another set might be needed for other listeners. When giving a speech, you should reinforce your main points.

Resources for Review and Skill Building

Summary

Because language has great power, the words that you use in a speech should be chosen with care and sensitivity. Always use language that is appropriate for your particular audience and occasion, avoiding words that might be misinterpreted by your audience.

To use words accurately, you must be sensitive to both denotation, which is a word's dictionary definition, and connotation, which is the emotional significance of the word.

Be careful to use correct grammar. In business and professional life today, ungrammatical English causes many listeners to lower their estimate of a speaker's credibility.

You can achieve clarity in your language by choosing words that are simple, concrete, and precise. Beware of two types of doublespeak: euphemisms, which try to sugarcoat the unpleasant taste of reality, and inflated language, which exaggerates the importance of a person or a thing. Avoid using jargon, the specialized language of a group or a profession, unless all listeners are certain to know the meanings of the words used. If you must use jargon with an audience outside the industry, do so sparingly and be sure to define the terms.

You can make your language colorful and memorable by using imagery, metaphors, and similes, as well as rhetorical devices such as alliteration, antithesis, parallel structure, and repetition.

Oral language and written language are similar in many ways, but they should be treated differently in a speech. Oral language requires more elaboration than written language, and it needs repetition of key ideas.

Key Terms

abstract words, *245*

alliteration, *249*

antithesis, *249*

cliché, *249*

concrete words, *245*

connotation, *243*

denotation, *243*

doublespeak, *246*

euphemism, *246*

gender-biased stereotype, *241*

imagery, *248*

inflated language, *247*

jargon, *247*

metaphor, *248*

mixed metaphor, *249*

parallel structure, *250*

repetition, *250*

simile, *248*

Review Questions

1. Why might you alter the same speech for a different audience?

2. What is the difference between the denotation and the connotation of a word?

3. Why is incorrect grammar a handicap for a speaker?

4. What is the difference between concrete language and abstract language? Give an example of each.

5. What is the difference between euphemism and inflated language? Give an example of each.

6. Change the following metaphor to a simile: "Her life was a whirlwind of meetings, deadlines, and last-minute decisions."

7. Change the following simile by poet Robert Burns to a metaphor: "My love is like a red, red rose."

8. What is the term for the error the following sentence commits? "Learning is a spark in a person's mind that must be watered constantly."

9. Which rhetorical device is used in the following sentence? "Louise languished in the land of lilies and lilacs."

10. In what way should oral language be treated differently from written language?

Building Critical-Thinking Skills

1. Some sports teams are named after birds—in football, Philadelphia Eagles, Atlanta Falcons, Seattle Seahawks, and Arizona Cardinals; in baseball, Toronto Blue Jays, St. Louis Cardinals, and Baltimore Orioles. Why are teams named after these birds, and yet no teams are named after vultures, crows, or pigeons?

2. A book on automobile repair was once advertised under the headline "How to Repair Cars." When the advertising agency changed the headline to "How to Fix Cars," sales jumped by 20 percent. Why do you think sales increased?

3. In referring to poor people, a government official once spoke of "fiscal underachievers." What kind of language is this term, and why do you think he chose it?

Building Teamwork Skills

1. In restaurants, diners are more likely to select a dish if the menu describes it in appetizing terms, such as "topped with *zesty* garlic butter." In a group, create a list of at least 10 items for a menu. Pretending that you are managers of a restaurant, make the descriptions as tempting as possible.

2. An online poll asked people to cite what they considered the most beautiful words in the English language. Among the words mentioned were *lullaby, violet,* and *Chattanooga.* Working in a group, create a list of at least 10 words that group members think are especially beautiful. Discuss why the words are considered beautiful—is it the sounds of the words or the images the words evoke? If time permits, have group members who speak or have studied other languages contribute beautiful words from those languages.

Examining Your Ethics

Answer: A. This is a straightforward, honest statement. The other two responses use euphemisms that are designed to mislead the public about what really happened.

End Notes

1. Jeff Freier, "The Top 5: Knuckleball Quotes," *SB Nation New York*, https://newyork.sbnation.com (accessed December 9, 2015).

2. "R.A. Dickey on 'Winding Up' as a Knuckleballer," *NPR News*, www.nprnews.org (accessed December 9, 2015).

3. Charles T. Blair-Broeker and Randal M. Ernst, *Thinking about Psychology* (New York: Macmillan Higher Education, 2012), p. 418.

4. Anthony Pratkanis and Elliot Aronson, *Age of Propaganda: The Everyday Use and Abuse of Persuasion* (New York: Macmillan, 2001), p. 33.

5. Alex Mayyasi, "The Invention of the Chilean Sea Bass," Priceonomics, https://priceonomics.com (accessed January 15, 2016).

6. C. J. Ducasse Quotes, Goodreads, www.goodreads.com (accessed December 12, 2015).

7. D. Harsanyi, "This Isn't the Most Important Election of Your Lifetime," *Reason*, https://reason.com/2018/10/26/this-isnt-the-most-important-election-of/ (accessed February 9, 2020).

8. C. MacCabe and H. Yanacek, "The Politics of 'Political,'" *Oxford University Press Blog*, https://blog.oup.com/2018/11/politics-of-political/ (accessed February 9, 2020).

9. Edward T. Thompson, "How to Write Clearly," reprint of advertisement by International Paper Company, n.d.

10. William Zinsser, *On Writing Well*, 30th anniversary edition (New York: Harper Perennial, 2012), Kindle edition (no page numbers).

11. Sheldon Rampton and John Stauber, *Trust Us, We're Experts!* (New York: Jeremy P. Tarcher/Putnam, 2001), p. 292.

12. Peter Cashwell, *Along Those Lines: The Boundaries That Create Our World* (Philadelphia: Paul Dry Books, 2014), p. 199.

13. Lisa Rein, "The IRS Hung Up on Taxpayers 8.8 Million Times This Year," *The Washington Post*, www.washingtonpost.com (accessed December 15, 2015).

14. Colin McNairn, *In a Manner of Speaking: Phrases, Expressions, and Proverbs and How We Use and Misuse Them* (New York: Skyhorse Publishing, 2015), Kindle edition (no page numbers).

15. Henry Beard and Christopher Cerf, *Spinglish: The Definitive Dictionary of Deliberately Deceptive Language* (New York: Blue Rider Press/Penguin Random house, 2015), Kindle edition (no page numbers).

16. Stephanie Strom, "Lawyers from Suits against Big Tobacco Target Food Makers," *The New York Times*, www.nytimes.com (accessed December 17, 2015).

17. Samuel Abt, "Armstrong's Lead Unchanged after the Pyrenees," *The New York Times*, www.nytimes.com (accessed December 15, 2015).

18. Barack Obama's Keynote Address at the 2004 Democratic National Convention, www.pbs.org/newshour/show/barack-obamas-keynote-address-at-the-2004-democratic-national-convention (accessed February 16, 2020).

19. "Sir Boyle Roche," Bartleby.com, www.bartleby.com/344/338.html (accessed January 21, 2016).

Delivering the Speech

OUTLINE

OBJECTIVES

After studying this chapter, you should be able to

1. Explain the four methods of delivery.
2. Practice and deliver an extemporaneous speech.
3. Use effective vocal techniques in a speech.
4. Demonstrate effective nonverbal communication in a speech.
5. Conduct a question-and-answer period in a manner that encourages audience participation.
6. Utilize production methods in practicing a speech.
7. Use effective techniques when speaking in front of a camera.

MERRITT WEVER has starred in dozens of popular movies and TV shows, including *New Girl, The Walking Dead,* and *Birdman.* So she should be comfortable when speaking in public, right?

But when Wever was given the 2013 Primetime Emmy Award for Outstanding Supporting Actress in a Comedy Series, she gave one of the most infamous acceptance speeches of all time:

> *Thanks so much. Thank you so much. I gotta go. Bye.*

Interestingly, the abrupt speech fit the character of the ditzy nurse she played in *Nurse Jackie,* the role for which she was being honored. But her 11-word speech was unintentional. After the ceremony, the actress admitted, "It's hard to do those," later joking, "I have therapy next week." [1]

Wever won another Emmy in 2018 for her role in *Godless* and acknowledged her nervousness, saying, "I really hope that you don't mistake my fear for a lack of gratitude." A few seconds later, as she stumbled over her words, Wever said, "I came prepared and it's bombing already." [2]

The crowd laughed and gave her a rousing applause, and Wever finished her speech by thanking the other actresses and the person who inspired her role.

Although neither of her speeches would be considered prototypes for delivering acceptance speeches, they do exemplify an important trait of speeches—*actually deliver the speech*.

Wever's first speech still lives in infamy, immortalized in memes about brevity. The blunders in her second speech are barely remembered. Why? In her first speech, Wever caved into her nervousness and left the stage, making it the shortest acceptance speech in history. But her second speech, with all its imperfections, was delivered and the audience rallied behind her. Wever came off as charming and likable, and the audience wanted her to succeed.

Minneapolis Star Tribune/ ZUMA Press Inc/Alamy Stock Photo

The Key to Good Delivery

The key to good delivery is a strong desire to communicate with the audience. In her second acceptance speech, Wever started out shaky, but overcame her nervousness to get her message across.

Public speakers who care deeply about conveying their ideas to the audience almost always do an adequate job with their delivery—even if they lack professional polish and training. Virgin Group founder and celebrity billionaire Sir Richard Branson still gets nervous speaking in public, but he offers advice that he follows to help him overcome his nervousness: "speak from the heart."[3]

It is difficult to deliver a speech on a topic that is of no interest to you. There's no way to "speak from the heart" if the heart feels no passion about the topic. The speaker needs a desire to communicate to put the ideas of this chapter into proper perspective. The dozens of tips about delivery in the pages that follow are important, and you should study them carefully. But bear in mind that a strong desire to communicate with your audience gives you the power to deliver a speech with energy and effectiveness.

Methods of Speaking

Four basic speaking methods are used by public speakers today: memorization, manuscript, impromptu, and extemporaneous.

Memorization

Some speakers memorize an entire speech and then deliver it without a script or notes. Memorizing is a bad idea for most speakers, however, because of the following liabilities:

- You are forced to spend an enormous amount of time committing the speech to memory.

- At some point in your speech, you might suddenly forget what comes next. This could cause you to panic. Once derailed, you might be unable to get back on track.

- Even if you remembered your entire speech, you would be speaking from your memory, not from your heart. This could cause you to sound remote and lifeless—more like a robot than a human being.

Actors must memorize lines from a script to deliver a strong performance. But a speech is not a performance; it is a conversation with the audience. Memorizing a speech is not recommended.

Manuscript

manuscript method
delivery of a speech by reading a script.

Some speakers put their entire speech word for word on a **manuscript**, which they read aloud to the audience. In most cases, this is a poor method. Although a few people can read text effectively, most speakers lack spontaneity and enthusiasm. They fail to look at the audience, do not speak with adequate expression, and often read too quickly.

There are some occasions, however, when reading a manuscript is appropriate:

- In a highly emotional situation (such as delivering a eulogy at a funeral), having a script can give you stability and reassurance that you won't break down or ramble.

- If there is someone else relying on cues from your speech. For example, if someone else is operating your PowerPoint presentation, giving the person a manuscript and highlighting the moments to change slides would be preferred.

- Many government hearings and scientific conferences prefer manuscript delivery because each speaker's complete text is printed in a document or posted online.

If you use a manuscript, follow these guidelines:

- For ease of reading, print the document in large letters and leave generous spacing between lines.
- Print only on the top one-third of the page so that you don't have to bob your head.
- Use a yellow highlighter to mark key words and phrases.
- Underline words that need to be spoken with extra emphasis.
- Insert slanting lines to indicate pauses.
- Practice reading the document many times until you are thoroughly familiar with it.

If you are well-rehearsed, you should be able to look at your audience frequently and make gestures. Because you are using a method that is often monotonous, try to inject vigor and variety into your voice. Above all else, don't race through the manuscript.

Impromptu

Speaking **impromptu** means speaking on the spur of the moment—with no opportunity for extensive preparation. For example, without warning you are asked to give a talk to your fellow employees about your recent conference in Detroit. Or during a class, you are asked to summarize the week's readings.

impromptu method speaking with little or no preparation.

Because you have to respond immediately, impromptu speaking can be stressful. Just remind yourself that your listeners realize you are speaking off-the-cuff—they are not expecting a polished masterpiece. Here are some guidelines for impromptu success:

Decide your conclusion first.   Knowing how you will finish can prevent a long, drawn-out ending or a weak comment like "Well, I guess that's it."

Organize your speech.   You can use an organizational pattern from earlier chapters—for example, the problem–solution pattern—or you might consider one of the ready-made patterns shown in Table 1. These patterns are used by experienced speakers to quickly structure impromptu speeches.

Table 1 **Patterns for Impromptu Speeches**

Point-Support-Conclusion

- **Point** (State your point of view—that is, your key idea or objective.)
- **Support** (Give examples, stories, or other support material to explain or prove the point.)
- **Conclusion** (End with a restatement of the point and/or an appeal to action.)

PREP Method

- **Position** (State your position on the topic.)
- **Reason** (State your reason for taking the position.)
- **Example** (Give an example that helps illuminate or explain your reasoning.)
- **Position** (Summarize and repeat your position.)

Past-Present-Future

- **Point** (State your key point.)
- **Past** (Discuss what happened in the past.)
- **Present** (Talk about what is occurring today.)
- **Future** (Predict what will or could happen in the future.)
- **Point** (Drive home your key point.)

Let's explore one of the methods by imagining that you work for an accounting firm that has a standard 9-to-5 schedule, and you want to recommend staggered hours. At a staff meeting, you are asked to make your case. Having only a few moments to prepare, you decide to use the PREP template (Table 1). Here is a streamlined version of your remarks:

> Position—"I believe that all employees will be happier and more productive if they are permitted to work from 11 A.M. to 7 P.M. for one day a week."
> Reason—"With our present 9-to-5 system, many important services are unavailable to us."
> Example—"For example, we have no chance to renew a driver's license because the state license office is open only on weekdays from 9 A.M. to 5 P.M."
> Position—"Giving us one 11-to-7 day per week will improve morale because we will be able to meet both professional and personal responsibilities."

Don't rush.   Speak at a steady, calm rate. When beginning, and at various intervals, pause for a few seconds to collect your thoughts.

Whenever possible, link your remarks to those of other speakers.   When you take a statement made by a previous speaker and build upon it, you connect with your listeners and hold their attention.

Don't feign knowledge.   If you are asked to comment on the spot on a matter about which you know nothing, simply say, "I don't know." Don't try to "wing it." Some speakers think that admitting ignorance will hurt their credibility, but the opposite is often true: if you fail to admit your ignorance and try to hide it behind a smokescreen of verbal ramblings, you can look insincere and foolish. Instead say, "I don't know the answer to that, but I'll look into it and get back to you as soon as I can."

Be brief.   Some impromptu speakers talk too long, repeating the same ideas or dwelling on irrelevant matters. They usually do so because they are afraid they are omitting something important or because they lack a graceful way of closing the speech. Rambling on and on is certain to weaken a speech.

Try to foresee situations where you are likely to be called upon to speak impromptu. Plan what you will say. For example, driving back from a workshop, rehearse in your mind what you will say if the boss asks you to make a little presentation to your colleagues about what you learned.

Extemporaneous

extemporaneous method
delivery of a speech from notes, following extensive preparation and rehearsal.

The **extemporaneous method** is the most popular style of speaking in the United States today. Your goal is to sound as if you are speaking spontaneously, but instead of giving the clumsy, faltering speech that many off-the-cuff speakers give, you present a beautifully organized, well-developed speech that you have spent many hours preparing and practicing.

In extemporaneous speaking, you speak from notes, but these notes are not a word-for-word script. Instead, they contain only your basic ideas, expressed in a few key words. When you speak, therefore, you make up the exact words as you go along. You glance at your notes occasionally to remind yourself of your next point, but most of the time you look at the listeners, speaking to them in a natural, conversational tone of voice.

This conversational tone is valued in a speech because it is the easiest kind for an audience to listen to, understand, and remember. When you speak conversationally, you are speaking directly, warmly, and sincerely. Your manner is as close as possible to the way you talk to your best friends: your voice is full of life and color; your words are fresh and vital.

Speaking extemporaneously permits flexibility because you can easily make adjustments to meet the needs of an audience. If, for example, you see that some listeners don't understand a point, you can restate your message in different words. If you are the last speaker of the evening at a banquet and you sense that your audience is about to go to sleep because of the preceding long-winded speakers, you can shorten your speech by cutting out minor points.

Despite its advantages, the extemporaneous method can be flawed if used incorrectly. Here are some common scenarios:

- In a three-point speech, Speaker A looks at his notes, states the first point, and then elaborates on it at great length. He loses track of time—until he finally notices a clock and gallops through the remaining points, confusing the audience.

- Speaker B has notes with key points, but she talks on and on about *all* the points. This causes her to go 20 minutes over her time limit, much to the annoyance of her listeners.

- Speaker C works from carefully crafted notes, but because he has not practiced the speech, his delivery is hesitant and ragged.

To avoid such mistakes, you must spend a lot of time preparing an outline and notes, and then rehearsing your speech, using a clock to make sure you are not ad-libbing too much.

Voice

Some people think that to be an excellent speaker, you must have a golden voice, rich and resonant, that enthralls listeners. This is not true. Some of the greatest orators in history had imperfect voices. Abraham Lincoln's voice was described by his contemporaries as shrill and unpleasant[4] while Winston Churchill stuttered and had a slight lisp.[5] It is nice to have a rich, resonant voice, but other characteristics of the human voice are more important: volume, clarity, and expressiveness.

Volume

The larger the room, the louder you have to speak. You can tell if your volume is loud enough by observing the people in the back. Are they leaning forward with quizzical expressions as they strain to hear your words? Then obviously you need to speak louder. You may have to raise your voice to overcome noises, such as the chatter of people in a hallway or the clatter of dishes during a banquet.

Speaking loudly enough for all to hear does not mean shouting. It means *projecting* your voice a bit beyond its normal range. If you have never spoken to a large group or if your instructor tells you that you have problems with projecting your voice, practice with a friend. Find an empty classroom, have your friend sit in the back row, and practice speaking with extra force—not shouting—so that your friend can hear you easily.

In addition to projecting your voice, remember to speak in the direction of your audience. A common mistake speakers make is turning their attention away from the

When using a microphone, remember to speak continuously into the mic.

wavebreakmedia/Shutterstock

audience and to their visual presentation. For example, while pointing out an element on a PowerPoint slide, a speaker may begin talking in the direction of the screen, away from the audience. The same trap happens when speakers look at their notes for a lengthy period of time—they begin to talk into their notes, again directing their voice away from the audience.

In some environments you will have access to a microphone. If possible, it is a good idea to practice with a microphone; it can be quite intimidating to speak on a microphone for the first time, hearing your voice projected across the room. Adjust the microphone to your height so you can stand up straight and not awkwardly bend over. You should not adjust to the placement of the microphone, rather the microphone should be adjusted to your preference.

There are dozens of different styles and qualities of microphones. For most microphones, speak with your mouth about 6-12 inches away from it. The key component of using a microphone is to remember to keep speaking into the microphone—turning your head or moving away from the mic will make portions of your speech inaudible.

Although you have a microphone, you still should continue to project your voice. Obviously, you do not need to be as concerned about people hearing you, but it is still important to speak with emotion.

Dialects

dialect
a particular form of a language that is peculiar to a specific region or social group.

People from different regions of the world, and even from different regions of the country, speak with different **dialects**. This is especially true for people who speak English as a second language. It is important to recognize if you speak with a distinct dialect, understand the audience to whom you are speaking. If you know you struggle with certain words or phrases, practice saying them out loud. Another option is to include those words on your slide presentation. Be sure to speak in a conversational tone, not going so fast that your dialect becomes difficult for your audience to understand. Slow down when there are important points you want to emphasize. Remember, the overall goal is for your audience to understand your speech.

Clarity

Texting or messaging has become a very popular form of communication due to its non-invasive and brief nature. The texting lexicon has obliterated the English language, as acronyms, emoticons, and abbreviations have become more common. The following text exchange is considered pretty standard:

> Joe: WTH was up with that meeting?
> Carla: IMHO it was a waste of time. 2 hours of my life wasted!
> Joe: LOL
> Carla: U going to lunch?
> Joe: Yes! U should join me :-/
> Carla: OMW!
> Joe: :)

articulation
the act of producing vocal sounds.

Although there is nothing wrong with the above exchange, when giving a speech it is important to speak with clarity. A critical element for clarity is good **articulation**—the production of speech sounds by our vocal organs. In daily conversation, it is common to slur sounds, drop syllables, and mumble words. While poor articulation may not hurt us in conversation as long as our friends understand what we are saying, it can hinder communication in a speech. It is important to enunciate our words crisply and precisely to make sure that everything we say is intelligible.

If you tend to slur words, you can improve your speech by reading poems or essays aloud for 15 minutes a day for three weeks. Say the words with exaggerated emphasis, and move your mouth and tongue vigorously. Enunciate consonants firmly and make vowel sounds last longer than normal. In real situations, you should not exaggerate in this way, but the practice will help you avoid the pitfalls of slurring and mumbling.

While poor articulation stems from sloppy habits, poor **pronunciation** is a matter of not knowing the correct way to say a word. Examine the common pronunciation mistakes listed in Table 2.

pronunciation
correct way of speaking a word.

Be careful using words that you have picked up from books but have never heard pronounced. For example, you might be fascinated with the Sioux Indians and excited to give a speech about them, but have never heard the tribal name pronounced correctly. You might mistakenly call them the *sigh-ox* in your speech, rather than the correct pronunciation *sue.* Another common slip is to confuse words that sound alike. For example, in a speech about marriage you might encourage couples to make sure they are

Table 2 **Common Pronunciation Mistakes**

Word	Incorrect Pronunciation	Correct Pronunciation
across	uh-crost	uh-cross
athlete	ath-uh-lete	ath-lete
burglar	burg-you-lur	burg-lur
chef	tchef	shef
chic	chick	sheek
drowned	drown-did	drownd
electoral	e-lec-tor-ee-al	e-lec-tor-al
environment	en-vire-uh-ment	en-vi-run-ment
et cetera	ek-setera	et-setera
evening	eve-uh-ning	eve-ning
grievous	greev-ee-us	greev-us
height	hithe	hite
hundred	hun-derd	hun-dred
library	li-berry	li-brar-ee
mischievous	miss-chee-vee-us	miss-chuh-vus
nuclear	nu-cu-lar	nu-cle-ar
perspiration	press-pi-ray-shun	per-spi-ray-shun
picture	pitch-er	pick-shur
pretty	pur-tee	prit-ee
professor	pur-fess-ur	pruh-fess-ur
quiet	quite	kwy-et
realtor	reel-uh-tor	re-ul-tor
recognize	reck-uh-nize	rec-og-nize
relevant	rev-uh-lant	rel-uh-vant
strength	strenth	streng-th

compatible before they say their *vowels,* instead of *vows.* You can avoid such mistakes by practicing a speech in front of friends or colleagues and asking them to flag errors.

Expressiveness

A dynamic speaker has a voice that is warm and expressive, producing a rich variety of sounds. There are five basic elements of expressiveness: pitch and intonation, loudness and softness, rate of speaking, pauses, and conversational quality.

Pitch and Intonation

pitch
the highness or low-ness of a sound.

intonation
the use of chang-ing pitch to convey meaning.

The highness or lowness of your voice is called **pitch**. The ups and downs of pitch—called **intonation** patterns—give language its distinctive melody. Consider the following sentence: "I love you." The phrase can be said in a variety of ways and mean completely different things. In can be said with sarcasm after a friend tells a corny joke. It can be said with sincerity when hanging up the phone with a parent. It can be said with passion after receiving a meaningful gift from a significant other. Depending on the situation, the phrase is said using a different intonation pattern.

In conversation, almost everyone uses a variety of intonation patterns and empha-sizes particular words, but in public speaking, some speakers fail to use any variety at all. Instead, they speak in monotone—a dull, flat drone that will put many listeners to sleep. Even worse, they run the risk of appearing insincere. They may say something dramatic like "This is a terrible tragedy," but say it in such a flat way that the audience thinks they don't really mean it.

An absence of intonation also means that some words fail to receive the emphasis they deserve. For example, take a sentence like this: "Although they do the same job, Mr. Smith made $60,000 last year, while Mrs. Jones made $50,000." A speaker who talks in a monotone will say the two figures as if there were no difference between $60,000 and $50,000. But to help listeners hear the disparity, the speaker should let his or her voice place heavy emphasis on the $60,000.

Loudness and Softness

Besides using proper projection so that everyone in the audience can hear you speak, you should raise or lower your voice for dramatic effect or to emphasize a point. Try saying the following out loud:

> [*Soft*] "Should we give in to the kidnappers' demands? [*Switch to loud*] NEVER!"

Did you notice that raising your voice for the last word conveys that you truly mean what you say? Now try another selection out loud:

> [*Start softly and make your voice grow louder as you near the end of this sen-tence.*] "Edwin Arlington Robinson's character, Richard Cory, had everything that a man could want—good looks, lots of money, popularity." [*Now make your voice switch to soft.*] "But he went home one night and put a bullet through his head."

Changing from loud to soft helps the listeners *feel* the tragic discrepancy between Richard Cory's outward appearance and his inner reality.

Rate of Speaking

How quickly or slowly should you speak? It all depends on the situation. If you are describing a thrilling high-speed police chase, a rapid rate is appropriate, but if you are explaining a technical, hard-to-understand concept, a slow pace is preferred.

One of the biggest mistakes inexperienced speakers make is speaking too quickly. It is especially important that you speak at a deliberate rate during your introduction. Remember, the goal is to speak conversationally, and you want your audience to know what you are talking about. Give your audience a chance to get acquainted to you, your voice, and subject matter. If you race through your introduction, they may become lost and confused.

Speaking at a deliberate, unhurried pace helps you come across as someone who is confident and in control, as someone who cares about whether the listeners understand. This is especially important if you speak with a different dialect than your audience.

Pauses

When you read printed material, you have punctuation marks to help you make sense out of your reading. In a speech, there are no punctuation marks, so listeners must rely on your oral cues to guide them. One of these cues is the pause, which lets your listeners know when you have finished one thought and are ready to go to the next. Audiences appreciate a pause; it gives them time to digest what you have said.

A pause before an important idea or the climax of a story can be effective in creating suspense. Also, insert a pause when there is intended laughter:

> I'll never forget when I first moved from Chicago to the South. I was being introduced to my co-workers and one man shook my hand and asked, "Are you a Yankee?"

> I had no idea what he was talking about—the only Yankees I've ever heard of are the baseball players from New York. [*Pause*]

By pausing at this point, the speaker was giving space for the audience to laugh. The sincerity of the speaker makes listeners want to hear more of the story.

> "No sir. I'm a Chicago White Sox fan," I answered.

A pause also can be used to emphasize an important statement. It is a way of saying, "Let this sink in." Mark Twain said it best: "The right word may be effective, but no word was ever as effective as [*Pause*] a rightly timed pause."[6]

In some speeches, you may find yourself pausing not because you want to but because you have forgotten what you were planning to say next and you need to glance at your notes. Or you may pause while searching your mind for the right word. Such a pause seems like an eternity, and as humans we are naturally uncomfortable with silence when there is an expectation of conversation.

This is what leads many speakers to use **verbal fillers** such as "uh," "er," or "um." Such words can be incredibly distracting to the audience, and represent poor public speaking. Instead, remain silent, and don't worry that your silence is a "mistake." A few such pauses can show the audience that you are a conscientious speaker who is concerned about using the most precise words possible.

verbal fillers vocalized pauses in which a speaker inserts sounds such as "uh."

Conversational Quality

Some speakers give their speeches in a dull, plodding voice. Yet five minutes afterward, chatting with their friends in the hall, they speak with animation and warmth.

They need to bring that same conversational quality into their speeches. How can this be done? How can a person sound as lively and as "real" when talking to 30 people as when chatting with a friend? Here are two suggestions.

1. **Treat your audience not as a blur of faces but as a collection of individuals.** Here's a mental ploy you can use: at the beginning of a speech, look at one or two

How to Handle Tearful Situations

Sometimes a speech may include material that tugs at the heartstrings, and causes the speaker to tear up. For example, in a speech about pet adoption, a speaker might talk about his or her own experiences with pet adoption, bringing back memories of a deceased pet.

Some may avoid discussing topics that are emotional for them; however, speaking on such topics can be very powerful for the speaker and the audience. Emotion is a powerful element in a speech, and speakers should not avoid a topic just because they are concerned it will elicit tears.

Rather than avoid such topics, practice the speech and welcome the emotions as they come. If you need to cry, take the time to cry and do not worry about finishing the speech during this practice session. Practicing multiple times will help you get through the part that is eliciting the emotion.

Even with the practice, acknowledge that you may get emotional when giving the speech. However, because you already practiced the speech and allowed your emotions to come out, it is likely your emotions will be tempered during your speech. Be sure to have tissues on hand and deliver your speech.

Don't be afraid to show emotions. Listeners are very understanding, and some of them may join you in shedding tears.

One note of caution: Don't let tears cause you to end your speech prematurely. Pause, pull yourself together, and continue.

At a news conference on medical issues, Mike Hopkins of Covington, Georgia, wipes his face as he cries while talking about losing two of his children because of complications from seizures. Do you think that anyone in the room thought less of Hopkins because he cried?

David Goldman/AP Images

individuals in different parts of the room and act as if you are talking to them personally. You should avoid staring, of course, but looking at each face briefly will help you develop a conversational attitude. As the speech goes on, add other faces to your "conversation."

2. **Be yourself—but somewhat intensified.** To speak to an audience with the same natural, conversational tone you use with your friends, you must speak with greater energy and forcefulness. I am not talking now about projecting your voice so that the people can hear you but, rather, about *intensifying* the emotional tones and the vibrancy of your voice.

Being yourself in front of a large group of strangers does not come naturally to everyone. It doesn't always come naturally even if you personally know your listeners, such as classmates or colleagues. There are two ways to be a more intensified version of yourself when delivering a speech.

1. **Let your natural enthusiasm show.** If you have chosen a topic wisely, you are speaking about something you care about and want to communicate. When you stand in front of your audience, don't hold yourself back; let your voice convey all the

enthusiasm that you feel inside. Many speakers are afraid they will look or sound ridiculous if they get involved with their subject. "I'll come on too strong," they say. But the truth is that your audience will appreciate your energy and zest. Think back to the speakers you have heard. Didn't you respond best to those who were alive and enthusiastic?

2. **Practice loosening up.** Some novice speakers sound and look stiff simply because they have not had practice loosening up. Here is something you can try: find a private location and practice a speech you are working on, recite poetry, read from a book, or simply ad-lib. Whatever words you use, say them dramatically. Ham it up. Be theatrical. Act as if you are running for president and you are trying to persuade an audience of 10,000 people to vote for you. Or pretend you are giving a poetry reading to 500 of your most enthusiastic fans. You will not speak so dramatically to a real audience, of course, but the practice in "letting go" will help you break out of your normal reserve. It will help you learn to be yourself, to convey your natural enthusiasm.

Nonverbal Communication

Nonverbal communication consists of the messages that you send without words—what you convey with your eyes, facial expression, posture, body movement, and the characteristics of your voice (as discussed in the preceding section).

To be credible to your audience, your nonverbal communication must be synchronized with your words. If you say, "I'm very happy to be here," but your eyes are cast downward and your face is glum, your audience will think that you are not being honest. *Whenever there is a discrepancy between "body language" and words, listeners will believe the nonverbal signals instead of the verbal message.*[7]

To get your nonverbal signals synchronized with your words, show enthusiasm—with your eyes, facial expression, posture, and tone of voice—as you speak. If you do not feel like giving the speech or are extremely nervous, pretend. Yes, pretend to be confident in yourself and in your ideas. Pretend to be glad to appear before your audience. Pretend to be enthusiastic.

Yes, this is inauthentic, but that is okay. Humans put on different faces in different situations, without even thinking about it. You simulate cheerfulness and animation many times when you are not feeling up to it: a meeting with a professor, a conference with the boss, an important date with someone we love. By *acting* confident, poised, and enthusiastic, after a few minutes, the pretense gives way to reality. You will truly become confident, poised, and enthusiastic.

But even if this transformation does not happen, you should still pretend . . . and get through it. Think about a time when you were uncomfortable but still had to put on your "game face," such as a job interview. Even if you felt anxious throughout the entire process, you likely attempted to exude confidence and interest.

How can you make your body "lie" for you? By knowing and using the signals that the body sends out to show confidence and energy. The following discussion of the major nonverbal aspects of public speaking will help you become aware of these signals.

nonverbal communication
transmission of messages without words.

This nonverbal signal is used throughout the world. What does it mean?

FogStock/Alamy Stock Photo

At a U.S. Senate committee hearing, actor Ben Affleck shows that (1) dressing up is a sign of respect for your audience and (2) eye contact helps show your sincerity.

Bariskan Unal/Anadolu Agency/Getty Images

Personal Appearance

Your audience will size up your personal appearance and start forming opinions about you even before you open your mouth to begin your speech. You should be clean, well-groomed, and attractively dressed.

Janet Stone and Jane Bachner, who conduct workshops for women executives, have some good advice for both men and women:

> As a general rule of thumb, find out what the audience will be wearing and then wear something yourself that is just a trifle dressier than their clothes. The idea is to establish yourself as "The Speaker," to set yourself slightly apart from the crowd.[8]

Dressing up carefully is a compliment to the audience, sending the nonverbal message "You are important to me—so important that I dressed up a bit to show my respect for you."

Don't wear anything that distracts or diminishes communication. Baseball caps tend to hinder eye contact, and they suggest disrespect to some listeners. A shirt with a ribald or controversial slogan printed on the front may direct attention away from the speech itself, and it may offend some members of the audience.

You may regularly attend class in a T-shirt and pajama pants, and that may be okay. However, when you are presenting, you should show respect for your audience by dressing appropriately.

Eye Contact

Look at your audience 95 percent of the time. Good eye contact is important for several reasons: (1) It creates an important bond of communication and rapport between you and your listeners. (2) It shows your sincerity. We distrust people who won't look at us openly and candidly. (3) It enables you to get audience feedback. For example, did a number of listeners look puzzled when you made your last statement? Then you obviously confused them, and you need to explain your point in a different way.

The biggest spoiler of good eye contact is looking at your notes too much—a mistake that is usually made for these two reasons: (1) You are unprepared. This can be corrected by rehearsing your speech so that you need only glance at your notes to remind yourself of what comes next. (2) You are nervous. Some speakers are well-prepared and don't really need to look at their notes very often, but they are so nervous that they scrutinize their notes to gain security and avoid the audience. One way to correct this is to put reminders on your notes in giant red letters—LOOK AT AUDIENCE—to nudge you out of this habit.

Another security blanket speakers often rely on is their presentation. Be careful not to stare at the screen while talking. Not only does this eliminate your ability to make eye contact with the audience, but it also impacts the ability of the audience to hear you speaking since your voice is carrying to the screen instead of the audience.

In addition to making sure you are making eye contact, do not give your audience an opportunity to not look at you by distributing handouts before or during the speech. If you give listeners an eight-page packet during your speech, they will stare at that and you will lose eye communication.

Eye contact is more than glancing at the audience from time to time. It is more than mechanically moving your head from side to side like an oscillating fan. For a large audience, the best technique is to have a "conversation" with three or four people in different parts of the room (so that you seem to be giving your attention to the entire audience). For a small audience, look at *every* listener.

Facial Expressions

Let your face express whatever emotion is appropriate during your speech. The best facial expression—if it is appropriate—is a smile. Smiling can reduce your stress and lift the mood of both you and the audience, says Diane Windingland, a member of Toastmasters International and a presentation coach. "The contagious nature of a smile encourages listeners to smile back at you."[9]

A smile is one of the most powerful types of nonverbal communication.

Michaeljung/Shutterstock

Posture

Good **posture** conveys confidence. Stand up straight, with your weight equally distributed on your feet so that you appear stable and self-assured. Avoid two common pitfalls—slouching and drooping at one extreme, and being rigid and tense at the other extreme. Your goal should be relaxed alertness—in other words, be relaxed but not *too* relaxed.

> **posture**
> the position of your body as you sit or stand.

If you are speaking at a lectern, here are some things *not* to do: Don't lean on it. Don't slouch to one side of it. Don't prop your feet on its base. Don't rock back and forth with it.

Some speakers like to sit on the edge of a desk to deliver a speech. This posture is fine for one-hour classroom lectures because the speaker gets a chance to relax, and his or her body language conveys openness and informality. But for short speeches, especially the kind you are expected to deliver in a public speaking class, stand up. This will help make you alert and enthusiastic.

Movement

You don't have to stand in one place throughout your speech. Movement gives your body a chance to dissipate nervous energy. It also can be used to recapture your listeners' attention if they are getting bored or tired; an animated speaker is easier to follow than an unanimated speaker who stays frozen in one spot.

You can use movement to emphasize a transition from one point to the next. For example, walk a few steps to the left of the lectern as you say, "Now that we have examined the problem, let's discuss the solution." You can move *toward* your listeners when you plead for an immediate response (for example, "Please donate to help find a cure for cystic fibrosis").

Make sure that all movements are purposeful and confident—not random and nervous. Don't sway back and forth; don't rock on your heels. In short, make your movements add to your speech, rather than subtract from it. A good tip is to make movements during the transitions in your speech: the transition from the introduction to your first main point, the first main point to the second main point, and so on.

Using Notes

For classroom speeches, your instructor will tell you whether you may use notes. For speeches in your career, the note system that was explained in the chapter on outlining the speech is highly recommended.

Most professional speakers use cards or sheets of paper, and they have different ways of using them. Speakers who use a lectern place their notes in a stack on the lectern and consult one at a time, or they spread notes out so that several are visible at a time. Speakers who don't use a lectern prefer to hold their notes in one hand while gesturing with the other.

Tips for Your Career

Decide Whether and How to Use a Lectern

Experienced speakers disagree about whether a lectern should be used for career and community speeches. Some say that a lectern gives the speaker dignity and is a convenient stand for notes, especially on formal occasions such as an awards ceremony or a funeral. Others object that a lectern creates a physical barrier.

Here is a technique that is popular: using the lectern as "home base," walk a few paces to the left or right of it each time you make a point. In other words, glance at the notes on the lectern to remind yourself of the point you want to make, move away from the lectern a few paces, make the point, then walk back to the lectern to pick up your next point.

With some audiences, you can arrange for a remote or mobile microphone so that you can ignore the lectern or have it removed.

For a large audience, if the lectern is unmovable and has a stationary microphone, you have no choice but to stand behind it. Be sure not to lean on the podium and to adjust the microphone to your desired height.

doomu/Shutterstock

Whatever system you use, remember the earlier warning: *use notes sparingly.* Look at your audience 95 percent of the time.

Gestures

Making gestures with your hands and arms can add power to your words and cause you to look animated and engaged. Gestures should be natural and unplanned. They should occur spontaneously and be in harmony with what you are saying.

At all times, have at least one hand free to make gestures. To keep one hand available, abide by these rules: (1) Don't grip the lectern with your hands. (2) Don't clutch your notes with both hands. (3) Don't stuff both hands into your pockets.

If you use a lectern, don't let it hide your gestures. Some speakers rest their hands on the lectern and make tiny, flickering gestures that can be sensed but not seen by the audience. This makes the speaker look tentative and unsure.

When you make gestures, use all of your arm, advises British speech consultant Cristina Stuart:

> Don't tuck in your elbows to your waist or make jerky, half-hearted, meaningless gestures. I remember a tall woman in one of my courses who, through shyness, stood hunched up, making tiny movements with her hands. We advised her to stand tall, make eye contact, and use her arms to express her enthusiasm. The result was startling—she became regal and was very impressive. Without even opening her mouth, she looked like a self-confident, interesting speaker.[10]

Some speeches call for lots of gestures; some call for few or none. If you were describing your battle to catch a huge fish, you would find your hands and arms constantly in motion; if you were giving a funeral eulogy, you might not make any gestures at all.

While most gestures should occur naturally, there are a few occasions when it is appropriate to plan and rehearse them. If you have three major points to make, you can practice holding up the correct number of fingers. If you are discussing two contrasting ideas, you can hold up one hand when you say, "On the one hand . . ." and then hold up your other when you say, "On the other hand . . ."

The larger the audience, the more sweeping your gestures should be. Evangelists and political leaders who use broad, expansive arm movements when addressing multitudes in giant stadiums are doing so for a good reason: they are able to establish a bond with people who are hundreds of yards away. Small gestures would be lost in the vastness of the arena.

Some students worry too much about gestures. If you are the kind of person who simply does not gesture a great deal, don't be dismayed. Just be sure to keep at least one hand free so that if a gesture wells up, you will be able to make it naturally and forcefully.

One final note about your hands is to make sure they do nothing to distract the audience. Don't let them jingle keys, riffle note cards, fiddle with jewelry, adjust clothes, smooth your hair, rub your chin, or scratch any part of your body.

Fashion designer Zac Posen uses gestures effectively as he speaks at the Variety Power of Women conference in New York City.

Jemal Countess/Getty Images

Beginning and Ending

First impressions are important, especially in a speech where you have only one chance to make a first impression. You make this first impression as you walk to the front and say your first few words.

When you rise from your seat, walk to the front of the room with an air of confidence. Avoid the mistake of rushing forward and starting to speak even before you get to the front. Listeners need time to get settled for your speech, clear their minds of other things, and tune into you.

Face your audience and pause for a few seconds. Don't say a word—just stand in silence. Some inexperienced speakers are terrified by this silence; they think it makes them look too frozen with fear to speak. However, a brief period of silence is an effective technique that all good speakers use. It is a punctuation device, separating what went before from what is to come—your speech. It creates drama, giving the audience a sense of anticipation. In some cases, you may need to wait longer than a few seconds. If you are speaking at a community meeting, for example, and people are arriving late, it is best to wait until the noise created by the latecomers has settled down. Or if many members of the audience are chatting with one another, simply stand and wait until you have their attention.

During these opening moments of silence, you have a chance to make sure your notes are in order and to review once again what you will say in your introduction. The next step is very important. Before you say a word, give your audience a friendly, confident look (if possible and appropriate, smile), and then say your first few sentences. You should have practiced your introduction thoroughly so that you can say it without looking down at your notes. It is important to establish eye contact at this point. By looking at the listeners directly, your body language is saying, "I'm talking to you—I'm not up here just going through the motions of making a speech. I want to communicate. I want to reach out to you."

While first impressions are vital, final impressions are also important. Your conclusion should be well-rehearsed (though not memorized) so that you can say it without

Tips for Your Career

Deal with Distractions in a Direct but Good-Humored Manner

In classroom speeches, you should have an attentive, courteous audience, but at some point in your career, you may encounter an audience that contains listeners who chat among themselves while you are trying to speak, distracting other listeners.

Professional speakers stress that you should *not* ignore disturbances. Confront these listeners, but do so in a calm, friendly, good-humored manner.

One technique is to simply stop your speech and look directly at the rude listeners (try to look friendly and not irritated). This is often all it takes to get people to stop talking. Sometimes people sitting near the offenders will pick up on your cue and help you out by turning and saying, "shh."

In some cases, you might try asking, "Is there anything I can clarify or explain?" It could turn out that some of the listeners are confused about something you have said and they are discussing the matter among themselves. When you make your inquiry, you may unearth issues that the whole audience would appreciate your elaborating on.

If you are speaking and your phone rings (because you forgot to silence it), don't make a fuss about it. Just pull it out, turn it off, and keep going. The less said, the better.

Sometimes a speech is disrupted by the incessant crying of a baby. You should ask the parents to take the child out of the room—at least until he or she stops crying. You can explain that the distraction caused by the baby might prevent some listeners from receiving your message.

Some speeches are marred by listeners with electronic devices. For advice on how to handle these situations, see Tip 3, "Confront Electronic Rudeness," in the chapter on listening.

What would you do if a crying baby disrupted your presentation?
Halfpoint/Shutterstock

looking at your notes. At the end of your speech, pause a few moments, look at your audience, and if appropriate say, "I'll be happy to answer your questions now." Avoid gathering up your papers and leaning toward your seat—this sends a nonverbal message: "Please don't ask me any questions."

The Question-and-Answer Period

The question-and-answer period enables listeners to get clarification and further information about your topic. In classroom speeches, it usually involves only a small percentage of the total time spent in front of the audience, but in some career presentations—such as selling a product—it is the longest and most important part.

Many listeners are so accustomed to listener–speaker interaction that they will interrupt during a speech to ask questions. In some technical presentations or classroom lectures, such interruptions may be appropriate and acceptable, but in other speeches, they are a nuisance. The continuity of the speaker's remarks is broken because listeners are prematurely asking questions that will be answered later in the speech. If you feel that your speech would be marred by interruptions, you should

An audience member asks a question at the International Music Summit in Hollywood. Q & A sessions are considered an essential part of most presentations.

Dan Steinberg/Invision/AP Images

announce in the orienting material of your introduction, "I know many of you will have questions. I'd like to ask you to hold them until I finish my presentation, and then I'll be happy to try to answer them."

Don't feel defeated if you are not asked any questions. It could mean that you have covered everything so well that the listeners truly have nothing to ask.

Here are some guidelines for preparing for a question-and-answer period.

Planning

- Find out ahead of time if the person planning the program will want or permit a question-and-answer period, and if so, how much time will be allotted.

- Plan for the question-and-answer period by jotting down all the questions that might come from the audience and decide how you would answer them. Also discuss your speech with a few friends or associates and ask them to prepare a list of possible questions.

Fielding Questions

- Give the audience time to ask their questions. When you ask for questions, pause for as long as 10 seconds. If you get the feeling that no questions at all will be asked, you can say, "Thank you," and then sit down. But if you sense that the audience is simply shy, you can break the ice by saying, "One question that I am often asked is . . ." In some community and career contexts, you may want to involve listeners by asking *them* a question (for example, "What do *you* think of my proposal?").

- While a person is asking a question, look directly at him or her, but as you give your answer, look at the entire audience.

- In a large room, when a question is asked, repeat it for the benefit of listeners who may not have been able to hear it. Repeating it also gives you time to frame your answer. If a question is unclear to you, ask the listener to clarify it.

- Be consistent in how you respond. If you reward some questions with "That's a good question" or "I'm glad you asked that," the listeners who receive no praise may feel as if their questions have been judged inferior. Reward all questions—or none.

- If you don't know the answer to a question, say so. Your listeners will not think less of you. They *will* think less of you if you try to fake expertise. In some cases, you can ask the audience for help: "I don't know the answer; can anyone help us out?"

Handling Problems

- If a listener points out an inaccuracy or an omission in your material, don't be defensive. If the listener's point seems to have merit, say so. You can say something like "You may be right—that statistic could be outdated. I'll have to check it. Thanks." Such an approach is not only honest—it gains respect from listeners.

- Don't let any listener hog the question-and-answer period. If a person persists in asking one question after another or launches into a long monologue, it is your responsibility to intervene. You can say something like "Let's give others a chance to ask questions; if we have time later, I'll get back to you" or "Why don't you and I talk about this in greater detail after the meeting."

- Decline to answer questions that are not appropriate for a discussion in front of the entire audience—for example, questions that are too personal or that require a long, technical explanation that would bore most of the listeners. You can politely explain your reasons by saying something like "That's a little too personal—I'd rather not go into that" or "I'm afraid it would take up too much time to go into the details right now." In some cases, you might tell the questioner to see you afterward for a one-on-one discussion.

Ending the Session

- Don't let the question-and-answer period drag on. If you have been allotted an hour for both your speech and the Q & A period, end the session promptly at the end of an hour—even if some listeners still have questions. If you sense that some listeners would like to continue the session, you can say, "I'm stopping now because I promised I would take up only one hour of your time. However, if any of you would like to stay afterward, you can move to the seats here at the front and we'll continue our discussion."

- At the end of the Q & A session, provide a conclusion—not the conclusion you have already given in your speech, but a brief wrap-up—to give a sense of closure and provide one last look at your message. For example, you might say, "Thank you for letting me talk to you today about the need to get a flu shot every year. With flu season approaching, I hope each of you will get a flu shot as soon as possible."

Practice

After you have written your outline and made notes based on it, you should spend a great deal of time rehearsing your speech. Practice, practice, practice—it's a crucial step that some inexperienced speakers leave out. Practice makes you look and sound fluent, smooth, and spontaneous. Practice bolsters your confidence, giving you a sense of mastery and competence.

Here are some tips:

- Start early. If you wait until the night before your speech, you will not have enough time to develop and polish your delivery.

- Practice going through your entire speech at least four times. Spread your practice sessions over several days. Having time intervals between sessions will cause you to make greater progress.

- "Practice ideas, not words" is a popular saying in Toastmasters clubs. In other words, learn your speech point by point, not word for word. Remember that your goal in extemporaneous speaking is not to memorize or read a speech. Every time you say your speech (whether in practice or in delivery to an audience), the wording should be a bit different. The ideas will be the same, but not the exact words.

- Time yourself. If your speech exceeds the time limit set by your instructor or by the group that invited you, go back to your outline and notes and trim them down.

- During most of your practice sessions, go all the way through the speech. Don't stop if you hit a problem; you can work it out later. Going all the way through helps you see whether your ideas fit together snugly, and whether your transitions from point to point are smooth.

- Some speakers find it helpful to practice in front of a mirror or to record their rehearsals and watch or listen to them afterward. Whether or not you use one of these techniques, you should practice at least once in front of a *live* audience of friends or relatives who can give you a candid appraisal. Don't say, "Tell me how I do on this," because your evaluators will probably say, "Good job—I liked the speech," to avoid hurting your feelings. Instead give them a specific assignment: "Please note at least three positive things and at least three things that need improvement." Now your listeners have an assignment that they know will not hurt your feelings, and you are likely to get some helpful feedback.

- Some speakers find it helpful to make a trial run in the room in which they will deliver the speech. This is an especially good idea if you have visual aids and equipment, as you should test those in advance.

- In addition to practicing the entire speech, devote special practice time to your beginning and your ending—two parts that should be smooth and effective.

- Be sure that you don't put too many words on your notes. Have just key words that will jog your memory. Practice from the actual notes that you will use in the speech. Don't make a clean set right before the speech; the old, marked-up notes are more reliable because you're familiar with them from your practice sessions.

Time yourself in practice. If you are in danger of exceeding the time limit, trim your speech.

Gunnar Pippel/Shutterstock

Speaking in Front of a Camera

Chances are good that you will appear on video many times in the future, and sometimes you may have to create your own video using a video camera, tablet, or smartphone. You may be asked to record a speech for a class, participate in a video interview for a job, or take part in a meeting via video conference. Regardless of the situation, presenting through video presents some different challenges than presenting in person.

For video presentations, consider the following guidelines.

Dress conservatively.   The same rules apply for video that apply for in-person speeches. Show respect for your audience by dressing appropriately. Do not wear clothes with logos, pictures, or other distracting features. Avoid sparkling or noisy jewelry. If you notice your face looks shiny on camera, use face powder to cut down on shininess and glare.

Choose your background.   Make sure your background is uncluttered and contains no distractions. You want the viewer to be able to focus on you, not trying to figure out what is behind you. Avoid windows as backgrounds, as the light coming in can create an unwanted glare. Also, be sure you are in an environment where you will not be disturbed.

Whether you stand or sit, maintain a relaxed, confident posture.   As discussed earlier in the chapter, a rigid posture suggests nervousness and anxiety, while being overly casual suggests boredom and lack of interest. Be comfortable, yet alert, so that you project an image of confidence.

Determine whether your session is direct address or discussion.   In *direct-address* mode, you look straight into the camera and speak directly to the audience, while in *discussion* mode, you talk to an interviewer or have a conversation with others while the camera looks on.

1. For direct-address mode, look at the camera. If you fail to look straight at the lens, you come across to viewers as evasive, untrustworthy, or unprepared. As the only exception to this rule, you may glance down at notes occasionally and briefly.

2. For discussion mode, never look at the camera. Discussion mode creates the illusion that the viewer is eavesdropping on a conversation. Give your full attention to the interviewer or other participants.

Consider the angle of the camera.   If you are using a laptop, don't tilt the screen so far back that viewers can see your ceiling. This is disorienting for viewers, and it is often not the most flattering angle. You should look straight at the camera and position yourself so that you are framed in the video like a portrait, showing your head and upper body—not a close-up of your face.

Be sure that the camera is stable.   If you are filming yourself, your best options are to use either a laptop on a solid surface or a tripod stand for a video camera. Tripod stands are also available for smartphones and tablets. Do not record yourself by holding your computer, tablet, or smartphone at arm's length because your arm will waver. If someone is recording you without a tripod stand, have the recorder rest his or her elbows on a solid surface so that the video is not shaky.

Never assume that the eye of the camera is no longer on you.   During group discussions, some people assume that because another person is talking, the camera is no longer focused on them. Always assume that you are on camera until the session is officially over.

Always keep your "real" audience in mind.   It is easy to forget who your audience is if you are recording your speech in an empty room. Visualize your audience and speak conversationally, as if your audience is there.

Scale down movements and gestures.   The kind of vigorous movement and powerful gestures that are so effective in a speech to an auditorium of 500 people will make you look silly if repeated in front of a video camera. Any gestures you make should be small and low-key. Avoid sudden, swift movements such as crossing your legs rapidly; this can have a jarring effect on the viewers. If you must make such movements, do so very slowly.

Test your sound before recording.   Make sure you speak at a level that is appropriate—not too loud, not too soft. Enunciate clearly. Practice what you will say before you record the first time.

Resources for Review and Skill Building

Summary

The key to good delivery is a strong desire to communicate with the audience. Speakers who concentrate on getting their ideas across to their listeners usually find themselves using good delivery techniques.

There are four methods of delivering a speech: memorization, manuscript, impromptu, and extemporaneous. Of the four, extemporaneous is the most popular, and usually the most effective, because the speaker delivers a well-prepared, well-rehearsed speech in a lively, conversational manner.

When delivering a speech, your voice should be loud enough for everyone to hear, your words should be spoken clearly so that they are easily understood, and your voice should be expressive so that you sound interesting and lively. This is especially true if you have a dialect that is different than your audience.

Nonverbal communication is the message you give with your body by means of personal appearance, eye contact, facial expressions, posture, movement, and gestures. All these elements should convey confidence and a positive regard for the audience. Eye contact is of special importance. You should

look at your listeners during 95 percent of your speech to maintain a bond of communication and rapport with them and to monitor their feedback.

The question-and-answer period enables listeners to get clarification and further information. Anticipate what questions may be asked, and prepare your answers accordingly. Try not to be defensive if you are challenged by a listener, and be prepared to say "I don't know" if you don't have an answer—in other words, don't try to fake expertise.

Practice is a vital part in the success of your speech. You should practice the entire speech over and over again, at least once in front of a live audience, until you can deliver it with power and confidence.

When you speak in front of a camera, dress conservatively; plan an uncluttered background free of distractions; stand or sit in a relaxed, confident posture; decide if your session is direct address or discussion; consider the angle of the camera and make sure your camera is steady; always assume you're being recorded; keep your audience in mind; and scale down movement and gestures; and test your sound.

Key Terms

articulation, *260*

dialect, *260*

extemporaneous method, *258*

impromptu method, *257*

intonation, *262*

manuscript method, *256*

nonverbal communication, *265*

pitch, *262*

posture, *267*

pronunciation, *261*

verbal fillers, *263*

Review Questions

1. What are the differences among impromptu, manuscript, memorized, and extemporaneous speeches?

2. How should you begin your speech?

3. If there is a discrepancy between your words and your nonverbal behavior, which will the audience believe?

4. What should you do if you do not want to give a speech, but you are required to?

5. What are the characteristics of good eye contact?

6. How can gestures support your speech?

7. How should you handle a listener who casts doubt on some of your facts and figures?

8. What should you do if you do not know the answer to a question asked by someone in your audience?

9. Why should a speech be learned and practiced point by point, instead of word for word?

10. For recording and/or videoconferencing, what are some important considerations?

Building Critical-Thinking Skills

1. "If a man takes off his sunglasses, I can hear him better," says writer Hugh Prather. Explain the meaning of this statement in terms of public speaking.

2. Tennis coaches observe a phenomenon called "analysis equals paralysis." Players become so fixated on holding the racket correctly and swinging properly that they miss the ball. What lessons could public speakers draw from this phenomenon?

3. A newspaper reporter once wrote that an executive "read from a speech with the passion of an assistant principal announcing the week's school lunch menu." Describe how you think the speaker sounded.

4. While most instructors recommend against memorizing an entire speech, some recommend that you memorize short statements, such as a wedding toast or the last sentence of a speech. Do you think this is good advice? Defend your answer.

5. What nonverbal message is given by a person who goes to a funeral dressed in a T-shirt and jeans?

Building Teamwork Skills

1. In a group, create a list of six attributes of good delivery that are of utmost importance to group members when they are in an audience. Rank the attributes in order of importance. Then discuss why the top two attributes are more important than the others.

2. As a group, recount at least five experiences when you had to "pretend" to get through a social situation in which you initially did not feel comfortable. Discuss these situations. Did you eventually become comfortable in the environment? If not, how did you get through it?

Examining Your Ethics

Answer: **B.** An ethical speaker never uses deceit. Furthermore, if listeners learn about the ploy, the speaker's credibility is seriously damaged.

End Notes

1. Cynthia Littleton, "Merritt Wever Explains 'I Gotta Go' Speech," *Variety*, https://variety.com/2013/tv/news/emmys-merritt-wevers-surprise-is-showing-1200660288/ (accessed February 16, 2020).

2. J. Robinson, "A Complete History of Merritt Wever's Perfect Emmy Acceptance Speeches," *Vanity Fair*, www.vanityfair.com/hollywood/2018/09/merritt-wever-emmy-acceptance-speech-2013-2018 (accessed February 16, 2020).

3. R. Branson, "My Top Tips for Public Speaking," www.virgin.com/richard-branson/my-top-tips-public-speaking (accessed February 16, 2020).

4. Brian Lamb and Susan Swain, *Abraham Lincoln: Great American Historians on Our Sixteenth President* (New York: PublicAffairs, 2008), p. 52; Jackie Hogan, *Lincoln, Inc.: Selling the Sixteenth President in Contemporary America* (Lanham, Maryland: Rowman & Littlefield, 2011), p. 120.

5. Joseph S. Meisel, *Public Speech and the Culture of Public Life in the Age of Gladstone* (New York: Columbia University Press, 2012), p. 51.

6. Mark Twain, *Mark Twain at Your Fingertips: A Book of Quotations*, ed. Caroline Thomas Harnsberger (New York: Dover, 2009), p. 520.

7. Debi LaPlante and Nalini Ambady, "Saying It Like It Isn't: Mixed Messages from Men and Women in the Workplace," *Journal of Applied Social Psychology* 32 (2002), pp. 2435–57; Robert D. Ramsey, *How to Say the Right Thing Every Time: Communicating Well with Students, Staff, Parents, and the Public*, 2nd ed. (Thousand Oaks, CA: Corwin Press, 2008), p. 214.

8. Janet Stone and Jane Bachner, *Speaking Up* (New York: Carroll and Graf, 1994), p. 62.

9. Diane Windingland, member of National Speakers Association, telephone interview, January 5, 2016.

10. Cristina Stuart, *How to Be an Effective Speaker* (Lincolnwood, IL: NTC Business Books, 1990), p. 67. Reprint published as an ebook by Good Books for You, digital-contenters.com, 2015, no page numbers.

Speaking to Inform

OBJECTIVES

After studying this chapter, you should be able to

1. Prepare an informative speech.
2. Identify four types of informative speeches.
3. Explain how to make information interesting.
4. Explain how to help listeners understand and remember key information.

CHILDREN CAN DROWN, says Olympic swimming champion Cullen Jones, if their swimming instructors do not teach the proper techniques for breathing and staying afloat. In the photo, Jones points to his nose as he teaches breathing skills to students in Houston, Texas.

When Jones teaches swimming, he demonstrates a procedure and then has each student try it out. When he is satisfied that the student is performing correctly, he asks him or her to practice. "Practice is the most important part," he says, "because it causes you to swim the right way without thinking."[1]

Jones's approach is one of many techniques that you can use when you engage in informative speaking, a rewarding form of human communication. With an informative speech, you can enlighten your audience by explaining why some people become addicted to chocolate. You can enrich the lives of your listeners by discussing how to cook your mother's famous egg rolls. And you can even save lives by speaking about how to shut out distractions when you drive.

In this chapter, we will look at four types of informative speeches and then discuss guidelines to help you create informative speeches that are clear, interesting, and memorable.

Olympic champion Cullen Jones feels strongly that every child should learn how to swim.

Sharon Steinmann/AP Images

Goals of Informative Speaking

When you give an informative speech, your task is to be a teacher, and not a persuader, or an advocate, or a salesperson. Think of yourself as a reporter who gives facts, instead of a debater who makes arguments or a pundit who offers opinions. You have three major objectives:

1. **Convey fresh information.** Provide as much new material as possible to your audience. They will appreciate not hearing information they already know.

2. **Make your material interesting.** Use supports such as examples, stories, and visual aids.

3. **Help listeners remember important points.** Make your ideas clear and easily grasped. Repeat—in a graceful manner—key information.

Types of Informative Speeches

Informative speeches can be categorized in many ways, but in this chapter we will concentrate on four of the most popular types: definition, description, process, and explanation. A comparison of these types of informative speeches can be found in Table 1.

Definition Speech

Do you know what the term *bokeh* means? Unless you are a serious photographer, you probably don't. It is a Japanese word that is defined as "the effect created when the camera lens renders out-of-focus points of light."[2]

If you are still unsure of exactly what the term means, here are some elaborations:

- Figure 1 illustrates bokeh. The bamboo stalk is in focus, while the colorful autumn leaves behind it are blurred in a pleasant way that makes the overall picture more interesting and beautiful than if everything were in focus.

- A literal translation from Japanese is blur, but bokeh is more than just simple blurring of a photo. It is a soft, out-of-focus rendition of one part of an image—often the background. The result is aesthetically pleasing and heightens the attractiveness of the in-focus elements of a picture. A photographer can achieve bokeh by using certain lenses at optimal camera settings, and an advanced user

Table 1   **Informative Speech Types Comparison**

	Definition	Example
Definition Speech	Provides a longer, more meaningful extended definition of a term than what is found in a dictionary.	To define hockey for my audience, including the objective of the game, the rules, and common strategies
Description Speech	Describes in vivid detail a person, place, object, or event, using evocative language.	To describe for my audience the feeling of playing in a hockey game, including the coldness of the air, the biting of skate blades into the ice, and the sound of the audience
Explanation Speech	Explains a complex concept or situation, typically using in-depth research from credible sources.	To explain to my audience the safety concerns associated with playing hockey, including concussions and long-term brain injuries
Process Speech	Analyzes how to do or make something in a step-by-step manner.	To inform my audience of the step-by-step process to taking a perfect slapshot

Figure 1
This photo illustrates what is meant by the Japanese term *bokeh*.

Hamilton Gregory

of image-manipulation software like Photoshop can apply bokeh to a digital image and achieve the same result. Both the photographer and Photoshopper must use their tools carefully to avoid excessive or ugly bokeh.

These explanations and photograph constitute an **extended definition,** one that is richer and more meaningful than a dictionary explanation. That is what a **definition speech** is all about—giving an extended definition of a concept so that the listeners get a full, richly detailed picture of its meaning. While a dictionary definition would settle lightly on the listeners' brains and probably vanish overnight, an extended definition is likely to stick firmly. Here are some sample specific purpose statements for definition speeches:

extended definition
a rich, full elaboration of the meaning of a term.

definition speech
an oral presentation that gives an extended definition of a concept.

- To define for my audience "financial bubbles" in the world's economy
- To define for my listeners "Internet trolls"
- To define for my audience a "Pyrrhic victory" in business and politics

Any of the support materials that we discussed in the chapter on supporting your ideas and avoiding plagiarism (such as narratives, examples, vivid images, and statistics) can be applied to defining a topic. One student gave a speech on "phantom vibration syndrome," in which he defined the term by giving his own personal experience, as well as statistics and testimony from an expert:

- "I keep my cell phone on 'vibrate.' Many times during the day, I will be walking somewhere or driving in my car and I feel my phone vibrating. But when I check it, there is nothing—no text message, no phone call."
- Dr. Robert Rosenberger, a researcher at Georgia Tech, says the same thing happens to 9 out of 10 cell phone users—a phenomenon he calls "phantom vibration syndrome." He says it is surprisingly common for cell phone users to have "a vague tingling feeling which they think is their mobile phone indicating it has received a text message or call while on silent."[3]

Definition speech topic: Gambling addiction.

slpix/Shutterstock

Description speech topic: Outdoor art

imagenavi/iStockphoto/Getty Images

description speech
an oral presentation that describes a person, place, object, or event.

- Dr. Rosenberger says the feeling is a "hallucination" that is caused by anxiety. It is "a result of always being 'on-edge' to answer emails and text messages."[4]

Sometimes the best way to define a topic is to compare or contrast it with a similar item. If you were trying to define what constitutes child abuse, for example, it would be helpful to contrast abuse with firm but loving discipline.

Description Speech

A **description speech** paints a vivid picture of a person, a place, an object, or an event. As with all speeches, a description speech should make a point—and not be merely a list of facts or observations. Here are some specific purpose statements for description speeches:

- To describe to my listeners the Gulf Stream in the Atlantic Ocean
- To describe for my audience the "marijuana mansions" that drug dealers use in suburbs
- To describe to my audience the highlights of the life of civil rights leader Rosa Parks

If you were describing an object or a place, you might want to use the *spatial* pattern of organization. Here is an example of the spatial pattern as used in an outline describing New Zealand. The speaker travels from south to north.

Specific Purpose: To describe to my listeners the geographic variety of New Zealand

Central Idea: The two-island nation of New Zealand has more scenic variety than any other country on earth.

Main Points: I. The South Island—colder because it is closer to the South Pole—reminds visitors of Norway.

    A. The Southern Alps, with snowcapped peaks over 10,000 feet, extend the entire length of the island.

    B. Fjords, streams, and lakes are unspoiled and breathtakingly beautiful.

II. The North Island is like a compact version of the best of Europe, Asia, and the Pacific Islands.

    A. The cities suggest the elegance of Italy.

    B. The mountains and vineyards remind one of France.

    C. Active volcanoes look like those found in the Philippines.

    D. In the northernmost parts, the beaches and lush, tropical forests seem like Hawaii.

Describing a person, living or dead, can make a fascinating speech. You might want to use the *chronological* pattern to discuss the major events of a person's life in the order in which they occurred. Or you might prefer to use the *topical* pattern, emphasizing several major features of a person's life or career. The following is an example of the topical pattern as used in an outline describing the career of the United Farm Workers cofounder Dolores Huerta.

Specific Purpose: To describe to my audience the life and accomplishments of Dolores Huerta

Central Idea: Dolores Huerta is one of the most influential labor leaders in U.S. history.

Main Points: I. As cofounder of the United Farm Workers union, Huerta struggled to improve working conditions for migrant farmworkers.

II. She organized boycotts of grapes in the United States as a nonviolent tactic to revolutionize the agricultural industry.

III. Though Huerta practiced nonviolence, she endured much suffering.

A. She was arrested more than 20 times.

B. In 1988, she was nearly killed by baton-swinging police officers who smashed two ribs and ruptured her spleen.

Process Speech

A **process speech** covers the steps or stages by which something is done or made. There are two kinds of process speeches. In the first kind, you show the listeners how to *perform* a process so that they can actually use the skills later. (This is sometimes called a *demonstration* speech.) Here are some examples of specific purpose statements for this kind of speech:

- To demonstrate to my audience how to perform daily exercises to avoid and relieve back pain

- To show my listeners how to make low-fat pumpkin bread

- To teach my audience how to transform wine glasses into beautiful candle lamps

In the second kind of process speech, you provide information on "how something is done" or "how something works." Your goal is to tell about a process—not so that listeners can perform it themselves, but so that they can understand it. For example, let's say that you outline the steps by which counterfeiters print bogus money. You are showing these steps to satisfy the listeners' intellectual curiosity and to teach them how to spot a counterfeit bill, not so that they can perform the job themselves. Here are some samples of specific purpose statements for this kind of speech:

- To inform my audience of the process used to train horses to race in the Kentucky Derby

Examining Your Ethics

Which of these topics would be appropriate for an informative speech?

A. How to drive defensively so that you can avoid a traffic accident.
B. How to manipulate a friend into giving you money.
C. How to plagiarize a paper without getting caught.

For the answer, see the last page of this chapter.

process speech
an oral presentation that analyzes how to do something or how something works.

- To outline for my listeners the steps that astronomers take to find new stars in the universe

- To inform my audience of the process used by crime investigators to find and test DNA evidence

Here are some guidelines for preparing a process speech.

Use visual aids.   In some speeches, you can use a live demonstration. For instance, if you wanted to show how to treat a burn, you could use a volunteer and demonstrate the correct steps. In other speeches, PowerPoint slides and videos are effective. For example, a student speaker explained how to change a flat tire by using a video (with the sound off) to illustrate the steps in the process.

Involve the audience in physical activity whenever possible.   If you involve the audience in a physical activity, you capitalize on more than just the listeners' sense of hearing and seeing; you also bring in touch and movement, which aids in the retention of information. For an example, see Figure 2.

Process speech topic: How pearls are formed

Africa Studio/Shutterstock

There is an ancient Chinese proverb that says:

- I hear and I forget.

- I see and I remember.

- I do and I understand.

The wisdom of this saying has been confirmed by psychologists, who have found that of the three main channels for learning new information, the auditory is weakest, the visual is stronger, and physical action is strongest of all. The best approach is to bring all three together. For example, if you were explaining how to do stretching exercises, you could discuss the techniques (auditory) as you give a demonstration (visual); then you could have each listener stand and perform the exercises (physical action).

Figure 2

Aboriginal Australian Ron Murray (left) gives classes on how to throw a boomerang so that it returns to the thrower's hand. He lets each student practice until the technique is perfected.

William West/AFP/Getty Images

Some audience involvement can be accomplished while the listeners remain in their chairs; for example, if you are presenting on sign language, you can have the listeners practice the hand signals as you teach them.

Notes of caution: (1) Get your instructor's approval before you include physical activity in a speech. (2) Don't use an activity if it is likely to cause listeners to get so involved that they ignore you. (3) Don't ask listeners to do something that would be embarrassing or awkward for some of them.

In a process speech, one student provided simple steps for how to make flavored whipped cream.

piotrek73/Shutterstock

Proceed slowly.   Always bear in mind that much of what you say may be new to the listeners. If you are giving instruction about how to make leather belts, for example, you may be describing activities that are so easy for you that you could perform them blindfolded, but they are probably completely foreign to most members of the audience. That's why you should talk slowly and repeat key ideas if necessary. Give listeners ample time to absorb your points and form mental images.

Give warning of difficult steps.   When you are ready to discuss especially difficult steps, use transitions to give the listeners a warning. For example, you might say, "The next step is a little tricky," or "This next step is the hardest one of all." This alerts the listeners that they need to pay extra special attention.

Student speaker Junfeng Guan presented a process speech on how to make flavored whipped cream. Using the chronological pattern, he explained the basic steps. Here is the outline for the body of the speech, with each main point devoted to a different step in the process:

Specific Purpose: To demonstrate to my listeners how to make flavored whipped cream

Central Idea: Making flavored whipped cream is simple if you follow three easy steps.

Main Points:

(First Step)   I. Prepare ingredients and equipment to make two cups of whipped cream.

   A. Have 1 cup of heavy whipping cream and 2 tablespoons of confectioners' sugar.

   B. Set out your flavors.

      1. For chocolate, have a tablespoon of cocoa powder.

      2. For vanilla, have a teaspoon of vanilla extract.

      3. For a lemony taste, have a tablespoon of lemon zest.

      4. For almond, have a teaspoon of almond extract.

   C. Use a large bowl and a large whisk.

   D. Keep things cold.

      1. Refrigerate the cream.

      2. Put the bowl and the whisk in the freezer 10 minutes before you begin.

(Second Step)   II. Whip the cream with the whisk.

   A. Start as soon as the cream comes out of the fridge.

   B. Whip the cream briskly in a circular direction.

C. When the cream starts to thicken, add your flavoring and two tablespoons of confectioners' sugar.

(Third Step)   III. Toward the end, use precautions.

A. Limit the process to about 5 minutes to avoid creating butter.

B. If the mixture becomes lumpy, add a splash of cream and whisk it a few times until smooth.

If you look closely, you will see that Guan's outline really has more than three steps. There are a lot of minor steps underneath the three major steps. Did he make a mistake in not listing all these steps as main points? No, treating all steps as equal might have caused the audience to feel overwhelmed by technical details. By dividing his speech into three major sections, he makes the material more manageable—easier to grasp and remember.

Explanation Speech

explanation speech
an oral presentation that explains a concept or situation.

An **explanation speech** (sometimes called an oral report or a lecture) involves explaining a concept or a situation to the audience. For this type of speech, you often must conduct in-depth research, using books, articles, and interviews, rather than relying on your own experiences.

Here are examples of specific purpose statements for explanation speeches:

- To explain to the audience why works of art are highly prized as financial investments
- To inform my listeners of the reasons for the near extinction of mountain gorillas
- To explain to the audience the pros and cons of the Electoral College

For organizing an explanation speech, you can use any of the popular patterns (topical, chronological, spatial, etc.). One arrangement that is especially effective is the *statement-of-reasons* pattern, which lists reasons for a situation or an event. Student speaker Melissa Greenbaum uses this pattern in a speech on stolen cars. Here is the essence of her outline:

Specific Purpose: To inform my listeners of the reasons why old cars are stolen more frequently than new cars

Central Idea: The most frequently stolen cars in North America are Toyotas and Hondas that are about 10 years old.

Main Points:

(First Reason)   I. Stealing an old car is more profitable than stealing a new car because of the high demand for old-car parts.

(Second Reason)   II. New cars are harder to break into because of sophisticated security devices.

(Third Reason)   III. Old-car owners are less careful about locking up their vehicles.

Explanation speech topic: Why most male birds are more colorful than females

Daniel Dempster Photography/
Alamy Stock Photo

In her speech, Greenbaum developed each reason with examples and statistics. Another pattern is the *fallacy–fact* pattern, which also can be called *myth–reality*. In this pattern, the speaker cites popular fallacies and then presents facts that refute them. Student speaker Bob Metzger used this pattern to refute three popular misconceptions about nutrition:

Specific Purpose: To give my audience accurate information to overcome three common misconceptions about nutrition

Central Idea: Eggs, spicy foods, and frozen vegetables do not deserve their bad nutritional reputation.

Main Points:

(Fallacy)   I. "Eggs are bad for you" is a fallacy.

(Facts)   A. Eggs get a "bad rap" because they are high in cholesterol, but what's important is the level of cholesterol in the blood, not in the food.

                B. Saturated fat is what causes high cholesterol levels in the blood.

                C. Eggs are low in saturated fat, so they do not make a significant contribution to high cholesterol levels in the blood.

(Fallacy)   II. "Spicy food is bad for the stomach" is a fallacy.

(Facts)   A. Medical studies of healthy persons who eat spice-rich Mexican and Indian foods found no damage or irritation in the protective lining of the stomach.

                B. In a medical experiment in India, the stomach ulcers of patients who were fed spicy foods healed at the same rate as those of patients who were fed a bland diet.

(Fallacy)   III. "Frozen vegetables are not as nutritious as fresh" is a fallacy.

(Facts)   A. Quick freezing preserves all nutrients.

                B. In fact, if fresh vegetables have been sitting in the produce aisle too long, frozen vegetables are better.

Guidelines for Informative Speaking

In informative speaking, strive to make your message clear, interesting, and memorable. You can achieve these goals by applying the principles that we have covered so far in this book, as well as the following guidelines.

Relate the Speech to the Listeners' Self-Interest

Many listeners approach a speech with an attitude of "Why should I care? Why should I pay attention? What's in it for me?" The best motivator in a speech, therefore, is something that has an impact on their lives.

Let's say you are planning to give a process speech showing listeners how to clean their computers. How do you think your listeners will react when they discover what your topic is?

"B-o-r-ing!" they will probably say to themselves. "Why should I pay attention to this stuff?"

Your best strategy, therefore, is to appeal to their self-interest:

Imagine you sit at your computer all weekend working on a big research paper. You are almost through when suddenly your computer fails. Not only does it fail, but it deletes your entire report. To make matters worse, the technician who repairs your computer charges you $250.

This could happen to you if you don't clean and maintain your computer. Today I'd like to show you some easy steps you can take to safeguard your computer files and avoid repair bills.

Now that your listeners see that your information can have an impact on their own lives, they should perk up and listen carefully.

Make Information Interesting

The most important element in an effective speech, say many seasoned speechmakers, is relevant, interesting information.[5]

Many speeches are boring because the speakers deal primarily with *generalities,* which tend to be dull and vague. To make a speech lively, use generalities sparingly; and each time a generality is offered, follow it with lots of *specifics,* such as examples and anecdotes.

Student speaker Malaika Terry gave an informative speech on desserts in restaurants, and she began by showing the picture in Figure 3 on a PowerPoint slide. Then she said, "One of the most exciting things about dining out in a fine restaurant is enjoying a creative and tasty dessert. Imagine my surprise, then, when I recently learned that many restaurants don't want you to order dessert."

Terry followed her generality with lots of specifics, including personal experiences and testimony from experts:

- "I have noticed that almost no servers ask me if I want a dessert, even though I would probably order one if I were given a tempting offer," said Terry. "Now I know why."

- "Desserts just aren't very profitable for most restaurants. Tyler Cowen, an economics professor at George Mason University, says, 'It's hard to make money on desserts in the restaurant business today.'"[6]

- "Writer Laura Northrup says that because profit margins on desserts are very slim, most restaurants would prefer that you leave without dessert so that new customers

Figure 3
A Japanese chef presents a fruit dessert.
IAKOBCHUK VIACHESLAV/
Shutterstock

Tips for Your Career

For Long Presentations, Plan a Variety of Activities

Your boss asks you to conduct a three-hour workshop, scheduled for a Friday afternoon, to explain important procedures to a group of new employees. What do you do? Do you spend the entire three hours talking? No, not unless you want to put the group to sleep.

Provide a variety of activities to keep your audience awake and attentive during long presentations. Here are some suggestions.

1. **Invite audience participation.** At various intervals, or even throughout the entire presentation, encourage listeners to ask questions or make comments. By letting them take an active role, instead of sitting passively for three hours, you invigorate them and prevent them from daydreaming.

2. **Use visual aids whenever possible.** Visuals provide variety and sparkle, and they can clarify and reinforce key points.

3. **Give coffee breaks or stretch breaks at regular intervals.** A good rule of thumb for marathon sessions is to give a 15-minute break after every 45-minute period, even if the audience does not seem tired. In other words, don't wait until fatigue sets in. If you wait until the audience is drifting off, you might lose

their interest for the rest of the day. When you give a break, always announce the time for reassembly. When that time arrives, politely but firmly remind any stragglers that it is time to return to their seats. If you don't remind them, you will find that a 15-minute coffee break can stretch to 30 minutes.

4. **Call on people at random.** If your presentation is in the form of a lecture, you can use the teachers' technique of calling on people at random to answer questions. This causes every listener to perk up because he or she is thinking, I'd better pay attention because my name might be called next, and I don't want to be caught daydreaming. Call the person's name *after* you ask the question. (If you call the name before the question, everyone in the audience except the designated person might breathe a sigh of relief and fail to pay close attention to the question.)

5. **Encourage listeners to take notes.** Some speakers pass out complimentary pens and pads at the beginning of their presentations in the hope that the listeners will use them to write down key points. There is, of course, a side benefit: taking notes helps the listeners stay alert and listen intelligently.

can take the space. If you do decide to stick around, 'a restaurant would rather see you order sodas or mixed drinks instead of sharing a slice of cheesecake.' Drinks like coffee and soda are the most profitable things on the menu."[7]

Terry's speech was interesting because she chose good examples and quotations. She also used a valuable strategy: before she delivered her speech, she tested her content with friends and relatives, asking them to tell her which items were interesting and which were boring. (For more on testing your material, see Tip 1 in the chapter on the body of the speech.)

Avoid Information Overload

Give details, but not too many. You don't want to bore your audience with a tedious overload. "The secret of being tiresome," the French philosopher Voltaire said, "is in telling everything." Edit your material. Instead of giving all 14 examples that you have compiled for a point, cite just 2 or 3.

When students moan about all the wonderful material they must leave out, teachers offer a simple solution: put it on a handout or a USB flash drive that listeners can pick up after the speech and take with them. Many professional conferences allow speakers to upload their visual aids, handouts, and other documentation to a website where they can be downloaded later by interested listeners.

Tailor Information for Each Audience

A common mistake is to assume that your listeners possess the same knowledge that you possess. Consider these news items:

- You may know that the Earth revolves around the sun, but one in four adult Americans thinks that the sun revolves around the Earth, according to a study by the National Science Foundation.[8]
- In a survey of 1,416 adults by the Annenberg Public Policy Center of the University of Pennsylvania, only 36 percent could name all three branches of the U.S. government, and 35 percent couldn't even name one branch.[9]

Find out in advance what your audience knows and doesn't know on your topic, and then adapt your information accordingly. Whenever necessary, define words, explain concepts, and give background information.

What should you do when your audience is mixed, and some listeners know certain concepts already and some don't? How can you give explanations in a way that does not insult the intelligence of the listeners who already know the material? In some cases, you can give information in a casual, unobtrusive way. For example, let's say you are planning in your speech to cite a quotation by Adolf Hitler. Most college students know who Hitler was, but some may not. To inform the latter without insulting the intelligence of the former, you can say something like this: "In the 1920s, long before Adolf Hitler rose to power in Germany and long before he launched the German nation into World War II, he made the following prophetic statement. . . ." An indirect approach like this permits you to sneak in a lot of background information.

In other cases, you may need to be straightforward in giving definitions or explanations. For example, if you need to define *recession* for a speech on economic cycles, do so directly and clearly. Knowledgeable listeners will not be offended by a quick definition as long as most of your speech supplies them with new material; in fact, they probably will welcome a chance to confirm the accuracy of their own understanding of the term.

Use the Familiar to Explain the Unfamiliar

Ozone is an air pollutant, often known as smog, that harms the health of millions of people. How can it hurt you? When you inhale ozone, says the U.S. Environmental Protection Agency, it reacts chemically with your body's internal tissues. Prolonged exposure causes the equivalent of sunburn to your lungs.[10]

The chemical complexities of pollutants in our lungs are unfamiliar to most people, but we are all familiar with sunburn.

When you want to explain or describe something that is unfamiliar to your audience, relate it to something that is familiar. Use comparisons, contrasts, and analogies. If, for example, you point out that divers in Acapulco, Mexico, astound tourists by diving into water from rocks 118 feet high, that statistic does not have much impact unless you point out that a 118-foot plunge is equal to a dive from the roof of an 11-story building.

Similarly, to give listeners a mental picture of what the inside of a tornado is like, student speaker Dale Higgins said, "A tornado's funnel is like the vortex you see when you let water go down a drain." Since everyone has seen the swirling action of water going down a drain, the comparison helped the audience visualize a tornado's vortex.

Help Listeners Remember Key Information

To make sure that your audience retains important details, use the following techniques.

Engaging delivery techniques.   Just because you are giving an informative speech that avoids bias and persuasion doesn't mean your speech should lack engagement and personality. If you can use your passion about the topic to engage your audience, they will be more likely to remember the information you're trying to convey. Review the chapter on delivering the speech for more information.

Repetition.   Present key ideas and words several times.

Presentation aids.   Use the sensory channels discussed in the chapter on presentation aids—visual, hearing, taste, smell, touch, and physical activity.

Memory aids.   Provide listeners with shortcuts to remembering. Here are some samples:

- In financial news reports, you often hear the terms *bull market* and *bear market.* The former term means that stock values are trending upward; the latter means that values are trending downward. To help listeners distinguish between the two, you could tell them that "bull market" signifies an upward movement and ask them to visualize a bull's horns, which point upward. You can also show a visual like the photograph of a bull in Figure 4 to help solidify the association.

- In the United States, the color blue is often associated with one major political party and red with the other (red states vs. blue states). But which color goes with which party? The Republican Party is red, so just remember that *Republican* starts with an *R,* the same letter that starts *red.* That leaves blue for the Democratic Party. (By the way, a purple state is one that is a combination of red and blue, sometimes voting Republican, sometimes voting Democratic.)

- Acronyms are handy. For years students have recalled the names of the Great Lakes by using the word *HOMES,* each letter of which stands for a lake: Huron, Ontario, Michigan, Erie, and Superior. If you are speaking on how to treat injuries such as ankle sprains, you can help listeners remember the four steps of first aid by providing the acronym *RICE,* which stands for rest, ice, compression, and elevation.

Figure 4
This famous statue of a bull in New York City's financial district holds a key to remembering the meaning of the term *bull market.*

View a video of the speech "PPO or HDHP? How to Choose a Health Plan" in the online Media Library for Chapter 15.

Sample Informative Speech

One student delivered a speech on different types of health insurance plans. Below is the outline, followed by a transcript of the actual speech. The speaker uses the topical pattern to compare and contrast preferred provider organization (PPO) plans and a high deductible health plans (HDHP).

The Outline with Commentary

PPO or HDHP? How to Choose a Health Plan

COMMENTARY	SPEECH
	General Purpose: To inform
	Specific Purpose: To inform my audience about how to choose between a preferred provider organization (PPO) plan and high deductible health plan (HDHP).
	Central Idea: When deciding on a medical plan, consider the differences between a preferred provider organization (PPO) and high deductible health plan (HDHP) and choose the plan that best meets your needs.

INTRODUCTION

I. Attention Material

   A. Is it a common cold? The flu? Or something more severe? Do I need to go to the doctor? These are questions that might go through your head whenever you get sick.

   B. I find myself getting sick a few times a year and one thing that makes it easier for me is having good health insurance.

      1. Three years ago, I pinched a nerve in my neck and was faced with many hospital visits and even a major surgery.

      2. As a result, I became obsessed with understanding health insurance options to find what works best for me.

   C. Based on my class survey, 15 percent of the students here receive coverage under the university plan.

      1. This is consistent with the national average according to the American College Health Association (2019).

      2. Sixty-five percent of you have coverage under your parents' plan, and the rest—20 percent—are employed full-time and have a plan of your own.

   D. Matthew Frankel, writer for *USA Today*, mentions in his May 2018 article that the average American spends $4,612 in health care–related expenses per year including health insurance, medical services, and prescription drugs.

> The speaker previews the comparison to follow in the rest of the speech.

II. Orienting Material

    A. This is a potentially large investment, so getting the most out of your health care is important not only for your personal well-being but also your financial security.

    B. In our time together today, I want to tell you more about two major health insurance plans, the PPO–preferred provider organization plan, and the HDHP–high deductible health plan, so that you can choose the one that's right for you.

(*Transition*: First, I will provide brief descriptions of each plan and then move into the similarities and differences between them.)

BODY

I. Let us start with a brief definition of a PPO and an HDHP.

    A. A PPO plan is referred to as a preferred provider organization plan.

> The speaker refers to credible sources to bolster the point.

        1. According to health insurance provider Humana (n.d.), it is also known as a health maintenance organization.

        2. In general, a PPO plan provides a network of health care providers you may choose from.

        3. Smartasset.com, a financial technology website devoted to providing personal finance advice, says health care providers who are a part of this network will offer medical care at a negotiated rate determined by the health care provider and the insurance company (Dixon, 2019).

        4. That means you will pay a monthly premium for the insurance, but also co-pays at each visit throughout the policy term.

    B. An HDHP is referred to as a high deductible health plan.

        1. This plan also allows you to choose from a network of providers who will offer negotiated rates, lower than paying out of pocket.

        2. The monthly fee is much lower than a PPO's, and rather than co-pays, you will pay out of pocket for all health care expenses until you reach a certain dollar amount.

(*Transition*: There is a lot more to both plans, so let us dive in deeper by looking at the similarities and differences.)

II. First, let us consider the similarities between a PPO and an HDHP.

    A. In both plans, you will work with local medical providers that are considered in-network or that have a pricing contract with the insurer that is less expensive.

> The compare-and-contrast structure is reflected in the outline, and makes the logic of the speech very easy for listeners to follow.

    B. As a patient, you often have the option to elect out-of-network medical providers as long as you are willing to assume the extra out-of-pocket costs.

    C. Both plans also cover preventive services at full cost.

        1. Healthcare.gov, the U.S. government's health insurance exchange website, says these services may include routine physicals, blood pressure screenings, cholesterol screenings, immunization shots, and much more (U.S. Centers for Medicare & Medicaid Services, n.d.).

(continued)

2. It is important to check with your individual insurance provider to see what is considered preventive.

D. BlueCross BlueShield, another health insurance provider, says plans also cover discounts for some health and wellness programs as well as provide access to online tools that you can use to make healthier life decisions (BlueCross BlueShield of Texas, n.d.).

E. Also, each plan has an option for saving money for medical expenses that often comes with tax savings benefits.

(*Transition*: Now that we have considered the similarities, let's move on to the differences.)

III. When choosing a plan, you should consider some important differences between a PPO plan and an HDHP.

A. Cost is often the determining factor that impacts the decision for many people, so let's discuss the cost structure for each type of plan.

> Focusing on cost makes the speech especially relevant for the audience.

1. Most health insurance companies including BlueCross BlueShield and Humana describe a PPO as having lower deductibles, a co-pay for office visits and certain procedures, and higher monthly premiums.

2. By contrast, an HDHP has higher deductibles, few, if any, co-pays, and lower monthly premiums.

3. The monthly premiums vary based on negotiations between your insurance company and your company or institution's benefits department.

4. Additionally, monthly premiums vary based on selection of an individual plan or a family plan.

B. Make sure to consider carefully the deductible of the plan you choose.

1. With a PPO, typical deductibles may range from $500 to $1,000 or more and co-pays may range from $5 to $50 or more (Fay, n.d.).

2. PPOs usually have two different deductibles: one for services from providers in the network and another for services from providers outside the network.

> This information can be difficult to understand to an unfamiliar audience. The speaker takes time to provide a careful comparison between these plans, so the listeners have a clear picture of the differences.

3. For HDHP, the Internal Revenue Service (2020) says, in 2018, a high deductible plan must have a minimum deductible of $1,350 for single coverage and $2,700 for family coverage.

4. Since these are just the minimums, many plans have higher deductibles.

5. There are usually no co-pays since you are paying out of pocket until you meet your deductible.

C. As noted earlier, both plans offer savings accounts.

1. A PPO plan has an FSA, a Flexible Spending Account, and an HDHP has an HSA, a Health Savings Account.

> The speaker refers to the government website to bolster the claims.

2. Healthcare.gov says these accounts allow you to save money for out-of-pocket medical expenses with a tax savings (U.S. Centers for Medicare & Medicaid Services, n.d.).

3. Money is taken out of your paycheck before taxes, reducing what you pay in taxes overall.
4. You can use your account to pay for expenses related to co-pays, deductibles, prescriptions, medical equipment, dental work, and much more.
5. The Internal Revenue Service (2020) provides a full list of covered expenses on its website in IRS Publication 502.

(*Transition*: Now, you might ask yourself, which plan is right for me?)

IV. When you are deciding which plan to choose, consider both costs and your health.
   A. There are three questions you should ask yourself when choosing the right medical plan for you.
      1. Am I willing to plan for possible health care costs?
         a. If yes, the high deductible plan could save you the most money.
         b. If not, a higher premium that comes out of your paycheck may be better for you.
      2. Am I relatively healthy and visit the doctor on a limited basis?
         a. Remember, preventive care is free under both plans.
         b. If you're relatively healthy, an HDHP may be preferable over the higher monthly premium PPO.
      3. Do I have a chronic condition that requires continual care and repeated medical visits throughout the year?
         a. Smartasset.com says an HDHP may be suitable for someone who is younger and healthy without many medical needs throughout the year (Dixon, 2019).
         b. A PPO may be suitable for those who have many medical appointments, require ongoing medical care, or have regular prescriptions.
   B. Regardless of which plan you choose, Smartasset.com recommends you keep your individual or family medical needs in mind and review the cost of co-payments, deductibles, out-of-pocket maximums, and monthly medical premiums to determine which option may work best for you (Dixon, 2019).
      I. Since medical circumstances may change from year to year, it is a good idea to revisit your insurance needs each year to determine if a change is needed.
      II. Many organizations provide cost comparison calculators that allow you to compare the costs of an HDHP versus one that is not.
      III. MVP Health Care (n.d.) provides one that is relatively simple to use.

(*Transition*: As we wrap up today, choosing the right health insurance plan is not something to take lightly.)

CONCLUSION

I. Summary
   A. There are many plans out there, but the two we focused on are the PPO, preferred provider organization plan, and the HDHP, high deductible health plan.

(continued)

The speaker uses a parallel structure, asking three clear, simple questions to highlight the distinctions between the two plan types.

The speaker reviews the speech content in the conclusion.

> The final line drives home the importance of the content of the speech to the speaker's audience.

B. While both are similar, there are also significant differences, especially with regard to cost.

II. Clincher

A. It is important that you consider each plan carefully so that you choose the best one for your needs.

B. Regardless of the health insurance plan you choose, remember it is a major life decision and can impact your pocketbook, as well as your well-being.

REFERENCES

American College Health Association. (2019). *National College Health Assessment II–Spring 2019 reference group executive summary*. https://www.acha.org/documents/ncha/NCHA-II_SPRING_2019_US_REFERENCE_GROUP_EXECUTIVE_SUMMARY.pdf

BlueCross BlueShield of Texas. (n.d.). *Employer resources*. https://www.bcbstx.com/employer/resources/index.htm

Dixon, A. (2019, August 1). *10 health insurance terms you should know. SmartAsset*. https://smartasset.com/insurance/10-health-insurance-terms-you-should-know

Fay, B. (n.d.). *Health insurance premiums, deductibles, copays, and coinsurance*. Debt.org. https://www.debt.org/medical/health-insurance-premiums/

Frankel, M. (2018, May 8). How does the average American spend their paycheck? See how you compare. *USA Today*. https://www.usatoday.com/story/money/personalfinance/budget-and-spending/2018/05/08/how-does-average-american-spend-paycheck/34378157/

Humana. (n.d.). *What is a PPO?* https://www.humana.com/health-and-well-being/what-is-ppo

Internal Revenue Service. (2020, February 6). *About Publication 502, Medical and Dental Expenses*. https://www.irs.gov/forms-pubs/about-publication-502

MVP Health Care. (n.d.). *Which plan is right for me?* https://www.mywealthcareonline.com/mvphealthcare/Resources/HSA Resources/WhichHSAPlanisRightforme.aspx

U.S. Centers for Medicare & Medicaid Services. (n.d.). *Preventative care benefits for adults*. HealthCare.gov. https://www.healthcare.gov/preventive-care-adults/

> High-quality sources are used.

VISUAL AIDS

Venn diagrams showing similarities (four)
Venn diagrams showing differences (three)
IRS website
MVP Health Online website

> PowerPoint slides help illustrate and enliven the speech.

The Speech as Delivered

Here is a transcript of the speech as delivered.

PPO or HDHP? How to Choose a Health Plan

Is it a common cold? The flu? Or something more severe? Do I need to go to the doctor? These are questions that might go through your head whenever you get sick.

I find myself getting sick a few times a year and one thing that makes it easier for me is having a good health insurance. Three years ago, I pinched a nerve in my neck and was faced with many hospital visits and even a major surgery. As a result, I became obsessed with understanding health insurance options to find what works best for me.

Based on my class survey, 15 percent of the students here receive coverage under the university plan. This is consistent with the national average according to the American College Health Association. Sixty-five percent of you have coverage under your parents' plan, and the rest—20 percent—are employed full-time and have a plan of your own.

Matthew Frankel, writer for *USA Today*, mentions in his May 2018 article that the average American spends $4,612 in health care–related expenses per year including health insurance, medical services, and prescription drugs. This is a potentially large investment, so getting the most out of your health care is important not only for your personal well-being but also your financial security.

In our time together today, I want to tell you more about two major health insurance plans, the PPO–preferred provider organization plan, and the HDHP–high deductible health plan. [*Slide of the two plans appears on screen.*] First, I will provide brief descriptions of each plan and then move into the similarities and differences between them.

Let us start with a brief definition of each.

A PPO plan is referred to as a preferred provider organization plan. According to health insurance provider Humana, it is also known as a health maintenance organization. In general, a PPO plan provides a network of health care providers you may choose from.

Smartasset.com, a financial technology website devoted to providing personal finance advice, says health care providers who are a part of this network will offer medical care at a negotiated rate determined by the health care provider and the insurance company. That means you will pay a monthly premium for the insurance, but also co-pays at each visit throughout the policy term.

An HDHP is referred to as a high deductible health plan. This plan also allows you to choose from a network of providers who will offer negotiated rates, lower than paying out of pocket. The monthly fee is much lower than a PPO's, and rather than co-pays, you will pay out of pocket for all health care expenses until you reach a certain dollar amount.

There is a lot more to both plans, so let us dive in deeper by looking at the similarities and differences. First, the similarities.

In both plans, you will work with local medical providers that are considered in-network or that have a pricing contract with the insurer that is less expensive. As a patient, you often have the option to elect out-of-network medical providers as long as you are willing to assume the extra out-of-pocket costs.

Both plans also cover preventive services at full cost. Healthcare.gov, the U.S. government's health insurance exchange website, says these services may include routine physicals, blood pressure screenings, cholesterol screenings, immunization shots, and much more. It is important to check with your individual insurance provider to see what is considered preventive.

BlueCross BlueShield, another health insurance provider, says plans also cover discounts for some health and wellness programs as well as provide access to online tools that you can use to make healthier life decisions.

Also, each plan has an option for saving money for medical expenses that often comes with tax savings benefits.

(continued)

Now let us move on to some of the major differences between a PPO plan and an HDHP with a focus mostly on cost. This is often the determining factor that impacts the decision for many people.

Most health insurance companies including BlueCross BlueShield and Humana describe a PPO as having lower deductibles, a co-pay for office visits and certain procedures, and higher monthly premiums. By contrast, an HDHP has higher deductibles, few, if any, co-pays, and lower monthly premiums. The monthly premiums vary based on negotiations between your insurance company and your company or institution's benefits department. Additionally, monthly premiums vary based on selection of an individual plan or a family plan.

With a PPO, typical deductibles may range from $500 to $1,000 or more and co-pays may range from $5 to $50 or more. PPOs usually have two different deductibles: one for services from providers in the network and another for services from providers outside the network.

For an HDHP, the Internal Revenue Service says, in 2018, a high deductible plan must have a minimum deductible of $1,350 for single coverage and $2,700 for family coverage. Since these are just the minimums, many plans have higher deductibles. There are usually no co-pays since you are paying out of pocket until you meet your deductible.

As noted earlier, both plans offer savings accounts. A PPO plan has an FSA, a Flexible Spending Account, and an HDHP has an HSA, a Health Savings Account. Healthcare.gov says these accounts allow you to save money for out-of-pocket medical expenses with a tax savings. Money is taken out of your paycheck before taxes, reducing what you pay in taxes overall. You can use your account to pay for expenses related to co-pays, deductibles, prescriptions, medical equipment, dental work, and much more. The Internal Revenue Service provides a full list of covered expenses on its website in IRS Publication 502.

Now, you might ask yourself which plan is right for me? There are three questions you should ask yourself when choosing the right medical plan for you.

1. Am I willing to plan for possible health care costs?

   If yes, the high deductible plan could save you the most money. If not, a higher premium that comes out of your paycheck may be better for you.

2. Am I relatively healthy and visit the doctor on a limited basis?

   Remember, preventive care is free under both plans. If you're relatively healthy, an HDHP may be preferable over the higher monthly premium PPO.

3. Do I have a chronic condition that requires continual care and repeated medical visits throughout the year?

   Smartasset.com says an HDHP may be suitable for someone who is younger and healthy without many medical needs throughout the year. A PPO may be suitable for those who have many medical appointments, require ongoing medical care, or have regular prescriptions.

Regardless of which plan you choose, Smartasset.com recommends you keep your individual or family medical needs in mind and review the cost of co-payments, deductibles, out-of-pocket maximums, and monthly medical premiums to determine which option may work best for you. Since medical circumstances may change from year to year, it is a good idea to revisit your insurance needs each year to determine if a change is needed.

Many organizations provide cost comparison calculators that allow you to compare the costs of an HDHP versus one that is not. MVP Health Online provides one that is relatively simple to use.

As we wrap up today, choosing the right health insurance plan is not something to take lightly. There are many plans out there, but the two we focused on are the PPO, preferred provider organization plan, and the HDHP, high deductible health plan. While both are similar, there are also differences especially with cost. Regardless of the health insurance plan you choose, remember it is a major life decision and can impact your pocketbook, as well as your well-being.

Resources for Review and Skill Building

Summary

The goals of informative speaking are to convey fresh information, make material interesting, and help listeners remember key points. Four types of informative speeches were discussed in this chapter:

- *Definition* speeches give an extended definition of a concept so that listeners get a full, richly detailed picture of its meaning.

- *Description* speeches paint a vivid picture of a person, a place, an object, or an event.

- *Process* speeches explain the steps or stages by which something is done or made.

- *Explanation* speeches involve explaining a concept or a situation to the audience.

In developing an informative speech, keep these guidelines in mind: (1) Relate the speech to the listeners' self-interest, if at all possible. Show them explicitly the connection between your material and their personal lives. (2) Make the information interesting by going beyond generalities to give lots of specifics, such as examples and anecdotes. (3) Avoid information overload. (4) Tailor information for each audience. (5) Use the familiar to explain the unfamiliar. (6) Help listeners remember key information.

Key Terms

definition speech, *281*

description speech, *282*

explanation speech, *286*

extended definition, *281*

process speech, *283*

Review Questions

1. What is an extended definition? Why is it preferable in a speech to a dictionary definition?

2. Which two organizational patterns would be most appropriate for a speech on the life and achievements of astronaut Sally Ride?

3. What are the two kinds of process speeches?

4. In a process speech, at what point should you give listeners a warning?

5. Which organizational pattern would be most appropriate for a speech aimed at dispelling misconceptions about wolves?

6. Why is it important to relate a speech, if possible, to the listeners' self-interest?

7. Why is the issue of generalities versus specifics an important matter in informative speaking?

8. What should you do if some members of an audience know the meaning of a term but others do not?

9. A speaker says, "The lungs of a heavy smoker look like charred meat." What principle of informative speaking is the speaker using?

10. "Rhythm Helps Your Two Hips Move." By recalling this sentence and noting the first letter of each word, you can know the correct spelling for the word *rhythm*. This is an example of what kind of device?

Building Critical-Thinking Skills

1. A bad résumé can prevent an applicant from getting a job. If you conducted a three-hour workshop on how to create effective résumés, what techniques would you use to keep your audience awake and engaged?

2. A handout from a dog-obedience class reads, "Training a well-behaved dog takes time and practice. The more repetitions you do on a regular basis, the quicker your dog will understand. However, do not bore him. Keep your training sessions fun and interesting." Do you think this advice would apply to training humans? Justify your answer.

3. For a speech on hurricanes, how could you make the topic interesting for your listeners?

4. It is important to avoid overdosing on the fat-soluble vitamins A, D, K, and E. Create a memory aid to help an audience remember them.

Building Teamwork Skills

1. If improperly developed, the topics below can be boring. In a group, brainstorm ways that each topic could be made interesting.

    a. Teaching methods
    b. Citizenship
    c. Transportation

2. The text advises that you relate a topic to listeners' self-interest. In a group, brainstorm how the following topics can be presented in a way that would satisfy a listener's attitude of "What's in it for me?"

    a. Social Security
    b. Destruction of rainforests
    c. Secret video surveillance of employees
    d. Solar energy
    e. Homeless people

Examining Your Ethics

Answer: A. This is a positive topic and a service to the audience. Topics B and C are unethical. A speaker should not give advice on how to cheat, defraud, or manipulate.

End Notes

1. Cullen Jones, Olympic Gold Medalist, telephone interview, November 10, 2010.

2. "Using Field Blur in Photoshop," Planet Photoshop, planetphotoshop.com (accessed January 21, 2016).

3. Colin Fernandez, "Nine in Ten Feel Phantom Phone Vibrations," *Daily Mail*, www.dailymail.co.uk (accessed January 12, 2015).

4. "Do You Have Phantom Vibration Syndrome?" British Broadcasting Corporation, www.bbc.com (accessed January 14, 2016).

5. "Public Speaking—Essential Tips and Advice," Self Help Education Arena, selfhelpeducationarena.com (accessed January 22, 2016).

6. Roberto A. Ferdman, "Why Many Restaurants Don't Actually Want You to Order Dessert," *The Washington Post*, www.washingtonpost.com (accessed January 13, 2016).

7. Laura Northrop, "Dessert Is Good for Your Taste Buds, Bad for Restaurants' Profit Margins," *Consumerist*, https://consumerist.com (accessed January 13, 2016).

8. Samantha Grossman, "1 in 4 Americans Apparently Unaware the Earth Orbits the Sun," *Time*, https://time .com (accessed January 13, 2016).

9. "Americans Know Surprisingly Little about Their Government, Survey Finds," Annenberg Public Policy Center, www.annenbergpublicpolicycenter.org (accessed January 13, 2016)

10. "Ground-Level Ozone: Health Effects," U.S. Environmental Protection Agency, www3.epa.gov /ozonepollution/health.html (accessed January 13, 2016).

Speaking to Persuade

OUTLINE

Goals of Persuasive Speaking

Types of Persuasive Speeches

Patterns of Organization

Sample Persuasive Speech

After the Persuasive Speech

OBJECTIVES

After studying this chapter, you should be able to

1. Prepare a persuasive speech.
2. Identify two major types of persuasive speeches.
3. Understand how to discuss controversial topics in a civil manner.
4. Identify four patterns for organizing a persuasive speech.
5. Understand what to do after the speech.

ANGELINA SUJATA, a college student in Columbia, South Carolina, suffered severe, permanent injuries when the car she was driving rear-ended a car that had stopped abruptly in front of her. She says the crash caused her car's airbag to explode, sending sharp, metal fragments into her chest.[1]

After undergoing two surgeries, she sued Japan's Takata Corporation, the maker of the airbag. When she discovered that Takata airbags had caused five deaths and more than 100 injuries, she joined a campaign aimed at forcing the company to recall its defective airbags, and she went to Washington to try to persuade federal regulators and members of Congress to put pressure on Takata.

Finally, after three years of refusing to acknowledge that its airbags were defective, Takata capitulated, admitted error, and agreed to recall airbags in 34 million vehicles.[2]

The success of Sujata and her fellow campaigners demonstrates the power of persuasion. In a persuasive speech, you act as an advocate, a person who argues on behalf of an idea or a cause.

At first glance, persuasive speeches look like informative speeches, but that's because a persuasive speech must contain background information before it can make its case. The basic difference is that an informative speech is aimed at reporting, while a persuasive speech is aimed at winning over the audience.

To illustrate the two types of speeches, let's take the topic of solar-powered cars. For an informative speech, you would just give the facts—how the car works, how much the battery pack costs, and so on. For a persuasive speech, you would give some of the same facts, but you also would try to convince listeners that a solar-powered car is superior to a gasoline-powered vehicle and to persuade them to buy and drive a solar car.

In this chapter, we will examine types of persuasive speeches and how you can organize them. In the next chapter, we will look at persuasive strategies.

Angelina Sujata, flanked by several members of Congress, speaks out as part of a campaign to persuade lawmakers and regulators to pressure the Takata Corporation to recall defective air bags in 34 million vehicles.

Pablo Martinez Monsivais/ AP Images

Examining Your Ethics

Wendy, a software developer for an accounting firm, gives speeches to high school students to persuade them to enroll in a certain four-year private college. She is a graduate of the college, and the college pays her to give her presentations. Which of the following would be most appropriate for her talks?

A. She makes no mention of being a graduate or being paid to speak.

B. She mentions being a graduate, but omits the fact that she is being paid to speak.

C. She mentions that she is a graduate and is being paid to speak.

For the answer, see the last page of this chapter.

Goals of Persuasive Speaking

Persuasion is the process of influencing, changing, or reinforcing what people think, believe, or do. There are three key goals in persuasive speaking:

1. **Win over your listeners.** In some cases, your objective may be to convince your audience to adopt your view. For example, you could use a persuasive speech to convince your audience to donate blood.

2. **Know your subject thoroughly.** You will have little chance of persuading listeners if you are not perceived as knowledgeable and competent with regard to your topic. Develop as much expertise as possible by doing careful, extensive research. In the above example, you would need to conduct research about blood donation, including how the blood donation process works, where people can donate blood, and why donating is critical.

3. **Maintain a high standard of ethical behavior.** Avoid any degree of manipulation and deceit. Use supports (such as examples and visual aids) that are accurate and truthful, and don't exaggerate or use half-truths. Be forthright in revealing to the audience your true goals and motives, and do not guilt your audience. For example, you may have people in your audience who—for medical reasons—cannot donate blood. You do not want those members of your audience feeling embarrassed or ashamed.

persuasion
the process of influencing, changing, or reinforcing listeners' attitudes, beliefs, or behaviors.

Types of Persuasive Speeches

Persuasive speeches can be categorized according to two objectives: (1) to influence thinking and (2) to motivate action. Sometimes these categories overlap; for example, you often have to influence thinking before you can motivate action.

Speech to Influence Thinking

speech to influence thinking
an oral presentation aimed at winning intellectual assent for a concept or proposition.

The **speech to influence thinking** is an effort to convince people to adopt your position on a particular subject. If some listeners agree with your ideas even before you speak, your job is to reinforce what they already think.

Here are some sample specific purpose statements for this kind of speech:

- To convince my audience that marijuana should be legalized for recreational purposes

- To convince my audience that the capital gains tax should be lowered

- To convince my listeners that access to health care is a basic human right

speech of refutation
an oral counterargument against a concept or proposition put forth by others.

A subcategory of the speech to influence thinking is the **speech of refutation**, in which your main goal is to convince the audience that an opposing argument is flawed. In this type of speech, the objective should not be to attack what another speaker has said, but rather provide an alternative way of thinking that more aligns with your beliefs.

Here are some sample specific purpose statements for speeches of refutation:

- To persuade my audience to reject the viral spread of "deepfake" videos on social media

- To convince listeners to reject widespread conspiracy theories about the government

- To persuade my audience to disbelieve claims that American elections are rigged

Refuting an argument is easier when you are dealing with facts than when you are dealing with deeply held beliefs. Suppose, for example, that you want to challenge the idea that brown sugar is more natural and therefore healthier than white sugar. You can refute this idea by citing nutrition experts who say that brown sugar offers no nutritional advantages because it is simply white sugar with small amounts of molasses or burnt sugar added for coloring. Since this assertion involves verifiable chemical facts, your persuasive task is easy.

But suppose that you wanted to persuade an audience to reject the idea that human life begins at conception, and therefore abortion should remain legal. A topic like abortion has so many layers attached to it, including religion and questions of morality. Such core beliefs are extremely difficult to change. Attempting to refute a person's core belief is almost impossible.

This isn't to say that contentious topics should be avoided in persuasive speeches. To the contrary—a healthy debate about such issues is vital to a well-informed citizenry. And examining divisive issues in speeches is a much better way to explore opposing viewpoints than reading opinion pieces. A psychology study by University of California-Berkeley researchers found that "hearing a person explain his or her beliefs makes the person seem more mentally capable—and therefore seem to possess more uniquely human mental traits—than reading the same content."[3]

When tackling controversial topics in a speech to influence thinking, there are three characteristics that should be followed: be respectful of opposing viewpoints, avoid emotionally charged language, and attempt to find areas of common ground.

To *be respectful of opposing viewpoints* requires you to acknowledge opposing viewpoints and offer your appreciation and respect for them. This can be done at the beginning of the speech. For example, in the beginning of your speech about abortion you might say, "I want to discuss a topic that I know people have strong feelings about. I respect your opinion on this topic. My goal is not to start an argument, but rather to facilitate a discussion."

During your speech, you *avoid using emotionally charged language* that may instantly upset members of your audience who disagree with you. For example, if you were against abortion, you want to avoid making a statement like, "Abortion is murder." In this example, it takes just three words to cast severe judgment on those who disagree with your opinion on this issue. Even if you truly believe that abortion is murder, in a speech to influence thinking your goal is to have your audience consider your viewpoint. By accusing those who are pro-choice of being pro-murder, you have instantly shut down any opportunity to influence the thinking of the people you are trying to influence.

Your ultimate goal when speaking about controversial issues is to *attempt to find areas of common ground*. Speech consultant and debate coach Julia Dhar notes that "The way to reach people is by finding common ground."[4] For a topic like abortion, it is unlikely that you will change your audience's mind on the core issue of abortion. However, you might find common ground in other areas of this contentious issue. For example, you might try to convince your audience to support efforts that reduce unwanted pregnancies, such as the availability of free birth control and/or better sex education programs in high schools.

Speech to Motivate Action

speech to motivate action
an oral presentation that tries to impel listeners to take action.

Like the speech to influence thinking, the **speech to motivate action** tries to win people over to your way of thinking, but it also attempts one of the most challenging tasks of persuasion: getting people to take action. Your goal is to get listeners to respond in one or more of these ways: *start* a behavior (start taking first aid lessons), *continue* a behavior (continue donating blood), or *stop* a behavior (stop smoking).

Here are some sample specific purpose statements for speeches to motivate action:

- To persuade my listeners to sign a petition aimed at requiring drivers over 75 to be retested each year for their driver's license
- To persuade my audience members to stop overspending on their credit-card accounts
- To persuade my listeners to contact their representatives in Congress to demand mandatory background checks on all gun purchases

Speech to motivate action: "To persuade my listeners to visit the Martin Luther King Jr. Monument in Washington or go to its website."

Dave Newman/Shutterstock

Sometimes you want prompt action from your listeners ("Please vote for my candidate in today's election"); at other times, you simply want them to respond at any appropriate point in the future ("Whenever you see a child riding a bike, please slow down and drive very cautiously").

Here are some suggestions for motivating action.

Ask for the precise action that you want. Don't just "give the facts" and assume that your listeners will know what action to take. Say *exactly* what you want them to do.

If you are speaking on the importance of donating blood, don't just outline the need for blood in certain areas of the country. Tell your audience members that you want them to participate in an upcoming blood drive, and give them instructions on how to donate.

Whenever possible, get a response before listeners leave the room. Often a speaker gets listeners fired up over an issue and asks them to go home and write an e-mail to the appropriate agencies. Listeners leave the room determined to write that e-mail, but unfortunately very few ever do. Everyone has good intentions, but life is busy and there are urgent personal matters to be taken care of. After a couple of weeks, the vows are forgotten.

To avoid this problem, try to get an immediate response. In the above example, you can have a signup sheet ready for your audience to sign up for time to donate blood.

Researchers have verified that if you persuade a person to take a positive step, you increase that person's commitment to your cause.[5] He or she now has made an

Tips for Your Career

Use Role Play to Change Behavior

Role play is a powerful way to modify behavior. If possible, make a video of a session. All participants can view the video and discuss strengths they see, as well as areas that need improvement.

If you own a restaurant and you want to persuade your servers to respond in a friendly manner toward obnoxious customers, you can give them examples of how to treat diners, you can urge them to be friendly, and you can show training videos. But none of these techniques will be as effective as having your employees engage in role play. One person plays the role of the crabby complainer ("There's too much dressing on this salad!") while a server acts out the correct response (saying, with a smile, "I am so sorry—let me bring you another salad"). After each server's performance, give a critique and, if anything is wrong, ask him or her to try again.

auremar/Shutterstock

investment of time and energy. If opponents try to persuade the person to believe the opposite of what you have espoused, he or she will be highly resistant to change (unless, of course, there is some compelling counterargument). Why? Because human beings feel a strong need to be consistent.[6] Going over to the other side would be inconsistent with an action such as signing your petition.

Let's examine some on-the-spot responses that can help strengthen your listeners' support of your position.

- **Phones and social media.** Although cell phones and electronic devices should not be turned on during a speech, some speakers at the end of a presentation ask listeners to pull out their devices and take action on the spot. For example, listeners can be asked to log on to Facebook or Twitter to join a national crusade against abuse of workers in an American corporation. If it is appropriate, they can also be told how they can send a text message to make a donation to a worthy cause.

- **Petition.** Whether on paper or online, petitions are an effective way to get large numbers of people to demand action. You can set up a laptop or other device in the back of your meeting room, and as people leave, they can type in their names and addresses at an online petition site. Molly Katchpole, who was working two part-time jobs in Washington, DC, heard that Bank of America was planning to charge customers a $5 monthly fee for using their debit card. This made her angry, and she launched an online petition to urge the bank to cancel the fee. In just a few weeks, her petition received more than 300,000 signatures, causing Bank of America to cancel the fee.[7]

- **Show of hands.** Having listeners raise their hands can be helpful in building assent for your cause.[8] Ask for a show of hands only when you're sure that most listeners will be eager and unembarrassed to make a public commitment.
- **Sign-up sheet.** To garner commitment for some future activity such as volunteer work, you can ask people to write down their names and e-mail addresses. This strategy can be effective because even if their enthusiasm cools, most people will honor their promise to help when called upon later.

Don't pressure listeners.   No matter how much you want audience action, don't browbeat, manipulate, or beg. Don't single out and embarrass those listeners who decline to take action. Listeners who feel pressured might become so resentful that they will decline to support your cause simply out of spite.

Patterns of Organization

Organizing a speech effectively can enhance your persuasiveness. While any of the organizational patterns covered in the chapter on the body of the speech can be used, four patterns are especially strong in persuasive speeches: the motivated sequence, the problem–solution pattern, the statement-of-reasons pattern, and the comparative-advantages pattern. The motivated sequence pattern is often the most difficult for speakers to understand fully, so an extended example appears in the following section.

Motivated Sequence

motivated sequence
a series of steps designed to propel a listener toward accepting the speaker's proposition.

The **motivated sequence** is an effective approach to persuasion that was developed by Purdue University professor Alan H. Monroe in the 1930s.[9] The pattern is especially useful when you want to sell a product or service, or when you want to mobilize listeners to take a specific action (vote for your candidate, stop smoking). It has the virtue of being suitable for any type of audience—unaware, hostile, apathetic, neutral, or favorable. There are five steps in this pattern.

1. **Attention.** Grab the audience's attention at the beginning of your introduction, as discussed in the chapter on introductions and conclusions.

2. **Need.** Show your audience that there is a serious problem that needs action.

3. **Satisfaction.** Satisfy the need by presenting a solution, and show how your solution works.

4. **Visualization.** Paint a picture of results. Your scenario can be *positive:* help listeners visualize the good things that will happen when your solution is put into effect. Or it can be *negative:* show them the bad results if your solution is rejected.

5. **Action.** Request action from the listeners. Be specific: "Sign this petition" or "Write your legislators today—here are their addresses" or "You can volunteer in Room 211 this afternoon."

Table 1 gives an example of how the steps work. While these steps seem simple enough, some have trouble knowing how to fit the sequence into a speech outline. To clarify the matter, the following annotated outline demonstrates how one speaker placed the steps of the motivated sequence at logical places.

Table 1   Example of the Motivated Sequence

Step 1. Attention
Grab the listeners' attention.
"This photo shows cars parked in a hot parking lot on a summer day. The windows are rolled up, and when the owners return, they will have to endure stifling heat until their air-conditioning cools the interior."

Yorkman/Shutterstock

Step 2. Need
Describe a problem that needs action.
"In this parking lot, the cars, asphalt, and concrete are absorbing the sun's energy and retaining heat, making an 'urban heat island.' We need to find a way to keep our cars cool and stop wasting all of this solar energy—and instead use it to our advantage."

Shutterstock/Nikola Bilic

Step 3. Satisfaction
Satisfy the need by presenting a solution.
"The solution is to park our cars under a solar canopy that protects them from blazing heat, and at the same time converts all that solar energy into electricity. This solar canopy is one of four canopies that protect 600 cars at federal buildings in Denver, Colorado. They save the U.S. government about $500,000 in electricity costs each year, and they provide plug-in charging stations for electric cars."

Source: Courtesy of the U.S. General Services Administration

Step 4. Visualization

Help the audience visualize the results.
"With solar canopies at a mall, this couple can
drive away in a car that doesn't need a blast of
air-conditioning to cool down. Not only are they
comfortable, but they are saving money on the
cost of gasoline to power the air conditioner."

bikeriderlondon/Shutterstock

Step 5. Action

Request audience action.
"Please sign my petition to request solar canopies
for our campus. The petition includes information
about how many millions of dollars the college
can save in electricity bills in the coming decades.
And it also includes a request for plug-in charging
stations so that students can get free electricity
supplied while they are in class."

Nerthuz/Shutterstock

Relieving Eye Strain

COMMENTARY

Attention
(Grab the listeners' attention.)

SPEECH

INTRODUCTION

I. Did you know that you can experience eye problems if you
stare too long at the screens of your electronic devices?

II. Text-messaging devices like smartphones are the worst, but
you can also suffer from staring at a computer screen.

BODY

I. "Computer vision syndrome" afflicts millions of Americans who stare at a screen for long periods of time.

    A. Symptoms include dry, irritated eyes, headaches, sensitivity to light, and blurred vision, according to Dr. Kent Daum, associate professor of optometry at the University of Alabama–Birmingham.

    B. The syndrome can cause long-term deterioration of visual acuity.

> **Need**
> (Describe a problem that needs action.)

II. Doctors recommend a simple solution—the 20/20/20 rule.

    A. "Every 20 minutes, take a 20-second break and focus on something 20 feet away," says Dr. Jeffrey Anshel of Encinitas, California, who is a consultant on visual ergonomics for American Airlines.

    B. The simple technique not only rests your eyes, but it also keeps them moist and prevents them from "locking into a close-up."

> **Satisfaction**
> (Satisfy the need by presenting a solution.)

III. The 20/20/20 rule is effective.

    A. Dr. Amy Greer of Dallas, Texas, recommended the rule to patients who were suffering from headaches and eyestrain caused by staring at small screens.

    B. All of the patients who tried the technique said that it eliminated their problems.

> **Visualization**
> (Help the audience visualize the results.)

CONCLUSION

I. Prolonged staring at a screen can cause "computer vision syndrome," with symptoms such as blurred vision, dry and irritated eyes, and headaches.

II. The solution is simple: Every 20 minutes, take a 20-second break and focus on something 20 feet away.

    A. I challenge all of you to follow the 20/20/20 rule.

    B. Your eyes will thank you.

> **Action**
> (Request audience action.)

For another speech that uses the motivated sequence, see the sample outline and transcript in the next section.

Problem–Solution Pattern

For many audiences, the most persuasive approach is the **problem–solution pattern**. You show that a problem exists, and then you present the solution. This pattern is especially

problem–solution pattern
an arrangement of material that explores a problem and then offers a solution.

effective when listeners either don't know about the problem or don't know how serious it is. Here an example:

Specific Purpose: To persuade my audience to avoid using plastic bags when shopping

Central Idea: Use alternatives to plastic bags when grocery shopping to help reduce the amount of plastic bag waste.

Main Points:
(Problem)   I. Plastic bags are destroying our environment.

  A. Plastic bags can take up to 1,000 years to decompose in landfills.

  B. The average American family uses 1,500 plastic bags each year.

  C. Only 5 percent of plastic bags are recycled.

(Solution)   II. Find alternatives to plastic bags.

  A. Paper bags are better, but not the answer. They consume a tremendous amount of energy to produce (more than plastic bags).

  B. Use reusable bags. The average reusable bag has a life span of more than 700 plastic bags.

In the speech itself, under the first main point, the speaker showed some striking statistics. Under the second main point, the speaker gave specific examples of how enforcement should be carried out.

For a transcript of a speech that uses the problem–solution pattern, see the chapter on persuasive strategies.

Statement-of-Reasons Pattern

statement-of-reasons pattern
a variation of the topical pattern in which a speaker gives reasons for an idea.

The **statement-of-reasons pattern**, a variation of the topical pattern (discussed in the chapter on the body of the speech), gives reasons for the speaker's argument. It can be used for any persuasive speech, but it is especially useful when the audience leans toward your position yet needs some justification for that leaning. Here is an example:

Specific Purpose: To persuade my listeners about the importance of getting a flu shot

Central Idea: Getting a flu shot not only benefits you, but also may help the most vulnerable people in the community.

Main Points:
(First Reason)   I. You reduce your chance of getting the flu.

(Second Reason)   II. Even if you get the flu, your symptoms will likely not be as severe.

(Third Reason)   III. You will be reducing the chance that the flu will spread, especially important for infants and others with medical conditions not allowing them to get a flu shot.

Comparative-Advantages Pattern

comparative-advantages pattern
an organizational scheme that shows the superiority of one concept or approach over another.

When listeners already agree with you that a problem exists but aren't sure which solution is best, you can use the **comparative-advantages pattern** to show that your recommended solution is superior to others. Let's say that your listeners agree with you that

Tips for Your Career

View Persuasion as a Long-Term Process

Persuasion is sometimes a one-shot event aimed at a quick decision, as when you urge listeners to vote for a certain candidate. But in your career, persuasion often takes a long time—weeks, months, or even years. You need to gently nudge people toward a goal, giving them time to trust you and evaluate your recommendations.

Imagine a real estate agent who meets a young couple who are in the market for a new house. Instead of pressing for a quick sale, he gets to know them and truly listens to their needs. He takes them to visit many different houses, making notes on which features the couple like and dislike. After a long process of friendly collaboration, he is able to match the couple with a house that truly satisfies their needs.

Whether you succeed or fail in persuasion often comes down to one key question: are you trustworthy? Before people will buy your ideas, products, or services, they want to know whether they can trust you to guide them in the right direction. Proving your reliability may take

time, but one factual error or unethical move can eliminate any chance at persuasion.

bikeriderlondon/Shutterstock

medicine is needed for alleviating the symptoms of the common cold, but they don't know whether herbal remedies or conventional medicines would be better. If you feel that the latter is the preferred option, you could use the comparative-advantages pattern:

Specific Purpose: To convince my audience that conventional medicines are superior to herbal remedies in treating a common cold

Central Idea: Conventional medicines are more likely than herbal remedies to relieve symptoms of the common cold.

Main Points:
(First Advantage)   I. Unlike herbal remedies, conventional medicines are tested and given FDA assurance of safety and purity.

(Second Advantage)   II. Unlike herbal remedies, conventional medicines are required to list possible side effects.

(Third Advantage)   III. Conventional medicines act more quickly than herbal remedies to lessen discomfort.

Each main point shows the superiority of conventional medicines over herbal remedies.

Sample Persuasive Speech

Using the motivated sequence, this speaker argues that schools should be required to offer anti-bullying programs. Below is the outline of the speech, which is accompanied by a commentary. Following the outline is a transcript of the speech.

The Outline with Commentary

Bullying

COMMENTARY	SPEECH

General Purpose: To persuade

Specific Purpose: To persuade my audience to support anti-bullying education.

Central Idea: Anti-bullying education should be mandated in public schools.

INTRODUCTION

I. Attention Material

    A. Reference scene/show clip from *Bully* documentary

    B. I have been a victim of bullying.

    C. 64 percent of those who are bullied never report it (Curtin).

> In the **attention** step of the problem–solution, the speaker tries to arouse curiosity.

(*Transition:* I'm here to argue today that anti-bullying education should be mandated in our public schools. First, we'll take a look at the rampant problem with bullying, and then we'll move more into the solution of mandating these education programs in our schools.)

> The speaker enhances his credibility by admitting that he has experienced bullying.

BODY

I. Bullying is a major problem

    A. Bullying is widespread in the United States.

        1. Victims typically are bullied because of race, ethnicity, gender identity, religion, sexual orientation, or disability.

        2. Bullying comes in two forms: face-to-face and cyber.

    B. Bullying is a problem on school grounds, with one-fourth of all students experiencing bullying on school property, 74 percent of bullying instances among 8- to 11-year-olds happening at school, and a child is bullied every seven minutes ("Facts").

> For the **need** step, the speaker explains a problem.

        1. 160,000 kids will skip school on any given day to avoid being bullied ("Do Something").

        2. One in 10 students will drop out of school due to repeated bullying ("Do Something").

        3. Bullying victims are 2 to 9 times more likely to consider suicide ("School Bullying").

           a. A 9-year-old Denver boy committed suicide due to bullying in 2018 (O'Kane).

> In the outline, the names of sources are placed in parentheses, but in the actual speech, they will be woven into the fabric of the speaker's remarks.

           b. A 10-year-old Kentucky boy killed himself after repeated bullying (Li).

(*Transition:* How can we help reduce bullying?)

II. It's time to start mandating anti-bullying education in our public schools.

   A. Olweus Bully Prevention Program at Clemson—most researched and best-known program ("The Olweus")

     1. Students who complete the program show a 50 percent reduction in bullying or being bullied.

     2. Participating students also show reductions in antisocial behavior.

     3. Classroom social environment is improved.

   B. Steps to Respect—another successful bully-prevention program

     1. 26 classrooms across six different Seattle elementary schools piloted the program in 2011.

     2. Was developed to reduce the harmful gossip that leads to bullying

     3. Resulted in 72 percent decrease in gossip (McElroy)

       a. Emphasizes empathy and assertiveness

       b. Teaches that bullying is not the social norm

       c. Involves entire school community, from students to bus drivers to teachers

   C. Anti-bullying education works to reduce bullying in schools (McElroy).

(*Transition:* Research indicates that had there been an anti-bullying education program in Alex's middle school, he likely wouldn't have to had suffer in silence for as long as he did.)

III. Three years later, the Libby family moved to Edmond, Oklahoma.

   A. Alex had a new life.

     1. He become a national spokesperson for bullied kids.

     2. His new beginning has given him a newfound confidence.

(*Transition:* What can you do?)

IV. Join me today and help me advocate for anti-bullying education programs in our public schools.

   A. I have cards on the back desk with more information about how you can help spread the word.

   B. Phone numbers are provided to call our local legislators.

CONCLUSION

Together, we can put a stop to this.

BIBLIOGRAPHY

Bully. Produced by S. Foudy et al., directed by L. Hirsch, 2011. United States: Cinereach.

Curtin, M. "Want Your Kids to Be Strong Leaders? Teach Them This about Bullying Immediately." *Inc.com, 29* June 2016,

---

The **satisfaction** step presents a solution to the problem.

Citing sources gives your argument more credibility.

Referring back to the anecdote in the beginning of the speech is a nice tactic to connect the introduction to your call-to-action.

In the **action** step, the speaker spells out exactly how listeners can help.

Because the body of the speech is necessarily long, it is appropriate to have a brief, to-the-point conclusion.

(continued)

www.inc.com/melanie-curtin/this-striking-statistic-on-bullying
-could-turn-your-kid-into-a-very-strong-leade.html.

"Do Something about Bullying." *DoSomething.org,* www
.dosomething.org/us/causes/bullying.

"Facts about Bullying." *Bully Free,* www.bullyfree.com/free
-resources/facts-about-bullying.

Li, D. "10-Year-Old Kentucky Boy Who Killed Himself Was
Bullied." *NBC News,* 23 Jan. 2019, www.nbcnews.com/news
/us-news/10-year-old-kentucky-boy-who-committed-suicide
-was-bullied-n961936.

McElroy, M. "33 Percent Drop in Physical Bullying in Schools
Using 'Steps to Respect.' " *UW News,* 21 Sept. 2011, www
.washington.edu/news/2011/09/21/33-percent-drop-in-physical
-bullying-in-schools-using-steps-to-respect/.

O'Kane, C. "9-year-old Denver Boy Dies by Suicide after Being
Bullied at School." *CBS News,* 27 Aug. 2018, www.cbsnews
.com/news/9-year-old-denver-boy-dies-by-suicide-after-being
-bullied-at-school-mother-says/.

"The Olweus Bullying Prevention Program." *Violencepreventionworks
.org,* www.violencepreventionworks.org/public/olweus_bullying_
prevention_program.page.

"School Bullying Statistics." *Bullyingstatistics.org,* www
.bullyingstatistics.org/content/school-bullying-statistics.html.

VISUAL AIDS

Clip from *Bully* documentary
PowerPoint slides

> The speaker relies on highly credible sources.

The Speech as Delivered

Here is a transcript of the speech. Notice the ideas of the outline do not match the exact wording of the speech. In an extemporaneous speech, a speaker does not read or memorize a speech but speaks from brief notes.

Bullying

Public Schools Should Mandate Anti-bullying Education

Upon discovering that her 12-year-old son was being bullied by his classmates on a daily basis, and saddened over why he did not speak about it sooner, a mother asks her son, "Does it make you feel good when they punch you? Or kick you? Or stab you?"

Unable to look his mother in the eyes, the young man replies saying, "No . . . I don't know. I'm starting to think I don't feel anything anymore." These words belong to Alex Libby, one of the central figures in *Bully,* the 2012 documentary film directed by Lee Hirsch, himself a victim of cruel and violent childhood bullying.

The fact that Alex doesn't tell anybody about what is happening to him comes as no surprise. In a 2016 article on Inc.com, writer and activist Melanie Curtin says that 64 percent of those who are bullied never report it. The only reason Alex's parents eventually find out is because Director Hirsch presents them with live video footage showing their son being beaten and abused on the school bus.

I, myself, have been a victim of bullying. And even today, experience it from time to time. I want to put a stop to this and thus, have conducted research and continue to read as much as I can about the topic.

I'm here to argue today that anti-bullying education should be mandated in our public schools. First, we'll take a look at the rampant problem with bullying, and then we'll move more into the solution of mandating these education programs in our schools.

Let's focus on the problem.

Bullying is a widespread problem in the United States. Victims are typically bullied because of their race, ethnicity, gender, religion, sexual orientation, or disability. Bullying comes in two main forms: one, the traditional face-to-face encounters involving physical and/or verbal assaults and two, virtual encounters known as cyber-bullying.

The website Bully Free, which is dedicated to bullying prevention, says one-fourth of students across all grades experience bullying or harassment on school property. When 8- to 11-year-olds are bullied, it happens at school 74 percent of the time. And a child is bullied on a school playground every seven minutes.

According to statistics on DoSomething.org, a digital platform powering offline actions, 160,000 kids will skip school on any given day to avoid being bullied. One in 10 students will drop out of school because of repeated bullying. The bullying can become so extreme that the victims are driven to suicide. Bullyingstatistics.org says that based on a study by Yale University, bullying victims are 2 to 9 times more likely to consider suicide than nonvictims.

Bullying-related suicide hits children of all ages. *CBS News* says that a 9-year-old Denver boy killed himself after being bullied in 2018. Even more recently, *NBC News* reports that in early 2019, a 10-year-old Kentucky boy killed himself after experiencing repeated bullying by his peers. How many more victims of bullying do we need to hear or read about before we seriously and effectively address the problem?

Something has to be done to stop this.

We've taken a look at the problem. Now let's move on to the solution. It's time to start mandating anti-bullying education in our public schools.

One successful anti-bullying education program is the Olweus Bully Prevention Program housed at Clemson University. Violencepreventionworks.org says that this is the most researched and best-known bullying prevention program available today. According to the same website, students who have completed this program reported a 50 percent reduction in being bullied or bullying others, as well as reductions in antisocial behaviors and positive increases in the overall classroom social environment.

Another successful bullying prevention program is Steps to Respect. In 2011, 36 classrooms across six different Seattle elementary schools piloted the program, which was developed to reduce the kind of harmful childhood gossip that often leads to more serious forms of bullying. The University of Washington observed this program for three months, and found that it resulted in a 72 percent decrease in gossip among the students.

Steps to Respect worked as well as it did for a few reasons: It emphasized empathy and assertiveness, and it taught that bullying is not the social norm. It also asked administrators to take stock of their schools' anti-bullying policies. It involved all the adults from bus drivers to teachers and eventually all the students in the classrooms. The Campbell Collaboration, an international research network, asserts that anti-bullying education does in fact help in preventing bullying in our schools. Almost 10 years later this program is still in action in helping to reduce bullying.

Clearly, school-place bullying is a grave concern that deserves proper attention. Research indicates that had there been an anti-bullying education program in Alex's middle school, he likely wouldn't have to had suffer in silence for as long as he did. Three years after the filming of *Bully* and dissatisfied with how their school district handled the case, the Libby family moved from their native Sioux City, Iowa, to Edmond, Oklahoma. There, Alex had a new life for himself. He also became a national spokesperson for bullied kids, an experience that has given him a newfound confidence, a new beginning, and most of all, a respected voice.

Join me today and help me advocate for anti-bullying education programs in our public schools. If interested, I have cards on the back desk with more information about how you can help spread the word, as well as phone numbers for our local legislators. Together, we can put a stop to this.

For other persuasive speeches, see the sample outlines in the chapter on the body of the speech and the chapter on introductions and conclusions; also see the sample speech in the chapter on persuasive strategies.

After the Persuasive Speech

In a classroom environment, once you finish your persuasive speech, you likely are finished with the assignment. All that's left is to wait for the grade from your instructor. However, when you complete a persuasive speech in the professional world, your persuasive task is far from finished. The goal is to have your word spread from the people in the room to their colleagues, supervisors, and other relevant decision makers. One way to accomplish this is to provide "leave-behinds"— materials that are distributed at the end of your question-and-answer period. Make sure each listener receives a set. Leave-behinds can be a variety of things:

1. *Summary.* A condensation of your key information will help listeners recall your points later, and it will provide a good abstract for those who could not attend. The summary must be brief—no more than one page.

2. *Memory aids.* A popular technique is to provide cards that can be slipped into a wallet or purse for future reference. Figure 1 shows a sample card.

3. *Graphics.* Copies of graphs, diagrams, and tables provide visual support.

Figure 1

This memory aid was given to listeners by a student speaker at the end of a speech on dangerous mercury levels in fish. The card could be kept in a wallet or purse and pulled out at a restaurant or grocery store to help identify the types of fish containing high levels of mercury. (The student derived his information from the Natural Resources Defense Council.)

Shutter_M/Shutterstock

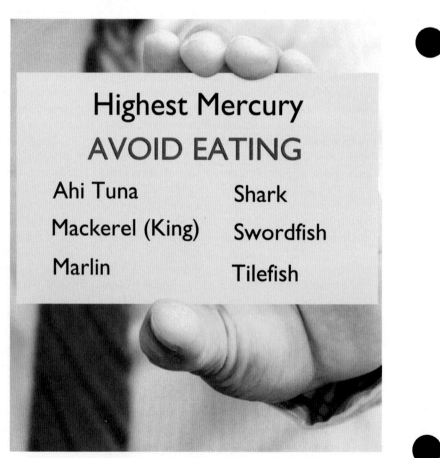

4. *New points.* If your time limit prevents you from covering all the points you want to discuss, you can focus on just a few points in the speech and cover the others on a leave-behind.

5. *Sources and websites.* For listeners who want to pursue your subject further, provide a piece of paper giving your sources and relevant websites.

6. *Samples.* A sample product is a tangible reminder of your message. For example, if you are selling herbal skin lotion, you can give each listener a small tube of the product.

7. *Multimedia.* Provide a USB flash drive with information that can provide bonus material in an enjoyable format.

8. *File folders.* Consider providing labeled file folders containing your materials. The folders help listeners keep material together and make it easy to share with others.

For all important presentations, use leave-behinds. They enable your audience to take your message far beyond the meeting room to influence many people.

Resources for Review and Skill Building

Summary

Persuasion means influencing, changing, or reinforcing what people think, believe, or do. When you give a persuasive speech, you should have three key goals: (1) Win over your listeners so that they adopt your view or take a certain action. (2) Know your subject thoroughly. (3) Maintain a high standard of ethical behavior.

There are two major types of persuasive speeches: the speech to influence thinking and the speech to motivate action.

In the speech to influence thinking, your primary goal is to convince people to adopt your position. A subcategory of this kind of speech is the speech of refutation, in which your aim is to convince the audience that an opposing argument is flawed. In this type of speech, the objective should not be to attack what another speaker has said, but rather provide an alternative way of thinking that more closely aligns with your beliefs. When tackling controversial topics, there are three characteristics that should be followed:

be respectful of opposing viewpoints, avoid emotionally charged language, and attempt to find areas of common ground.

In the speech to motivate action, you should tell your listeners exactly what action you want them to take. Whenever possible, encourage them to take some action—even if it's a small, token action—immediately.

Of the many patterns that can be used for the persuasive speech, four are especially effective: the motivated sequence, problem–solution pattern, statement-of-reasons pattern, and comparative-advantages pattern.

After you have finished presenting your speech and answering any questions, leave your audience with some material that will remind them of your message so that they can possibly spread it to others. Leave-behinds can include cards, memory aids, graphics, new information, sources, samples, multimedia, and other documents.

Key Terms

comparative-advantages pattern, *312*

motivated sequence, *308*

persuasion, *304*

problem–solution pattern, *311*

speech of refutation, *304*

speech to influence thinking, *304*

speech to motivate action, *306*

statement-of-reasons pattern, *312*

Review Questions

1. What is the ultimate goal in a speech of refutation?

2. In a speech to influence thinking, how can you effectively argue controversial topics?

3. In a speech to motivate action, why should you try to get listeners to take action immediately?

4. Give three examples of immediate, on-the-spot audience action.

5. Briefly explain the four steps of the motivated sequence.

6. Which organizational pattern is useful when listeners don't know how serious a problem is?

7. When is the statement-of-reasons pattern especially effective?

8. When is the comparative-advantages pattern most effective?

9. How can you ensure your message is carried on after your persuasive speech?

Building Critical-Thinking Skills

1. Charities often give instructions like these to their fund-raisers: "If people decline to contribute, ask them to give just a token amount, such as a quarter or one dollar." These instructions are sometimes effective in building support for an organization because they follow one of the successful persuasive techniques discussed in this chapter. What is the technique?

2. Political discussions can be very polarizing, whether among politicians in Congress or among family at the dinner table. How can we discuss controversial topics in a more civil manner?

3. Before sponsoring a proposed law, some legislators hire what is called a "devil's advocate" to argue forcefully *against* the proposal (in private, of course). Why do you think this approach is taken? What can be gained?

4. Which organizational pattern would work best for a speech on why short résumés are better than long ones? Defend your answer.

Building Teamwork Skills

1. Think of a controversial issue that often elicits passionate debate. Appoint a neutral moderator from your group and split the rest of the team into the two sides of the debate. Using a white board, poster paper, or some other method that both sides can see, the moderator should draw a line down the middle of the page and write down one side on the left of the line and another on the right.

   A. Discuss why each side feels so passionately about the issue with the moderator summarizing the arguments on the appropriate side *(Note: Avoid charged language that insults the opposing viewpoint.)*

   B. After a list of at least eight reasons are listed for each side, look for commonalities among the arguments. For example, in a debate on gun rights, the gun enthusiast side might argue "personal safety and protection," while the gun control side might argue argue "keep children safe." Here, "safety" would be a commonality.

   C. After commonalities are found, discuss how the group might find solutions that both sides can agree on.

2. Working in a group, create a brief synopsis for an original television commercial that uses the motivated sequence. Here are some possible topics:

   a. Buying a certain brand of toothpaste
   b. Exercising at a gym
   c. Donating blood to the Red Cross
   d. Buying a smartphone

Examining Your Ethics

Answer: C. Wendy could say something like this: "I am a graduate of the college, and in the interest of full disclosure, I want you to know that I am being paid to give this presentation. However, let me add that even if I were not being paid, I would still recommend this college as an ideal school for you."

End Notes

1. Roddie Burris, "Chapin Woman Files First SC Claim against Honda Airbag Maker," The State, www.thestate.com (accessed January 18, 2016).

2. Jeff Glor, "Major Airbag Recall Leaves Questions Unanswered," CBS News, www.cbsnews.com (accessed January 18, 2016).

3. J. Schroeder, M. Kardas, and N. Epley, "The Humanizing Voice: Speech Reveals, and Text Conceals, a More Thoughtful Mind in the Midst of Disagreement," *Psychological Science*, 2017, https://doi.org/10.1177/0956797617713798 (accessed February 20, 2020).

4. J. Dhar, "How to Disagree Productively and Find Common Ground," October 2018, TED Talks, www.ted.com/talks/julia_dhar_how_to_disagree_productively_and_find_common_ground (accessed February 20, 2020).

5. Stuart Oskamp and P Wesley Schultz, *Attitudes and Opinions* (New York: Psychology Press, 2005), p. 238.

6. "The Need for Consistency," Changing Minds, changingminds.org (accessed January 18, 2016).

7. Linette Lopez, "This 22-Year-Old Is Leading a Huge Campaign against Bank of America," *Business Insider*, www.articles.businessinsider.com (accessed January 23, 2016).

8. Jesse Scinto, "5 Tips for Powerful Audience Participation," *Fast Company*, www.fastcompany.com (accessed January 18, 2016).

9. Alan Houston Monroe, *Principles and Types of Speech* (Chicago: Scott, Foresman, 1935).

Persuasive Strategies

OUTLINE

OBJECTIVES

After studying this chapter, you should be able to

1. Describe how to analyze listeners, using a persuasion scale.
2. Explain how to build credibility with an audience in a persuasive speech.
3. Explain how to marshal convincing evidence in a persuasive speech.
4. Distinguish between deduction and induction as tools of reasoning in a persuasive speech.
5. Identify 10 fallacies in reasoning.
6. Select motivational appeals for a persuasive speech.
7. Explain how to arouse emotions in a persuasive speech.

SHOULD YOU GET A FLU SHOT EACH YEAR? In 2018, more than 800,000 Americans were hospitalized with the flu, and the virus killed roughly 60,000 people.[1] But many of these hospitalizations and deaths could have been prevented with the flu vaccine. According to the Mayo Clinic, the flu vaccine can be up to 60 percent effective in adults, and even if a vaccinated adult gets the flu, the severity of the illness is typically lessened.[2]

Some might argue that in a year like 2018, the flu shot was not effective. Indeed, that year the vaccine was only 30 percent effective, significantly lower than in most years. But Dr. Kathleen Neuzil, director of the Center for Vaccine Development at the University of Maryland School of Medicine, says, "That's still 30 percent of people who were not spreading the flu to anyone else. The vaccine prevents significant morbidity and mortality in tens of thousands of lives annually, if not more."[3]

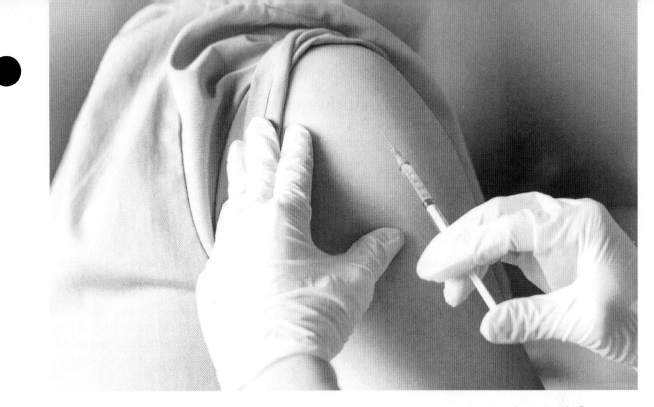

Increases in flu vaccinations have led to a decrease in the spread of the virus.

Pornpak Khunatorn/iStock/Getty Images

So what happened in 2018? After a steady increase in the percentages of people getting vaccinated over the past decade, vaccinations took a huge dip in 2018, with only 37.1 percent of adults receiving the vaccine (down from 43.3 percent in 2017).[4]

The Centers for Disease Control and Prevention (CDC) responded with a massive promotional campaign to promote vaccinations in the following years. The efforts seemed to have paid off. In 2019, a record 45.3 percent of adults were vaccinated. Vaccinations among children also hit a record high, with 62.6 percent getting the flu shot in 2019.[5]

The increase in vaccinations led to the decrease in the spread of the virus. Hospitalizations due to the flu dropped from 800,000 in 2018 to 490,000 in 2019, and flu-related deaths dropped from 61,000 to 34,000.[6]

Why did this campaign work? In this chapter we will examine strategies that can work in persuasive campaigns, and in persuasive speeches.

Knowing Your Audience

The first step in persuasion is to understand your listeners. To truly understand them, you must get inside their minds and see the world as they see it. For example, the CDC conducted several surveys and interviews among Americans to examine why so many people were not getting a flu vaccine. It found three main reasons:

- The flu vaccine can give you the flu.
- The vaccine is ineffective, so it's unnecessary.
- The flu is not a serious illness—it's like catching a cold.

Understanding these reasons, the CDC was able to craft a promotional campaign that countered some of these misbeliefs.

In a public speaking class, you may already know your audience on a series of topics. For example, your audience likely shares your concerns about college affordability. But for other topics that are not as clear, you might consider conducting a survey of your classmates to see how they feel about specific issues. One way to do this is to have all students in the class collaborate on a survey that will provide information for each student's persuasive speech.

In addition to surveys, the following are some other strategies for understanding your audience.

Analyze Listeners

How can you find out where listeners stand? In a professional environment, knowing the demographics of your audience can help. The environment of your speech can give a lot of clues as well. For example, if you are speaking at a Chamber of Commerce function, you will likely have a lot of business-oriented people on hand. If your speech is about raising the minimum wage, you know it will likely be a tough sell.

In the classroom, you should have been listening to your classmates give speeches on a variety of topics throughout the semester. This should give you some insight into where your audience stands. Based on your classroom experience, you might select a few individual members of your class to interview, finding out how much they know about your subject and what their beliefs and attitudes are. This can be used to help formulate an audience survey.

Use a Persuasion Scale

For analyzing an audience, consider using the persuasion scale in Table 1. On the scale, mark where the listeners are in relation to your specific purpose *before* you speak. Then mark where you hope they will be *after* you speak. Knowing a starting point and an ideal finishing point can help prevent you from giving a speech that fails to connect with your audience.

Table 1 Persuasion Scale

1	2	3	4	5	6
Unaware of the issue	Aware of the issue but opposed to your view	Aware of the issue but apathetic	Informed and interested but neutral on your view	Convinced of your view	Ready to take action

TIP 1

Tips for Your Career

Don't Expect Universal Success

One of the greatest orations in American history—the Gettysburg Address—was a failure, in the opinion of some of Abraham Lincoln's contemporaries. An editorial in the *Chicago Times* on the day after his speech said, "The cheek of every American must tingle with shame as he reads the silly, flat and dishwatery utterances of the man who has to be pointed out to intelligent foreigners as the President of the United States."

Career Track, a company that sponsors business speeches and seminars throughout the United States, asks listeners to evaluate each of its speakers. No speaker has ever received 100 percent satisfaction. No matter the speaker, no matter the subject matter, at least 2 percent of listeners are dissatisfied. Even popular spellbinders can please no more than 98 percent.

In your career, do your best, try to meet the needs of all listeners, but remember that you can give an oration equal in greatness to the Gettysburg Address and still fail to please that intractable 2 percent.

Sources: Clifton Fadiman, ed., *The American Treasury, 1455–1955* (New York: Harper & Brothers, 1955), p. 152; Lilly Walters, *Secrets of Successful Speakers* (New York: McGraw-Hill, 1993), p. 37.

If your goal is to persuade your audience to switch from diet sodas to healthier beverages, it might be a mistake to assume that audience members are at Stage 5 (convinced of your view and wanting tips on how to find healthy substitutes). Perhaps they are really at Stage 1 (unaware of the long-term health hazards of diet sodas). In that case, you should start at Stage 1 and move toward Stage 5 and ultimately end up at Stage 6.

Set a realistic goal. You are not a failure if your listeners fall short of Stage 6. With some listeners, persuading them to move from Stage 2 to Stage 4 is a great triumph.

Plan Your Strategy

While some audiences may fit neatly into one category or another, many audiences are segmented—that is, you may find 16 listeners opposed to your view, 15 apathetic, 8 already convinced, and so on.

When you have several different segments, to which group should you devote your energies? An obvious answer is to try to meet the needs of everyone. While this is an admirable goal, it cannot always be achieved. For example, if most listeners know a great deal about your topic but a few are totally uninformed, it would be foolish to spend almost all of your time focusing on the needs of a tiny minority.

The best approach is to try to meet the needs of all listeners, but when this is impossible, choose the group that is most important. If, for example, your pre-speech analysis shows that 21 listeners want guidance on how to manage student loan debt and 3 listeners don't think the issue is relevant to their lives, don't focus most of your time and energy on those 3 listeners.

Despite the difficulty of meeting the needs of several different segments, there are some strategies you can employ. Using the persuasion scale, let's examine how to reach listeners with *starting* points at each of the six stages. As we proceed, study Table 2, which shows an example of how to apply these strategies.

1. **Unaware of the issue.** For people in the dark on your topic, start by explaining the situation and showing why your ideas are important. Later in the speech, try to convince them to adopt your view.

Table 2   Using the Persuasion Scale

Situation: A speech aimed at persuading listeners to use reusable bags for grocery shopping.

Position on Scale	Strategy	Example
1. Unaware of the issue	Explain the problem.	"Single-use plastic grocery bags can take up to 500 years to decompose, longer than any consumer-use product including Styrofoam, disposable diapers, and cigarette butts."
2. Aware of the issue but opposed to your view	Refute opposing arguments or schemes.	"You may think that the solution is to recycle plastic bags, but despite most grocery stores offering plastic bag recycling bins, only about 5 percent of plastic bags are recycled each year."
3. Aware of the issue but apathetic	Show that the issue can affect listeners' lives.	"Maybe this is an issue you don't feel impacts you, but did you know that up to 12 million metric tons of plastic waste wash up on the shoreline every year? Plastic—including bags—contains chemicals that ends up in your drinking water."
4. Informed and interested but neutral on your view	Show that your proposal offers the best solution to the problem.	"Consider using reusable shopping bags on your grocery trips. Each reusable bag has the life span of 700 plastic bags! And in cities that have banned plastic bags in grocery stores, they have seen an 89 percent reduction in plastic bag litter in nearby rivers and streams."
5. Convinced of your view	Reinforce existing beliefs and give new reasons for supporting your view.	"Many of us already use reusable shopping bags for our grocery store shopping trips, but what happens at the gas station when we are purchasing a candy bar and drink? Many times the attendant puts them in a plastic bag. Kindly say, 'I don't need a bag.'"
6. Ready to take action	Show how, when, and where to take action.	"I am giving each of you a reusable shopping bag to get started on this journey. Thank you."

2. **Aware of the issue but opposed to your view.** Find out the listeners' reasons for opposing your view and then aim at refuting them. When listeners are strongly skeptical or hostile to an idea, a smart plan often is to delay divulging your central idea until the end of your speech. (This idea will be discussed later in this chapter in the inductive reasoning section.)

   Always show respect for opponents and their views. *Never* insult or belittle those who disagree; sarcastic or belligerent remarks make people defensive and will shut down their listening of your speech. Try to persuade these people, but if that fails, be content if you can move them a few inches closer to your side. Sometimes the best you can hope for is to plant some seeds of doubt about their position that might someday sprout into full-blown conversion to your side.

3. **Aware of the issue but apathetic.** "Who cares?" is the attitude of listeners in this category. To break through their apathy, show how the issue affects their own lives.

4. **Informed and interested but neutral on your view.** People at this stage need little background information; you can plunge directly into convincing them that your position is correct or superior to other views.

5. **Convinced of your view.** For listeners who agree with you, try to reinforce their belief and, if possible, give them new reasons for supporting your position. Although they agree with your view, some listeners may not have considered or endorsed a plan of action. With them, your task is to demonstrate that your plan offers the best approach.

6. **Ready to take action.** For speeches aimed at motivating action, this is the stage you want all listeners to reach (although you may not be able to bring every listener this far). Tell listeners how, when, and where to take action.

As previously noted, it is difficult to meet the needs of all listeners when their starting points are at different stages on our scale. But sometimes you can do so. All the examples in Table 2 could be integrated into one speech, permitting you to meet the needs of listeners at all six stages.

Building Credibility

Everyone encounters moments in life when they acknowledge they don't know all the answers. Whether it's fixing your car, doing your taxes, or undergoing surgery, there have been moments when you've fully trusted someone else—even a stranger—to take care of you or something important to you. Why did you trust that person? Because the person has credibility in his or her field. Through education, training, and experience, the person has developed credibility in his or her line of work.

In public speaking, before listeners can accept your ideas, they want to know whether you have **credibility.** Although you don't necessarily have to be an expert in the field to give an effective persuasive speech about a topic, credibility in public speaking means you must be reliable, competent, and trustworthy. In your career, when you want to persuade people who know you well, your credibility boils down to how they assess your ability and your character. If you are a person who is known for honesty, fairness, and competence, you enter the speech with a powerful asset. If you are known for dishonesty, unfairness, or incompetence, you enter with a heavy liability.

In the speech itself, credibility is enhanced if your delivery is enthusiastic and if your speech is clear, well-organized, and well-reasoned. In addition, you can build credibility by adhering to the following guidelines.

credibility
audience perception of a speaker as believable, trustworthy, and competent.

Explain Your Competence

If you have special expertise, let your audience know about it—modestly, of course. Don't boast; just give the facts. This enhances your credibility because it shows that you are speaking from personal experience. It says, "I've been there—I know what I'm talking about." Explaining personal experiences can build credibility. For example, if you are trying to persuade your audience about the importance of adopting shelter animals, discussing your own experience with pet adoption makes you a credible source (of course, as long as it is true).

If you lack personal experience on your topic, you can still enhance your credibility by showing that you have chosen competent sources. For example, if you are speaking on business innovation, you might use quotes from Steve Jobs and Jeff Bezos.

Be Accurate

Getting facts and figures wrong or taking quotes out of context can undermine your credibility. In the business world, it can ruin a career and even a company, unintentionally hurting thousands of people. Adam Neumann, cofounder and former CEO of office

Chris Herren, former basketball player for the Boston Celtics and a former heroin addict, speaks at a fire station in Massachusetts to try to persuade drug users that it is possible to break their addiction and lead healthy, productive lives. If you give a speech on addiction, you enhance your own credibility by quoting a former addict like Herren.

Elise Amendola/AP Images

space sharing company WeWork, transformed a small co-working space into a multibillion-dollar company in just 10 years. But as the company was ready to go public in 2019, potential investors learned that the company was inflating profits, spending carelessly, and that Neumann was secretly profiting from company dealings (such as personally purchasing a trademark, then selling that trademark to the company). After this information became public, WeWork's valuation plummeted from $47 billion to $10 billion, the company laid off 2,400 employees, and Neumann was dumped from the company he helped create.[7]

Although an inaccuracy in a public speaking class won't likely tank your career, it can tank your speech (and maybe your grade). When listeners believe you are wrong on one point, even when it's a small matter, they will have little faith in anything else you say.

Show Your Open-Mindedness

Showing confidence in your ideas is a good thing, of course, but some speakers go to an extreme—they become arrogant and inflexible, refusing to admit any possible problems with their argument.

Audiences distrust fanatical know-it-alls. They prefer a speaker who is open-minded and capable of admitting error or exceptions. Think about your own experiences with people. You likely tend to avoid people who never admit mistakes or fault and never apologize.

In a persuasive speech, you might be trying to convince your audience about the importance of funding the military. If you have no military background, it would be a good idea to acknowledge that at the beginning of your speech (followed up with why you still have credibility on the issue).

TIP 2

Tips for Your Career

In a Debate, Be Reasonable and Fair

Your boss knows that you strongly oppose a proposed policy, and she asks you to debate the issue with a colleague at the next staff meeting. What is your best approach? Should you demolish your foe with a slashing, take-no-prisoners assault? No, that approach is actually counterproductive.

Debaters who are overly aggressive come across as unreliable to many listeners. By contrast, speakers who are reasonable and fair and truly listen to opposing arguments sometimes win respect or at least sympathy for their views.

Avoid cheap shots—personal abuse or ridicule. For example, a speaker at a public forum on air pollution ridiculed environmentalists as "mushroom pickers who weep at the thought of a butterfly dying." If you throw such poisoned barbs, listeners who agree with you may laugh and applaud your cleverness, but those who are neutral or opposed to your position (the very people you want to win over) may discount everything you say. In fact, your unfairness may elicit sympathy for the other side.

Debate plays an important part in politics. In a contest for a city council seat in San Jose, California, attorney Linda Nguyen, left, gestures during a debate with school board member Madison Nguyen, right.

©Paul Sakuma/AP Images

It is especially important to be reasonable and open-minded during the question-and-answer period. Some speakers will do a good job in their speeches, but when they are asked questions, they become rigid and defensive. They refuse to admit error or to concede that a listener has a good point. These speakers severely damage their own credibility and undo much of the persuasiveness of their own speeches.

Show Common Ground with Your Audience

When you are introduced to someone at a party, you try to find things that you have in common. You ask each other questions ("What is your major?" "Where are you from?") until you hit upon some interest that you share. We try to find common ground because it not only helps us make conversation but also helps us feel comfortable with another person.

In a speech, listeners tend to respect and trust a speaker who is similar to themselves, so your job is to show how you are like your listeners. This does not mean compromising your beliefs; it means highlighting those characteristics you share with the audience. This is especially important if some of the listeners are hostile to your ideas. Imagine that you are speaking on gun control, and you know that half the listeners are already against your position. Here's what you can say:

> I'm talking on gun control today. I know that a lot of you are opposed to the position I'm going to take. I ask only that you hear me out and see if my arguments have any merit whatsoever. Though we may disagree on this subject, you and I have at least one thing in common: we want to see a reduction in the number of violent, gun-related crimes in our society.

With this kind of statement, you not only pinpoint common ground (opposition to crime) but also appeal to the audience's sense of fair play.

One of the best ways to build credibility is to show listeners that you share (or have shared) their experiences or feelings. It's well known that if you attend an Alcoholics Anonymous meeting, you will introduce yourself as, "Hi. My name is . . . And I'm an alcoholic." That introduction automatically relates you to everyone else in the room, regardless of your differences.

In public speaking, if you were giving a speech on the importance of seeking help for mental health issues, you might recount a time in your life when you sought help from a therapist. Such admissions automatically bond you with your audience.

Providing Evidence

evidence
the facts, examples, statistics, testimony, and other information that support an assertion.

When you make an assertion in a speech, it is not enough to say, "Trust me on this," or "I know I'm right." The audience wants **evidence**, or proof. Evidence can be presented in the forms discussed in the chapter on supporting your ideas and avoiding plagiarism, such as narratives, statistics, examples, and testimony. For each main point in your speech, choose the evidence that is most likely to prove your point with a particular audience. Ask yourself these questions:

1. Is the evidence *accurate?* Erroneous information would obviously undermine the credibility of your entire speech.

2. Is the evidence *up-to-date?* A research study conducted in the field of medicine in 1986 is almost certain to be outdated.

3. Is the evidence *typical?* An athlete may attribute his success to consuming five banana milkshakes a day, but is his diet common among athletes, or is he probably the only one in the world with such a diet?

Here are some tips on using evidence.

Choose evidence from credible sources.   For example, would you believe the following information if it was presented in a speech?

> Scientists have discovered how to build robots that have empathy. They can understand human emotions and respond appropriately. Right now, the robots are not completely ready for widespread distribution, but in the future, as they become more and more sophisticated, these robots may become our caregivers and our friends.

This seems highly improbable, right? Sure, Alexa and Siri are nice "robot assistants," but they cannot emulate human emotion. But what if the speaker continued:

> This new technology was reported by Dr. Pascale Fung, a professor of electronic and computer engineering at the Hong Kong University of Science and Technology, in an article titled "Robots with Heart" in *Scientific American*.[8]

Now this does not seem that far-fetched. Although more details are needed, the speaker's information is more credible because it is based on an article written by a highly respected robot developer and published in a prestigious scientific publication.

Evidence—especially the hard-to-believe variety—becomes much more convincing to the audience if you cite a reliable source. Be sure to give specific details; instead of saying, "a judge," give her name and title: "Sharon Brown, chief justice of our state's Supreme Court."

Provide a variety of evidence.   In some cases, a single example or statistic may be sufficient to bolster an argument, but in most persuasive situations, a speaker needs multiple sources of support.

Use a vivid personal narrative whenever possible.   Imagine that you are planning a speech on drunk driving. If you want to convince your listeners that they could be victimized by a drunk driver, which of the following would be the more persuasive piece of evidence?

1. You tell about an automobile crash in which a drunk driver hit your car and killed one of your passengers.

2. You cite the fact that 25,000 people are killed in America each year in alcohol-related car crashes.

Though you would need to use both of these items in your speech, item #1 would be more persuasive for most listeners. But, you might ask, how can one solitary case be more persuasive than a statistic encompassing 25,000 people? Psychologists have conducted scores of experiments that indicate that one vivid narrative, told from the speaker's personal experience, is much more persuasive than its statistical status would imply. As social psychologist Elliot Aronson puts it: "Most people are more deeply influenced by one clear, vivid personal example than by an abundance of statistical data."[9]

Television personality Rocsi Diaz (Figure 1) gives talks to high school students about the dangers of anorexia nervosa, an eating disorder characterized by self-starvation and excessive weight loss. There are grim statistics that high school students should

Figure 1
Rocsi Diaz tells high school students about her battle with an eating disorder.

Paul Morigi/Getty Images for Get Schooled/Getty Images

learn, such as the fact that 5 to 20 percent of people who struggle with anorexia nervosa will die.[10] To convince people of the dangers of eating disorders, Diaz's most persuasive strategy is to relate her personal struggles with the disorder. "When I was in high school and in junior high, I used to starve myself," she says. "I was a cheerleader, and I was completely obsessed with trying to be skinnier and skinnier. I would do crunches till my abs hurt. I almost killed myself taking diet pills. I was addicted to diet pills. I was creating this hole in my heart."[11]

Using Sound Reasoning

reasoning
using logic to draw conclusions from evidence.

Reasoning, the act of reaching conclusions on the basis of logical thinking, is a part of everyday life. If you take an umbrella with you on a walk because you notice heavy clouds massing in the sky, you are using reasoning to prevent yourself from getting soaked by the rain that may soon fall. While it is true that people are not always logical and rational, it is also true that they frequently can be persuaded by a message that appeals to their powers of reasoning.[12]

Let's look at two popular types of reasoning and then examine some common fallacies of reasoning.

Deduction

Imagine that you are driving a car 15 miles per hour over the speed limit. Suddenly you see a police car parked behind a billboard, with a radar device protruding. You slow down, but you know it is too late. Sure enough, you glance in your rear-view mirror and see a second police car with lights flashing.

deduction
reasoning from a generalization to a specific conclusion.

How did you know that you were going to be stopped? By using **deduction**—a chain of reasoning that carries you from (1) a generalization to (2) a specific instance (of the generalization) to (3) a conclusion. In formal logic, this chain of reasoning is expressed in a form of argument known as a **syllogism**:

syllogism
a deductive scheme consisting of a major premise, a minor premise, and a conclusion.

Major Premise (Generalization):	Motorists who are speeding when they pass a radar point are stopped by police.
Minor Premise (Specific Instance):	I was speeding when I passed a radar point.
Conclusion:	Therefore, I will be stopped.

Deductive reasoning with a syllogism is one of the most powerful tools of persuasion that a speaker can use. If you can convince your listeners to accept the major and minor premises, the conclusion is inescapable. The listeners are compelled by logic to accept it.

Until her death in 1906, Susan B. Anthony fought for the right of women to vote—a right that was not fully secured until 1920, when the Nineteenth Amendment to the Constitution granted nationwide suffrage to women. In speeches delivered throughout the United States, Anthony used deductive logic as her persuasive strategy. If we put the essence of her speeches in the form of a syllogism, it would look like this:

Major Premise (Generalization):	The Constitution guarantees all U.S. citizens the right to vote.
Minor Premise (Specific Instance):	Women are U.S. citizens.
Conclusion:	Therefore, women have the right to vote.

To us today, this syllogism looks simple and obvious. How could Anthony have failed to persuade every listener? But bear in mind that when Anthony fought for women's rights, many people viewed women as less than full-fledged citizens. In her speeches, Anthony had to convince her audience of both the major premise and the minor premise. Those listeners whom she won over were then obliged by force of logic to accept her conclusion.

In a speech, deductive reasoning is convincing *only if both premises are true and are accepted by the audience as true.*[13] Would an audience be likely to accept the following chain of reasoning?

Major Premise: Cardiovascular exercise improves your ability to spell words correctly.

Minor Premise: Jogging is a form of cardiovascular exercise.

Conclusion: Therefore, jogging improves your ability to spell words correctly.

The minor premise is true, but the major premise is false, so the entire syllogism is flawed. An audience would reject the conclusion.

Now let's turn to the correct use of deductive reasoning: Let's say you wanted to speak about the desire of wind energy producers to expand their footprint on unused land to produce more energy. You need to ask the question, "Why would my audience care about wind farms?" This syllogism can help construct your argument:

Major Premise (Generalization):   Renewable energy sources are better for the environment and result in lower energy costs than fossil fuel sources.

Minor Premise (Specific Instance):   Wind energy companies are looking to make deals with governments across the country so they can install wind turbines to produce energy.

Conclusion: So its citizens can save money, and to promote a cleaner environment, governments should make sensible deals with wind energy companies. If listeners believed both the major premise and the minor premise, they are more likely to accept this conclusion.

Induction

While deduction moves from the general to the specific, **induction** proceeds from the specific to the general. Imagine that you are a pediatrician seeing patients one January morning in your office:

induction
reasoning from specific evidence to a general conclusion.

- The first patient, age 9, complains of a runny nose, a sore throat, a headache, and muscle aches. She has a fever of 103° Fahrenheit.
- The second patient, age 7, has similar complaints and a fever of 102° Fahrenheit.
- The third patient has the same symptoms, plus a fever of 101.5° Fahrenheit.
- The fourth patient has similar complaints and a fever of 102.5° Fahrenheit.
- The fifth patient has similar symptoms and a fever of 103° Fahrenheit.

You know from your medical training that these complaints are classic symptoms of influenza (or flu). You know that influenza is a communicable disease, striking many people in a community, usually in winter. On the basis of what you have seen, you reason inductively that your community is experiencing an influenza outbreak. You use *specific* evidence (or isolated observations) to reach a *general* conclusion. In reaching this conclusion, however, you must take an *inductive leap*. You cannot prove that there is a flu outbreak simply because of your five patients. You are probably right, but your conclusion has to remain tentative (until further evidence is gathered and the county health department declares an outbreak), because there is always the chance that some other explanation can account for your five patients' illness. Perhaps they have nasty colds or suffer from some new virus; perhaps no other patients with those symptoms will show up at your office during the remainder of the week. The chances are overwhelming that an influenza outbreak *is* the explanation, of course; but the point is that induction, unlike deduction, never leads to a certain conclusion, only a *very likely* one.

The Usefulness of Induction

The inductive method is used frequently by scientists. They make isolated observations and then form a hypothesis. They may note, for instance, that the average temperature is rising each year in Sydney, Tokyo, Cairo, Rome, Copenhagen, Montreal, Lima, Mexico City, and Los Angeles. Therefore—now they take an inductive leap—the entire globe is warming up. A scientific induction will often lead to further research to confirm the hypothesis.

The inductive method has often led to useful discoveries. In World War II, British fighter planes had cockpit covers made of plastic. During combat, a cover would sometimes shatter, causing small pieces of plastic to become lodged in the pilots' eyes. In pilot after pilot, a British physician observed that the eyes were not damaged or infected by the plastic fragments. This observation led to the use of plastic to make artificial lenses for people's eyes following cataract surgery.[14]

How to Construct an Inductive Argument

Public speakers can construct their inductive arguments by following three steps: (1) ask a question, (2) answer the question by collecting as much specific evidence as possible, and (3) reach a conclusion based on the evidence. Here is an example:

If the first three crackers in a package are too salty for your taste, you can use inductive reasoning to conclude that all the crackers are too salty.

aberration/123RF

Question:	Are scientists finding some animals that were believed to be extinct?
Evidence:	
Item 1:	Scientists have photographed a type of monkey—the Bouvier's red colobus monkey—that was assumed to be extinct because it had not been seen since the 1970s. Two primatologists snapped a photo of an adult female and an infant in the Republic of Congo. The monkey has no fear of humans and therefore is vulnerable to hunters.[15]
Item 2:	A tree frog species in India, believed to be extinct for more than a century, was found recently in the foothills of the Himalayas. The tiny, golf-ball-size frog—*Polypedates jerdonii*—was found by biologist Sathyabhama Das Biju, who said, "We heard a full musical orchestra coming from the tree tops. It was magical. Of course we had to investigate."[16]
Item 3:	Australian scientist Blanche D'Anastasi recently found two presumably extinct sea snakes, the leaf-scaled sea snake and the

short-nose sea snake, in Shark Bay off Western Australia—the first time the creatures had been seen alive in about 15 years.[17]

Conclusion: Some animals that were thought to be extinct have been found alive.

If you were using this material for a speech, you would need to flesh it out with additional facts, of course, but the construction of the argument gives you a framework and helps you think logically.

When you use inductive reasoning, you will convince an audience only if your evidence is strong. If you have weak evidence, your conclusion will be weak.

A Special Use for Inductive Reasoning

Earlier in this text, you were advised to state your central idea in the introduction of your speech. There is, however, an important exception to this guideline: if listeners are likely to have a negative reaction to your central idea, a wise strategy is to lead them through an inductive chain, saving the central idea for the latter part of the speech.

Let's say you are planning a speech to a group of parents who are enthusiastic supporters of their children playing sports like soccer and football. You want to convince the parents that if a child suffers a brain concussion on the playing field, he or she should be immediately removed from play and not allowed to return until several weeks have passed and a neurologist gives approval. You know from interviews with your future audience that many parents regard a concussion as a minor, non-serious matter. So you fear that if you state your central idea in the introduction, the parents will react negatively and fail to take your speech seriously. A wise course is to withhold your key idea and instead build your case one block at a time:

- "Within our skulls, our brain floats in a protective cushioning fluid, but a blow to the head or violent shaking can override the protection, causing a brain injury called a concussion. You can suffer a concussion while playing a sport like soccer or football."

- "With proper care, most people recover fully from a concussion, according to Dr. Beth Ansel, an expert on rehabilitation research at the National Institutes of Health. 'But in some cases,' she says, 'a concussion can have a lasting effect on thinking, attention, learning, and memory.'"[18]

- "Until recently, the prevailing wisdom among sports doctors was that a person who suffered a concussion could return to a game quickly. Today that 'wisdom' has been replaced by an awareness that a concussion is not a minor injury and that injured persons should be removed from their activities as soon as they display symptoms (including dizziness, headache, nausea, and blurry vision)."[19]

- "I would like to share with you what the American Association of Neurological Surgeons says: 'Even mild concussions should not be taken lightly . . . In most cases, a single concussion should not cause permanent damage. A second concussion soon after the first one, however, does not have to be very strong for its effects to be deadly or permanently disabling.' Because a second concussion can be devastating, I urge all of you, if your child suffers a concussion, don't let him or her return to the playing field until a few weeks have passed and you get clearance from a neurologist."[20]

Your remarks might not win over every listener, but they should at least maximize the possibilities of your being successful. An inductive line of reasoning helps listeners

fallacy
an argument based on a false inference.

bandwagon fallacy
equating popularity with truth and proof.

hasty generalization
a conclusion that is based on inadequate evidence.

keep an open mind. When they watch you build your case block by block, they are more respectful and appreciative of the central idea when it is finally presented to them. This doesn't mean they will always agree with you, of course, but it does mean that those who are opposed to your ideas will probably see more merit to your case than they would if you announced your central idea in the introduction.

Quick tip: If you have trouble remembering the difference between deduction and induction, keep in mind that they travel in opposite directions. Deduction (think of the word *deduct* in the sense of taking *away*) leads *away* from a generalization; it goes from general to specific, applying a general principle to a specific case. Induction (think of the first two letters *in*) leads *into*, or toward, a generalization; it goes from specific to general, accumulating specific instances that point toward a general idea.

Everyone loves to win money at Gran Dolina Casino

This ad was created by the author to illustrate how a casino might use a bandwagon appeal to try to persuade people to come and gamble. Though the ad is fictitious, it is similar to the persuasion techniques that are widely used in advertising and politics.

Yuri/Getty Images

Fallacies in Reasoning

A **fallacy** is an error in reasoning that renders an argument false or unreliable. You should become adept at recognizing fallacies so that (1) you can avoid using them in your own speeches—an ethical speaker would never knowingly mislead an audience—and (2) you can prevent yourself from being influenced by them when you listen to the speeches of others. Here are some common fallacies.

Bandwagon

"Most voters in our community are supporting Sandra Dawkins for mayor, so jump on our bandwagon as we roll to victory." This is an example of the **bandwagon fallacy**, an argument based on popularity rather than on evidence and reasoning.

Some speakers use public opinion polls to create a bandwagon effect for their argument: "Over 80 percent of Americans believe that beef is an important part of a healthy diet." Although poll results may be interesting, a poll number by itself does not prove the value of anything. A speaker arguing for beef should use nutritional data and other evidence.

Hasty Generalization

A **hasty generalization** is a conclusion that is reached on the basis of insufficient evidence. In a speech on managing credit-card debt, a speaker might say, "All Americans are deeply in debt because of credit cards." Although it is true that credit cards cause debt, and that many Americans are in debt, it is a hasty generalization to assume the two are connected. Many other factors play into Americans' debt, including student loan debt, medical expenses, mortgages, and so forth.

Red Herring

In seventeenth-century England, according to legend, if criminals were being pursued by bloodhounds, they would drag a red herring (smoked fish) across the trail, confusing the dogs and making them veer off into a new direction.

A **red herring** argument distracts listeners from the real issue and leads them toward an irrelevant issue. This trick is frequently used in political debates. One legislator, for example, may argue for laws protecting the endangered species, and then an opponent counters, "How can we even think about animals when our most pressing problems deal with humans? Let's work on taking care of homeless people before we get all hot and bothered about animals."

red herring
diverting listeners from the real issue to an irrelevant matter.

Of course homelessness is a problem that should be addressed. But this politician was merely using it as a tactic to take attention away from the issue the speaker was trying to talk about. This politician is more than welcome to propose a law to take care of homeless people, but that is not what is being discussed now.

The red herring argument is also used in courtroom battles. If, say, a tobacco company is being sued by the government for endangering the health of citizens, a tobacco-company lawyer might try to divert the jury to a different subject: "Ladies and gentlemen of the jury, the government tells you that tobacco is poisonous, but they say nothing about alcohol. They say nothing about the 20,000 people killed each year by drunk drivers. I don't see the government suing whisky makers."

Even though lawyers and politicians often successfully employ this trick, ethical speakers should never use it.

Attack on a Person

Some speakers try to win an argument by attacking a person rather than the person's ideas. For example, a rival politician might say, "Fitzroy has lived in upper-class luxury all his life, so how can we believe anything he says about government assistance for the poor? He obviously knows nothing about poverty." This **attack on a person**, sometimes known as *argumentum ad hominem* (argument against the man), is unfair and unethical. Fitzroy's arguments should be judged on how sound his ideas are, not on any aspect of his personal life.

attack on a person
criticizing an opponent rather than the opponent's argument.

Attacks on a person are often used in the courtroom to discredit a witness ("Ladies and gentlemen of the jury, this witness admits that he's an atheist, so how can we trust him to tell us the truth?") and in politics to discredit a foe ("My opponent has gambled in Las Vegas at least five times. Do you want such a person to manage your tax dollars?"). Again, this tactic may be effective for politicians and lawyers, but the ethical speaker should never use it. It is not only dishonest and unfair, but it also can backfire and cause careful listeners to lose respect for the speaker.

False Cause

Beware of the fallacy of **false cause**—assuming that because events occur close together in time, they are necessarily related as cause and effect. A president takes office and four months later the unemployment rate goes up 1 percent. Can we say that the president's policies caused the rise in unemployment? It is possible that they did, but other factors likely caused the phenomenon—for example, the economic policies of the previous administration.

false cause
assuming that because two events are related in time, the first caused the second.

The fallacy of false cause also can occur when a speaker oversimplifies the causes of complex problems. Take, for example, a speaker who says that *the* cause of cancer is negative thinking. That explanation is simple and understandable—and wrong. While negative thinking may be a contributing factor in cancer, medical researchers say that no one thing has been isolated as *the* cause of cancer. The disease is probably caused by an inter-action of several factors, including genetic predisposition, susceptibility of the immune system, the presence of a carcinogenic virus, and environmental irritants. Cancer is too complex to be explained by a single cause.

Building on an Unproven Assumption

Some speakers act as if an assertion has been proved when in fact it has not. Suppose that a speaker tells an audience: "Since distance learning with a computer is more effec-tive than traditional classroom education, all of you should take your college courses on at home."

The speaker is acting as if the superiority of distance learning is an established fact, when in reality many people disagree. An ethical speaker would first try to prove the merits of distance learning and then urge the audience to support it.

The fallacy of **building on an unproven assumption** (which is also called "begging the question") makes careful listeners resentful. They feel as if they are being tricked into giving assent to a proposition that they don't believe.

building on an unproven assumption
treating an opinion that is open to question as if it were already proved.

False Analogy

When speakers use a **false analogy**, they make the mistake of assuming that because two things are alike in minor ways, they are also alike in major ways. Here is an example: "I played football through high school and no one was worried about concussions. These concerns about concussions today are overstated." This analogy quickly falls apart. When you played football, the medical community was not fully fully aware on the dangers of concussions. But as more information became available and as football players' brains were studied, we now have information that proves concussions can be very dangerous to an athlete.

false analogy
creating a comparison that is exaggerated or erroneous.

Either-Or Reasoning

The **either-or fallacy** occurs when a speaker offers only two alternatives, when in fact there are many. Here is an example: "Either we build a wall across our borders or we become overrun with immigrants." In reality, there are other options, such as improving immigration checkpoints and changing immigration policy.

Stating an argument in stark, either-or terms makes a speaker appear unreasonable and dogmatic. Most problems should be seen as a complex mosaic of many colors—not a simple choice between pure black and pure white.

either-or fallacy
presenting only two alternatives when in fact more exist.

Straw Man

To win arguments, some people create a **straw man**, a ridiculous caricature of what their opponents believe, and then beat it down with great ease. In a debate, imagine that you argue for standards that require cars to be more fuel efficient so that less CO_2 is released into the atmosphere. Your opponent replies, "What you really want is to kill off the automobile industry. What you really want is for everybody to walk or ride bicycles." Then your opponent spends the next 15 minutes attacking the notion of a world without automobiles. What he is saying about you is false, of course, but he is creating an easy target, made of straw. He can knock it down, smash it, and make himself look like a victor.

straw man
a weak opponent or dubious argument set up so that it can be easily defeated.

Slippery Slope

Imagine that you are standing at the top of a steep hill that is slippery with rain. You take a relatively small step downhill, but that step causes you to lose your footing and tumble to the bottom. This is an image of a **slippery slope**, the name for a fallacy that argues that if a certain event occurs, it will lead to a chain of events that ultimately ends in tragedy. The slippery slope fallacy was used in the gay marriage debate. Some who opposed gay marriage would say, "If we allow gay people to get married, what's next? Will humans be able to marry animals?" Such an argument is ridiculous and offensive, as it equates being gay with bestiality. Just like the above fallacies, the goal of people using the slippery slope fallacy is to change the argument you intended to discuss to something completely absurd, painting you in a corner as supporting the absurd.

slippery slope
one action will initiate a chain of events that will result in a tragic ending.

Appealing to Motivations

Motivations are the needs, desires, or drives that impel a person toward a goal or away from some negative situation. People have hundreds of motivations, including love, happiness, and health. If you show your listeners how your ideas can help them satisfy such needs and desires, you increase your chances of persuading them to adopt your point of view. Here are some examples of how speakers can appeal to the motivations of their audiences:

motivations
the impulses and needs that stimulate a person to act in a certain way.

- To persuade listeners to support cancer research, a speaker appealed to the motivation of health, noting statistics show that half the people in the room will have cancer in their lives.

- To persuade listeners to put money aside for retirement, a speaker appealed to the motivation of financial security, noting that most older Americans have little more than a year's salary stashed away in retirement savings.

- To persuade listeners to think seriously about marriage, a speaker appealed to the motivation of love and esteem, citing statistics that show married people tend to live longer and have less stress.

Some Common Motivations

Some of the common motivations that audiences have include:

- Love and esteem
- Success
- Recreational pleasure
- Social acceptance
- Health
- Financial security
- Altruism
- Adventure
- Safety
- Self-improvement
- Curiosity
- Creativity

Figure 2

Maslow's Hierarchy of Needs

Psychologist Abraham Maslow organized human motivations in a hierarchy that ranged from basic biological needs (at the bottom) to self-actualization needs (at the top).

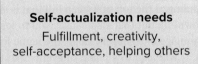

Self-actualization needs
Fulfillment, creativity, self-acceptance, helping others

Esteem needs
Respect, recognition, success

Love and belonging needs
Friendship, family, being loved and accepted

Safety needs
Shelter, safety from violence, secure income, comfort, tranquility

Physiological needs
Water, food, sleep, clothing, medical care

Maslow's hierarchy of needs
a ranking of human needs from simple to complex.

self-actualization
the need of humans to make the most of their abilities.

A popular model for analyzing motivations is **Maslow's hierarchy of needs**, created by the late Abraham Maslow, an American psychologist. As shown in Figure 2, the hierarchy starts at the bottom with the most basic human needs and ranges upward to more and more sophisticated levels.[21]

At the top is **self-actualization**, where one realizes his or her full potential as a human. Maslow believed that when lower-level needs are present, they will usually take precedence. For example, if you are sleep-deprived and sick (lowest level), you probably will have no energy to engage in a creative activity such as violin playing (highest level).

Models such as Maslow's hierarchy can't cover all human needs, but they do remind us of the multiple motivations that can be found in our listeners.

Multiple Motivations

Whenever possible, appeal to more than one motivation. Listeners who are not reached by one appeal may be influenced by another. Suppose, for example, that you are trying to persuade your listeners to take up bicycling. Table 3 shows some of the motivations that you could identify, coupled with appropriate appeals.

By appealing to more than one motivation, you increase your chances of persuading the audience. For example, the listener who is already in superb health may not be reached by any of the first three items but might be swayed by one of the last three.

Table 3 Motivations and Appeals

Motivation	Appeal
Feeling good	Bicycling works out tension and makes you feel energetic and happy.
Looking good	Bicycling burns lots of calories, so it's ideal for weight control. It also tones up leg muscles.
Long-term health	Bicycling is excellent exercise for the heart and lungs, thus helping prevent cardiovascular disease.
Friendship	Being on a bicycle is an instant passport to the world of cyclists. It's easy to strike up conversations with other riders, and you can often make new friends. Cycling also provides an enjoyable activity to share with old friends.
Adventure	With a bicycle, you can explore out-of-the-way places, travel long distances in a single day, and experience the thrill of flying down a steep mountain road.
Competition	If you enjoy competing, there are bicycle races in almost every city or town.

Arousing Emotions

Emotions are spontaneous feelings that can be either positive (amusement, love, joy) or negative (fear, anger, sadness). You can use emotional appeals to stimulate listeners and rouse them to action.

How can emotions be evoked? By using support materials (such as provocative narratives) or powerful language (such as vivid metaphors).

As an example of how emotions can be used effectively, here is an excerpt from a speech on how con artists target older adults:

> A recent news report from the Rochester, New York, area told of an elderly couple who were bilked out of their entire life savings of over $100,000. It all started when a man who claimed to be a contractor stopped by their home and offered to do some minor work, like cleaning the gutters. Then he warned the couple that he had discovered some serious problems with the roof and chimney—problems that needed extensive repairs. The husband and wife were very scared, and since they believed the contractor, they gave him all of their savings. Later, when the contractor was arrested on charges of second-degree grand larceny, police said that he admitted that he never did any of the work that he was paid in advance to do. This case is just one example of how con artists prey on the elderly in communities throughout the United States.[22]

This story was effective in eliciting disgust—an appropriate emotion for listeners to experience as they learned of the outrages that are sometimes committed by con artists.

Here are some tips on arousing emotions.

Always combine emotional appeals with rational appeals.   If you appeal only to emotions, you give the audience only one underpinning for a belief. Let's say you are arguing against the practice of keeping a dog chained up all day. If you focus on the suffering of the dog, you create an argument that appeals only to the heart. For a stronger case, add an appeal to the mind: chaining a dog sometimes causes the animal to become aggressive. If it breaks free someday, it might attack a neighbor or passerby.

While people can be swayed by emotional appeals, they also need to think of themselves as rational. They need to have justification for the feelings and passions they embrace in their hearts. If you use logic and emotion together, you have a more powerful speech than if you use either one alone.[23]

Examining Your Ethics

Eliciting strong fear would be an appropriate and ethical goal for which of the following speech topics?

A. Dressing correctly for a job interview
B. Voting for the Republican candidate for U.S. Senator
C. Protecting yourself in a thunderstorm
D. Sending or receiving text messages while driving a car

For the answer, see the last page of this chapter.

Know how to use fear.   Over the years, communicators have wondered how much fear one should evoke in trying to persuade people. For example, if you want to convince an audience to avoid tailgating on the highway, would you be more successful with some low-fear visual aids, such as a chart on traffic fatalities, or with some high-fear graphics, such as a gory, full-color videotape of victims of a terrible car wreck? Research favors the latter. Professor Kaylene C. Williams of California State University, Stanislaus, says, "In general, the more frightened a person is by a fear appeal, the more likely he or she is to take positive preventive action." Other research, she pointed out, indicates that high-fear messages are most effective when they are coupled with specific instructions on how to take action. For example, a high-fear message on rabies would be more persuasive if it included instructions on how to avoid the disease than if it left out such instructions.[24]

Use emotional appeals ethically.   Any emotion can be exploited in the wrong way. Fear and loathing, desirable when targeted at an infectious disease, are repugnant when aimed at a minority group. Unfortunately, some politicians have demonstrated that creating or exploiting fears and hatreds can win elections. If you are an ethical speaker, however, you will never let short-term gain entice you into using such tactics. If, for example, you are trying to mobilize public opinion to save an endangered species of bird, you will not demonize homebuilders who want to build on the bird's natural habitat; you will not incite hatred by falsely portraying them as merciless killers. Instead, you will channel emotional appeals in appropriate ways—by generating sadness over the possible disappearance of the bird or by appealing to the happiness listeners might feel over saving endangered creatures.

To determine whether you are acting ethically, identify each emotion you want to arouse and then answer the following questions:

- Do you avoid scapegoating any person or group?
- Does the emotion reinforce, rather than replace, solid evidence and sound logic? (If not, is it because your case is unsupportable and illogical?)
- In arousing this emotion, are you treating the issue and the opposing side with fairness? (Put yourself in the shoes of an opponent and see if your treatment looks fair from that perspective.)

If you cannot answer yes to all three, your ethical footing is shaky. You should omit the emotional appeal or alter the speech.

Develop the emotional appeals inherent in some pieces of evidence.   Often you don't need to hunt for emotional appeals to add to your accumulation of evidence. All you need to do is develop the evidence already collected so that it moves the listeners. Let's say that while preparing a speech on domestic violence, you found this statistic: in the United States nearly 20 people are physically abused *each minute* by an intimate partner.[25] You can state that figure in your speech and then develop it for emotional impact: "By the time I finish this sentence, a woman will be slapped . . . a woman will be grabbed . . . a woman will be punched . . . a woman will be beaten . . . and a woman will be raped." By expressing a fact in this dramatic way, and slowing down at each action to let the point sink in, you help your listeners feel the magnitude of the problem.

Sample Persuasive Speech

The following speech by Alexandra Morton uses the problem–solution pattern. The outline is presented first, with a commentary in the margin.

connect

View a video of the speech "Sleep Deficiency" in the online Media Library for Chapter 17.

The Outline with Commentary

Sleep Deficiency

COMMENTARY	SPEECH

General Purpose: To persuade

Specific Purpose: To persuade my audience to take necessary steps to achieve good sleep

Central Idea: Sleep deficiency is a major problem, but it can be overcome by changing priorities and strategies.

INTRODUCTION

I. Attention Material

    A disturbing news report makes an effective attention-grabber.

    A. An air traffic controller is a vital person in your life if you are on a commercial airplane.

    B. The Federal Aviation Administration recently confirmed 7 cases of controllers sleeping on the job.

    C. In 3 of the cases, planes had to land without assistance.

II. Orienting Material

    A. These reports illustrate a major problem—millions of Americans failing to get adequate sleep.

    B. We will look at the problem and then discuss the solution.

(*Transition:* Let's start with the problem.)

BODY

I. About two-thirds of Americans fail to get adequate sleep, causing health problems. (National Sleep Foundation)

    The speaker devotes the first half of the body to the problem.

    A. Adults need 7 to 8 hours of sleep each night. (Dr. Lawrence Epstein, Harvard Medical School)

        1. If you get only 4 to 6 hours for several nights in a row, you build up a sleep deficit.

        2. You will probably become irritable and groggy.

        3. You will have reduced energy and alertness.

    A complete-sentence outline helps speakers organize material intelligently. For actual delivery, however, a speaker should not read the outline but, instead, use brief notes that are based on the outline.

    B. If you go for longer periods without enough sleep, you develop chronic sleep deprivation.

        1. You are more likely to overeat and gain weight. (Dr. Epstein)

        2. You are at higher risk for colds and infections.

        3. In some cases, you are at risk for depression, diabetes, heart disease, and obesity.

(continued)

C. Insufficient sleep reduces alertness and can cause mistakes at work and accidents on the highway.
   1. Each year at least 100,000 car crashes are due to drowsy drivers. (National Highway Traffic Safety Administration)
   2. 40,000 drivers are injured, 1,500 are killed.
D. Centers for Disease Control and Prevention says 60 percent of college students frequently have sleep disturbances.
   1. They don't sleep well or wake up feeling tired.
   2. Sleep-deprived students often have poor grades and stress-related illness.
   3. When stressed out, they avoid what they need the most—sleep.

(*Transition:* Now that we've looked at the problem, let's talk about the solution.)

II. People who have sleep problems need to change priorities or learn new strategies.
   A. Many of us have our priorities out of order because we consider sleep a waste of time.
      1. We consider sleep a necessary evil or nuisance—something that should be shortened.
      2. Instead, we should consider sleep "a fundamental biological need"—a top priority.
   B. Here are strategies recommended by the National Sleep Foundation. (Rosenberg)
      1. Each night, go to bed at the same time, and each morning, get up at the same time.
      2. Stop drinking caffeine and alcohol 5 hours before bedtime.
      3. Stop exercising at least 3 hours before bedtime.
      4. Don't eat large meals right before bedtime.
      5. Stop looking at screens (TV, tablet, computer) 1 hour before bedtime.
         a. They contain "blue spectrum light."
         b. The light suppresses production of the brain hormone that helps us go to sleep.
      6. Before bedtime, wind down and relax—perhaps read in dim light or listen to music.
      7. If you're worried, imagine a calm and peaceful place or play comforting music.

(*Transition:* Let's sum up.)

CONCLUSION

I. Summary
   A. Lack of adequate sleep, a major problem in America, can lead to irritability, reduced energy, and less alertness.
   B. If chronic, a sleep deficit can result in traffic accidents, weight gain, and an increase in infections.
   C. The solution is to make sleep a priority and use strategies such as reducing caffeine late in the day and turning off screens 1 hour before bedtime.

Statistics from a reputable source are effectively used.

The second half of the body is devoted to the solution.

Listeners always appreciate tips that can help them improve their lives.

The speaker did more than just warn against looking at screens—she explained why.

A summary does not need to be long, but it should give the highlights of the speech.

Figure 3
An interesting quotation
makes a good finale for
the speech.

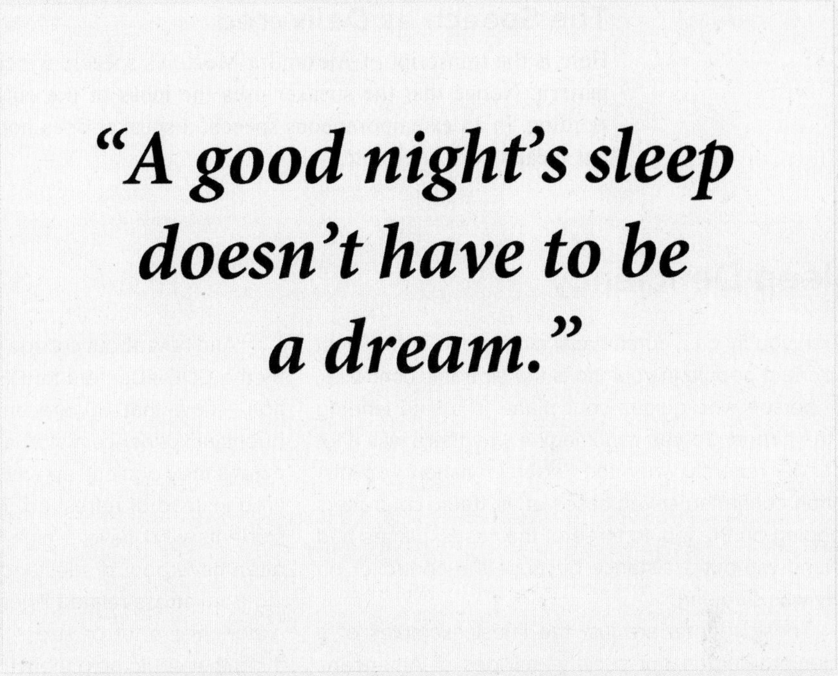

"A good night's sleep doesn't have to be a dream."

II. Clincher
    A. If you or your friends or relatives are sleep-deprived, I
       want to give you hope.
    B. (Show poster.) [See Figure 3] In the words of Janet
       Kennedy, a sleep specialist: "A good night's sleep
       doesn't have to be a dream."

The speech closes with a graceful
finale—a memorable quotation.

See the chapter on locating information for details on how to prepare works
cited and references lists.

WORKS CITED

Ahmed, Quanta. "Re: Sleep Disorders." Message to Alexandra
    Morton, 4 July 2011.

Centers for Disease Control and Prevention. "Sleep
    Deprivation." 4 Mar. 2011, cdc.gov/mmwr/preview/
    mmwrhtml/mm6008a3.htm.

Epstein, Lawrence. *The Harvard Medical School Guide to a Good
    Night's Sleep*. McGraw-Hill, 2006.

National Highway Traffic Safety Agency. "Research on Drowsy
    Driving." 16 Apr. 2011, one.nhtsa.gov/Driving-Safety/Drowsy-
    Driving/Research-on-Drowsy-Driving.

Rosenberg, Russell. "Annual Sleep in America Poll." *National
    Sleep Foundation*, 7 Mar. 2011, National Sleep Foundation.
    7 March 2011, sleepfoundation.org/press-release/
    annual-sleep-america-poll-exploring-connections-
    communications-technology-use-and.VISUAL AIDS

VISUAL AIDS

Poster with Janet Kennedy quotation

The Speech as Delivered

Here is the transcript of Alexandra Morton's speech, which uses the problem–solution pattern. Notice that the speaker uses the ideas of the outline without using the exact wording. In an extemporaneous speech, a speaker does not read or memorize a speech but speaks from brief notes.

Sleep Deficiency

When you fly on a commercial airline, one of the most important people in your life is the air traffic controller, the person who guides your plane to a safe landing at the airport. So you can imagine why there was a lot of anger recently when the Federal Aviation Administration confirmed seven cases of air traffic controllers sleeping on the job. In three of the cases, planes had to land without assistance because the controller on duty was sleeping.

These reports are just the latest examples of a major problem in our society—millions of Americans simply don't get enough sleep. I'd like to talk to you about the extent of this problem, and then give you some solutions, which might involve changing your priorities and strategies.

Let's start with the problem. According to the National Sleep Foundation, about two-thirds of all Americans fail to get enough sleep, and this problem is hazardous to their health.

How much sleep does a person need? Dr. Lawrence Epstein of the Harvard Medical School says that adults need seven to eight hours of sleep every night. If you get only four to six hours for several nights in a row, you're building up a sleep deficit, he says, and you're likely to become irritable and groggy, and you'll have a reduction in energy and alertness.

If you go for even longer periods without adequate sleep, you develop what is known as chronic sleep deprivation. Dr. Epstein says you're more likely to overeat and gain weight, and you're more susceptible to colds and infections. In some cases, you're at risk for depression, diabetes, heart disease, and obesity.

When you don't get adequate sleep, your alertness is reduced, which can cause mistakes at work and at school, and can lead to traffic accidents. The National Highway Traffic Safety Administration says that every year there are at least 100,000 car crashes due to drowsy drivers—40,000 people get seriously injured and 1,500 are killed.

And how about college students? Studies reported by the CDC—Centers for Disease Control and Prevention—show that 60 precent of college students frequently experience disturbances during the night. That means they don't sleep well, and they wake up feeling tired instead of refreshed. The studies also show that students who have a high level of sleep deprivation often have poor grades and are more prone to suffering from stress-related illnesses. When these students experience a lot of stress, they often avoid the one thing that could help them the most—sleep.

So now that we've examined the problem, how can we solve it? The solution is for people to either change their priorities in their busy lives or change their strategies for going to sleep. First let's talk about priorities. Dr. Quanta Ahmed, of New York's Winthrop Hospital Sleep Disorders Center, says that too many of us consider sleep a waste of time. We all have busy lives, and we tend to think of sleep as a necessary evil or a nuisance—something to be shortened if possible. This is a big mistake, she says. We need to change our attitudes toward sleep and think of it as, quote, "a fundamental biological need." So sleep should become a priority in our lives.

Now let's discuss people who have trouble falling asleep or who have trouble getting a full, restful sleep. I'd like to share some strategies recommended by the National Sleep Foundation.

- Go to bed at the same time each night, and get up at the same time each morning.
- At least five hours before bedtime, stop drinking caffeinated beverages and alcohol. Some people say that if they don't stop drinking coffee by noon, their sleep gets disrupted.
- Don't exercise within three hours of bedtime.
- Avoid large meals before bedtime.
- This next tip is very hard—for me and probably for a lot of you: About 1 hour before bedtime, stop looking at screens—TVs, tablets,

computers, and so on. All these devices contain "blue spectrum light" and it suppresses the production of a hormone in our brains that helps us nod off at night.

- Allow time to wind down and relax before bed. Perhaps you can read in dim light or listen to music.
- If worries keep you from sleeping, relax your mind by imagining a calm and peaceful place. Or distract yourself from your troubles by playing comforting music.

Now let's summarize. We've seen that most Americans fail to get adequate sleep—a problem that leads to irritability, reduced energy, and less alertness.

If a sleep deficit becomes chronic, it can lead to traffic accidents and increased risk of weight gain and infections. The solution to the problem is to make sleep a priority and use the recommended strategies, such as avoiding caffeine late in the day and cutting off electronic devices 1 hour before bedtime.

If you or the people you care about are among the ranks of the sleep-deprived, I'm here to give you hope. [*The speaker displays the poster in Figure 3.*] In the words of Janet Kennedy, a sleep specialist:

"A good night's sleep
doesn't have to be
a dream."

Resources for Review and Skill Building

Summary

To be effective in persuasion, you must have a thorough *knowledge of the audience.* Find out exactly where your listeners stand concerning your view. Are they opposed, apathetic, neutral, or already convinced? Then plan a strategy to move them toward your position.

During a persuasive speech, enhance *credibility* with the audience by explaining your competence, by being honest and careful with speech material, by remaining open-minded, and by showing common ground with listeners.

Build your case by using strong *evidence* (such as statistics, examples, and testimony) that is accurate, up-to-date, and typical. Try to use a variety of sources, all of them reliable and reputable.

Use sound *reasoning* as a powerful tool of persuasion. Two popular forms are deductive reasoning, in which you take a

generalization or a principle and apply it to a specific case, and inductive reasoning, in which you observe specific instances and then form a generalization. In using logic, avoid these fallacies: bandwagon, hasty generalization, red herring, attack on a person, false cause, building on an unproven assumption, false analogy, either-or reasoning, straw man attacks, or slippery slope arguments.

Whenever possible, appeal to listeners' *motivations*—their needs, desires, and drives that impel them toward a goal or away from some negative situation. Focus on the listeners' needs, not your own. If possible, appeal to more than one motivation, and anticipate conflicting needs.

Finally, try to arouse the listeners' *emotions,* making sure that you always combine emotional appeals with rational appeals, and that you always use emotions ethically.

Key Terms

attack on a person, *337*

bandwagon fallacy, *336*

building on an unproven
assumption, *338*

credibility, *327*

deduction, *332*

either-or fallacy, *338*

evidence, *330*

fallacy, *336*

false analogy, *338*

false cause, *337*

hasty generalization, *336*

Review Questions

1. Why are sarcastic remarks inappropriate when directed toward listeners who are hostile to your view?

2. Why is it a good idea in many cases to tell the audience why you are competent to speak on your particular subject?

3. How is an audience likely to react if you are misrepresent your facts?

4. Which is more persuasive with the typical audience: one vivid personal narrative or a series of statistical data?

5. What is the difference between deduction and induction?

6. What is a "red herring" argument?

7. What is the "straw man" fallacy?

8. What is the "slippery slope" fallacy?

9. List at least five motivations that listeners have.

10. Why should emotional appeals always be accompanied by rational appeals?

Building Critical-Thinking Skills

1. One of the most influential books in American history, *Silent Spring,* was published in 1962 as a warning against the health hazards of pesticides. Its author, Rachel Carson, had her credibility attacked by a scientist who questioned her concern for future generations because she was an unmarried woman with no children. What fallacy of reasoning was the scientist using? Why was the scientist's criticism invalid?

2. A TV commercial shows a video of an attractive young couple running barefoot on a beach while a voice says, "ABC multivitamin supplements—just one a day for the rest of your life." Identify the motivational appeals contained in the commercial.

3. Name some arguments used by politicians—on both sides of the aisle—that use the persuasive fallacies discussed in this chapter. Name the fallacy.

4. During the first-year student orientation at some colleges, an administrator says something like this, "Look at the person seated next to you. One of you won't be here next year." Do you think this is an effective motivator to get students to study hard? Defend your answer.

Building Teamwork Skills

1. In a survey reported by *Health* magazine, 89 percent of adults said they know they should exercise three times a week for good health, but only 27 percent actually do. In a group, compile a list of excuses that people might use for not exercising. Then brainstorm strategies that a speaker could use to discourage listeners from using each excuse.

2. Working in a group, list the motivations that students in a typical high school class are likely to have. Then brainstorm how an army recruiter could appeal to each motivation in a speech aimed at persuading the students to join the military.

Examining Your Ethics

Answer: C and D. These are life-or-death topics, and eliciting strong fear could save a listener's life. For topics A and B, intense fear would be out of place.

End Notes

1. "Estimated Range of Annual Burden of Flu in the U.S. since 2010," Centers for Disease Control and Prevention, www.cdc.gov/flu/about/burden/index.html (accessed February 22, 2020).

2. "Flu Shot: Your Best Bet for Avoiding Influenza," Mayo Clinic, September 12, 2019, www.mayoclinic.org /diseases-conditions/flu/in-depth/flu-shots/art-20048000 (accessed February 22, 2020).

3. "The 2018 Flu Vaccine Was Only 29% Effective—but Experts Still Recommend It," Healthline, www .healthline.com/health-news/flu-vaccine-had-another -disappointing-year-will-this-year-be-different#Flu-shot -still-prevents-illness (accessed February 22, 2020).

4. "Flu Vaccination Coverage, United States, 2018–19 Influenza Season," Centers for Disease Control and Prevention, www.cdc.gov/flu/fluvaxview/coverage -1819estimates.htm (accessed February 22, 2020).

5. "Flu Vaccination Coverage, United States, 2018–19 Influenza Season," Centers for Disease Control and Prevention, www.cdc.gov/flu/fluvaxview/coverage -1819estimates.htm (accessed February 22, 2020).

6. "Estimated Range of Annual Burden of Flu in the U.S. since 2010," Centers for Disease Control and Prevention, www.cdc.gov/flu/about/burden/index.html (accessed February 22, 2020).

7. R. Aydin, "The WeWork IPO fiasco of 2019," *Business Insider*, October 22, 2019, www.businessinsider.com /wework-ipo-fiasco-adam-neumann-explained-events -timeline-2019-9 (accessed February 22, 2020).

8. Pascale Fung, "Robots with Heart," *Scientific American*, November 2015, pp. 61–63.

9. Elliott Aronson, quoted by *Manner of Speaking*, mannerofspeaking.org (accessed January 22, 2016).

10. "Anorexia Nervosa," National Eating Disorders Association, www.nationaleatingdisorders.org (accessed January 22, 2016).

11. "Rocsi Opens Up on Eating Disorder," *Entertainment Tonight*, November 17, 2013, www.etonline.com /news/140880_Rocsi_Diaz_on_Her_Struggle_with_ Anorexia (accessed January 22, 2016).

12. Kenneth T. Broda-Bahm, Daniela Kempf, and William J. Driscoll, *Argument and Audience: Presenting Debates in Public Settings* (New York: International Debate Education Association, 2004), p. 186.

13. Aristotle, Analytica Posteriora, Book I, in *Introduction to Aristotle* (New York: Modern Library, 1947), pp. 9–34.

14. Anahad O'Connor, "Harold Ridley, Eye Doctor, 94, Early Developer of Lens Implants," *The New York Times*, www.nytimes.com/2001/06/06/world/harold-ridley-eye -doctor-94-early-developer-of-lens-implants.html (accessed January 28, 2016).

15. Jim Algar, "Photo Captured of Rare Monkey Thought to Be Extinct Proves Species Is Alive and Kicking," *Tech Times*, www.techtimes.com (accessed January 22, 2016).

16. "'Extinct' Tree Frog Rediscovered in India after 137 Years," *BBC News*, January 21, 2016, www.bbc.com (accessed January 22, 2016).

17. "Two Species of Sea Snake Feared Extinct Found off WA," *The Daily Mercury* (Australia), www.dailymercury .com.au (accessed January 22, 2016).

18. "A Bang to the Brain: What We Know about Concussions," *NIH News in Health*, National Institutes of Health, newsinhealth.nih.gov (accessed January 22, 2016).

19. Radiological Society of North America, "Single Concussion May Cause Lasting Brain Damage," *Science Daily*, March 12, 2013, www.sciencedaily.com (accessed January 22, 2016).

20. "Patient Information," American Association of Neurological Surgeons, www.aans.org (accessed January 22, 2016).

21. Abraham H. Maslow, *Motivation and Personality* (New York: Harper & Row, 1970).

22. The speaker derived the material from Brett Davidsen, "Contractor Accused of Stealing Couple's Life Savings," *WHEC News* (Rochester), www.whec.com (accessed January 22, 2016).

23. Virginia Hughes, "Emotion Is Not the Enemy of Reason," *Phenomena/National Geographic*, phenomena .nationalgeographic.com (accessed January 22 2016).

24. Kaylene C. Williams, "Fear Appeal Theory," *Research in Business and Economics Journal*, February 2012, pp. 1–21.

25. National Coalition Against Domestic Violence, https:// ncadv.org/statistics (accessed February 23, 2020).

Speaking on Special Occasions

OBJECTIVES

After studying this chapter, you should be able to

1. Prepare an entertaining speech.
2. Prepare a speech of introduction.
3. Prepare a speech of presentation.
4. Prepare a speech of acceptance.
5. Prepare a speech of tribute.
6. Prepare an inspirational speech.
7. Identify potential pitfalls in using humor in a speech.

ANDERSON COOPER, AN ANCHOR FOR CNN, stood on a stage in Los Angeles during "CNN Heroes: An All-Star Tribute" and paid tribute to Malala Yousafzai, whom he described as "the Pakistani teenager who was shot by the Taliban because of her support for girls' right to education in her home country." He went on to share, "Malala is recovering from the attack, and she has a message for her supporters."

Cooper read the message written by Malala: "'Thank you so much for the outpouring of love and support. I thank the people who supported me without distinguishing religion and color. People have actually supported a cause, not an individual. Let's work together. Let's work together to educate girls around the world.'"[1]

Cooper's tribute is an example of a special kind of speech that will be discussed in this chapter. Though most of the speeches you will give in your lifetime will probably be informative or persuasive, there are occasions when you may be called upon to give other kinds—an entertaining speech at a banquet, a brief speech introducing the main speaker at a convention, a few words announcing the presentation of an award, a eulogy at a funeral to honor a close friend or family member, an acceptance speech to thank an organization for giving you an award, or an inspirational speech to lift the morale of your subordinates or fellow employees.

While delivering a speech of tribute, CNN anchor Anderson Cooper stands in front of a photograph of Malala Yousafzai.

Michael Buckner/Staff/WireImage/ Getty Images

Entertaining Speech

entertaining speech
an oral address designed to amuse or engage listeners.

An **entertaining speech** provides amusement or diversion for the audience. It can be given in any setting, from classroom to convention hall. It is sometimes referred to as an "after-dinner speech" because it is often given after a meal. People who have just eaten want to sit back, relax, and enjoy a talk. They don't want to work hard mentally. They don't want to hear anything heavy and negative.

An entertaining speech can contain a few elements of persuasion and information; however, the primary goal is not to persuade or inform but to create an interesting diversion—an enjoyable experience—for the audience.

Techniques for Entertaining

To entertain, do you have to tell jokes that elicit loud laughter? Not necessarily. Joke telling is just one option among many. Other devices you can use to entertain an audience include anecdotes, examples, quotations, narratives, and descriptions.

Humor

One common way to entertain your audience is to interject humor throughout your speech. Laughing relaxes your audience and puts them in a position to be more engaged in what you have to say. Humor is typically more appropriate during informal speeches, like addressing an audience at a banquet hall. Humor should not be used to mock opposing

---

Special Techniques

How to Use Humor

If used effectively, humor is a good way to keep an audience interested in your speech. It creates a bond of friendship between you and the listeners, and it puts them into a receptive, trusting mood. Here are some guidelines for using humor.

1. **Use humor only when it is appropriate.** A speech about a solemn and/or controversial subject such as assisted suicide would not lend itself to an injection of humor.

2. **Tell jokes at your own risk.** A joke is a funny story that depends on a punch line for its success. If you are an accomplished humorist, you may be able to use jokes effectively, but novice speakers should typically avoid them, for the following reasons:

   - Jokes usually don't tie in smoothly with the rest of the speech.
   - A joke that is successful with your friends might bomb with a large audience.
   - Listeners may not be in a receptive mood to hear a joke.
   - A joke that isn't received well can damage a speaker's morale and lessen the impact of the speech.

"But it looks so easy on TV," some students say. It looks easy and *is* easy because TV joke tellers have advantages that most speakers lack: they have studio audiences that are predisposed to laugh at virtually any joke the comedians tell. They have writers who test the jokes out before they are used. Most important of all, they are talented performers who have years of joke-telling experience.

3. **Use low-key humor.** A mildly amusing story, quotation, or observation—although not as spectacular as a side-splitting joke—can be effective. The best thing about low-key humor is that it's safe. While the success of a joke depends on the audience laughing immediately after the punch line, the success of a light story or a witty observation does not depend on laughter—or even smiles. Sometimes the only audience response is an inner delight. In a speech on the elaborate cheating systems that some students use on tests, student speaker Henry Mandell said:

   There is one method of cheating that guarantees that you won't be caught. The night before a test, make a cheat sheet. Memorize it. Then tear it up to destroy the evidence. The next morning, you'll do well on the test.

viewpoints. If you are not comfortable using humor in a speech, do not attempt to do so without practicing in front of a trial audience to gauge reactions. For more tips on how and when to use humor, see the Special Techniques feature "How to Use Humor."

Anecdotes, Examples, and Quotations

Using a single theme, some speakers string together anecdotes, examples, or quotations as if creating a string of pearls—one bright jewel after another. In a speech on the crackpot predictions that so-called experts have made over the centuries, a student speaker gave her audience one astonishing quotation after another. Here's one example:

> When women began to enter all-male professions at the beginning of the 20th century, many prominent men warned that such work would be disastrous for women. Here's what a professor at Berlin University, Hans Friedenthal, said in 1914: "Brain work will cause [the 'new woman'] to become bald, while increasing masculinity and contempt for beauty will induce the growth of hair on the face. In the future, therefore, women will be bald and will wear long mustaches and patriarchal beards."[2]

Narratives

An interesting journey, an exciting adventure, or a comical sequence of events can make a speech enjoyable, even if the story is serious. Here are some examples:

- A speaker related her encounter with a grizzly bear while backpacking in the Rocky Mountains.

Mandell was using the kind of wry humor that does not depend on belly laughs. It was not a joke. If the listeners laughed or smiled, fine; if they didn't, no harm was done. It was still enjoyable.

4. **Always relate humor to the subject matter.** Never tell an amusing story about, for example, a farmer, unless your speech is about farming and the story ties in with the rest of the speech.

5. **Never use humor that could possibly offend any person in the audience.** Avoid humor that is sexual. Avoid humor that targets members of any group in society (racial, ethnic, religious, political, gender, and so on). Even if the audience contains no members of a particular group, you are unwise to ridicule that group because you risk alienating listeners who dislike such humor.

6. **Never let your face show that you expect laughter or smiles.** If you say something that you think is hilarious, don't stand with an expectant grin on your face, waiting for a reaction. If no one smiles or laughs, you will feel very foolish. And remember, failure to get any smiles or laughs doesn't necessarily mean that the listeners did not appreciate your humor.

7. **Consider using self-deprecating humor in some situations.** Many good speakers tell humorous anecdotes at their own expense because it builds rapport with the audience. Benjamin Franklin was a speaker who was willing to poke fun at himself in a speech. For example, he liked to tell audiences about an incident that occurred in Paris while he was attending a public gathering that featured many speeches. He spoke French, but he had trouble understanding the formal, rhetorical language of French orators. Wishing to appear polite, he decided that he would applaud whenever he noticed a distinguished woman, Mme. de Boufflers, express satisfaction. After the meeting, his grandson said to him, "But Grandpapa, you always applauded, and louder than anybody else, when they were praising you."

Self-deprecating humor has two bonuses: (1) When you tell about something you did or said, there is no danger that the audience has heard it before. (2) You don't risk offending anyone—your target is yourself, not some group.

However, there are also two cautions to exercise with self-deprecating humor: (1) Don't poke fun at your nervousness because then your audience will focus on it, and it will undermine your effectiveness as a speaker. (2) Don't use self-deprecating humor if your expertise or authority has not been established. For example, if you are a new employee who is making a presentation to the board of directors, self-effacing humor could weaken your credibility.

Source: Edmund Fuller, ed., *Thesaurus of Anecdotes* (New York: Avenel, 1990), p. 21.

Tips for Your Career

Move Listeners Together

If your listeners are spread apart in a large room or an auditorium, try to move them together if possible. Let's say you have 15 people scattered about in a large hall. It will be easier to make contact with them if you ask them to move to seats at the front and center.

Moving them together is especially important for entertaining talks. Nightclub comedians make sure tables are pushed close together because they know that patrons are more likely to laugh if they are jammed together in warm coziness. Some comedians are reluctant to tell jokes to an audience widely scattered in a large room. People feel isolated, and they are afraid that if they laugh, they will be conspicuous. Have you ever noticed that funny movies are funnier if you see them in a packed theater than if you see them in a sparsely attended theater?

- A police officer gave an hour-by-hour account of the extraordinary security measures taken by the Secret Service when a presidential candidate made a campaign stop in one city.
- One speaker told of the mishaps and misunderstandings that caused her to arrive late and frazzled at her wedding.

Descriptions

You can entertain with vivid descriptions of fascinating places, interesting people, or intriguing objects. Here are some examples:

- To give her audience an impression of the bright colors and exotic varieties of birds in the Amazonian rainforest, one speaker showed color slides she had taken of birds in a Brazilian zoo.
- At the meeting of a culinary club, the chef of a gourmet restaurant gave an after-dinner talk in which he described various French pastries. As the chef discussed each type of pastry, a sample was served to each listener.

An entertaining speech does not need to be as elaborately structured as an informative or persuasive speech, but it should have a unifying theme. In other words, all your material should tie together, and it should have the standard three parts of a speech: (1) an introduction to gain the attention and interest of the audience, (2) a body that develops the theme in satisfying detail, and (3) a conclusion that provides a graceful finale.

Choose a topic that you find enjoyable, and as you deliver your speech, try to share your enjoyment with the audience. Be light and good-natured. Have fun along with your listeners.

Sample Entertaining Speech

This section contains a sample entertaining speech, delivered by student speaker Elise Chang.[3]

Slimehead for Dinner?

A few weeks ago, I was reading the *Washington Post* on my tablet, and I saw a headline that read, "Baby Carrots Are Not Baby Carrots." This made me curious, so I read the story, which says that the highly popular little carrots [see Figure 1] that we buy at the store and serve as appetizers and snacks are not baby carrots.

The baby carrot is an example of a clever marketing ploy, and I'd like to tell you about some of the most successful marketing ploys that we see in our food industry today.

There is such a thing as baby carrots, but these tasty little veggies are not baby carrots. In the words of *Washington Post* writer Roberto Ferdman, they are "milled and sculpted from the rough, soiled, mangled things we call carrots." True baby carrots are regular carrots that are harvested before they reach maturity.

In the 1980s, a carrot farmer from California named Mike Yurosek invented the so-called baby carrots you buy at the store. At that time, carrot crops were not very profitable. More than half of the carrots grown by farmers were considered ugly and unfit for grocery store sales. In 1986, Yurosek wanted to find a way to sell them. Instead of throwing them away, he carved them into something that looked more appetizing. And then he came up with a marketing gimmick that was brilliant. He called them baby carrots.

These little sculptures became a big success— one of the best-selling vegetables in the United States, responsible for almost 70 percent of all carrot sales.

David Just, a professor of behavioral economics at Cornell University, says most consumers don't know the origin of the carrots. "There are so many people who honestly believe there are baby carrot farmers out there who grow these baby carrots that pop out of the ground perfect and smooth."

The baby carrot is just one of many triumphs of clever marketing. Consider portobello mushrooms. Until the 1980s, they were just simple brown

Figure 1
What are baby carrots?
Shutterstock/AnjelikaGr

mushrooms—unglamorous and almost worthless. In many cases, they had to be thrown out because growers couldn't sell them. But then, according to writer Gholam Rahman, "some PR genius got a bright idea: Why not give them a fancy name with a vague Italian sound and set a stiff price on them as if they were some rare gourmet stuff? The name chosen was *portobello,* something picked right out of thin air."

Portobello mushrooms became a big success, and today they are more expensive than steak. They are highly prized at gourmet restaurants, and in some dining establishments, they have become a popular replacement for ground beef in burgers.

Our next food [Figure 2] was known as Chinese gooseberry, an unappetizing name for a fruit that looks like a fuzzy ball. It is grown in New Zealand, and it did not sell well until a marketing genius, Frieda

Caplan of Los Angeles, changed its name to kiwifruit in honor of the kiwi bird, the national symbol of New Zealand. Now kiwifruit is popular throughout the world and is known for its nutritious qualities.

The list of marketing successes goes on. A fish called "slimehead" was unwanted until it was rebranded as "orange roughy." It became so popular that environmental groups now recommend that you refrain from ordering it in restaurants because it has been overfished and could become endangered. A small yellow fruit called "Cape gooseberry" has been marketed as a Peruvian superfood. In honor of the lost Incan civilization at Machu Picchu, it is now called "picchuberry" or "Golden Incan berry."

What do all of these marketing success stories add up to? I think they just might prove an old saying: "With good marketing, you can sell anything."

Figure 2
Chinese gooseberry or kiwifruit?

Be Good/Shutterstock

Speech of Introduction

The **speech of introduction** is designed for one speaker to introduce another to an audience. Here are a couple of examples:

- At a meeting of her civic club, Paula Moreno spoke briefly on why she was supporting a particular candidate for Congress and then turned the lectern over to the candidate.

- Theodore Lansing, a university librarian, stood up in front of 1,500 delegates at a national librarians' convention and introduced the keynote speaker, a renowned writer of science fiction.

When you introduce one friend to another, you want them to get interested in each other and to like each other. When you introduce a speaker to an audience, you want to achieve the same goal. You want speaker and audience to be interested in each other and to feel warmth and friendliness.

An introduction should mention the speaker's name several times (so that everyone can catch it), and it should give background information to enhance the speaker's credibility with the audience. Your tone of voice and facial expression should convey enthusiasm for the speech to come.

Here are some guidelines for speeches of introduction.

Interview the speaker in advance.   Ask him or her exactly what should be covered in the introduction. For example, should you discuss the significance of the topic to help prepare the audience for the speech? Should you tell the audience to hold questions until the end of the presentation?

Verify name and pronunciation.   Ask the speaker the following questions:

- "What name do you want me to use?" If you are introducing Dr. Elizabeth Wilson, don't assume that she prefers to be called "Dr. Wilson." Perhaps she prefers the informality of "Elizabeth" or even her nickname, "Liz."
- "How do you pronounce your name?" If you aren't familiar with Greek pronunciation, you probably need help introducing a speaker with a name like Neophetos Apostolopoulos. Practice saying it in advance so that you don't stumble during the introduction. For easier names, don't always assume you know the correct pronunciation. A speaker named Mia may pronounce her name ME-UH, or she may prefer MY-UH. Similarly, Eva can be pronounced EE-VUH or EH-VUH.

Tell the speaker what you plan to say.   By doing so, you can avoid this nightmare: a speaker is about to talk to an audience of 1,000 people, and suddenly she realizes that the person introducing her is telling the very anecdote that she had carefully planned as the opener of her speech. Such nightmares actually happen, say experienced speakers, but they won't happen to you if you reveal your plans to the speaker to avoid repetition.

Set the proper tone.   When you introduce someone, you help set the tone for the speech to follow. Be careful to set the right tone—a humorous tone for a humorous speech, a serious tone for a serious speech.

Keep it short.   A good rule of thumb is to keep an introduction under three minutes. After all, an audience wants to hear the speaker, not the introducer.

Avoid exaggeration.   If you exaggerate the speaker's abilities or credentials, you build up unrealistic expectations in the audience. Consider this kind of introduction: "Our speaker tonight is so hilarious, he'll have you laughing so hard you'll be rolling in the aisles." Here is another example: "The speaker will give us insights that are wise and brilliant." Such statements can cause speakers to become overly anxious because they feel pressure to live up to the excessive praise.

The following introduction of Joseph Conte was delivered at a meeting of a genealogical society; the introducer had consulted with Conte in advance to make sure that he did not steal any of the speaker's speech.

Our speaker tonight, Joseph Conte, will talk to us about how to set up a computerized ancestry record. Mr. Conte brings a lot of personal experience to this subject. The great-grandson of immigrants from Italy, he has traced his own family roots back to Florence. Mr. Conte has a background of expertise in scholarly detective work: for the past decade he has been a researcher for the National Archives in Washington, DC, specializing in nineteenth- and twentieth-century immigration. Mr. Conte, welcome to our society, and thank you for taking the time to share your knowledge with us.

Consider another example, in which a college president introduces the keynote speaker of a graduation ceremony:

Graduates, students, alumni, and Bearcats family, we are pleased to welcome Dr. Francis Bartholomew to Hillsman University today. Dr. Bartholomew achieved renown for leading cutting-edge cancer research efforts while practicing at the Memorial Sloan Kettering Medical Center in New York City. In his recent memoir, *My Life with Cancer,* Dr. Bartholomew reflects honestly on the lessons he's learned as a lifelong researcher, doctor, father, and husband. Now, Dr. Bartholomew will share his insights and advice for embarking on a well-lived postcollegiate life. Let's all give Dr. Bartholomew a warm Bearcat welcome!

Speech of Presentation

Awards or honors are often bestowed upon individuals for their service to business, institution, community, place of worship, charity, or club. It is customary for a brief speech to be made before the award is presented.

speech of presentation
an address designed to formally present an award or honor.

The **speech of presentation** should include the following elements: (1) any background information that would help the audience understand the purpose of the award, (2) the criteria used for selecting the recipient, and (3) the achievements of the recipient.

In many cases, it is customary to withhold the name of the recipient until the very end of the speech, as a way of building suspense.

Humor is usually inappropriate. If you try to make a joke about the recipient, you may seem to be belittling him or her. At one company banquet, a department head gave an award for 10 years of service to a subordinate and used the occasion to tease him with a mock insult: "The only reason we keep him on the payroll is because his father worked here for 40 years." The "humor" was similar to the kind of bantering that the boss and the subordinate engaged in during a typical workday, but at the awards banquet, with his family present, the subordinate felt humiliated.

Consider this example, in which a speaker presents a community service award at a local church:

As many of you know, Doris Anthony represented the best of our congregation, and exemplified the great values of our church: humility in action, advocacy for the needy, and service to all people. The Doris Anthony Community Service Award commemorates her lifelong commitment to the church and community by recognizing an individual who shares her heartfelt passion for helping others with selflessness and love. This year, the selection committee is proud to present this award to an individual who spent so much time at the food pantry this year that by June, she was managing it all on her own. She also expanded our typical Thanksgiving and Christmas food basket drives, making them a monthly event to serve the hungry. As one houseless beneficiary of her service told me, "I wouldn't be alive today if she hadn't been there for us." On behalf of the selection committee, I am pleased to present this year's Doris Anthony Community Service Award to Megan Russell.

Speech of Acceptance

If you are ever given an award, a promotion, or some other sort of public recognition, you may be called upon to "say a few words." Giving a **speech of acceptance** is difficult because you want to sound appreciative without being syrupy, and you want to sound deserving without being egotistical. Here are some guidelines.

speech of acceptance oral remarks made by the recipient of an award or honor.

Thank those who played a part in your achieving the honor.   If a few individuals made your recognition possible, mention them by name; if a lot of people did, mention the most important contributors to your success and say something like this, "There are many others but they are too numerous to name. Nevertheless, I am grateful to all of them."

Thank the organization giving you the award and recognize the work it is doing.   If, for example, you are cited by the United Way as top fund-raiser of the year, spend a few moments extolling its great work.

Be brief.   I have seen some ceremonies marred because an award recipient viewed the acceptance speech as a chance to expound on his or her favorite ideas. If you deliver a lengthy oration, the people who are giving you the honor may regret their choice. Make a few sincere remarks—and then sit down.

Here is a sample acceptance speech given by Rita Goldberg, who was honored by a chapter of the Lions Club for her work on behalf of people with disabilities.

> I want to thank you for choosing me to receive your Distinguished Service Award. I couldn't have accomplished half of what I did in the past year without the help of Henry and Judith Fletcher. I am grateful to them for their valuable assistance. And I am grateful to you Lions for setting up programs for those who are visually impaired. Because of your compassion and your work, you have made it easy for volunteers like me to help people with disabilities. Again, thank you for this honor.

If you think you may be asked to speak at a ceremony in your honor, plan what you will say, and—above all else—be brief.

bikeriderlondon/Shutterstock

Speech of Tribute

A **speech of tribute** praises or celebrates a person, a group, an institution, or an event. It conveys gratitude, respect, or admiration. For example, the leader of a veterans' organization might pay tribute on Memorial Day to comrades who died in combat. At a retirement banquet, you might give a brief talk lauding the work of a colleague who is stepping down after 25 years.

A speech of tribute should be completely positive. It is never appropriate to point out faults or dredge up old disputes.

Let's examine three popular types of tribute speeches—wedding speeches, toasts, and eulogies.

Wedding Speeches

Weddings are celebrated in many ways, depending upon religious, ethnic, and family traditions. Many of these traditions call for brief speeches of tribute at the rehearsal dinner and the wedding reception. The remarks may be delivered by members of the wedding party, parents, grandparents, siblings, and friends. Here are some guidelines.

Focus on the couple.   Instead of dwelling on your own experiences and emotions, talk mostly about the wedding couple and their love and future happiness.

Be brief, but not too brief.   If you speak for only 15 seconds, saying that the honorees are wonderful people whom everyone likes, you are not giving them the respect that they deserve. Say something specific and heartfelt, but keep your remarks under three minutes.

Don't say anything that could embarrass anyone in the room.   You've seen the movies in which a wedding celebration is marred when the best man reveals humiliating

details about the groom or says something that is insulting to the bride. Such behavior is not limited to the movies. In real life, people make major blunders. Never mention ex-boyfriends or ex-girlfriends. Never tease about past misdeeds, goofy habits, or unfortunate shortcomings. For this occasion, focus entirely on the positive.

Consider using an appropriate poem or quotation.   Anthologies and the Internet are full of apt quotations, such as this one by the ancient Chinese philosopher Lao Tzu: "To love someone deeply gives you strength. Being loved by someone deeply gives you courage."[4] Or you can use a lighter touch by reciting a humorous poem or quotation.

If you create videos, make them short and tasteful.   A speech of tribute accompanied by photos and favorite pieces of music can be a delightful part of the occasion if you keep it short, and if you avoid surprise photos that might embarrass someone. Concentrate on the couple, using upbeat, happy images.

End with a toast.   It's customary, and the perfect way to complete your speech. (In the next section, we will discuss the art of toasting.)

Jamie Grill/Getty Images

Wedding speeches can vary in length; here is an example of a shorter one, delivered by the best man for a happy couple:

> Thank you, family and friends, for coming today to celebrate the marriage of John and Bert. As I look around, I recognize people I've known my entire life, and some folks I just met a few hours ago— but today, we are all one family, brought together by the great love between these two individuals.
>
> Everyone who knows John understands that he is a quiet and contemplative person. I've watched him stare at the calmness of a lake while fishing for hours on end, pondering how to make the world a better place. He likes to think through every consequence before he acts, and to develop a comprehensive strategy before he undertakes a new challenge. But Bert gives him the balance he needs; he's spontaneous, he's fun-loving, and he always has a good joke or a funny quip to make light of a tense situation. John once told me that Bert helps him live in the moment. He's done things he never dreamed of doing—like skydiving—because Bert was there, not only to push him, but to make him feel safe, secure, and comfortable. Likewise, John told me that he recently dragged Bert to his favorite art history museum for a daylong event on impressionist art—and that Bert even enjoyed it!
>
> Their relationship represents what we all desire in love. They care for one another, in sickness and in health. They complement one another, helping each other grow and flourish. They are honest, kind, and generous with one another— and, most importantly, they love one another, fiercely and proudly.
>
> Let's raise a glass and toast to John and Bert. May we all find a love as great as theirs.

Ethical Issues Quiz

In a wedding speech by the father of the bride, which of the following remarks is most appropriate?

A. A humorous account of the "losers" the daughter dated in the past.
B. Lighthearted teasing about the daughter's clumsiness
C. An amusing anecdote about one of the daughter's childhood birthday parties.

For the answer, see the last page of this chapter.

Toasts

A toast is a short tribute spoken as glasses are raised to salute people, occasions, or things. Toasts are offered at graduation celebrations, family get-togethers, class reunions, retirement dinners, wedding celebrations, and many other events. Here is an example:

> I'd like to propose a toast to Miriam Steele, who has devoted 27 years to this company, giving us creativity, integrity, and a friendly ear to tell our troubles to. Miriam, we will miss you, and we hope your retirement years are filled with much happiness and abundant good health.

Traditionally, in the United States and Canada, the glasses contain wine, but at most events, any beverage is acceptable—even water. In other countries or with international guests, don't toast with water, because some cultures interpret it as disapproval of the toast.[5]

Announce a toast by raising your glass and saying, "I'd like to propose a toast." Participants show their agreement by raising their glasses and, at the end of the toast, lightly "clinking" them against the glasses of those nearby. Then everyone takes a sip to "seal" the toast.

Here are some guidelines.

Strive for sincerity, warmth, and brevity.   At a party celebrating a college graduation, a classmate gave this toast: "Here's to Paul. May your future be filled with work that you enjoy and friends that bring you as much happiness as you have brought to us."

When is it a bad idea to use water for a toast?

Phil Date/Shutterstock

Don't read a toast.   Prepare your toast and practice it at home, but don't bring a manuscript to the table.

Avoid all forms of teasing.   A toast honoring a couple on their 35th anniversary should not include references to memory lapses, wrinkles, and weight gain.

Browse the Internet for ideas.   You can combine your own words with toasts that are found on the Internet. For example, at a wedding celebration, a friend of the newlyweds gave this toast: "Maggie and Zack, may your days be filled with wonder and grace, and (to quote a wedding toast popular in Mexico) I wish you health, love, happiness—and enough money to enjoy them."

Eulogies

eulogy

a laudatory oration in honor of someone who has died.

An especially important kind of tribute speech you may be asked to make is a **eulogy**—a speech of praise for a friend, relative, or colleague who has died. A eulogy should be dignified, without exaggerated sentimentality. If it is appropriate, you may use humor, such as anecdotes about how a grandmother created elaborate and fun-filled surprises for her grandchildren.

A eulogy should focus on the *significance* of the person's life and deeds, rather than on a mere recital of biographical facts. In other words, how did this man or woman enrich our lives? What inspiration or lessons can we draw from this person's life?

As we discussed in the chapter on delivering the speech, a script is usually not recommended for speeches, but an exception may be made for a eulogy. Because the death of a relative or friend often causes grief and disorientation, reading a script can give you stability and reassurance that you won't break down or ramble.

Carolyna De Laurentiis talks about her father (as her sister Dina listens) at the funeral of Italian filmmaker Dino De Laurentiis in Los Angeles. Sometimes joy and humor are appropriate at a funeral as loved ones share fond memories of the deceased.

Reed Saxon, Pool/AP Images

Inspirational Speech

The goal of the **inspirational speech** is to stir positive emotions—to help people feel excited, uplifted, and encouraged. You may need to give inspirational speeches at various times in your life. Let's say, for example, that you are the manager of an office or a department, and you give your staff members an upbeat "you-can-do-it" speech to motivate them to do their best work. Or imagine you coach a children's soccer team, and you give the boys and girls a "pep talk" before a game to encourage them to play well.

inspirational speech
an address that tries to stimulate listeners to a high level of feeling or activity.

The inspirational speech is similar to the persuasive speech, with their purposes often overlapping. The main difference is that in the inspirational speech, you devote yourself almost solely to stirring emotions, while in the persuasive speech, you use emotional appeals as just one of many techniques.

Delivery is an important dimension of inspirational speaking. To inspire other people, *you* must be inspired. Your facial expression, your posture, your tone of voice—everything about you must convey energy and enthusiasm.

An inspirational speech should tap the emotional power of vivid language. An example of effective use of language can be found in a speech delivered by Dan Crenshaw to a support group of parents of children with developmental disabilities. Here is a section from the speech:

> We must learn to live fully and joyfully in the here and now, setting aside all our pain from the past and all our worries about the future. Fulton Oursler said, "We crucify ourselves between two thieves: regret for yesterday and fear of tomorrow."
>
> If we live in the past or in the future, we miss what today has to offer. We miss the glistening beauty of a puddle of water. We miss the soothing melody of a love song. We miss the glint of wonder in a child's eyes. We miss the beautiful arrangement of clouds in the sky. We miss the satisfaction of petting a dog's fur.
>
> The past is over. Think of it as a bullet. Once it's fired, it's finished. The future is not yet here, and may never come for us. Today is all we have. Treasure *today,* celebrate *today,* live *today.*

Crenshaw made effective use of the techniques of *repetition* and *parallel structure* (discussed in the chapter on wording the speech).

Resources for Review and Skill Building

Summary

While informative and persuasive speeches are the most frequent types of speeches, there are occasions when a speech must serve other purposes. When you need to entertain an audience, as in an after-dinner talk, your remarks should be light and diverting; any elements of information or persuasion should be gracefully woven into the fabric of entertainment. One device for an entertaining speech is to string together anecdotes, examples, or quotations on a single theme. Extended narratives or descriptions also can be entertaining.

Using humor in a speech is an effective way to create a bond of warmth and friendliness with an audience. Be cautious in telling jokes because they can be risky, and listeners may not respond as you hope they will. A safer type is low-key humor, such as a mildly amusing story, quotation, or observation. Whatever humor you use should relate to the topic and not be offensive to any person in the audience.

When you are asked to introduce a speaker, convey enthusiasm for the speaker and the topic, and give whatever background information is necessary to enhance the speaker's credibility.

When you make a speech of presentation, focus your remarks on the award and the recipient.

When you are called upon to "say a few words" in acceptance of an award or a promotion, thank the people who gave you the honor and acknowledge the help of those who made your success possible.

When you give a speech of tribute, praise the person, group, institution, or event being honored, avoiding any negativity or embarrassing remarks. Three types of tribute speeches are wedding speeches, toasts, and eulogies.

When you speak to inspire an audience, devote yourself to stirring emotions, using a dynamic delivery to convey your energy and enthusiasm.

Key Terms

entertaining speech, *352*

eulogy, *362*

inspirational speech, *363*

speech of acceptance, *359*

speech of introduction, *356*

speech of presentation, *358*

speech of tribute, *360*

Review Questions

1. Why would an informative speech on a difficult, highly technical subject usually be inappropriate for an after-dinner audience?

2. What are the risks that a speaker takes when telling a joke?

3. In what situation is self-deprecating humor inadvisable?

4. If you are asked to introduce a speaker, why should you coordinate your remarks beforehand with those of the speaker?

5. When introducing a speaker, some introducers use the speaker's first name, others use the last name. How would you know what name to use?

6. In which kind of special occasion speech does the speaker often withhold an honoree's name until the last sentence?

7. List three guidelines for the speech of acceptance.

8. What is the function of the speech of tribute?

9. What should be the focus of a eulogy?

10. What is the main difference between an inspirational speech and a persuasive speech?

Building Critical-Thinking Skills

1. One speaker told his audience, "Before I left for this speech, my wife gave me some advice: 'Don't try to be charming, witty, or intellectual. Just be yourself.'" What kind of humor is the speaker using, and in what kind of situations do you think it is acceptable?

2. Psychologists have discovered that humor can improve a person's problem-solving abilities. Why do you think humor has this effect?

3. "Our speaker tonight," says the master of ceremonies, "will outline the five key steps in rescuing a person who is in danger of drowning. Let me give you a quick preview of these steps." What mistake is the master of ceremonies making? If you were the master of ceremonies in this scenario, what would you say to introduce this speaker?

4. If you are asked to deliver a eulogy for a co-worker who was always helpful to you but was known at work as a difficult and argumentative person, should you speak about the work-related problems? Explain your answer.

Building Teamwork Skills

1. Working in a group, decide on a topic and then prepare
    and deliver an entertaining talk, with each member of the
    group speaking in turn. Here are some possible topics:

    a. An embarrassing moment
    b. Good vacation spots
    c. The weird behavior of pets

2. In a group, choose a person (living or dead) whom every-
    one admires. Create a speech of tribute to that person.

Examining Your Ethics

Answer: C. A story about a childhood event could illustrate the
father's fondness for his daughter. Answers A and B would be
embarrassing.

End Notes

1. Anderson Cooper, CNN anchor, in a speech at "CNN
    Heroes: An All Star Tribute" at the Shrine Auditorium in
    Los Angeles on December 2, 2012.

2. Mark Leigh, Epic Fail: *The Ultimate Book of Blunders*
    (London: Virgin Books/Random House, 2013), p. 199.

3. The speaker derived her information from Roberto A.
    Ferdman, "Baby Carrots Are Not Baby Carrots," *The
    Washington Post,* www.washingtonpost.com (accessed
    January 26, 2016); Gholam Rahman, "The Name's the
    Thing," *West Palm Beach Post,* www.palmbeachpost
    .com (accessed January 26, 2016); Jessica Belasco
    and Ellery Jividen, "Would You Eat Slimehead?," *San

Antonio Express-News, www.expressnews.com (accessed
January 26, 2016); Janet Fletcher, "The Mushroom That
Grew," SFGATE, www.sfgate.com (accessed January 26,
2016); Sharon Tyler Herbst and Ron Herbst, "Portobello
Mushroom," *Food Encyclopedia,* www.foodterms.com
(accessed January 26, 2016).

4. "Wedding Quotations," Famous-Quotes-And-Quotations.
    Com, www.famous-quotes-and-quotations.com (accessed
    January 26, 2016).

5. Lillian Hunt Chaney and Jeanette S. Martin, *The Essen-
    tial Guide to Business Etiquette* (New York: Greenwood
    Publishing Group, 2007), pp. 100–101.

Speaking in Groups

OUTLINE

Meetings

Group Presentations

OBJECTIVES

After studying this chapter, you should be able to

1. Serve as a leader or a participant in a small-group meeting.

2. Describe the responsibilities of both leaders and participants in small groups.

3. Identify and explain the seven steps of the reflective-thinking method.

4. Prepare and deliver a presentation as a member of a team.

5. Participate in a symposium.

6. Serve as moderator or panelist in a panel discussion.

YOU CAN BOLSTER YOUR CAREER if you know how to work well in a group. Here is what research shows:

- If you show that you have had experience working on a team, you improve your chances of getting a job.[1]
- Once employed, if you establish a reputation as an effective team member, you enhance your chances for promotion.[2]

Why is working on a team so important? Much of the work of society is done by small groups, such as a team of scientists who develop new medicines, a committee of educators who improve a curriculum, a group of neighbors who try to reduce crime, and a crew of workers who devise a labor-saving method of production.

Small groups have some advantages over the individual. Members of small groups can pool their resources, ideas, and labor. They can catch and correct errors that

might slip past an individual. According to Yale psychologist Robert Sternberg, a group often has an IQ (or intelligence level) that is higher than the IQ of any individual in the group.[3]

The power of working in groups can be seen by looking at members of the Farmington High School (Minnesota) Robotics Team. The team worked together to build a customized, powered wheelchair for a five-year-old boy in their community who suffered from a rare form of dwarfism. The students modified a mini-powered toy car into a wheelchair, customizing it to his height and needs. Wearing their "Rogue Robotics" team shirts, the students were invited to present the wheelchair to the child in a ceremony sponsored by First Lady Melania Trump.[4]

In this chapter, we will look at working in groups and then discuss making presentations as a group.

Meetings

A meeting is often the best way for small groups to plan and carry out their collective work. It sounds simple, but there is a problem: the majority of business and professional people say (in surveys) that most meetings are unproductive and a waste of time.[5]

Fortunately, this problem can be solved. To have a productive meeting, group leaders and participants should follow well-established principles of effective group communication, as explained below. Let's start with the role of group leaders.

Responsibilities of Leaders

No matter what kind of group you are asked to lead—whether a committee to plan the office holiday party or a classroom group presentation—your general responsibilities will be the same.

Make Sure You Need a Meeting

It is a mistake to hold a meeting just because "we always have a staff meeting every Friday afternoon." If there is nothing significant to discuss or act upon, a meeting is a waste of valuable time. If you simply need to share information, use e-mail. You should call a meeting when

- You need to develop ideas, gain consensus, plan, and follow up.
- You must share information that is sensitive, emotionally charged, or could be misinterpreted.
- You need to build teamwork and cooperation.

Make Sure Group Members Know Purpose and Scope

In advance of the meeting, all participants should be clearly informed of the purpose of getting together. Otherwise, people will walk in saying "Why are we meeting?" Letting people know in advance gives them the opportunity to be thinking about the task.

Just as important, make sure group members know how their work will be used. Does the group have the authority to make and carry out a decision, or is it merely being asked to make a recommendation? Can the group's decisions be overruled by a higher authority? Understanding the group's purpose and power can help save time and frustration down the road.

When the meeting begins, you should quickly review the group's purpose and scope of power in order to refresh everyone's memory.

Set the Agenda and Length of Meeting

agenda
document listing what is to be accomplished during a meeting.

An **agenda** is a list of items that need to be covered in a meeting (see Figure 1). When there is no agenda, groups are unfocused—they spend time and energy on minor items and never get around to the major issues. A study of meetings by the 3M Corporation found that "a written agenda, distributed in advance, is the single best predictor of a successful meeting."[6]

You don't need to set the agenda by yourself. Ask participants in advance to submit their ideas and concerns. You will not only get good ideas but also assure the participants that their input is valued and will be heard.

Arrange the agenda so the most important items are discussed first. Consider allocating an appropriate amount of time for each item.

Early in the meeting, get the group's approval of the agenda in case new issues have come up that need to be addressed.

AGENDA
Advertising Committee

December 5, 2019, 2:00–2:55 P.M.
Frazier Conference Room

Committee Chair:	Janice Moss
Committee Members:	Amin Abraham-Quiles, Dale Van Cantfort, Joe Dennis, Melissa Jackson, Grafton Tanner, and Melissa Tingle
Objective:	To decide the best outlet for our spring advertising campaign
Agenda Items:	

1. Welcome and call to order
2. Approval of last meeting's minutes
3. Approval of agenda
4. Discussion of TV advertising options (10 minutes)
5. Discussion of social networking opportunities (10 minutes)
6. Discussion of magazine options (10 minutes)
7. Vote on our recommendation to the company president
8. Suggestions for next meeting's agenda
9. Committee chair's summary
10. Adjournment

Figure 1
Sample Agenda

Many people automatically schedule meetings for one hour. Instead of automatically assuming you need one hour, estimate the time you really need. Holding quick meetings (sometimes with everyone standing up) can be an effective way to keep the group focused (see Figure 2).

While short meetings can be effective, they are not always ideal. When you have a long agenda, or complex issues, having one long session can be more effective than several meetings that break up your momentum.

Start on Time

Start your meetings on time and thank those who are there. When latecomers arrive, tell them where you are on the agenda and let them catch up. Waiting to start your meeting until everybody shows up is almost always a mistake.

- It rewards the latecomers, effectively "training" them—and those who arrived on time—to come later and later.
- It wastes the time of those who arrived on time and tells them you don't appreciate their punctuality.

Of course, there are sometimes valid reasons for starting late, such as a traffic jam or an office emergency. When this happens, make sure your group knows the reason for the delay and invite them to take a break and return at a specified time.

Set the Tone

Greet people as they arrive. Set an appropriate tone. Usually it will be friendly and upbeat, but it will be more serious if the purpose of the meeting is to share bad news. In any case, always thank your participants for coming.

Figure 2

Some companies insist that all participants stand up during an entire meeting. "This ensures that our meetings are short," said one manager. "We get our work done quickly and efficiently because no one wants to dawdle or engage in idle chit-chat. Stand-up meetings boost our productivity."

alvarez/Getty Images

If some of the participants are newcomers, make sure they are introduced to every-one else.

Make Sure Minutes Are Kept

minutes
written record of what occurred at a meeting.

If the group is not a formal committee with a previously designated recorder, appoint someone to take notes and later prepare **minutes** of the meeting. Minutes are a record of what was discussed and accomplished during a meeting. They should be circulated to group members after the meeting, as soon as possible. While minutes are obviously valu-able for absentees, they are also important for people who were present to remind them of their responsibilities for the next meeting. Minutes should consist of five elements: (1) agenda item, (2) decision reached, (3) action required, (4) person(s) responsible for taking action, and (5) target date for completion of action. At each meeting, the minutes of the previous session should be briefly reviewed to make sure that tasks have been completed.

Guide—Don't Dominate—the Discussion

Your challenge is to set the direction of the meeting while encouraging free and produc-tive group participation. This is more than politeness; it's good strategy. Group members feel a commitment to the plans and decisions if they have helped to formulate them. Now it is *their* idea, *their* policy. Here are some guidelines for guiding the discussion:

- Don't let anybody take over the conversation, including yourself. If any one person is doing most of the talking, you may have to gently but firmly intervene: "Those are excellent points . . . I'd like to hear how others are reacting to what you just said."

- Draw out participants who aren't speaking up—but don't put them on the spot: "Janice, you've had experience with writing proposals. Are you seeing anything we're overlooking?"

- Encourage free discussion, but don't permit attacks on people or ideas.

- Address side conversations directly: "Dale and Melissa, it looks as if you've come up with something interesting. Could you share it with all of us?" They will either grin sheepishly and return to the group or share their thoughts—and they may be shy and welcome the invitation to give their input.

- Summarize periodically. Sum up what has and has not been decided, saying just enough to help the participants keep their bearings: "Okay, we've decided to recommend A and B to the board for approval, but it looks like we're stuck on C until Amin gets numbers from Finance. Let's move on to item D."

- When you near the agreed-upon time to end the meeting, summarize what the group has accomplished, set the time and place for the next meeting, and make sure all participants know their assignments for the next meeting. Express appreciation for the work that the group has done.

Responsibilities of Participants

While leadership of a small group is important, the participants themselves play a vital role. People working together can combine their insights and energies to achieve goals that would be unattainable by a single person. The key is cooperation. "The secret of a successful team is not to assemble the largest team possible, but rather to assemble a team that can work well together," says Dean Kamen, founder of FIRST (For Inspiration and Recognition of Science and Technology).[7]

Here are guidelines to keep in mind.

Prepare for Every Meeting

Take time to review the agenda and the key players. Do whatever research, background reading, and interviewing you need to strengthen your position on issues to be discussed. Bring any documentation needed.

Arrive Early

Show up a few minutes before the meeting time. You'll look—and be—more in command. It will also give you a chance to touch base with others before the meeting begins.

Be Respectful

As soon as the meeting begins, put down your smartphone or any other items that may distract you from paying attention. It's a sign of disrespect when you are looking at your phone or working on something non-meeting related on your computer as the meeting continues. You're essentially saying to your co-workers around the table, "You are not important to me and deserving of my attention." Although you may not realize it, such behavior is noticed by your colleagues and even your supervisor.

Participate

Join the discussion and contribute your ideas and opinions. It can be as simple as voicing agreement with a team member or asking a question. If you tend to be shy in group settings, speak up early. The longer you wait, the harder it will be.

Watch your body language. Nonverbal behaviors, such as facial expressions and posture, speak more powerfully than words. If you slump in your chair and don't make eye contact, people will assume you are bored or negative. Instead, sit in an alert but relaxed

Examining Your Ethics

While at a meeting for your neighborhood block association, you find yourself disagreeing on an issue on which all of your neighbors agree. Which of the following would be an acceptable reason for you to concede and go along with the others?

A. Your block association's bylaws stipulate that decisions must be unanimous, and you don't feel strongly enough about the issue to delay a group decision.
B. You want to avoid conflict.
C. You want to see a quick decision reached so that the meeting doesn't drag on and you can go home.
D. You know that standing in the way of a unanimous decision might cause your neighbors to be frustrated with you.

For the answer, see the last page of this chapter.

posture with an open, friendly expression. Make eye contact with those speaking. Smile and nod in agreement when appropriate—everyone who speaks up appreciates positive feedback.

Have the Courage to Disagree

You've undoubtedly been part of a group in which everybody seemed to agree with an idea or an approach until one member expressed reservations—and then almost everybody jumped in to say they, too, had concerns. A good way to open the conversation to receive many points of view is to ask a question that separates the issue from the person making the argument. Focus on the *issue,* not on people: "How can we be sure we draw a big enough audience to justify the expense?" As group members respond, they may realize that the idea *is* unworkable—or you may realize it has merit. You can help your group avoid making a decision in false unanimity.

Don't Work from a Hidden Agenda

hidden agenda
an ulterior motive.

A group's work can be sabotaged if some members pretend to be committed to the goals of the group but in reality have **hidden agendas**—that is, unannounced private goals that conflict with the group's goals. One frequent hidden agenda is the desire to win the favor of a superior. One or more members of a committee will agree with the chairperson—the boss—even though they feel strongly that the boss's ideas are flawed. They would rather see the committee's efforts fail than go on record as disagreeing with their superior.

Don't Carry On Private Conversations

A whispered conversation by two or three participants is rude and insulting to the speaker. It is also damaging to the work of the group, since it cuts off teamwork and undermines cooperation. Be considerate, and stay focused on the task at hand.

The Reflective-Thinking Method

The American essayist H. L. Mencken said that for every human problem, "there is always an easy solution—neat, plausible, and wrong." Unfortunately, some business and professional groups leap at easy but wrong solutions. In the 1980s, when Coca-Cola was losing ground to Pepsi, the "neat, plausible" solution was to change the Coca-Cola formula and make it as sweet as Pepsi. The solution seemed reasonable, but it was a huge blunder. Sales plummeted because millions of Coca-Cola lovers disliked the new taste. Soon the embarrassed company resumed making the original formula (which was sold as Coca-Cola Classic).

reflective-thinking method
a structured system for solving problems.

An effective technique for avoiding mistakes like this is to use the **reflective-thinking method**, a step-by-step approach derived from the writings of the American philosopher John Dewey.[8] Follow the steps in this order.

1. **Define the problem.** Doing so clearly and precisely can save time and money. Here are some tips:

   - Phrase the problem in the form of a question. Instead of making a statement— "We have traffic jams on our campus"—ask, "How can we eliminate traffic jams after the 2 P.M. and 3 P.M. classes?"
   - Avoid wording that suggests a solution. If you say, "How can we finance the hiring of more security officers to eliminate traffic jams on campus?," you are stating that you already know the best solution to the traffic jam problem. You risk cutting off discussion that might lead to a different solution—one that is even better than hiring more security officers.
   - Be specific about the problem. If it is litter, say so. Instead of "How can we improve our campus?" ask, "How can we discourage littering?"

2. **Analyze the problem.** You must get a clear picture of the full dimensions of a problem before the problem-solving process can continue. Ask these questions:

   - What are the causes of this problem?
   - What are the effects of this problem?
   - How severe is it? Are many people affected? Or just a few?

   If you own a restaurant, and some of your customers have complained about slow service, your problem-solving team should focus on causes. Is slow service caused by the servers? If so, is it because they are careless and unprofessional, or is it because each of them is assigned too many tables? Or can the slow service be blamed solely on the cooks? If so, is it because they are lazy or inefficient? Or are they understaffed?

3. **Establish criteria for evaluating a solution.** Imagine you are employed by a company that assigns you and four others to work on a team to solve this problem: Many employees complain that the indoor air quality is very poor, causing headaches and fatigue. After hours of research and discussion, your team recommends installation of an air-filtration system costing $400,000. But the idea is quickly shot down by senior management because it's four times what the company can afford. Now it's back to the drawing board. Your team could have saved itself much time and effort if it had known that the spending ceiling was $100,000.

   This scenario shows why a group should write down the criteria—the standards or conditions—by which to judge a solution. To establish criteria, a group should ask these key questions:

   - What must the proposed solution do?
   - What must it avoid?
   - What restrictions of time, money, and space must be considered?

4. **Generate possible solutions.** One of the best techniques for putting potential solutions on the table is **brainstorming**. People in the group express their ideas, which are captured—preferably on a visible board—and later discussed and analyzed. Many of the ingenious products that we use daily were invented or improved as a result of brainstorming. For example, consider the digital camera that we use to take photos. The image-capture chip in the camera was invented in a one-hour brainstorming session by two engineers who were under pressure to produce or lose their funding.[9]

   For brainstorming to work effectively, there must be an atmosphere of total acceptance—no one analyzes, judges, ridicules, or rejects any of the ideas as they are being generated. Nothing is too wild or crazy to be jotted down.

brainstorming
generating many ideas quickly and uncritically.

In a brainstorming session, executives at a novelty company in Connecticut came up with the idea of putting pumpkin faces on leaf bags, transforming the bags from unsightly trash containers into autumn decorations. The company has sold millions of them. Brainstorming is one of the best ways for small groups to solve problems and create new ideas.

© Hamilton Gregory

Total acceptance is vital because (1) it encourages the flow of creative thinking and (2) an idea that seems far-fetched and impractical at first glance might eventually prove to be a good idea.

5. **Choose the best solution.** After the brainstorming session, a group should analyze, weigh, and discuss its ideas to come up with the best solution. It may be a combination of the ideas generated, or something new generated by the analysis and discussion. Regardless, the solution chosen must meet these standards:

- The solution must satisfy the criteria previously established.
- The group must have the authority to put the solution into effect—or recommend a way to do so.
- A solution must not create a new problem.

6. **Implement the solution.** For this important step, decide how to put the solution into action. For example, if your committee has come up with a way to discourage littering on campus, you should go to the appropriate administrators and give detailed instructions on exactly what needs to be done (such as installation of more conveniently located trash receptacles).

7. **Evaluate the solution.** Many groups hammer out a solution to a problem but never follow up to determine whether their solution really solved the problem. Make sure you design a way to evaluate your recommendation at the time you make it. For example, let's say your group recommends hiring more security officers to solve traffic jams on campus. You need to set up an evaluation that will contrast *before* with *after:*

   • What was happening *before* the solution was implemented: Student motorists required about 15 minutes to exit the campus after 2 P.M. classes let out.
   • What must happen *after* the solution: The average exit time must be less than 7 minutes.

   If the goal is not met, your group needs to go back to Step 4 and proceed through Step 7 until the correct solution is found.

Group Presentations

In your classroom, career, or community life, you are likely to speak publicly as part of a group. Three popular ways of presenting are the team presentation, the symposium, and the panel discussion.

Team Presentation

Teams play an important role in the business and professional world, and sometimes they are called upon to deliver a presentation to an audience. A **team presentation** is like a speech given by an individual except that the content is divided, with each member delivering a different section. For effective team presentations, here are some guidelines.

team presentation
a well-coordinated presentation made by members of a group who focus on a common goal.

Designate Roles

To keep the group on track, choose a project leader. He or she should conduct meetings (along the lines discussed earlier in this chapter) to determine key issues: Who will do the various research tasks? Who will deliver which section of the presentation? When will the assignment be due?

Prepare Content

Use all the steps you have learned for an individual speech. Analyze your audience, create a specific purpose and a central idea, develop an outline, and gather materials (especially visuals).

Plan Your Time

Going over your time limit can destroy your credibility and irritate your audience. Time every minute of your presentation. Leave plenty of time for questions and discussion.

Practice, Practice, Practice

It is more important to rehearse when you do a group presentation than when you present alone. Practice many times, using all of the equipment and visual aids that you will be using on the big day. If you must travel to another city to give the presentation, take your own equipment—it can be risky to use unfamiliar equipment. In some situations, your team

TIP 1

Tips for Your Career

Strive to Improve Communication Skills

As you give speeches during your career, I hope that you will try to become better and better as a communicator. Here are two suggestions.

1. **Seek opportunities for speaking.** The best way to improve your skills is to actually give speeches, so look for opportunities in your career and in your community. An excellent place to practice is in a Toastmasters club, where your speaking skills will be critiqued in a friendly, supportive atmosphere. To find the name, specific website, and phone number of the club nearest you, visit www.toastmasters.org.

2. **Be a lifetime student of public speaking.** You can improve your own speaking skills by studying the speechmaking of others. Whenever you listen to a speech, make notes on what does and doesn't work. Which delivery techniques were effective? Which were ineffective? What speech material seemed to please the listeners? What seemed to bore them? Keep your notes in a file for future reference so that you can profit from both the successes and the failures of others.

members may live in different parts of the globe, communicating by e-mail, telephone, or videoconference. To avoid being out of sync with one another, you and your teammates should come together several days before a presentation to practice together in the same room.

Get Feedback during a Practice Session

This is a critical—and commonly overlooked—key to success. Find at least one person who is typical of your audience and who has not heard your presentation so he or she can provide a fresh, unbiased viewpoint. Use the feedback to make necessary alterations.

Prepare for the Question-and-Answer Period

Compile a list of likely questions from the audience. For each question, decide the best answer and designate which team member will deliver it.

Plan for Emergencies

Identify potential problems such as equipment failure or a cancelled flight, and how you will manage them. For example, be ready to provide printed copies of your PowerPoint slides in case the multimedia projector malfunctions.

Support One Another

Strive for harmony in the presentation. It looks bad if one team member contradicts or criticizes another in front of the audience. I once saw a team of architects give a presentation, at the end of which the senior architect on the team rose and apologized for the poor speaking skills of a young team member. His remarks were unnecessary—a gratuitous slap in the face—and they reflected poorly on him and the firm.

Listen to the Presentation Attentively

While your teammates are presenting, don't review your notes, check your smartphone, or whisper comments to others. These distractions signal to your audience that what's being said isn't important.

Symposium

A **symposium** is a series of brief speeches on a common topic, each usually discussing a different aspect of the topic. Every year, for example, Mount Sinai School of Medicine in New York City holds a symposium on autism, with five to eight medical researchers speaking on various aspects of autism. One might discuss diagnosis, another might recommend a certain treatment, and another might explore possible causes.

Unlike the team presentation, the speakers in a symposium do not necessarily agree with one another. Sometimes they are not required to coordinate their remarks, although it is a good idea to do so, to avoid excessive duplication of material.

A symposium is conducted by a moderator, who gives a brief introduction of each speaker and manages a question-and-answer period after the speeches.

Symposium speeches are supposed to be brief, and each speaker should be careful to stay within time limits. If a speaker is long-winded, the moderator should intervene and politely ask him or her to yield to another speaker in the interest of fairness.

When you prepare and deliver a speech as part of a symposium, use the same skills and techniques as those of solo speechmaking, with an introduction, a body, and a conclusion.

symposium
a meeting featuring short addresses by different people on the same topic.

Panel Discussion

In a **panel discussion**, a team converses on a topic in front of an audience. A panel is usually made up of three to eight members and is led by a moderator. A common pattern is for panelists to give a brief opening statement and then discuss the subject among themselves, with the moderator guiding the flow. At the end of the discussion, the audience is usually invited to ask questions.

Because of the variety of viewpoints and the liveliness of informed conversation, audiences enjoy a good panel discussion.

panel discussion
consideration of a topic by a small group in the presence of an audience.

American journalist Roxana Saberi, who was imprisoned for five months in Iran's notorious Evin Prison, speaks on a panel in New York City about human rights abuses in Iran.

Spencer Platt/Staff/Getty Images

Guidelines for the Moderator

Much of the success (or failure) of a panel discussion is determined by the moderator. He or she must keep the discussion moving along smoothly, restrain the long-winded or domineering panelist from hogging the show, draw out the reticent panelist, and field questions from the audience. Here are some guidelines to follow when you are a moderator.

Arrange the setting.   You and the panelists can be seated at a table facing the audience. Or, even better, you can be seated in a semicircle so that all members of the panel can see one another while still remaining visible to the audience. A large name card should be placed in front of each panelist so that the audience will know the participants' names.

Brief panel members in advance.   Well before the meeting, give panel members clear instructions on exactly what they are expected to cover in their opening remarks. Are they supposed to argue the "pro" or the "con" position? Are they supposed to speak on only one aspect of the topic? For information-giving discussions, you may want to assign each panel member a subtopic according to his or her area of expertise so that there is not much overlap among speakers. Instruct the panelists not to bring and read written statements, but tell them that they are free to bring notes.

Before the meeting, prepare a list of items that you think should be discussed.   This ensures that no important issues are inadvertently omitted. If the discussion begins to lag or go off into irrelevancies, you will have fresh questions ready.

Prepare and deliver an introduction.   At the beginning of the program, introduce the topic and the speakers, and explain the ground rules for the discussion; be sure to let listeners know if and when they will be permitted to ask questions.

Moderate the discussion.   Give each panelist a chance to make an opening statement (within the time constraints previously announced) and then encourage the panelists to question one another or comment upon one another's remarks. Be neutral in the discussion, but be prepared to ask questions if there is an awkward lull or if a panelist says something confusing or leaves out important information. Listen carefully to what each panelist says so that you don't embarrass yourself by asking questions on subjects that have already been discussed.

Maintain friendly, but firm, control.   Don't let a panelist dominate the discussion. During the question-and-answer session, don't let a member of the audience make a long-winded speech; interrupt kindly but firmly and say, "We need to give other people a chance to ask questions." If a panelist exceeds the time limit for opening remarks or monopolizes the discussion time, gently break in and say, "I'm sorry to interrupt, but let's hear from other members of the panel on their ideas concerning . . ." If a reticent panelist says very little, draw him or her out with specific, pertinent questions.

Be respectful of all panelists, including those with whom you disagree.   Think of yourself not as a district attorney who must interrogate and skewer criminal defendants but as a gracious host or hostess who stimulates guests to engage in lively conversation.

Ask open-ended questions.   For example, ask "How can we make sure our homes are safe from burglars?" rather than "Is burglary on the increase in our community?"

End the program at the agreed-upon time.   Wrap up the proceedings on time and in a prearranged way, perhaps by letting each panelist summarize briefly his or her position. You may want to summarize the key points made during the discussion. (To do this, you would need to take notes throughout the program.) Thank the panelists and the audience for their

Tips for Your Career

Remember the Essentials

Prepare an "elevator speech" that can explain your expertise in 30 seconds, or about the length of an elevator ride. For example, if asked to break down the most important elements of public speaking, one might use this elevator speech:

- Focus on the audience—their interests, needs, and desires—and not on yourself.

- Tell stories. They can be the most powerful and memorable part of a speech.
- Bear in mind that speaking over your time limit is not a small matter—it is a big mistake.

---

participation. If some members of the audience are still interested in continuing the discussion, you may want to invite them to talk to the panelists individually after the program is over.

Guidelines for Panelists

If you are a member of a panel, here are some guidelines to keep in mind.

Prepare for the discussion in the same way you prepare for a speech. Find out all that you can about the audience and the occasion: On what particular aspect of the topic are you expected to speak? Who are the other panelists and what will they cover? Will there be questions from the audience? What are the time constraints?

Prepare notes for the panel, but not a written statement. If you read your remarks, you will spoil the spontaneity that is desired in a panel discussion. In addition to notes, you may want to bring supporting data (such as bibliographical sources or statistics) from which to draw in case you are asked to document a point.

Respect the time limits set by the moderator. If, for example, you are asked to keep your opening remarks under two minutes, be careful to do so.

In the give-and-take of the discussion, be brief. If the other panelists or listeners want to hear more from you, they will ask.

Stay on the subject. Resist the temptation to ramble.

Be respectful and considerate of your fellow panelists. Don't squelch them with sarcasm, ridicule, or an overbearing attitude. Don't upstage them by trying to be the one to answer all the questions from the audience.

Listen carefully to the comments of other panelists and members of the audience. If some people disagree with you, try to understand and appreciate their position instead of hastily launching a counterattack. Then be prepared to follow the next guideline.

Be willing to alter your position. If you listen with an open mind, you may see merit in others' views, and you may decide that you need to modify your original position. Though such a shift may seem like an embarrassing loss of face, it actually causes the audience to have greater respect for you. It shows you are a person who possesses intellectual courage, flexibility, and integrity.

Resources for Review and Skill Building

Summary

Small groups are important elements in business and professional life, and much of the work of small groups is done in meetings. To lead a meeting, establish an agenda and make sure that it is followed; encourage all members to participate in group discussions; and guide the discussion to make sure that it stays on the subject. When you are a participant in a small-group meeting, enter the discussion with a positive attitude and an open mind.

One of the most effective agendas for problem solving is known as the reflective-thinking method. It involves seven steps: defining the problem; analyzing the problem; establishing criteria for evaluating a solution; generating possible solutions; choosing the best solution; implementing the solution; and evaluating the solution.

Sometimes groups appear in public to discuss or debate an issue. Three popular formats are team presentations, the symposium (a series of brief speeches on a common topic), and the panel discussion (an informal presentation involving a moderator and panelists).

Key Terms

agenda, *368*

brainstorming, *373*

hidden agenda, *372*

minutes, *370*

panel discussion, *377*

reflective-thinking method, *372*

symposium, *377*

team presentation, *375*

Review Questions

1. Why is an agenda necessary for a meeting?

2. What elements should a meeting's minutes include?

3. Why is nonverbal behavior important in a group meeting?

4. What is a hidden agenda?

5. What are the seven steps of the reflective-thinking method?

6. What does a group do when it brainstorms?

7. In what ways does a team presentation resemble an individual speech?

8. What is a symposium, and how does it differ from a team presentation?

9. What are the duties of the moderator in a panel discussion?

10. What are the duties of panelists in a panel discussion?

Building Critical-Thinking Skills

1. A football huddle is a type of group meeting. Fran Tarkenton, former star quarterback for the Minnesota Vikings, says, "Many of my best plays were the result of input by other team members. For example, outside receivers often told me that they could run a specific pattern against the defense, and we adjusted to run those plays. I would guess that 50 percent of my touchdowns came about by my receivers suggesting pass patterns." How could Tarkenton's insights be applied to business meetings?

2. Some communication experts say that group meetings lose a great deal of their effectiveness when group members number more than 12. Assuming that this statement is true, what would account for a decline in effectiveness?

3. Researchers at Stanford University estimate that in a typical meeting, an effective agenda prevents at least 20 minutes of wasted time. And yet most meetings use no agenda. Why do you think agendas are not used?

4. How should a team handle the possibility of one member being sick and absent on presentation day?

Building Teamwork Skills

1. In a group, use the steps of the reflective-thinking method (as shown in this chapter) to discuss how to solve a problem on your campus or in your community. Choose a leader to guide the discussion.

2. Using guidelines from your instructor, conduct either a symposium or a panel discussion to present the findings from the problem-solving assignment in item 1.

Examining Your Ethics

Answer: A. Going along when unanimity is required is often a good choice so that the work of the group is not stymied by one person, although there may be cases when you should refuse to go along—for example, if you have good reason to believe that the group is about to make a terrible mistake. The other answers (B, C, and D) are weak reasons for capitulating.

End Notes

1. Gloria J. Galanes and Katherine Adams, *Effective Group Discussion: Theory and Practice*, 14th ed. (New York: McGraw-Hill, 2013), pp. 1–19.

2. Lauren M. Hug and Andrew H. Hug, *The Professional Woman's Guide to Getting Promoted* (Birmingham, England: Impackt Publishing, 2015), p. 18.

3. "The Art of Creativity," *Psychology Today*, www .psychologytoday.com (accessed January 27, 2016).

4. Deanna Weniger, "Melania Trump Honors Farmington Robotics Team at the White House," TwinCities.com, May 7, 2019, www.twincities.com/2019/05/07/melania -trump-honors-farmington-robotics-team-at-the-white -house/ (accessed February 23, 2020).

5. "The State of Meetings Today," EffectiveMeetings.com, www.effectivemeetings.com (accessed January 27, 2016).

6. Andy Goodman, "The Single Best Predictor of a Successful Meeting Is . . . ," The Goodman Center, www .thegoodmancenter.com (accessed January 27, 2016).

7. "ASME Guide to Starting a FIRST Team," American Society of Mechanical Engineers, www.asme.org (accessed January 27, 2016).

8. John Dewey, *How We Think* (Boston: Heath, 1933), pp. 106–115.

9. Guy Gugliotta, "1-Hour Brainstorm Gave Birth to Digital Imaging," *Washington Post,* February 20, 2006, p. A-09.

Glossary

A

abstract words words that name qualities, concepts, relationships, acts, conditions, and ideas.

abstract summary of key information.

adaptation adjusting one's material and delivery to meet listeners' needs.

adrenaline a hormone, triggered by stress, that stimulates heart, lungs, and muscles and prepares the body for "fright, flight, or fight."

agenda document listing what is to be accomplished during a meeting.

alliteration repetition of the beginning sounds of words.

analogy resemblance in some respects between things that are otherwise dissimilar.

antithesis balanced juxtaposition of two contrasting ideas.

articulation the act of producing vocal sounds.

attack on a person criticizing an opponent rather than the opponent's argument.

attention material the part of the introduction designed to capture audience interest.

attitude a predisposition to respond favorably or unfavorably toward a person or an idea.

audience analysis collecting information about audience characteristics.

audience-centered speaker one who tries to establish a meaningful connection with listeners.

average a single value that represents the general significance of a set of unequal values.

B

bandwagon fallacy equating popularity with truth and proof.

bar graph a visual that contrasts two or more sets of data by means of parallel rectangles of varying lengths.

blog frequently updated online log.

brainstorming generating many ideas quickly and uncritically.

bridge a transitional device that links what went before with the next part of a speech.

building on an unproven assumption treating an opinion that is open to question as if it were already proved.

C

cause–effect pattern a scheme that links outcomes (effects) and the reasons for them (causes).

central idea the key concept of a speech.

channel the pathway used to transmit a message.

chronological pattern an arrangement of information in a time sequence.

citation basic facts about a source.

clarifying question a question designed to clear up confusion.

cliché an overused word or phrase.

clincher a final statement in a speech that drives home the key concept of the speech.

closed question a question requiring only a short, specific response.

comparative-advantages pattern an organizational scheme that shows the superiority of one concept or approach over another.

comparison showing how two or more items are alike.

complete-sentence outline a systematic arrangement of ideas, using complete sentences for headings and subheadings.

concrete words words that name persons and things that we can know by our five senses.

connotation the emotional overtones of a word that go beyond a dictionary definition.

contrast showing how two or more items are different.

copyright infringement unauthorized use of legally protected material.

correlation the degree of relative correspondence between two sets of data.

credibility audience perception of a speaker as believable, trustworthy, and competent.

customize to make or alter to a customer's specifications.

D

deduction reasoning from a generalization to a specific conclusion.

definition speech an oral presentation that gives an extended definition of a concept.

definition a statement of the meaning of a word or phrase.

denotation the thing or idea to which a word refers.

description speech an oral presentation that describes a person, place, object, or event.

dialect a particular form of a language that is peculiar to a specific region or social group.

doublespeak language that is designed to confuse or to be misunderstood.

E

either-or fallacy presenting only two alternatives when in fact more exist.

entertaining speech an oral address designed to amuse or engage listeners.

ethnocentrism judging other cultures as inferior to one's own culture.

eulogy a laudatory oration in honor of someone who has died.

euphemism a mild, indirect, or vague word used in place of one that is harsh, blunt, or offensive.

evidence the facts, examples, statistics, testimony, and other information that support an assertion.

example an instance that serves to illustrate a point.

explanation speech an oral presentation that explains a concept or situation.

extemporaneous method delivery of a speech from notes, following extensive preparation and rehearsal.

extended definition a rich, full elaboration of the meaning of a term.

F

fair use allowable and reasonable exceptions to copyright rules.

fallacy an argument based on a false inference.

false analogy creating a comparison that is exaggerated or erroneous.

false cause assuming that because two events are related in time, the first caused the second.

feedback verbal and nonverbal responses made by a listener to a speaker.

field research firsthand gathering of information.

flip chart a large pad of paper consisting of blank sheets (hinged at the top) that can be flipped over to present information sequentially.

follow-up question a question designed to stimulate elaboration.

full text every word of a document.

G

gender-biased language words based on gender stereotypes.

gender-biased stereotype generalization that assigns roles or characteristics to people on the basis of gender.

general purpose the broad objective of a speech.

H

handout material distributed to an audience as part of a speaker's presentation.

hasty generalization a conclusion that is based on inadequate evidence.

hearing the process by which sound waves are received by the ear.

hidden agenda an ulterior motive.

hypothetical illustration an imaginary scenario that illuminates a point.

hypothetical narrative imaginary story related to help listeners visualize a potential situation.

I

imagery words that evoke mental pictures or images.

impromptu method speaking with little or no preparation.

induction reasoning from specific evidence to a general conclusion.

infinitive a verb form beginning with "to."

inflated language words designed to puff up the importance of the person or thing being described.

inspirational speech an address that tries to stimulate listeners to a high level of feeling or activity.

interference anything that obstructs accurate communication of a message.

interlibrary loan sharing of materials and services among libraries.

internal summary a concise review of material covered during the body of a speech.

intonation the use of changing pitch to convey meaning.

J

jargon the technical language of a group or profession.

L

line graph a visual consisting of lines (charted on a grid) that show trends.

linear a sequence that proceeds from beginning to end.

listener the receiver of the speaker's message.

listening the act of interpreting and evaluating what is being said.

M

main points key assertions made by a speaker to develop his or her central idea.

manuscript method delivery of a speech by reading a script.

margin of error a statistic expressing the amount of random sampling error in a survey's results.

Maslow's hierarchy of needs a ranking of human needs from simple to complex.

mean in a set of numbers, the sum of all figures divided by the number of figures.

median the number that falls in the middle of a numerical ranking.

message whatever is communicated verbally and nonverbally to the listener.

metaphor a comparison implying similarity between two things.

minutes written record of what occurred at a meeting.

mixed metaphor incongruously combined metaphors.

mode the figure that appears most frequently in a set of figures.

motivated sequence a series of steps designed to propel a listener toward accepting the speaker's proposition.

motivations the impulses and needs that stimulate a person to act in a certain way.

N

narrative a story that illustrates a point.

non-linear an overall map that permits zooming in and out.

nonverbal communication transmission of messages without words.

O

open-ended question a question that permits a broad range of responses.

opinion a conclusion or judgment that remains open to dispute but seems true to one's own mind.

oral footnote a spoken citation of the source of one's material.

orienting material the part of the introduction that gives listeners the information they need to fully understand and believe the rest of the speech.

overt-response question a question asked to elicit a direct, immediate reply.

P

panel discussion consideration of a topic by a small group in the presence of an audience.

parallel language equivalent grammatical forms to express equivalent ideas.

parallel structure equivalent grammatical forms used to express ideas of equal importance.

paraphrase to restate material, using different words.

percentage a rate or proportion per hundred.

persuasion the process of influencing, changing, or reinforcing listeners' attitudes, beliefs, or behaviors.

pictorial graph a visual that dramatizes statistical data by means of pictorial forms.

pie graph a circle showing a given whole that is divided into component wedges.

pitch the highness or lowness of a sound.

plagiarism stealing the ideas or words of another and passing them off as one's own.

positive imagery visualization of successful actions.

positive nervousness useful energy.

posture the position of your body as you sit or stand.

preview a preliminary look at the highlights of a speech.

problem–solution pattern an arrangement of material that explores a problem and then offers a solution.

process speech an oral presentation that analyzes how to do something or how something works.

progressive revelation piece-by-piece unveiling of a visual.

pronunciation correct way of speaking a word.

public domain what is owned by the community at large; unprotected by patent or copyright.

Q

quote verbatim to cite the exact words used by a source.

R

reasoning using logic to draw conclusions from evidence.

red herring diverting listeners from the real issue to an irrelevant matter.

reference librarian a specialist in information retrieval.

reflective-thinking method a structured system for solving problems.

repetition repeating words or phrases for emotional effect.

rhetorical question a question asked solely to stimulate interest and not to elicit a reply.

royalty-free devoid of restrictions or fees.

S

scapegoat an individual or a group that innocently bears the blame of others.

scholarly journal a publication that contains peer-reviewed research conducted by experts in the field.

search engine a service that lets you search for keywords on Web pages throughout the world.

self-actualization the need of humans to make the most of their abilities.

signpost an explicit statement of the place that a speaker has reached.

simile a comparison, using *like* or *as,* of otherwise dissimilar things.

situation the setting in which communication takes place.

slippery slope one action will initiate a chain of events that will result in a tragic ending.

spatial pattern an arrangement of information in terms of physical space, such as top to bottom.

speaker the originator of a message sent to a listener.

speaking notes brief reminders of the points a speaker plans to cover during a speech.

specific purpose the precise goal that a speaker wants to achieve.

speech of acceptance oral remarks made by the recipient of an award or honor.

speech of introduction a brief talk that introduces a speaker to an audience.

speech of presentation an address designed to formally present an award or honor.

speech of refutation an oral counterargument against a concept or proposition put forth by others.

speech of tribute an oration in praise of someone or something.

speech to influence thinking an oral presentation aimed at winning intellectual assent for a concept or proposition.

speech to motivate action an oral presentation that tries to impel listeners to take action.

spotlight a device that alerts listeners to important points.

statement-of-reasons pattern a variation of the topical pattern in which a speaker gives reasons for an idea.

statistics numerical facts assembled to present significant information about a subject.

stereotype an oversimplified or exaggerated image of groups of people.

straw man a weak opponent or dubious argument set up so that it can be easily defeated.

summarize to give the substance of a statement in condensed form.

support materials elements that illustrate or substantiate a point.

syllogism a deductive scheme consisting of a major premise, a minor premise, and a conclusion.

symposium a meeting featuring short addresses by different people on the same topic.

synchronous existing or occurring at the same time; frequently used to refer to online meetings that happen in real time.

T

table numbers or words arranged systematically in rows and columns.

taboo an act, word, or object that is forbidden on grounds of morality or taste.

team presentation a well-coordinated presentation made by members of a group who focus on a common goal.

testimony statement by a knowledgeable person, used by a speaker to explain or bolster a point.

topic outline a systematic arrangement of ideas, using words and phrases for headings and subheadings.

topical pattern a division of a topic into components, types, or reasons.

transition an expression that links ideas and shows the relationship between them.

V

verbal fillers vocalized pauses in which a speaker inserts sounds such as "uh."

visual presenter a device capable of producing images of both two- and three-dimensional objects.

vivid image a description that evokes a lifelike picture within the mind of the listener.

Index